More praise for *Asia's New Battlefield*

'Combining lucid analysis with rich data and elegant prose, Heydarian's book provides a tour d'horizon of the central dynamics that are shaping Asia's strategic landscape. A must-read for anyone who is interested in the future of Asia.'

Alexander Vuving, Asia-Pacific Center for Security Studies

'A valuable source for policy makers, academics, researchers and those who would like to understand the dynamics among the powers in Southeast Asia and the possible dangers that might arise.'

Wilfrido Villacorta, former Philippine ambassador and permanent representative to ASEAN

About the author

Richard Javad Heydarian is an assistant professor in political science and international relations at De La Salle University, the Philippines, and served as a foreign policy adviser at the Philippine House of Representatives from 2009 to 2015. He has also been a consultant for various national and international institutions, advising on economic and foreign policy issues concerning the Philippines and East Asia. He has written for and/or been interviewed by, among other major publications, *Foreign Affairs, Aljazeera, ABC, BBC, Bloomberg, CNN, The New York Times, The Financial Times, The Wall Street Journal, The Nation, The National Interest,* and contributed to leading think tanks such as the Center for Strategic and International Studies (CSIS), S. Rajaratnam School of International Studies (RSIS), and the Norwegian Peacebuilding Resource Centre (NOREF). The *Manila Bulletin*, one of the Philippines' leading newspapers, has described him as 'one of the country's foremost foreign affairs and economic analysts'. His previous works include *How Capitalism Failed the Arab World: The Economic Roots and Precarious Future of the Middle East Uprisings* (Zed Books, 2014).

ASIA'S NEW BATTLEFIELD

The USA, China and the struggle
for the Western Pacific

Richard Javad Heydarian

Foreword by Walden Bello

Zed Books
London

To my loving mother, Evangeline Pe Benito Foronda,
who has always been there for me ...

And to my long-time mentor Walden Bello, who has been a
great source of intellectual nourishment throughout the years ...

Asia's New Battlefield: The USA, China and the Struggle for the Western Pacific
was first published in 2015 by Zed Books Ltd, The Foundry, 17 Oval Way,
London SE11 5RR, UK

www.zedbooks.co.uk

Copyright © Richard Javad Heydarian 2015

The right of Richard Javad Heydarian to be identified as the author
of this work has been asserted by him in accordance with the
Copyright, Designs and Patents Act, 1988.

Typeset in Plantin and Kievit by Swales & Willis Ltd, Exeter, Devon
Index by Rohan Bolton
Cover designed by Dougal Burgess
Printed and bound by CPI Group (UK) Ltd, Croydon CR0 4YY

A catalogue record for this book is available from the British Library.

ISBN 978-1-78360-313-8 hb
ISBN 978-1-78360-312-1 pb
ISBN 978-1-78360-314-5 pdf
ISBN 978-1-78360-315-2 epub
ISBN 978-1-78360-316-9 mobi

MIX
Paper from
responsible sources
FSC
www.fsc.org   FSC® C013604

CONTENTS

FIGURES AND TABLES

Figures

Tables

ACKNOWLEDGEMENTS

This book is the product of years of intensive research, active participation in various regional and international experts' workshops and conferences, and extensive exchanges – many on the record – with a wide and diverse range of academics, journalists and policy-makers across the Asia-Pacific region and beyond.

Let me begin by thanking Walden Bello, for whom I worked as a foreign policy adviser at the Philippine House of Representatives for more than five years (2009–15) – an extremely enriching experience, I must say. It was through our various collaborations that I was able to gradually hone my understanding of (and be inspired to further explore) the policy-making aspects of the South China Sea, and be exposed to challenges and dilemmas of policy-making. I also want to thank my friends and colleagues in academe, government and media for helping me to navigate a series of highly complex and contentious issues covered by this book. Obviously, ensuring (maximum-possible) objectivity and (much-needed) comprehensiveness was by no means easy, so I naturally had to rely on materials from and extensive discussions with experts (from varying disciplinary backgrounds) and policy-makers from various countries.

I would also like to thank my kind and supportive editors at *The National Interest*, particularly Harry Kazianis, and *Asia Times Online* (for which I wrote a long series of reports on South China Sea disputes from 2012 to 2014) for kindly giving me permission to use some excerpts from my previous works for this book. I would also like to thank my friends at the Asia Maritime Transparency Initiative of the Center for Strategic and International Studies (CSIS), particularly the director of the programme, Mira Rapp-Hooper, for so kindly allowing me to use a number of high-resolution, up-to-date images of China's extensive construction activities in the South China Sea.

I would also like to thank Asia experts at the CSIS headquarters in Washington, from Ernest Bower to Bonnie Glaser and Gregory Poling, who kindly shared their views on the geopolitical dimensions of the East and South China Sea disputes during a visit to Washington, DC, in early December 2014. The same goes for good friend Jay Batongbacal, director of the University of the Philippines' Institute for Maritime Affairs and Law of the Sea (IMLOS), for sharing his balanced and tempered legal views on Philippine–China maritime disputes. I must also thank colleagues and friends from other think tanks across South-East Asia, from the S. Rajaratnam School of International Studies (Singapore) to the Scientific Research Institute of Sea and Islands (Vietnam) and the Center for Strategic Studies and International Development (Vietnam). Special thanks also go to other friends in academe, from my former colleagues Alma Salvador and Diana Mendoza at Ateneo De Manila University, to Chester Cabalza of the National Defense College, for taking the time to share their views on Philippine defence policy and/or Chinese domestic politics. In terms of better understanding the strategic behaviour and motivations of middle powers such as India, Japan and Australia, I am also very grateful to exchanges with Srikanth Kondapalli (professor of Chinese studies at Jawaharlal Nehru University), Saturo Nagao (research fellow at the Tokyo Foundation and lecturer at Gakushuin University) and Carl Thayer (emeritus professor at the University of New South Wales), who were all kind enough to share their views on the record. I must also thank David Fluharty, associate professor at the University of Washington, for sharing his expertise in the realm of environmental and marine sciences, which further opened my eyes to the other less appreciated dimensions (and costs) of the ongoing South China Sea disputes.

Friends in the media have also been very helpful in shaping my understanding of the domestic politics behind the foreign policy predisposition of the Philippines and China. In particular, I am grateful to veteran journalists such as Chito Sta Romana, a long-term journalist based in Beijing, who has certainly played a great role in aiding mutual understanding between the Philippines and China, as well as Ellen Tordesillas, a seasoned journalist, who has closely covered the South China Sea disputes for years. I am also grateful to many friends, especially those from China, who helped me to better understand Chinese domestic politics.

I became even more familiar with the UN Convention on the Law of the Sea (UNCLOS) thanks to a series of exchanges (1–19 December

2014), under the International Visitor Leadership Program (IVLP) of the United States government, with a number of leading experts in Washington, DC, New York, Seattle and Hawaii. In particular I would like to thank professors Anthony C. Arend (Georgetown University), John Norton Moore and Myron H. Nordquist (Virginia University), Mathew Waxman (Columbia University) and James Hsiung (New York University), as well as several law-of-the-sea experts at the United Nations and the Asia-Pacific Center for Security Studies, among other legal scholars. I also want to thank Professor Alexander Proelss (University of Trier) for so kindly sharing his views on China's historical rights claims, the implications of the *Philippines v. China* arbitration at The Hague, and prospects for cooperation in the South China Sea, on the sidelines of an international conference on the law of the sea in Hanoi.

Lastly, I would like to thank numerous policy-makers and diplomats from across the Asia-Pacific region, who, over the years, were kind enough to share their governments' points of view with me. My exchanges with them certainly helped me to better understand the strategic dilemma of many important powers and stakeholders directly or indirectly affected by the territorial disputes in the Western Pacific. I am also grateful to Roilo Golez, former national security adviser of the Philippines, and friends in the Philippine Coast Guard, particularly Deputy Commander Rudyard Somera, who agreed to share their views on the record. I would also like to thank top officials in the Philippine Department of Foreign Affairs, including Foreign Secretary Albert Del Rosario, as well as the Taiwanese Foreign Ministry and most especially President Ma Ying-jeou, who so kindly shared their views with me on the sidelines of conferences and workshops I have been invited to in recent months.

I sincerely hope this book will make some contribution, no matter how small, to a better and more balanced understanding of the relevance, roots, evolution and trajectory of the ongoing disputes in the Western Pacific. In my own humble ways, I hope I have provided some guidance for much-needed policy reforms to avoid armed conflict and manage existing disputes through the language of reason and the art of diplomacy.

FOREWORD BY WALDEN BELLO

The East Asia/Western Pacific region is one of the most volatile regions in the world today. Here, classic geopolitics is at work. Two great powers confront each other, a declining power seeking to contain a rising one, with a number of smaller states manoeuvring between the two to ensure their survival.

With the central element of its Grand Strategy being the prevention of the rise of a regional power in the Eurasian landmass that would threaten its global superiority, the USA under the Obama administration has put into motion the containment of China via military and economic means. The so-called Pivot to Asia has involved the refocusing of Washington's strategic assets, especially its naval power, on the region, while the Trans-Pacific Partnership aims to constrain the rise of China's economic might. Meanwhile, although China does not aim for global hegemony, it does aim for it at a regional level, and the US military assets and allies on the East Asian littoral and island-chain pose a major obstacle to this ambition.

Some smaller states in North-East Asia and South-East Asia, caught between this great power rivalry, seek to maximize their political and economic independence by playing off one against the other, though with a weak hand that, as in the case of the Philippines, leads to subordination to the goals of the power it chooses to ally with. Another middling state, North Korea, has chosen to ensure national survival not so much by taking sides as by developing its own nuclear arsenal and adopting a posture of deliberate unpredictability.

Then there is Japan, an economic power but a military protectorate distrusted by most of its neighbours that is engaged in the dangerous game of using the Chinese threat as an excuse to rearm and eventually throw off both its strategic subservience to the United States and military inferiority to China.

Richard Heydarian does a brilliant job of illuminating the complex dynamics of this multi-sided regional competition and warning of its perilous consequences, both direct and collateral. One of the younger generation of Asian political analysts, Heydarian has few peers when it comes to bringing us to an understanding of the policies, motivations and interaction of the actors in what analyst Barry Posen describes as the most geopolitically dynamic part of the globe.

Washington's imperial 'pivot', China's aggressive moves and Japan's opportunistic moves add up to a volatile brew. Many observers note that the Asia-Pacific military-political situation is becoming like that of Europe at the end of the nineteenth century, with the emergence of a similar configuration of balance-of-power politics. It is a useful reminder that while that fragile balancing might have worked for a time, it eventually ended up in the conflagration that was the First World War. None of the key players in East Asia today may want war. But nor did any of the Great Powers on the eve of the First World War. The problem is that in a situation of fierce rivalry among powers that hate one another, an incident like a ship collision – intended or unintended – may trigger an uncontrollable chain of events that may result in a regional war, or worse.

Hopefully this book will make a contribution not simply to academic analysis but to policy changes that will lead to an easing of tensions in the region.

Walden Bello
11 May 2015

INTRODUCTION

On 12 March 2015, London shocked the world when it decided to break ranks and join the Beijing-backed Asian Infrastructure Investment Bank (AIIB) as a founding member. Soon, all major American allies and strategic partners followed suit, puncturing a months-long American-led boycott against the Chinese proposed investment institution. It was nothing less than a strategic *coup de grâce*, highlighting Washington's declining global economic influence – and the gradual emergence of China as the economic pivot of Asia.

The participation of the United States' closest (European) ally as a founding member of the AIIB paved the way for long-standing European partners, from Germany to Italy to France, and leading Asia allies, particularly Australia and South Korea, to jump on the China economic bandwagon. Even Japan, which saw the AIIB as nothing less than a direct challenge to the Asian Development Bank (ADB), was forced to reconsider an initial boycott. It didn't take long before the World Bank, the International Monetary Fund and the (Japan-dominated) ADB also expressed their support for the establishment of the AIIB as a necessary institutional response to close the huge infrastructure spending gap in Asia, estimated at more than US$8 trillion in the 2010–20 period, which has inundated the financing capacity of existing regional and international intergovernmental development agencies (Asian Development Bank 2012). Prior to London's strategic mutiny, Washington delicately managed to successfully stage a collective boycott against the AIIB, leaving the China-backed bank stacked with mostly developing countries with limited capital to spare. At some point, Chinese officials began wondering whether the AIIB would make any commercial sense at all, shifting their attention to more financially viable options, such as the proposed Maritime Silk

Road initiative (Sun 2015). Formally, Washington has raised concerns over the AIIB's compliance with existing good governance, transparency and environmental sustainability standards, which are supposedly embodied by the World Bank, the ADB and the IMF. In reality, however, the key concern is whether China will use the AIIB as a Trojan horse for its broader strategic interests in Asia, utilizing the prowess of its financial resource to buy the loyalty of its neighbours. After all, if China was really interested in bridging the infrastructure spending gap in Asia, sceptics point out, it could have simply increased its contribution to the (Japan-dominated) ADB. And there are concerns that China, as the major donor, will wield effective veto power within the AIIB and deploy the new institution as an instrument of its national power. As prominent Chinese scholar Yan Xuetong (in Nikkei 2015) bluntly put it: 'The policy now is to allow these smaller [neighbouring] countries to benefit economically from their relationships with China. For China, we need good relationships more urgently than we need economic development. We let them benefit economically, and in return we get good political relationships. We should "purchase" the relationships.' The world was by now witnessing Chinese president Xi Jinping's 'Peripheral Diplomacy' initiative in action (see Chapter 3), a strategy that was first announced in a late 2013 high-profile gathering, the Peripheral Diplomacy Work Conference, in Beijing, but really gained pace after the Chinese Communist Party's Foreign Affairs Leading Group meeting in late 2014, the first in eight years.

In light of the AIIB fiasco, which clearly marked a major symbolic victory for Chinese *soft power*, the United States responded with sound and fury. Senior American officials bluntly expressed their outrage over the UK's decision, stating how Washington was 'wary about a trend toward constant accommodation of China, which is not the best way to engage a rising power' (*Economist* 2015). A statement by the National Security Council expressed Washington's 'concerns about whether the AIIB will meet these high standards, particularly related to governance, and environmental and social safeguards', encouraging China to ensure the AIIB will 'complement the existing architecture, and to work effectively alongside the World Bank and

Asian Development Bank' (Stewart 2015). With the World Bank, the International Monetary Fund and the ADB also expressing their support for the AIIB, Washington had no choice but to soften its criticism of the China-led body. Recovering from a major strategic setback, top American officials, such as Treasury Secretary Jack Lew, stated that the United States 'welcome[s] China having a significant role in the global economic and financial architecture', provided, of course, it will 'complement existing international financial institutions ... and share the international community's strong commitment to genuine multilateral decision making and ever-improving lending standards and safeguards' (Asia Society 2015).

Pledging US$50 billion out of its own pocket, China was proposing a new intergovernmental development bank to provide necessary funds and expertise to developing countries, specifically in the realm of infrastructure spending. Despite its relatively limited initial funding, the AIIB, at least in symbolic terms, represented a rival to existing institutions under the post-Second World War Bretton Woods System (BWS), namely the IMF, the World Bank and its Asian counterpart, the ADB. In fairness, China's decision to challenge the BWS by establishing new initiatives, such as the AIIB, the New Development Bank and the New Silk Road initiative (see Chapter 3), was partly driven by emerging powers' deepening frustration with the lack of much-needed reforms to reflect the shifting poles of global economic power in the World Bank and the IMF. Largely thanks to the unwillingness of the US Congress to ratify proposed reforms in 2010, the BWS has continued to artificially deflate the actual economic prowess of countries such as China, which have voting shares comparable to mid-size European countries, while magnifying the voting power of Western countries, especially the USA, which still effectively wields a veto power in the IMF (Mayeda 2015). With almost US$4 trillion dollars in its coffers, China – the world's biggest economy in purchasing power parity terms – is in a strong position to bridge the US$8 trillion infrastructure spending deficit in Asia. Given the inherent volatilities of currency markets, China is interested in redirecting its financial reserves towards more tangible, commercially viable investment opportunities (Dreyer 2015; Heydarian 2014d, 2015a). Asian triumphalists, such as Kishore Mahbubani, author of *The Great Convergence: Asia, the West, and the Logic of One World*, have happily embraced the AIIB – and China's rising economic profile on the global stage. For Mahbubani (2015), 'this new [economic] competition between America and China to produce better multilateral institutions will be good for the world'. The former Singaporean diplomat adds, '[i]t does not matter whether America wins or China wins. Either way, we will see an improvement in the standards of managing institutions of global governance.' The intensifying Sino-American rivalry ultimately means, Mahbubani argues, 'the Asian people will be better off. And the Asian century will arrive faster.' Fears over China's supposed plans to manipulate the AIIB as an extension of its national interest are most likely overblown. China has offered to forgo its veto power within the Beijing-based AIIB (Wei and Davis 2014). More importantly, the participation of wealthy and/or influential countries such as Australia, South Korea, Germany, France, the UK, Saudi Arabia, Singapore, India and Indonesia, among others, will almost certainly make the AIIB more diverse, multipolar and depoliticized in its design, decision-making structure and day-to-day operation. It's highly unlikely that China will try or even be able to impose its will on such powerful collection of countries. Although, technically China (with 26% of the voting shares) will still have a (latent) veto on issues that will require supermajority vote. But the AIIB episode reveals the growing ability of Beijing to isolate Washington over economic matters and entice its major economies to join alternative institutions outside the Western-dominated BWS. The circumstances surrounding the creation of the AIIB stand as a powerful testament to China's financial prowess, and its ability to assemble new economic blocs at the expense of its key regional rival, the USA.

The seismic shift

While Washington emerged as the undisputed global hegemon after the utter devastation of European powers and Japan in the Second World War, China's purported bid for hegemony is anchored by an unprecedented period of prosperity in East Asia and the emergence of Beijing as an indispensable economic partner for the West as well as the developing world.

After almost seven decades of American geopolitical primacy in Asia, the inexorable rise of China has gradually reshaped the regional strategic landscape. Two decades into the post-Cold War era, pre-cipitating a relatively brief period of American *hyperpower*, it became painfully clear that the United States' ever-expanding global interests – and its myriad of imperial engagements across multiple continents – were precariously anchored by ever-diminishing marginal improve-ments in the country's economic prowess. It did not take long before Washington – beginning in the latter years of the Bush administra-tion, but gaining more prominence under the Obama administration – realized its declining global influence and its diminishing appetite to respond to multiple crises across the world. It marked the end of the 'unipolar moment', with a growing proportion of American people opposing proactive American intervention in global affairs. In late 2013, a Pew Research poll showed that a majority of US respondents said their country 'should mind its own business internationally and let other countries get along the best they can on their own'. As many as 80 per cent agreed that the USA should 'not think so much in inter-national terms but concentrate more on [its] own national problems'. According to a mid-2014 poll by CNN, 63 per cent of the respondents expressed their gloomy outlook for the American economy by sharing their belief that the succeeding generation of Americans will be worse off than their parents (Polling Report 2014).

In fact, the gravity of America's problems has led to an interesting phenomenon: there are indications of a surprising convergence of perceptions between the ordinary Americans and the country's foreign policy establishment. Reflecting on America's foreign policy commitments in Asia, for instance, Elbridge Colby and Brad Glosserman (2012), senior experts from the Center for New American Security (CNA) and the Center for Strategic and International Studies (CSIS) respectively, succinctly captured the prevailing *zeitgeist* in the country by stating:

> The roots of a stronger external posture, then, lie in a reinvigorated effort to address America's internal problems. This is what most Americans want, too: a political system that starts grappling with the big problems that could mean the difference between solvency and insolvency, and an economic system that regains the vigor that Americans took for granted in the 20th century. Addressing these

challenges is especially important as, above all in the Pacific and Asia, increasingly competitive and assertive nations are rising. We cannot afford to fixate on secondary problems and allow our economic and ultimately military advantages to be overtaken.

This is not the first time that the USA has confronted severe scepticism at home, among both experts and ordinary Americans. But there are serious indications of genuine decline in American global standing. Historically, there were at least five waves of 'declinist debates', as identified by political scientist Samuel Huntington, beginning with fears sparked by the Soviet Union's technological leaps in the late 1950s, the disastrous impact of the Vietnam wars of the late 1960s, the stagflation caused by the Arab countries' coordinated oil embargo in the early 1970s, the seeming resurgence of Soviet power (after its invasion of Afghanistan, which coincided with the collapse of the powerful Iranian monarchy) in the late 1970s, and the economic uncertainties of the 1980s (Colby and Lettow 2014). Reflecting on the latest wave of declinist arguments vis-à-vis American power in recent years, Elbridge Colby and Paul Lettow (ibid.), a former member of the US National Security Council, argue that America's relative decline is largely driven by the resurgence of non-Western powers, potentially upending a two-centuries-old order:

> This anxiety is real and justified, and it lies behind much of the public's support for withdrawing from the world, for retrenchment … For the first time in 200 years, most growth is occurring in the developing world, and the speed with which that shift – a function of globalization – has occurred is hard to fathom … This shift reorders what was, in some sense, a historical anomaly: the transatlantic dominance of the past 150 years.

The shift in economic poles of power, from the West to the global South, is startling: as early as 1990, only 14 per cent of cross-border flows of services, commodities and finances originated in rapidly developing countries, also known as emerging economies (EMs). Within two decades, the figure has increased to nearly 40 per cent (ibid.). Worried by the purported re-emergence of the early-twentieth-century American isolationism, neoconservative thinkers such as Robert Kagan (2014) have portrayed a pessimistic outlook for the international system, where the absence of proactive American global leadership has supposedly paved the way for a dystopian world – characterized by an upsurge of regional conflicts, from Ukraine in eastern Europe to Syria and Iraq in the Middle East – that serves as 'a sign that something is changing, and perhaps more quickly than we may imagine ... [a] transition into a different world order or into a world disorder of a kind not seen since the 1930s'.

While China managed to maintain robust rates of economic growth – and rapidly augment its military capabilities along the way – the USA, in turn, confronted what British historian Paul Kennedy described as 'imperial overstretch'. A decade of military interventions, particularly in Afghanistan (2001) and Iraq (2003), tarnished the American image around the world and undermined the fiscal foundations of the American economy, eventually forcing the Pentagon to consider across-the-board budget cuts, amounting to as much as US$1 trillion, in the second decade of the twenty-first century (Olson 2014). Similar to the heady aftermath of the Vietnam War – which deeply divided the American citizenry and exacted tremendous economic and military costs on the USA – *strategic retrenchment* has once again become a foreign policy imperative, forcing the Obama administration to contemplate a new 'Nixon Doctrine', whereby the USA would (i) reassess its overseas priorities; (ii) delegate more strategic autonomy to regional allies to uphold the liberal international order, and (iii) reduce defence spending and foreign policy commitments (Porter 2013).

The 2007/08 Great Recession – which exposed the structural vulnerabilities of Anglo-Saxon capitalism, and precipitated the deepest economic crisis since the Great Depression in the early twentieth century – marked both a relative and absolute decline in America's global standing. While Western economies were battered by a vicious combination of financial crisis and economic contraction, proactive economic interventions allowed China to avoid a hard landing. Launching a massive US$586 billion programme of fiscal and monetary stimulus, the Asian powerhouse managed to quickly close its economic gap with the world's leading power. As early as

2000, the USA's GDP was ten times bigger than China's (Colby and Lettow 2014). In 2007, the USA's gross domestic product (GDP) was almost four times bigger than China's. Within four years, the USA's (nominal) GDP was only twice as big, with China poised to become the world's biggest economy in purchasing power parity terms in late 2014 (Pei 2014). In *The Post American World*, Fareed Zakaria, one of America's most celebrated foreign policy experts, eloquently outlined how the emerging global order was more undergirded by the rise of the rest rather than the absolute decline of the West. After the Great Recession, however, the West was confronting absolute economic decline, while emerging powers such as China managed to cruise ahead and sustain above-average growth rates.

Compared to other great powers in human history, China has been arguably the most successful economic power in its first three decades of 'catch up' (with the leading powers of the time). Figures 0.1, 0.2 and 0.3 show the key economic and military indicators (e.g., GDP growth, share of global GDP, share of global trade and share of global military spending) of the five most successful rising powers in recent history. While the rise in China's share of global defence spending has been relatively modest (see Figure 0.3), it has experienced the most

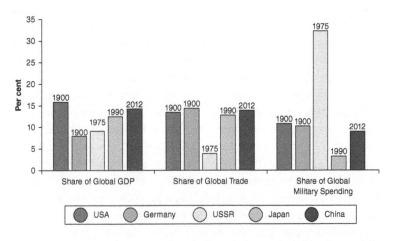

0.1 Rising powers' key economic and military indicators in their peak years (%) (*source*: World Bank, Stockholm International Peace Research Institute).

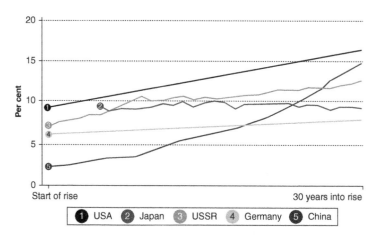

0.2 Five rising powers' share of global GDP in their peak decades (%) (*source*: World Bank).

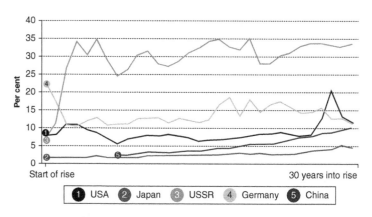

0.3 Five rising powers' share of global military spending in their peak decades (%) (*source*: Stockholm International Peace Research Institute).

rapid increase in its share of global GDP and global trade (see Figures 0.1 and 0.2) compared to Imperial Japan, the Kaiser's Germany, the Soviet Union (USSR) and the USA in their respective first three decades of rapid growth.

This rapid economic transformation of China has had immense geopolitical repercussions. It was during this period of accelerated catch-up that China began to more confidently express its misgivings vis-à-vis the global architecture of governance. For instance, Chinese leaders began calling for the displacement of the dollar as the global currency and the overhaul of the World Bank and the IMF. In Asia, Chinese leaders became increasingly more assertive in advocating an end to unimpeded American naval patrols across the East and South China Seas, specifically within China's 200-nautical-mile exclusive economic zone. Slowly but surely, the Asian theatre inched closer to a game-changing power transition, pitting China's revisionist ambitions against a US-led liberal order. With the world's largest population and standing army, China's growing economic might enabled it to emerge as a key contender to American hegemony; this trend was most prominent in China's own backyard, East Asia.

An inscrutable challenge

China's purported bid for leadership in Asia is complicated by a myriad of domestic economic and socio-political challenges (see Chapters 2 and 3), which may, especially in the long run, undermine the country's willingness and wherewithal to upend the existing order in the region. An additional source of complexity is the distinct nature of great power rivalry in the region. In contrast to the USSR, which represented the greatest threat to American hegemony in Asia during the height of the Cold War, China is engaged neither in a full-blown ideological warfare nor in an overt military confrontation with the USA. China's relations with its historical rival, Japan, and the global superpower, the USA, are shaped by conditions of simultaneous rivalry and cooperation – a hallmark of structural interdependence among leading global actors in an era of economic globalization. No wonder it is easy to dismiss any suggestion that the world is in the midst of a new Cold War, with China and the USA as the main protagonists.

The late Lee Kuan Yew, Singapore's founding father and a long-time adviser to both American and Chinese leaders, aptly distinguished the fundamental differences between the Sino-American rivalry and the Cold War by arguing: 'Unlike U.S.–Soviet relations during the Cold War, there is no irreconcilable ideological conflict between the U.S. and a China that has enthusiastically embraced the market. Sino-

American relations are both cooperative and competitive. Competition between them is inevitable, but conflict is not' (Mearsheimer 2014a). There is hardly any indication that Washington is replicating the Cold War 'containment' strategy, which was conceptualized and advocated by no less than George Kennan (1947), who argued:

> In these circumstances it is clear that the main element of any United States policy toward the Soviet Union must be that of a long-term, patient but firm and vigilant containment of Russian expansive tendencies ... In the light of the above, it will be clearly seen that the Soviet pressure against the free institutions of the Western world is something that can be contained by the adroit and vigilant application of counterforce at a series of constantly shifting geographical and political points, corresponding to the shifts and maneuvers of Soviet policy, but which cannot be charmed or talked out of existence ... This would of itself warrant the United States entering with reasonable confidence upon a policy of firm containment, designed to confront the Russians with unalterable counterforce at every point where they show signs of encroaching upon the interest of a peaceful and stable world.

The complexity of Sino-American relations, and their attendant strategic uncertainties, was succinctly captured by no less than the US National Security Advisor, and former US ambassador to the United Nations, Susan Rice, who, in a 2013 speech at Georgetown University, said: 'When it comes to China, we seek to operationalize a new model of major power relations. That means managing inevitable competition while forging deeper cooperation on issues where our interests converge – in Asia and beyond' (White House 2013). One could argue that what the world is witnessing today is a historically unique form of great power rivalry, portending a transition from a unipolar order towards a more complex multipolar system, with China, among a diverse group of emerging powers in the global South, standing as the most promising contender for leadership in Asia. While the USA stands as the only country in human history to have achieved global superpower status (Mearsheimer 2014a), China, in turn, is poised to become the world's biggest-ever economy, equipped with an unprecedented reservoir of military, technological and demographic assets (Jacques 2012).

But it is more than just a question of size, and the geographic extent of the two powers' influence. Oscillating between 'strategic rivalry' and 'strategic cooperation' – depending on the issue at hand, the configuration of power relations in the international system, and the nature of bilateral relations at a particular historical juncture – Sino-American relations in recent decades have been largely guided by a 'neither friends nor foes' principle (Pei 2014). Far from pursuing a communist utopia, modern-day China epitomizes the brutal efficiency of state capitalism in the twenty-first century. Decoupled from its revolutionary past, when Beijing served as a leading patron of communist movements across South-East Asia, today's China represents a large, competitive neo-mercantilist state, which is primarily interested in large-scale access to raw materials, advanced (civilian and military) technology and global consumer markets. Fully integrated into the global chains of production, China stands as the pivot of the global capitalist system: it serves as a leading manufacturing hub, a market for intermediate-capital goods, and a source of affordable financing as well as cheap labour for the industrialized West. Struggling with anaemic growth at home, major corporations and industries in the West and Japan have placed their hopes in China's insatiable desire for foreign direct investments (FDIs), technological imports and luxury products. A post-ideological China, primarily driven by national interest, has become an indispensable economic partner to the West.

After three decades of relentless economic growth, however, China is yet to emerge as a full-spectrum competitor to the USA. While one could argue that China has achieved economic dominance in Asia, emerging as the biggest trading partner of all major economies in the region, the USA continues to be the pre-eminent naval power in the region, with Japan and Australia acting as key elements of Washington's 'hub and spokes' alliance structure in the Asia-Pacific theatre (see Chapter 6). In short, China's pursuit of regional leadership is yet to assume its most compelling form. At times, international affairs may seem to be a fluid struggle for dominance among competing powers. In the late 1970s, for instance, leading scholars, from Robert Gilpin to Paul Kennedy and Ezra Vogel, discussed the possibility of an economically ascendant Japan fully challenging American hegemony in Asia. In the following decade, however, Japan would suffer an economic meltdown, giving birth to the so-called 'Lost Two Decades' (1995–2007). Since then, Japan has struggled to regain its economic dynamism, with deflation, stagnating productivity and demographic decline severely undermining the country's competitiveness. In short, the decline of the USA, specifically in recent years, does not necessarily guarantee a permanent slump in Western power – and portend the emergence of China as the new global superpower.

It is far from clear whether China will ever attain the kind of economic and military dominance enjoyed by the USA in the immediate decades following the Second World War and the collapse of the USSR in 1991. Acting as an offshore balancer, reluctantly intervening in the Eurasian wars once its national interests were perceived to be directly threatened by revisionist powers (Wilhelmite and Nazi Germany in Europe, and Imperial Japan in the Pacific), the USA emerged out of the two world wars relatively unscathed, given the utter destruction suffered by Japan and western Europe throughout the Second World War. Responsible for almost half of the global economic output by the middle of the twentieth century, and equipped with a nuclear arsenal, the USA was in an unprecedented position to fully shape the architecture of global governance for decades to come. Even if China manages to become the world's biggest economy (in nominal terms) in the coming years, it is unlikely that it will become dominant enough to single-handedly outshine all its peers the way the USA managed to do after the destructive conflicts of the twentieth century. If anything, other emerging powers such as India, Brazil, Russia, Turkey, Indonesia and Iran are also intent on translating their expanding capabilities into greater influence within their immediate neighbourhood and the wider international system. Despite suffering a relative decline in their global status, the USA, Japan and western European powers, meanwhile, will continue to wield considerable influence and military-economic power in the coming decades. Yet even if one assumes that China will most likely fall short of fully displacing *Pax Americana*, especially in East Asia, and emerge as the new global superpower in the foreseeable future, recent years have seen a perceptible uptick in Sino-American tensions, especially in the western Pacific. And it is this theatre of competition which may set ablaze three decades of relentless economic growth and regional integration in Asia, which were built under the auspices of American hegemony and a surprisingly symbiotic relationship between Washington and Beijing. As Sinologists Evan S. Medeiros and M. Taylor Fravel point out (2003): 'A great irony, unacknowledged by many Chinese, is that China's economy has benefited enormously from U.S. military primacy and American efforts to maintain stability in Asia over the last 20 years.' In his groundbreaking work *The End of History*, Francis Fukuyama (1992: 1) emphasized the need to distinguish between 'what is essential and what is contingent or accidental in world history'. Against the backdrop of relative American decline, and absolute reduction in its military expenditures, China's emergence as a regional powerhouse has gained greater salience. But does this mean that we have entered a truly post-American era? Has *Pax Americana* given way to a *Pax Sinica*, especially in Asia? Are we witnessing the re-establishment of a Sino-centric Asian order? Are we living in a second Cold War, portending an inevitable conflict between the world's most powerful states? Or instead, are we witnessing a unique historical period, dominated by two capitalist rivals with distinct strategic cultures, political systems and economic visions? These are just among a number of important questions, which have been raised with greater urgency and vividness in recent years, to examine whether Asia is on the cusp of a genuine strategic transformation. In this regard, the book aims to shed light on the intensifying rivalry embedded in and the complex evolution of Sino-American relations in Asia in recent decades (see Chapters 1 and 2).

Asia's new battlefield

The emergence of China as an economic powerhouse should be largely welcomed as a positive development, especially as it democratizes the international structure of governance and provides new sources of capital and expertise for the developing world. The problem with Mahbubani's (2015) argument, however, is that it treats

Sino-American rivalry in Asia like a free-market competition between corporate giants, paving the way for global multipolarity. But the case at hand is not a microeconomic scenario of efficient, profit-driven firms competing for market shares. As China grows richer, becoming 'moderately prosperous', it will naturally, similar to great powers in recent memory, become more concerned with prestige, influence and the pursuit of the 'China Dream' – restoring China to its position of historical glory, potentially recreating the Sino-centric order in Asia (see Chapter 3). Peripheral diplomacy, many of China's neighbours suspect, is primarily about challenging American hegemony – and deepening China's strategic depth in its backyard. Ultimately, however, the key litmus test for China's rise, on whether it will be peaceful or destabilizing, is the intensified territorial disputes in the western Pacific (see Chapters 4 and 5), which have placed an ascendant China on a collision course with regional neighbours, from Japan to the Philippines and Vietnam, as well as the putative anchor of the liberal international order, the USA. In recent years, China's economic charm offensive has gone hand in hand with its accelerated construction activities across the South China Sea, as it gobbles up contested maritime features and resources in the area, as well as challenging Japan's age-old hold over the Senkaku (*Diaoyu* to China) islands in the East China Sea (see Chapters 3–5). Not only the USA, but also many of its allies are wondering whether China's growing economic muscle will continue to provide greater ammunition for its territorial and maritime ambitions in East Asia. After all, China's astonishing economic expansion has allowed it to increase its (announced) annual defence spending from US$10 billion in 1997 to roughly US$145 billion in 2015. This marks one of the most dramatic defence build-ups in human history, understandably raising alarm bells among China's neighbours and rivals, which have anxiously watched Beijing's ever-expanding (paramilitary and military) presence in the western Pacific and economic influence across the globe. Since China conceals many of its off-the-books defence-related expenditures, and doesn't reveal expenses for arms imports, research and development and subsidies to defence industries, many suspect that China's true defence spending could be twice as large as the announced figures (Bitzinger 2015).

In the long run, others are wondering whether Beijing's prospective domination of adjacent waters will pave the way for a more globally assertive China, which will not shy away from vigorously challenging American interests beyond the East Asian theatre. No wonder the ongoing maritime disputes are increasingly treated as a proxy for tracing the trajectory of China's long-term ambitions and behaviour. The rise of China and its brewing rivalry with the USA are paving the way for the establishment of a new order in the Asia-Pacific region. There are serious concerns that China is beginning to move from what the early-twentieth-century Italian thinker Antonio Gramsci identified as 'War of Position', patiently building the foundations of influence, to 'War of Manoeuvre', directly confronting the status quo, for hegemony[1] (see Chapter 6). Recognizing the nexus between domestic politics and broader international developments in shaping foreign policy (Moravcsik 1997; Putnam 1988), the book also looks at the interface of domestic political calculations and balance of power dynamics in the Asia-Pacific theatre. To further contextualize the relevance and direction of the ongoing maritime battle in the western Pacific, the book, throughout the following chapters, examines the roots of the ongoing maritime disputes in Asia, especially the South China Sea, and the perilous explosion in nationalistic fervour among claimant states (see Chapter 3); the role of middle powers in the territorial showdown in the western Pacific (see Chapter 5); the ever-increasing stakes in preventing a regional armed conflict; and, finally, the prospects for a post-American order in the Asia-Pacific theatre (see Chapter 6). Astonishingly, many forget how, just a few decades ago, Sino-American relations enjoyed remarkable stability and symbiosis – a core element of regional prosperity and stability in East Asia. Understanding the circumstances and policies that facilitated rapprochement between the two powers in the past may guide our current and future efforts at exploring possible mechanisms for managing the deepening geopolitical competition in the western Pacific and trace the potential trajectory of Sino-American relations in the coming decades. And this is where our analysis should begin.

---

[1] For a summary of these terms in Gramsci, see Egan (2014).

1 | THE GREAT CONVERGENCE: SINO-AMERICAN SYMBIOSIS

Victorious warriors win first and then go to war, while defeated warriors go to war first and then seek to win.

Sun Tzu

One must change one's tactics every ten years if one wishes to maintain one's superiority.

Napoleon Bonaparte

With the decisive collapse of the USSR in 1991, the USA entered a period of unparalleled global dominance, reinforcing its long-held bid to achieve full-spectrum hegemony. Interestingly, the American-centred unipolar order emerged amid a largely symbiotic relationship between Washington and Beijing – an astonishing result of significant reconfigurations in the strategic orientation of both powers, aided by a historic leadership transition in China. In the USA, the Clinton administration played a decisive role in further integrating China into the international liberal order, transforming the Asian country into a pillar of the global economy – and an indispensable strategic partner for the USA. While the Nixon administration took the initial decisive steps to forge a mutually satisfying strategic understanding between the two powers, arguably it was the Clinton administration, perhaps more than that of any other American president in recent decades, which most proactively pursued a viable strategic partnership with China, particularly in the realm of trade and investments. On China's part, the post-Mao leadership progressively, albeit with certain setbacks along the way, pushed the boundaries of economic reforms at home and consciously sought improved ties with neighbouring states, including historical rivals such as Japan, as well as the USA. The fateful entente between Beijing and Washington underpinned a period of relative stability and unprecedented capitalist expansion in Asia, especially in China, strengthening the pillars of a US-led liberal order in the region and beyond. The seemingly symbiotic Sino-American relationship, however, concealed deep geopolitical faultlines, with the two powers repeatedly teetering on the verge of collision.

The liberal experiment

Committed to a liberal vision, wherein interstate cooperation and economic interdependence define international relations, the Clinton administration was an enthusiastic advocate of progressive reduction in trade barriers and frictionless flow of investments across state borders. The whole liberal-institutionalist paradigm, embraced by the Clinton administration, was predicated on the following assumptions: that individual states value absolute gains of economic cooperation, that military power has become increasingly superfluous as an instrument of foreign policy, and that international organizations are capable of autonomously facilitating rule-based behaviour by rewarding cooperation and penalizing non-compliance vis-à-vis existing norms in the international system (Keohane 1982; Nye 2004). This marked the era of *economic globalization*, with the establishment of the World Trade Organization (WTO), regional trading regimes such as the North American Free Trade Agreement (NAFTA), and pan-regional platforms such as the Asia-Pacific Economic Cooperation (APEC) Economic Leaders' Meeting serving as the pillars of a new order, wherein economics and trade stood as the ultimate preoccupation of interstate affairs. Intent on preventing the re-emergence of Cold War rivalries, the Clinton administration advocated the integration of post-Soviet Russia and post-Mao China into the liberal international order. The strategic rationale behind the Clinton administration's accommodating approach was the perceived necessity to transform China and Russia into benign, responsible powers by increasing their economic and geopolitical stake in the stability and perpetuation of the existing global order. Guided by the belief that the forces of globalization could tame historical animosities and discipline the ambitions of former Cold War rivals, the Clinton administration sought to co-opt non-Western powers by appealing to the capitalist instincts of their ruling classes. Just as the post-Second World War 'Marshall Plan', and its variants in East Asia, allowed Washington to integrate former rivals such as Germany and Japan into the Western order, the latest wave of economic globalization, in turn, carried the promise of eliminating late-twentieth-century rivalries with communist powers. In Europe, the Clinton administration pushed for the enlargement of the European Union (EU) into the ex-Soviet space, downplaying the necessity for active containment of Moscow. To assuage Russia's insecurities, and underscore its commitment to building a new relationship with the heir of the Soviet empire, Washington expanded the Group of Seven (G7) to the Group of Eight (G8), inviting Moscow to join the world's most exclusive club of industrial powers. In Asia, Clinton assiduously supported China's desire for greater economic interaction with the industrialized powers, vehemently advocating China's membership of the WTO as well as the large-scale inflow of investments and technology into the Asian country. Despite facing tremendous pressure from the (Republican-dominated) US Congress, which maintained a critical stance on China's political system and trading practices, the Clinton administration sought to decouple trade from human rights issues, declaring in 1994 that such an approach would 'place [the Sino-American] relationship into a larger and more productive framework' (Shirk 2008: 225). Such efforts were predicated on decades of carefully built rapprochement between Beijing and Washington, which commenced with the Nixon administration's back-door diplomacy in the early 1970s, but suffered a huge, albeit temporary, setback after the 1989 Tiananmen massacre. Guided by the principles of realpolitik, which emphasizes the pragmatic importance of overcoming ideological differences for the pursuit of material gains, the Nixon administration sought to exploit the Sino-Soviet split (1960–89) to create a new concert of powers against Moscow. The strategy was also born out of the painful realization that the material, political and humanitarian costs of the Vietnam War dramatically undermined the foundations of American power, highlighting the necessity for creative diplomatic overtures vis-à-vis rising powers such as China. In the 1990s, however, the Clinton administration was reaching out to China from a position of strength, supposedly making Washington's efforts look more sincere and benevolent in nature. China, meanwhile, was still grappling

with the political aftershocks of the 1989 democratic uprising at home –
and the horrific crackdown on student protests in Beijing and across the
country that followed – which provoked unprecedented divisions within
the political class, undermining the internal coherence and domestic
legitimacy of the Chinese Communist Party (CCP). No wonder China
was more than happy to reciprocate the Clinton administration's
efforts, hoping to end Beijing's political isolation and aid a decade-
and-half-long experiment with economic liberalization, which took off
under the leadership of Deng Xiaoping, China's paramount leader from
the late 1970s to the mid-1990s. In the twilight years of the twentieth
century, the Clinton administration seemingly became the harbinger
of the end of history, with capitalist prosperity becoming the ultimate
obsession of the world's leading powers – and the pivot around which
international relations revolved and took their form. After all, the
Clinton administration was confident that globalization was a game that
the USA – as the world's most advanced country with the most powerful
military – could win (Bello 2006). But what were China's calculations,
as it welcomed a more cooperative relationship with China?

China's soul-searching

The collapse of the USSR was a sobering moment of reflection
for the CCP, presenting new sets of challenges and opportunities for
China's one-party system. On one hand, China benefited from the
(temporary) elimination of a powerful rival to the north. For centuries,
Moscow represented a major source of national security threat to
Beijing, with the balance of power rapidly shifting in the former's
favour, especially in the nineteenth and twentieth centuries (Jacques
2012). The revolutionary upheavals of the early twentieth century
fell short of permanently resetting age-old rivalries between the two
nations. Despite sharing a common belief in communism, and Stalin's
financial and logistical assistance to Maoist China, the two powers
adopted divergent interpretations of Marxist ideology,[1] with Beijing

---

[1] In contrast to Leninist-Marxist Russia, Mao Zedong, who took over
a backward feudal-agricultural country, emphasized the importance
of mobilizing the peasant class as the core constituency of communist
revolutionary emancipation.

constantly fearful of Moscow's territorial ambitions in Central Asia and the north-western frontiers of China. Also, Maoist China constantly refused to subordinate itself to Moscow's leadership claims over the communist world, eventually leading to an increasingly overt split in the 1960s, which brought the two powers close to armed confrontation over territorial tensions in North-East Asia. In the latter decades of the Cold War, which saw greater strategic understanding between Beijing and Washington, China was predominantly concerned with a joint Soviet–Vietnamese invasion from the south. The disappearance of the Soviet threat dramatically reduced the likelihood of large-scale land-based warfare on China's northern borders, consolidating China's position as a continental power. This allowed the Asian powerhouse to shift its strategic orientation towards maritime domains to the east and south (Garver 1992; Nan 2010; Kaplan 2010; Kissinger 2011; Jacques 2012).

Analysing the geography of China's rising global ambitions, Robert Kaplan (2010), a leading geopolitical thinker, explains the post-Cold War geography of China's rising global ambitions, and the rapidly shifting balance of power between Moscow and Beijing:

> China today is consolidating its land borders and beginning to turn outward ... During the Cold War, border disputes between China and the Soviet Union brought hundreds of thousands of troops to this Siberian back of beyond and sometimes ignited into clashes ... The Russian state expanded its reach into [China's northern frontier] during the nineteenth century and the early twentieth century, while China was weak. Now, China is strong, and the Russian government's authority is nowhere as feeble as it is in the eastern third of the country.

The collapse of the USSR, meanwhile, also marked the ideological bankruptcy of communism as a state ideology. And the 1989 protests reflected the growing discontent among China's intelligentsia and middle classes against the single-party rule of the CCP, which stubbornly held on to power with a combination of brute force, ideological indoctrination and, particularly under Deng's leadership, the provision of material prosperity. The 1989 pro-democracy protests underscored the fragility of Deng's performance-based mode of political legitimization, forcing China's paramount leader to consider a tenuous cocktail of repressive political measures and economic liberalization schemes. No less than Zhao Ziyang, China's highest-ranking official and the CCP's general secretary, stood as one of the most prominent critics of Beijing's response to the democratic protests. His call for political liberalization, and outright opposition to the brutal crackdown in Tiananmen in favour of dialogue, led to his political downfall. Yet he repeatedly refused to recant. Under house arrest, he sought to justify his position by smuggling out his personal journals, which culminated in *Prisoner of the State: The Secret Journal of Chinese Premier Zhao Ziyang* (Nathan 2009).

The end of the Cold War also meant that the capitalist West, especially the USA, was placed in a position of unrivalled ascendancy, leaving China in a particularly vulnerable position. The 1991 Gulf War, which saw the rapid devastation of Iraq's massive army by the Western coalition forces, served as a wake-up call for the Chinese political leadership. Saddam's Iraq boasted one of the largest armies in the world, but its antiquated Soviet hardware stood no chance against the technology-intensive armed forces of the North Atlantic Treaty Organization (NATO). Like Iraq's, China's military hardware was largely a derivative of Soviet technology, with the Western arms embargo on China, instituted after the 1989 Tiananmen massacre, depriving the Asian country of sustained, large-scale access to advanced defence technology. The RAND Corporation, a leading security think tank, argued (Cliff et al. 2011): 'The 1991 Persian Gulf War sent shockwaves throughout China's military community and accelerated the People's Liberation Army's (PLA) modernization and shifts in strategy. The United States' overwhelming dominance in that conflict led Chinese military leaders to push for advanced military technologies.' A few years earlier, the RAND Corporation similarly described (Kazianis 2014) how Chinese strategists anxiously analysed the 1991 Gulf War: 'airpower received attention [from Chinese observers] for its ability to destroy air defense and command-and-control nodes [of Soviet-armed Iraq], while the U.S. use of stealth aircraft and cruise missiles highlighted the difficulties [China's armed forces] would have in defending [themselves] against an attack from an advanced air force'.

During the 1995/96 Taiwan Crisis, the third in a series of cross-strait exercises in military brinkmanship since the end of the Second World War, China was once again reminded of its palpable military inferiority, when the USA tried to defend Taiwan by resorting to its strongest display of military power in the region since the Vietnam War. As Harry Kazianis,[2] an expert on China's military affairs, explains:

> China has studied with great interest the wars in Iraq, Afghanistan and in the Balkans over the last two decades as well as Beijing's own clashes with Washington (the 1995–1996 Taiwan crisis and 2001 Hainan Island controversy). The lesson is quite clear: China, for the foreseeable future, will not be able to match America carrier for carrier, sub for sub etc. So they have invested in anti-access capabilities to raise the cost of entry into a conflict in places like the South China or East China Seas as well as near and around Taiwan. As time passes, Beijing will have the capabilities to create an ever increasing 'no-go zone' – as Toshi Yoshihara has called it – extending out to as far as the second island chain in the years to come. Would America be willing to trade a carrier – and the thousands of men and women aboard – for a disputed island or reef? China's goal is to deter America just as much as win if a kinetic conflict ever occurred.

The Clinton administration deployed two aircraft carriers, USS *Nimitz* and USS *Independence*, amid a rise in hostilities between mainland China and Taiwan. Beijing vociferously opposed pro-independence sentiments among the Taiwanese political leadership. Kazianis (2014) argues that the event once again underscored how 'Chinese strategists simply had no solution in negating [America's] power projection capabilities ......' Recognizing the USA's indisputable superiority in military prowess, the Chinese leadership responded to the post-Cold War strategic environment with legendary pragmatism. No less than Deng himself stood at the centre of China's pragmatic turn. As China's paramount leader, who took over Mao's helm in the late 1970s after being purged twice by the conservative factions of the

---

[2]   Interview with the author, 29 July 2014.

CCP, he constantly emphasized the necessity for strategic patience in a fluid domestic and regional environment and the wisdom of pragmatic accommodation with external powers, no matter how seemingly undesirable such an approach seemed, especially to hardline factions within the party. Deng advised caution to his colleagues and future Chinese leaders by famously stating: 'hide your strength, bide your time'. Viewing the international system as a Darwinian struggle for survival and power, Deng lamented how 'development is the only hard truth ... [and] if we do not develop, then we will be bullied' (Kissinger 2011). Deng's heterodox approach to governance was born out of this cold, calculating admission of China's relative backwardness and insecurity. But instead of resorting to propaganda and ideological delusions, as many autocratic leaders tend to do in periods of crisis and relative decline, Deng sought to confront China's precarious situation by humbly taking on the country's challenges with utmost patience and legendary perseverance.

The architect of reform

Despite his notoriety for being the architect of two devastating social upheavals, namely the Great Leap Forward and the Cultural Revolution, which led to the deaths of tens of millions of innocent citizens, Mao Zedong took an increasingly pragmatic position in the twilight years of his rule. In the 1970s, Deng's tenuous return to power, and his perilous lobbying for structural reforms in China's governance paradigm, took place within a fluid milieu, where Mao's more pragmatic instincts stood against a backdrop of revolutionary zeal, disastrous socio-economic experiments, and factional warfare within the CCP. It took drastic actions by the People's Liberation Army (PLA), the military wing of the CCP, to prevent the disintegration of China by the late 1960s (Shirk 2008: 13). The Sino-American rapprochement in the 1970s, however, served as a powerful springboard for decisive political reforms in China – paving the way for Deng's emergence as China's paramount leader at the expense of Mao's anointed successor, Hua Guofeng, who took a more conservative position by opposing outright ideological break with the Maoist orthodoxy (Kissinger 2011). In retrospect, though cataclysmic, Mao's radical policies prepared China for Deng's reforms, which were no less revolutionary in their transformation of Chinese society. Together, Mao and Deng played a central role in the transition of China from a backward feudal polity into a modern industrial powerhouse. As Henry Kissinger (ibid.: 321) aptly puts it: 'Mao destroyed traditional China and left its rubble as building blocks for ultimate modernization. Deng had the courage to base modernization on the initiative and resilience of individual Chinese. He abolished the communes and fostered provincial autonomy to introduce what he called "socialism with Chinese characteristics".'

It was precisely such a dialectical relationship between the two paramount leaders – with Mao's orthodoxy negating the Chinese feudal past, and Deng's 'economic modernization' synthesis, in turn, representing a negation of Mao's radical anti-feudalism – which has allowed China to reclaim its place among the great powers, after centuries of decline under pre-modern dynastic regimes. China experts Orville Schell and John Delury (2013) eloquently captured the Hegelian dimension of China's transition under Mao and Deng when they argued:

> No leader in 20th-century China was more totalistic and unrelenting in attacking traditional culture than Mao … it may have been precisely those periods of Mao's most uncompromising nihilism that demolished China's old society, freeing Chinese from their traditional moorings … [serving as an] essential, but paradoxical, precursor to China's subsequent boom under Deng and his successors, catapulting the Chinese into their present single-minded and unrestrained pursuit of wealth and power.

Towards the end of their lives, China's paramount leaders, Mao and Deng, displayed growing concerns for the stability and well-being of communist China. In Mao's case, he was concerned with the prospects of a full-scale war with the USSR. Domestically, Mao could not but be alarmed by the disastrous legacy of his socio-economic experiments, the Great Leap Forward and the Cultural Revolution, and the risks of his manipulative exploitation of inter-factional politics within the CCP, which became increasingly vicious in the 1970s. This provided an auspicious backdrop for the Nixon administration's efforts to explore a rapprochement with China. More pragmatic than Mao, and committed to an overhaul of China's unsustainable state-controlled economic system, Deng hoped to lay down the foundations of a prosperous China. Nevertheless, he preserved the state apparatus, and its party-centred bureaucratic architecture, constructed under Mao. In the twilight years of his rule, Deng pushed for an increasingly more accommodating relationship with neighbours as well as Washington, hoping to strengthen China's bid to re-emerge as a legitimate leader in Asia. Between 1979 and 1984, in a series of important statements, Deng provided a blueprint for managing long-standing territorial disputes with neighbouring states by stating: 'sovereignty remains ours; shelve disputes; pursue joint development' (Fravel 2013). Deng sought to find a diplomatic formula, which would allow China to normalize and strengthen relations with neighbouring states without necessarily dropping the country's historical claims (Kissinger 2011).

The Cold War saw China (directly and indirectly) participating in multiple theatres of war, namely the Korean War and the Vietnam War, and providing (logistical and financial) support to communist insurgencies across the world, from Myanmar and Cambodia in Indochina to a whole host of countries in Latin America, Africa and the Middle East (Kurlantzick 2007: 13–14). Meanwhile, Sino-Vietnamese tensions culminated in the 1979 Chinese invasion of its southern neighbour, and two bloody skirmishes over the Paracels (1974) and the Spratly (1988) chain of islands in the South China Sea (see Chapter 3). Recognizing Vietnam's regional isolation, Deng calculated that military operations against Hanoi would draw minimal regional and international backlash. Deng's rise to power coincided with improved relations with the USA, which was also increasingly alarmed by Soviet–Vietnamese designs in South-East Asia. After all, the USA fought a bloody conflict in Vietnam, and failed to deter communist Vietnam from conquering pro-American South Vietnam. Both China and the USA were opposed to a Soviet strategic footprint in East Asia and considered military countermeasures against a prospective Greater Vietnam in Indochina (Kissinger 2011). The post-

Cold War period, however, saw an economically ascendant China, which downgraded its support to overseas communist rebellions – what Mao considered 'righteous struggles' – and declined to invade any neighbouring country. Instead of resorting to large-scale deployment of military force, China instead employed a 'salami-slicing' tactic – the calibrated use of paramilitary forces to lay claim to contested maritime territories and intimidate rival states without triggering full-scale armed conflict – to gradually consolidate its claims in the adjacent waters (see Chapter 3).

Eager to transform China into a vibrant economic power, without loosening the grip of the CCP on the political system, Deng carefully studied the economic miracles in fellow autocratic neighbours such as Singapore and South Korea. China's currency reserves were heavily depleted, and the country was in deep need of economic revival lest its national security be endangered (Naughton 2006; Jacques 2012). The impressive transformation of China's neighbours provided a blueprint for Deng's economic reforms at home, featuring, on a gradual and geographically limited basis, Special Economic Zones (SEZs) on China's favourably located south-eastern coastal provinces such as Guangdong and Fujian. Initially, the Chinese diaspora, especially in places like Hong Kong, which bemoaned labour cost increases, served as a significant source of foreign capital for the development of these SEZs. Hong Kong businessmen were responsible for almost half of the entire foreign capital from 1978 to 1991 (Walker and Buck 2007). This trend accelerated in the post-Cold War period: from 1990 to 2002, investments from South-East Asia, dominated by the Chinese diaspora, were responsible for as much as US$90 billion in FDIs, with some studies suggesting the Chinese diaspora collectively contributed as much as 80 per cent of all the FDIs in the country (Kurlantzick 2007: 76). This went hand in hand with political decentralization, relaxation of previous restrictions on private entrepreneurship, partial privatization of the state-owned enterprises (SOEs), and the decollectivization of agricultural practices, which gave rise to township and village enterprises (TVEs) (Andreas 2008, 2010, 2012; Walker and Buck 2007). American sociologist Joel Andreas (2010) sums up the outcome of the first stage of reform (1978–92):

There were two great sectors: a public sector that was still largely based on socialist production relations and a private sector in which family production relations prevailed. Looking a little closer, in urban areas, the public sector was dominant, with a thriving family economy at the margins, while in rural areas, the family economy was dominant, with a growing township and village enterprise sector, which harboured both socialist and small-scale capitalist production relations.

The capitalist revolution By the early 1990s, when China entered a second stage of more vigorous pro-market reforms – which saw, among other things, banking system reforms and the progressive streamlining of SOEs – major multinational companies and foreign investors from across the world began to pour in capital and technology, transforming China into the 'world's workshop'. North-East Asian industrialized countries such as Japan, South Korea and Taiwan were able to move up the ladder of economic development by largely depending on domestic capital and the systematic expansion of their nascent industries, which benefited from strategic protectionist barriers and favourable access to export markets. China's development pattern, however, increasingly resembled that of South-East Asian tiger cubs such as Thailand, which relied heavily on FDIs and supply chain trade (Baldwin 2013; Rawski and Brandt 2008; Jacques 2012). Deng's reforms paid off: in the 1978–2005 period, China's annual GDP growth stood at 9.5 per cent, twice that of the pre-reform era (Rawski and Brandt 2008: 1; Jacques 2012: 177). By 2003, China surpassed the USA as the largest recipient of FDI, which had accounted for 4–5 per cent of Chinese GDP in recent decades. Since 1978, China has received over US$500 billion in FDI, ten times the amount Japan attracted from 1945 to 2000 (Jacques 2012: 182). In a few decades, China became a trading powerhouse, with the trade-to-GDP ratio jumping from 10 per cent prior to Deng's reforms to a whopping 63.9 per cent in 2005 (Rawski and Brandt 2008: 2). Capital stock increased at an astonishing rate of 20 per cent per year from 1978 to 1994 (Walker and Buck 2007). Tables 1.1. and 1.2. show China's impressive performance compared to other major countries.

By dissociating itself from communist insurgencies across South-East Asia, and downplaying its maritime disputes with neighbouring states, Deng's China patiently built strategic and economic bridges with the broader neighbourhood. The presence of prosperous, influential Chinese minorities across South-East Asia provided an additional instrument for (peacefully) reinforcing burgeoning ties between China and its smaller neighbours (Shirk 2008; Kurlantzick 2007). Over the years, Singapore, a Chinese-majority city-state, would emerge as a key interlocutor between China, on the one hand, and the broader East Asian neighbourhood and the West, on the other. For the Singaporean leadership, the transformation of China from a revolutionary cause into a pragmatic state actor provided a unique opportunity to (once again) unlock the vast economic potentials of one of the world's greatest civilizations – presenting untold investment opportunities for industrialized, export-oriented neighbouring states such as Singapore, Taiwan and Japan.

TABLE 1.1 China's GDP as a percentage of GDP for other major economies (1952–2004)[a]

	1952	1978	1990	2000	2004
United States	9.5	13.6	27.9	51.7	64.0
Japan	78.5	38.5	70.5	165.9	219.2
Germany	n.a.	50.8	113.3	244.8	322.1
India	63.9	78.0	122.2	190.6	203.1[b]

Source: Heston, Summers, and Aten (2006).
a Calculated at purchasing power parity.
b Based on date for 2003.

TABLE 1.2 China's GDP per capita as a percentage of figures for other major economies (1952–2005)[a, b]

	1952	1978	1990	2000	2005
United States	2.7	3.2	6.3	11.6	15.7
Japan	11.8	4.6	7.7	16.7	21.3
Korea	25.4[c]	15.0	16.4	25.5	30.1
India	42.6	53.7	90.3	151.4	188.5

Source: Data for 2005 are World Bank measures in current international dollars; data for earlier years from Heston, Summers, and Aten (2006).
a Measured at purchasing power parity.
b Annual figure for each comparator nation equals 100.
c Figures refer to 1953.

Intent on turbo-charging China's industrialization, Deng eagerly pursued broader trade and investment ties with arch-rival Japan – and much later Taiwan – which welcomed a more pragmatic leadership in China. As Taiwan and Japan entered the mature stages of their export-driven capitalist development, rising production costs at home became increasingly challenging. Throughout the 1970s, a debilitating stagflation in centre economies and multiple oil shocks, due to armed conflicts and political upheavals in the Middle East in 1973 and 1979, further undermined the 'developmental state' economic models in East Asia. The 1985 Plaza Accord, a historic agreement that led to the revaluation of Japan's currency, encouraged major Japanese conglomerates to explore investment opportunities in neighbouring countries, which provided more favourable production costs (Yergin 2008).

The flying geese South-East Asian countries such as Malaysia, Thailand and Indonesia were among the biggest beneficiaries of Japan's manufacturing outsourcing. But China represented an incomparably large investment destination for Japanese and Taiwanese businessmen, who were eager to take advantage of the economic dividends of China's pragmatic foreign policy turn. No wonder that, over the decades, Japan and Taiwan would emerge as among the largest foreign investors in China. In many ways, Japan played a pivotal role in China's economic modernization. In 1972, under Mao's watch, China and Japan established diplomatic relations. Reflecting his eagerness to establish a new partnership with Japan, which showed its willingness to downgrade its relations with Taiwan and was similarly concerned with Soviet designs in East Asia, Mao went so far as to forswear any Japanese reparation for the Second World War atrocities. In exchange, Tokyo expressed its remorse for the atrocities of Imperial Japan in a joint communiqué, which reflected the country's 'keenly conscious responsibility for the serious damage that Japan caused in the past to the Chinese people through war, and deeply reproaches itself' (Shirk 2008: 158–9). The aim was to put behind them historical animosities in favour of a new chapter in their bilateral relations. Deng built on Mao's efforts by visiting Japan in 1978, the first visit of its kind by the People's Republic of China. Later on, he even asked several Japanese experts to serve as China's economic advisers, creating the Sino-Japanese Economic Knowledge Exchange Association. The two countries also signed a Treaty of Peace and Friendship, with Japanese prime minister Nakasone displaying a willingness to revise Japan's controversial historical textbooks to more accurately reflect Imperial Japan's historical atrocities against China (Shirk 2008: 159–60). The economic dividends of Sino-Japanese rapprochement were compelling: by the late 1970s, Japan accounted for about a quarter of China's trade, which grew to almost 30 per cent over the next decade. In the 1979–99 period, Japan–China trade increased by a factor of ten. After signing the bilateral investment protection pact in 1988, Japanese FDI in China accelerated, rising from US$479 million in 1990 to US$4.1 billion in 1995 (Burns 2000). More crucially, in the 1979–99 period, the Overseas Economic Cooperation Fund (OECF), Japan's state development financing agency, provided almost US$25 billion in soft loans to China, while Japan's External Trade Organization (ETO) facilitated the establishment of training programmes by Japanese firms to facilitate capital investment in and (limited) technology transfer to China (Keck 2014a).

As for Taiwan, (geographical and cultural) proximity to China's SEZs provided an excellent opportunity for the Taiwanese business class, who were interested in expanding their production facilities, enhancing their economies of scale, and facilitating growing economic interdependence between the two Chinese nations, which intermittently came close to armed conflict. Thus, a greater Taiwanese economic footprint in China was seen as an economic as well as a strategic opportunity for better cross-straits relations. Taiwanese investments in post-Mao China, however, were initially constrained by domestic regulatory restrictions. By 1986, Taiwanese FDI in China amounted to only US$20 million. After a series of high-stakes negotiations under the auspices of the General Agreement on Tariffs and Trade (GATT) – the world's (then) main platform for trade negotiations and the precursor of the World Trade Organization (WTO) – China further liberalized its FDI-related regulations. Within two years, Taiwanese investment jumped to US$420 million. Domestic economic reforms in Taiwan further encouraged investments in China, which reached US$9.9 billion in 1993. By 1996, Taiwan had invested as much as US$40 billion, equivalent to 5 per cent of Taiwan's entire GDP. Increasingly, the sheer size of Taiwanese exposure to China meant that it was integrated into the mainland's larger economic system (Brown et al. 2010: 13). Pragmatic circles in Taiwan as well as in the USA were largely sanguine vis-à-vis this phenomenon, hoping that greater cross-strait economic interdependence would dissuade Beijing from coercively pursuing its long-held desire for reunification with the island nation. The USA, meanwhile, emerged as China's most important export market, facilitating the sustained expansion of the Asian country's industrial base and productive capacities. On the supply side, China benefited from Japan's know-how and the Chinese diaspora's capital. On the demand side, China benefited from American markets. It was a triangular economic relationship, underwriting a burgeoning strategic alliance against Soviet expansionism in Asia.

As China's economy picked up, however, its ambitions went beyond just building robust economic ties with the world's leading economies. In August 1994, Deng Xiaoping called for a more muscular diplomacy, anchored by two principles: 'First, to oppose hegemonism and power politics and safeguard world peace; second, to build up a new international political and economic order' (Brzezinski 1998). Beyond normalizing frayed ties, he was interested in transforming China into a regional leader. And this required a major overhaul in China's foreign policy strategy. It was one thing to heal historical wounds with neighbouring states to facilitate much-needed economic ties; but it was another thing to make China a legitimate contender for regional leadership, capable of creating a new order in Asia. Up until the nineteenth century, China comfortably stood as the most powerful state in Asia, with the world's biggest economy; for almost an entire millennium, from AD 500 to 1500, China was arguably the world's most powerful political entity (Kurlantzick 2007; Jacques 2012). But the task of upgrading China's status within the regional and international order would fall largely on the shoulders of Deng's protégé, Jiang Zemin, who took over the leadership of all the country's important pillars, namely the Communist Party, the state and the central military commission (CMC), in the early 1990s.

China's charm offensive

Jiang's assumption of power represented the first peaceful transfer of leadership in communist China, and came on the heels of rapid economic growth, with per capita income levels having risen by a factor of three across the country and a factor of five in urban centres since the commencement of economic reforms in 1978 (Kissinger 2011: 479). It also marked China's transition from personalistic leadership (by the founding fathers of the communist revolution) to an increasingly institutionalized one, based on consensus-building and collective decision-making among the heirs of Deng (Shirk 2008; Nan 2010). Under Jiang, the CCP's membership was more democratized, integrating former ideological foes, particularly reform-minded individuals and ambitious entrepreneurs, who came to play a more prominent socio-economic role in a quasi-capitalist China (Kissinger 2011: 480). One could argue, however, that the pluralization of the CCP's membership was part of a broader strategy of co-opting new economic forces, particularly the salaried middle class and the business elite, who could form a potentially formidable counter-elite if they felt significantly excluded from the system. By integrating new economic forces into the political class, the CCP transformed its potential rivals into formidable interest groups, who became heavily invested in the status quo. What emerged was a vibrant quasi-capitalist system guided and stabilized by the visible hand of the CCP (Kurlantzick 2009).

Once again, domestic political changes went hand in hand with a transformation in China's foreign policy. The nexus between domestic politics and foreign policy is a key feature of the CCP's evolution. By now, the communist regime was entering its third phase of foreign policy evolution. Under Mao, China largely shunned the international order, dismissing it as the artificial construct of Western capitalist powers, while emphasizing the importance of building ties with fellow developing countries and supporting revolutionary movements across the 'Third World'. Deng dispensed with Mao's revolutionary bombast and combative language, prioritizing economic ties with neighbouring states and stable relations with the West. Rather like Mao, however, he was averse to China's participation in international organizations and forums, viewing them as unnecessary entanglements, which could jeopardize the country's (fragile) rise. But Deng acknowledged the possibility of greater Chinese assertiveness in regional and international multilateral arrangements, provided China achieved a degree of stability at home and reached a certain stage of economic development, which would require more proactive protection of Chinese interests abroad. As China experts Taylor Fravel and Evan Medeiros (2003) argue, from the mid-1990s onwards China's foreign policy entered a new stage, characterized by 'an attempt by China's [new] leaders to break out of their post-Tiananmen isolation, rebuild their image, protect and promote Chinese economic interests, and enhance their security', which, following Deng's August 1994 dictum, also served the purpose of 'hedg[ing] against American influence around the world'. China was now moving beyond Deng's earlier caution that CCP leaders should 'keep a low profile and never take the lead', since the country was now in a better position to shape its external environment and – as China embarked on a sustained phase of capitalist expansion with ever-growing dependence on international trade and commodity imports – to increasingly protect its emerging global interests (Kurlantzick 2007: 16).

Under the leadership of Jiang Zemin and his successor, Hu Jintao, China developed a new mantra for its foreign policy, filled with ideas such as 'new security concept' and 'peaceful development', which emphasized the importance of cooperation, diplomacy and multilateralism to pursue win-win relationships between China and the wider world. While the Jiang administration was more focused on great power relations with Washington, the Hu administration, in turn, was more interested in deepening China's strategic depth in East Asia (Shirk 2008:111). The Asian power's voracious appetite for raw materials, to feed its booming industrialization at home, also precipitated a huge infusion of Chinese capital into resource-rich Africa, the Middle East and Latin America, which came to benefit from ever-expanding economic and strategic ties with Beijing. It didn't take long before China emerged as the pre-eminent economic player in long-neglected continents such as Africa, with China watchers boldly proclaiming the dawn of a second 'scramble for Africa' – reminiscent of Western competition over the resource-rich continent in the colonial era – under the auspices of an Asian power. Gradually, China's deepening footprint in Latin America was seen as a challenge to the USA's centuries-old hegemony in South America, under the Monroe Doctrine. While the Bolivarian bloc of radical-leftist South American regimes, under the leadership of Hugo Chávez, utilized deeper economic ties with Beijing to confront what they saw as American imperialism by establishing alternative solidarity-based regional integration mechanisms, other Latin American countries, such as Brazil and Argentina, in turn, saw an opportunity to diversify their trading relations and gain access to affordable capital and technology from China. From Africa to the Middle East, a whole host of autocratic regimes welcomed deeper economic ties with China (Kurlantzick 2007). Bereft of any missionary zeal à la American Manifest Destiny or French *mission civilisatrice*, China was primarily interested in business and access to raw materials. It couldn't care less about the political institutions of the host country. If anything, from a business point of view, autocratic regimes tend to be seen as more attractive owing to their relative predictability in policy-making. Unlike newly democratizing countries with multiple centres of power and unpredictable electoral cycles, autocratic regimes could represent greater policy continuity and political stability. China's successful blend of autocratic governance with capitalist prosperity proved to be an attractive model for many autocratic regimes across the developing world. Even democratic governments in the developing world, which suffered from decades of painful macroeconomic reforms and structural adjustment programmes under the auspices of international financial institutions (IFIs), welcomed China's economic rise as a viable alternative to the so-called 'Washington Consensus': the Western powers' and IFIs' emphasis on neoliberal economic reforms in exchange for trade, investment and financial incentives. China's no-strings-attached approach to international trade and investment relations would soon be called by Sinologist Joshua Cooper-Ramo the 'Beijing Consensus'.

Shifting the political discourse was an essential element of reshaping China's actual foreign policy. No longer just seen as an isolated, victimized nation, fighting an impossible war against imperialist and capitalist powers – a rhetoric that was common in the Maoist era of revolutionary upheavals – the country was now in need of new ideas to support its vision of a more charismatic, influential China. Fravel and Medeiros (2003) succinctly describe how the mid-1990s saw a perceptible shift in China's foreign policy:

> [China] expanded the number and depth of its bilateral relationships, joined various trade and security accords, deepened its participation in key multilateral organizations, and helped address global security issues. Foreign policy decision-making [became] less personalized and more institutionalized, and Chinese diplomats [became] more sophisticated in their articulation of the country's goals.

Building on Deng's legacy of calibrated compromise, which gained pace in the 1980s, China normalized ties and/or established formal diplomatic relations with eighteen countries in the 1988–94 period; confronting a new constellation of states emerging out of the ruins of the Soviet empire, China began establishing ties with newly created states in Central Asia and Europe, culminating in the 2011 Treaty of Good-Neighbourliness and Friendly Cooperation with Russia (Fravel and Medeiros 2003). Intent on deepening its strategic footprint in its historical backyard, South-East Asia, China progressively upgraded its bilateral relations with the Association of Southeast Asian Nations (ASEAN) and its members. By 1991, China had managed to establish formal relations with all members of ASEAN, while terminating aid to communist rebel groups in the region. In the same year, China's foreign minister, Qian Qichen, chose to attend the ASEAN Foreign Ministers Meeting (AMM). By 1994, he featured among the founders of the ASEAN Regional Forum (ARF), the leading platform for security dialogue in the Asia-Pacific region (Shirk 2008: 113). In the 1995–97 period, China began annual meetings with senior ASEAN officials, then advocated the 'ASEAN+3' initiative, which brought together the North-East Asian powers of South Korea, Japan and China under the aegis of the South-East Asian organization. Such initiatives were aimed at assuaging, among other things, ASEAN's lingering fears of a burgeoning economic rivalry with China, which became an increasingly more attractive destination for industrialized countries in Asia and the West. During the 1997/98 Asian financial crisis (AFC), China was particularly impressive. The crisis shattered South-East Asian economies such as Thailand and Indonesia, and severely undermined the Clinton administration's economic globalization project, specifically its focus on financial deregulation and capital mobility (Anderson 1998; Stiglitz 2003). Instead of exploiting the financial mayhem in neighbouring states by adjusting its interest rates and revaluing its currency, China chose to express solidarity with the region by advocating an Asia monetary fund and a web of currency-swap agreements as well as information-sharing mechanisms on capital movements to prevent and/or cushion against future financial contagion in the region. China also contributed to the IMF's financial aid package to help Thailand's post-crisis recovery. China's high-profile 'altruistic' display won acclaim across the region and beyond, with the Clinton administration praising such efforts and inviting China to attend the G8 finance ministers' meeting in 1998.

Displacing Japan Meanwhile, Japan was criticized for devaluing its currency during the AFC. During the late Cold War period, Japan was largely seen as the engine of development across East Asia, serving not only as an export destination for the commodity-based economies of South-East Asia, but also as a source of capital investment and manufacturing technology for its poorer neighbours. Intent on maintaining their competitiveness, especially after the revaluation of the Japanese currency in the mid-1980s, Japanese companies began outsourcing their production bases to neighbouring states on an increasingly growing scale. Under the so-called 'flying geese' phenomenon, Japan was seen as the core element of an elaborate network of vertically integrated production chains across East Asia, facilitating a series of economic miracles across the region. Constitutionally barred from developing its own offensive military capabilities, Japan's main source of influence was its economic prowess. The Asian Development Bank (ADB), headquartered in

Manila, served as a high-profile institutional framework to channel Japanese development aid across the continent (Anderson 1998). Analysing the roots of the AFC, Benedict Anderson (ibid.) provided an overview of Japan's role in the capitalist evolution of East Asia:

> Beginning in the Fifties, thanks to a series of war reparations agreements whereby Japan provided substantial funds to South-East Asian countries for the purchase of its manufactures, Tokyo's economic presence rapidly increased ... By the early Seventies, Japan had become the single most important external investor in the region, both as extractor of natural resources (timber, oil and so on) and in industrial and infrastructural development.

But a rising China was now chipping away at Japan's already waning economic influence, which was severely undercut by the deflationary spiral and economic stagnation that crippled the once ascendant Asian economy from the late 1980s onwards. The AFC undermined the whole economic paradigm, which underpinned the US–Japanese economic agenda in East Asia. For supporters of Beijing, China was not only an alternative pole of power, it also served as a much-welcomed balance against the neoliberal agenda of Tokyo and Washington. With respect to its South-East Asian neighbours, China quickly managed to achieve economic domination, displacing Japan as the historical top trading partner. From 2003, when China and ASEAN signed a strategic partnership agreement, two-way trade expanded more than sixfold over the next decade, its value reaching US$400 billion in 2012, with investments topping US$100 billion (Parameswaran 2013).

Recognizing the dearth of regional political integration in North-East Asia – where historical animosities and the legacy of the Cold War, such as the continued menace of North Korea, poison diplomatic relations among the regional powers – China also sought to create new diplomatic platforms for institutionalized engagement with Japan and South Korea, Asia's two most advanced economies. It also stepped up its participation in the Northeast Asia Cooperation Dialogue (NEACD). With APEC emerging as the premier platform for trade and economic diplomacy in the Indo-Pacific region, China deepened its participation in the organization, with Shanghai hosting the ninth APEC summit in 2001. With respect to Europe, China became the founding member of the transcontinental Asia-Europe Meeting (ASEM), which seeks to deepen political and economic engagements between the world's two leading regions by conducting summits and ministerial meetings annually. China also reached out to the European Union (EU), a major trade and investment partner, and the North Atlantic Treaty Organization (NATO), exploring new avenues for deeper strategic and security cooperation. The overarching objective was to weaken the USA's grip on the region by reaching out to American allies through a plethora of diplomatic initiatives and economic engagements. In fact, by 2005 Malaysia would host the East Asian Summit, which was largely seen as a Chinese-inspired effort to exclude the USA from the region (Shirk 2008: 120).

Responsible stakeholder Recognizing itself as a great power, China sought to underscore its commitment to international security by expanding its role within the United Nations, supporting peacekeeping operations in conflict zones such as East Timor and Congo, while acquiescing to, among other resolutions, UN Security Council Resolution 1441 on weapons inspections and disarmament in Iraq in 2002. China also ratified major non-proliferation and arms control agreements such as the Chemical Weapons Convention and the Treaty on the Nonproliferation of Nuclear Weapons. Despite its relative inferiority vis-à-vis Russia and the USA in terms of nuclear technology, China signed the Comprehensive Nuclear Test Ban Treaty in 1996, while agreeing to adhere to the basic principles of the Missile Technology Control Regime. China also became the convener of the Six-Party Talks on the North Korean nuclear issue, bringing together regional powers such as Japan, the USA and Russia to jointly manage the fragile security situation on the Korean peninsula. At times, China went so far as to censure and penalize North Korea, a long-time ally, for its provocative actions and brazen violation of international principles and agreements (Fravel and Medeiros 2003; Shirk 2008; Kurlantzick 2007). China also stepped up its military-to-military engagements with neighbours and regional powers. In 2002, the PLA started to dispatch observers to the Cobra Gold regional exercises, hosted by Thailand

and organized by the US Pacific Command. In 2003, China surprised the region when Chinese foreign minister Li Zhaoxing announced that his country was seeking a new security mechanism, under the auspices of the ARF, to increase communication among Asian militaries (Fravel and Medeiros 2003).

In 2006, China participated in a US-organized joint naval exercise in the Sea of Japan, featuring the region's leading naval powers cooperating in the prevention of the spread of nuclear weapons (Shirk 2008: 122). Long overshadowed by China's paramount leaders, especially Mao's revolutionary zeal and Deng's aversion to activist international diplomacy, the Chinese Ministry of Foreign Affairs (MFA) – now equipped with an educated and articulate personnel – began to emerge as an important arbiter of China's foreign policy. This led to the greater professionalization of China's approach to the external world, bringing a measure of predictability and transparency to Beijing's ambitions in the post-Cold War era. Beginning in 1996, Chinese scholars, in tandem with the MFA's Asia Department, explored a new conceptualization of national security and international affairs, hoping to counter the Cold War era emphasis on military balance and realpolitik. The result was the 'new security' concept, which emphasized 'mutual trust, mutual benefit, equality, and cooperation' as the cornerstone of China's foreign policy (Shirk 2008: 128). Through such initiatives, the MFA hoped to counter the influence of hardline bureaucratic-military factions and interest groups, which advocated a more muscular foreign policy to protect China's regional interests. In particular, territorial disputes with continental and maritime neighbours represented a daunting challenge. The Jiang administration, however, was determined to gain the goodwill of its neighbours and enhance bilateral relations with a constellation of established and newly created neighbours on its peripheries.

Charming neighbours With fourteen continental neighbours, six maritime neighbours and a precarious stand-off over a 'homeland dispute' over Taiwan, China confronts arguably the world's most difficult territorial conundrum. In his critically acclaimed book *Strong Borders, Secure Nation: Cooperation and Conflict in China's Territorial* *disputes*, Taylor Fravel elegantly shows how China skilfully and patiently resolved seventeen border disputes, abandoning claims to over 1.3 million square miles of land to facilitate diplomatic compromise. In the 1991–2003 period, China settled border conflicts with the Central Asian republics of Kazakhstan, Kyrgyzstan, Tajikistan and Russia, and south-east neighbours such as Laos and Vietnam. In most of these agreements, China settled for only 50 per cent or less of its original claims. China's concessions to Tajikistan were pretty dramatic: it accepted only 1,000 out of 28,000 square kilometres of contested areas in the Pamir mountains (Fravel and Medeiros 2003; Steele 2013). As Jonathan Steele, a former Moscow correspondent for the *Guardian*, succinctly puts it:

> Until the early 1990s Soviet Central Asia was hermetically
> sealed from China … When Central Asia unexpectedly became
> independent, Beijing and the three republics that have borders with
> China built on these foundations and border treaties were concluded
> within a decade. Although Mao had argued that the 19th-century
> tsarist treaties which set the borders were 'unequal', his successors
> accepted a deal that left 57 per cent of the territory China had
> claimed in Kazakh hands. In Tajikistan China took only 3 per cent of
> what it had asked for …

In South-East Asia, China sought to de-escalate maritime tensions with ASEAN members such as the Philippines by acquiescing to the 2002 Declaration on the Conduct of Parties in the South China Sea (DOC), which, among other things, encouraged rival claimants to (i) resolve their disputes through peaceful, diplomatic means and (ii) avoid the threat or use of force to consolidate their claims. China proposed the formula of 'joint development' as a confidence-building mechanism to manage the disputes without abandoning highly sensitive sovereignty claims (see Chapters 3 and 6). The Jiang administration was particularly interested in maintaining stable ties with Russia and India, the two great powers in China's continental neighbourhood. The 1962 Sino-Indian border war inspired mutual animosity, and severely undermined what initially looked like a blossoming relationship between Asia's two biggest countries, which served as the putative pillars of 'third world solidarity' in the first decade of the Cold War (Mishra 2013). Amid the Sino-Soviet tensions in the 1960s, the bitter war further pushed (non-aligned) India into the Soviet camp. Throughout the Cold War, India–China relations were essentially frozen. Under Deng, China tried to normalize ties with India, encouraging both sides to 'forget the unpleasant period in our past relations, and let us treat everything with an eye on the future' (Shirk 2008:116). Indian prime minister Rajiv Gandhi visited China in 1988, aiming to restore long-frayed bilateral relations. China also sought to assuage India by abandoning its earlier support for Pakistan over the Kashmir issue, a bitter source of conflict between Pakistan and India. However, China's long-standing alliance with Pakistan, India's arch-rival, among other things, did little to ease mutual suspicion and animosity. Beijing was also alarmed by India's development and testing of nuclear weapons in the late twentieth century. By 2000, bilateral trade stood at only US$3 billion, and there were no direct flights between the two countries up until 2002 – reflecting the poor state of relations between Asia's giant neighbours (ibid.: 115–16). In the mid-1990s, China pushed for a number of confidence-building measures, including troop-reduction agreements, over disputed land borders between China and India. With the border disputes in a state of hibernation, despite continued tensions between Chinese and Indian armed forces, the two countries were in a stronger position to contemplate expanded trade and investment relations. Within a decade, China became India's top trading partner, with the two countries aiming to increase their bilateral trade to as much as US$100 billion in 2015 (Krishnan 2011).

Meanwhile, the creation of the Shanghai Cooperation Organization (SCO) in 2001, after a series of border and military-related agreements among post-Soviet states and China, served three primary purposes. First, it acted as a symbol of stable and deepening relations among the member countries, most of them created out of the ruins of the Soviet empire. Secondly, it created an institutionalized mechanism for China, Russia and Central Asian countries to peacefully resolve their differences and enhance their cooperation, especially in the realm of counter-insurgency and Islamic fundamentalism, which represented a shared challenge to the autocratic rule of almost all of the SCO's members. Lastly, the SCO served as a Sino-Russian condominium for the joint management of their traditional spheres of influence in Central Asia, preventing the prospects of an overt, militarized competition between the two giants. Over time, however, the SCO began to resemble a burgeoning security regime, bringing together non-Western powers from across Asia and facilitating deeper strategic and military ties between Russia and China. Platforms such as the SCO and the Conference on Interaction and Confidence-Building Measures in Asia (CICA) allowed China to create alternative mechanisms for regional integration and security dialogue.

China's ambitious leaders also sought to leverage their country's cultural heritage and economic prowess. In particular, the Hu administration was committed to enhancing China's 'soft power', a term coined by American political scientist Joseph Nye. In his much-celebrated book *Soft Power: The Means to Success in World Politics*, Nye discussed the growing importance of soft power in the post-Cold War era, where complex interdependence and economic competitiveness shape, define and influence national aspirations in a highly globalized world. Soft power refers to the ability of nation-states to achieve desired outcomes through persuasion, attraction and co-optation rather than coercion and confrontation. As Nye (2004: 5) argues, soft power is based on the recognition that 'it is also important to set the agenda and attract others in world politics, and not only force them to change by threatening military force or economic sanctions'. A country's soft power is based on, Nye maintains, the attraction of its culture, the appeal and veracity of its political values, and the conduct and substance of its foreign policy (ibid.: 11). Following Nye's argument, to achieve hegemony a state can't rely on brute force (hard power) alone: the Soviet empire was a formidable military power, but it failed to achieve a global following, largely because it was seen as a threat (rather than an appealing partner) by the world's leading economies. The USA, meanwhile, was a more comprehensive power, which skilfully combined coercion with co-optation – akin to Antonio Gramsci's notion of ideological hegemony – to shape the post-Second World War architecture of global governance and integrate advanced economies in western Europe and East Asia into its sprawling network of military alliances.

Leading international relations scholars, and proponents of Hegemonic Stability Theory (HST), such as Robert Gilpin, for instance, emphasize the importance of the USA's willingness to provide/support global commons as essential to the stability of the post-Second World War order. Washington was not only responsible for massive aid programmes, which facilitated economic recovery in western Europe and Japan, it also played an indispensable role in the establishment of the BWS, which precipitated the 'Golden Age of Capitalism' in the mid-twentieth century. Despite the ebbs and flows of its military power, the USA's soft power facilitated its (self-serving) co-optation of international institutions and underpinned its ability to shape the strategic calculus of its allies. No wonder the Hu administration reckoned that China's emergence as a formidable economic power, supporting its accelerated military modernization programme, should be followed by greater influence and say in international institutions. The concept of new security was aimed not only at improving bilateral relations, but also projecting China as a new model of development and a source of cultural grandeur to the wider world.

'Culture has become a more and more important source of national cohesion and creativity and a factor of growing significance in the competition in overall national strength,' Hu said in a keynote speech to the 17th National Congress of the Communist Party of China (CPC) in 2007. He called upon the government to 'enhance culture as part of the soft power of [China] to better guarantee the people's basic cultural rights and interests' (Xinhua 2007). Under Hu's watch, China began expanding so-called Confucius Institutes – quasi-academic centres tasked with advertising China's culture and language – across the world, while increasing the number of scholarships to thousands of individuals around the world interested in studying in China's leading universities. After more than two decades of rapid economic growth, and relatively stable relations with the West and key neighbours such as Japan, China was finally ready to assume the status of a great power, while holding on to its self-image as a 'developing country'.

This dualistic identity presented complex challenges to China's relations with the outside world, especially with the USA. As a rising power, benefiting from the existing liberal international order, China saw increasing confluence between its interests and those of the USA. Both powers shared a common interest in the stability of the world economy, expanding trade and investment relations across borders, and the security of sea lines of communication (SLOCs) as well as hydrocarbon-exporting regions such as the Middle East. In aggregate terms, China's economy proudly stood among the largest in the world. In per capita terms, however, China remained a largely developing country with a deep sense of vulnerability – fuelling its self-image as a victim of American hegemony.

Signs of trouble

The Sino-American rapprochement, however, was challenged by multiple crises in the post-Cold War period. China's détente with the West and its neighbours had its limits, especially over contentious issues that Beijing considered as its 'core interest' (e.g., Taiwan, Tibet and Xinjiang). Under Deng, China's relationship with the USA, as Henry Kissinger (2011) puts it, transformed from ideological confrontation, culminating in the bloody Korean War, into combative coexistence: an uneasy agreement to postpone long-standing disagreements and focus on common interests for the foreseeable future. In the post-Cold War era, the Clinton administration upgraded bilateral relations by 'delinking' burgeoning economic and strategic cooperation between Beijing and Washington from their irreconcilable disagreements over domestic political concerns such as human rights and democracy, as well as geopolitical differences over, among other things, Taiwan and North Korea. The crisis in the Korean peninsula has been particularly challenging, with the USA repeatedly expressing its vexation at China's military and economic support to the North Korean regime, which has a mutual defence treaty with Beijing and, on multiple occasions, openly threatened a full-scale invasion of South Korea, an American treaty ally.

In the 1970s, the Nixon and Carter administrations, through successively negotiating the Three Joint Communiqués, were able to arrive at a modus vivendi with China over the status of Taiwan: the USA would shift its formal diplomatic recognition from Taiwan to communist China, depriving Taiwan of its seat on the UN Security

Council and in other international governmental organizations, in exchange for China's indefinite postponement of any form of coercive reintegration of Taiwan into Greater China. The whole gambit was based on Washington's shrewd recognition of the growing fissure between Beijing and Moscow, which culminated in a border war in 1969 that threatened a conventional (if not nuclear) showdown between the two communist powers (Osborne and Foster 2010). The USA acknowledged Beijing's aspirations for a unified, undivided China, but maintained robust economic and cultural ties with Taiwan (Kissinger 2011). As a form of confidence-building measure, both sides also had to refrain from any provocative action, which meant the USA had to downgrade, if not fully cease, military assistance to Taiwan. Both Washington and Beijing, however, had to contend with immense political pressure at home, with the Republican-dominated US Congress demanding full support for Taiwan, while nationalists in China constantly cited the importance of Taiwan to China's territorial integrity. It became practically impossible for the USA to fully eliminate its military support to Taiwan, thanks to the 1979 Taiwan Relations Act (TRA), which compels Washington to defend Taiwan against an invasion by mainland China and 'make available to Taiwan such defense articles and defense services in such quantity as may be necessary to enable Taiwan to maintain sufficient self-defense capabilities'. On China's part, it has not categorically ruled out the use of force if, among other things, Taiwan's political leadership opts for full independence – a development which would openly call into question China's stated sovereignty over Taiwan. In short, China and the USA would avoid an open confrontation over Taiwan if both sides refrained from introducing any large-scale military element into the equation and thwarted pro-independence sentiments in Taiwan (Shirk 2008; Kissinger 2011). Implicitly, both sides left open the possibility of the peaceful integration of Taiwan into China, similar to the case of Hong Kong and Macau, which, in accordance with the 'One Country, Two Systems' formula, were reunited with China in the late 1990s in exchange for a degree of political autonomy. At some point there were even proposals for a 'Once Country, Three Systems' formula, whereby mainland China, Hong Kong and Macau and Taiwan would maintain their unique governance systems under the sovereign jurisdiction of Beijing as the sole representative of the Chinese people (Shirk 2008: 198).

The stability of Sino-American ties was anchored by the suspension of Taiwan's full independence as a sovereign nation-state and the demilitarization of cross-strait relations. It demanded a fragile balancing act for both Beijing and Washington, which had to adopt considerable 'strategic ambiguity' to maintain a peaceful status quo. After the collapse of the autocratic order in Taiwan, the 1990s saw the resurgence of the pro-independence movement in Taiwan, which introduced new challenges to the Sino-American modus vivendi over the island nation. The situation reached a crisis point when mainland China threatened full-scale invasion in response to pro-independence parties' and political figures', who were now in a position of power, bid for a referendum on the country's sovereignty, and a quest for greater external support by internationalizing their quest for Taiwan's full independence (Shirk 2008; Kissinger 2011).

From the mid-1990s to the early 2000s, Sino-American relations would suffer setbacks from three major incidents, which deepened bilateral tensions, highlighted China's relative weakness, and intensi-fied anti-American sentiments in China. The Clinton administration was determined to turn Sino-American relations into a strategic part-nership. But two major crises tested Clinton's pro-China initiatives. The first was the 1995/96 Taiwan Strait Crisis, which brought the USA and China dangerously close to armed confrontation. Shortly before the crisis, President Jiang Zemin, who became China's top leader after elderly Deng became bedridden, offered to negotiate all issues with Taiwan's authorities on an equal, mutually respectful basis, known as 'Jiang's Eight Points', provided both sides acknowl-edged the existence of one China. This was a formal endorsement of the position of Taiwan's long-ruling party, the Kuomintang. Jiang hoped to build the foundations of a peaceful reintegration of Taiwan shortly after Macau's (1999) and Hong Kong's (1997) transfer from Portuguese and British control, respectively, to China. Jiang's control over the Chinese state apparatus and the CCP was far from con-solidated, and his overtures towards the USA and Taiwan unsettled hardline nationalist elements in the Chinese civilian and military leadership. Six months after Jiang's offer of comprehensive negotiations with Taiwanese authorities, the Clinton administration – under pressure from Congress– reversed a sixteen-year ban on visits by high-level Taiwanese officials to the USA by allowing Taiwan's president, Lee Teng-hui, to visit his alma mater, Cornell University, where he unabashedly described his country as a democratic sovereign nation, 'the Republic of China on Taiwan' (Shirk 2008: 188–9). Treating the issue as an unmistakable provocation, the hardliners pressured Jiang to acquiesce to a military response, which saw the PLA firing missiles dangerously close to Taiwan's north-eastern coastline. This was followed by a new round of missile and artillery tests as well as large-scale military exercises north of Vietnam. In March 1996, the PLA conducted its latest exercises on the eve of Taiwan's first presidential election. The USA responded by deploying two aircraft carrier battle groups to the vicinity of the area, which saw increased Chinese military mobilization and intimidation of Taiwan. Although China pushed ahead with a huge military exercise off the Fujian coast, refusing to immediately surrender to American counter-manoeuvres, the Clinton administration's show of force forced Beijing to cease further military provocations (ibid.: 189). The episode had a chilling impact on China's domestic politics, however, with a humiliated Jiang administration agreeing to an accelerated defence spending and military modernization programme, with a strategic focus on Taiwan, to appease the hardliners in the PLA and the CCP. This would have a profound impact on China's military posturing in the western Pacific, especially as territorial disputes in the South and East China Seas had reached a dangerous stage by the second decade of the twenty-first century (see Chapter 3). By 1999, military hardliners, who advocated defence build-up and modernization in preparation for a large-scale invasion of Taiwan in the future, received a second boost when Lee Teng-hui provoked a new round of cross-straits tensions by describing mainland China–Taiwan ties as 'state-to-state relations' – in effect proclaiming Taiwan as an independent nation-state (ibid.: 192). The election of pro-independence president Chen Shui-bian, who assumed power in 2000, stoked further tensions. Despite his initial efforts at striking a

modus vivendi with Beijing, he upped the ante by calling for a referendum to revise the Taiwanese constitution in 2006, to be ratified
by 2008, which would coincide with China's hosting of the summer
Olympics. Later, in 2006, he announced his plans for abolishing the
symbolically important National Unification Council, paving the way
for a declaration of full independence by the island nation. Though the
Taiwanese leader ultimately fell short of fulfilling his political agenda,
Sino-American relations were continuously tested by political developments in Taiwan, which were largely determined by the democratic
dynamics in the country (ibid.: 209). It was not until the 2008 election
of a new Taiwanese government, vowing to de-escalate tensions with
China and focus on deepening cross-straits economic ties instead, that
long-simmering tensions began to cool down.

In early May 1999, an American B-2 bomber, in the course of
the ongoing NATO operations against the Serbian regime, attacked
the Chinese embassy in Belgrade, mistaking it for a Yugoslav military structure. Naturally, China was infuriated, with anti-American
protests attacking the US embassy in Beijing, placing the American embassy's staff, including ambassador James Sasser, in danger.
The state-controlled Chinese media delayed the reporting of apolo-
gies by top officials in Washington and openly accused the US military of intentionally targeting the Chinese embassy in Belgrade.
Given the sophistication of American military hardware, which was
potently evident in the 1991 Gulf War, China found it very difficult
to accept Washington's 'unintentional mistake' narrative. The situation was exacerbated when President Clinton refused to sign a much-
anticipated WTO agreement, paving the way for China's membership in the global trading regime, upon Chinese premier Zhu Rongji's
visit to the USA. Confronting stiff opposition in Congress, which
resisted any economic incentives for China without major reforms
on the human rights and democracy front, the Clinton administration decided to release the draft agreement on the Internet to gain the
support of business groups. This upset the Chinese delegation, which
faced a firestorm of criticism at home, with some accusing Zhu of
being a 'national traitor' for negotiating a supposedly lopsided trade
agreement with the USA – reminiscent of criticisms of the late Qing

dynasty for its trade and territorial concessions to Japan and Western colonial powers (ibid.: 230). Mistrust towards China was repeatedly reinforced by these incidents, undermining Jiang's leadership and his long-standing preference for a strategic partnership with the USA. It didn't take long before a new administration in Washington faced a new crisis with China, when a US turboprop EP-3 surveillance aircraft, carrying out a routine reconnaissance mission over the South China Sea, collided with a Chinese jet fighter. The American aircraft was severely damaged, forcing it to land on a PLA navy airfield on China's southern province of Hainan. The death of the Chinese pilot and the perceived intrusion of the US aircraft into Chinese airspace provoked renewed anger among China's military and civilian leadership, who held on to the American aircraft's crew for eleven days and demanded a written apology from Washington. On all three occasions, the Chinese leadership had to refrain from full-scale diplomatic confrontation and pushed back against hardliners, which lobbied for a more forceful response immediately. But the psychological impact was visible: the USA was increasingly seen, among a growing number of officials and ordinary citizens, as an overbearing, oppressive hegemonic power. Envisioning stable Sino-American relations for an extended period became a daunting task. The USA's latest actions only reinforced long-standing reservations about closer Sino-American ties. As Bzrezinski, in his book *The Grand Chessboard*, argues: 'America is seen by China as the world's current hegemon, whose very presence in the region, based on its dominant position in Japan, works to contain China's influence' (Bzrezinski 1998: 177).

The Jiang administration's tireless efforts to avoid confrontation throughout a series of crises could be seen as a calculated move, which recognized the urgency of self-restraint in the short run, without necessarily ruling out a forceful response in the long run. After all, Deng Xiaoping didn't call for eternal submission to Western dominance, stating, 'Hide our capacities and bide our time, *but also get some things done* [author's own emphasis]'. The 'also get some things done' meant that short-term restraint should go hand in hand with proactive self-empowerment, both in military and economic terms. As John Mearsheimer (2014a) aptly put is: 'The reason it makes sense for

China to bide its time is that if it avoids trouble and merely continues growing economically, it will eventually become so powerful that it can just get its way in Asia'. China knew that time was on its side. Avoiding conflict in the short run was necessary to fulfilling China's dream of revival. The first decades after the Cold War, underpinned by economic globalization and American global policing, provided an unusually auspicious environment for Chinese economic expansion. But this era of unprecedented prosperity and capital accumulation was running against known limits, particularly China's demographic winter, which is poised to kick in after 2025 and reach a dangerous phase by the middle of the twenty-first century. As experts such as Barry Naughton famously observed, China could end up old before becoming rich enough to cope with and overcome its demographic dilemma (Shirk 2008: 20–21). In short, the Chinese leaders had the foresight to endure short-term humiliation to take advantage of a unique 'period of strategic opportunity'. More worryingly, China's economic rise could be delayed by the environmental and socio-political impact of its breakneck industrialization. A costly confrontation with a powerful adversary would distract the leaders from mounting domestic challenges and undermine China's economic transformation. But such self-imposed discipline would not last for long. Meanwhile, the George W. Bush administration's crude unilateralism and drive for full-spectrum American hegemony not only undermined Clintonite liberalism, which undergirded a largely symbiotic Sino-American relationship, but also weakened the very foundations of American power, paving the way for Chinese (and even Russian) resurgence amid the seeming breakdown of the international order.

2 | THE REVENGE OF HISTORY

> The dogmas of the quiet past are inadequate to the stormy present.
> The occasion is piled high with difficulty, and we must rise with
> the occasion. As our case is new, so we must think anew and act
> anew.
>
> Abraham Lincoln

> Who controls the past controls the future. Who controls the
> present controls the past.
>
> George Orwell

> History will be kind to me for I intend to write it.
>
> Winston Churchill

The exact origins of America's drive for global primacy, or *hegemony* in
Gramscian parlance, are a much debated issue, but it is widely believed
that a 1945 study, 'A security policy for post-war America', by the
Brookings Institution – endorsed by the most high-ranking members
of the defence establishment – set out Washington's growing interest in
and determination to prevent the emergence of any hostile dominant
power or coalition of powers in the Eurasian landmass (Porter 2013: 6).
The drive to sabotage the ambitions of indigenous powers to dominate
the Eurasian theatre was further crystallized during the Truman
and Kennedy administrations, as the Cold War (1947–89) entered
a dangerous phase of great power competition (ibid.: 6). With the
drive for primacy constituting the country's grand strategy, the USA's
foreign policy began to rely on what Zbigniew Brzezinski, a former
National Security Advisor (1977–81) and among the world's leading
strategic thinkers, characterized as the three imperatives of imperial
geo-strategy: 'to prevent collusion and maintain security dependence

among the vassals, to keep tributaries pliant and protected, and to keep the barbarians from coming together' (Brzezinski 1998: 40).

In the infamous 1992 'Defense Guidance' paper, the George H. W. Bush administration unabashedly celebrated America's status as the lone superpower – and its desire to remain in the position of ascendancy for the foreseeable future:

> Our [the USA's] first objective is to prevent the re-emergence of a new rival, either on the territory of the former Soviet Union or elsewhere, that poses a threat on the order of that posed formerly by the Soviet Union. This is a dominant consideration underlying the new regional defense strategy and requires that we endeavor to prevent any hostile power from dominating a region whose resources would, under consolidated control, be sufficient to generate global power … the U.S. must show the leadership necessary to establish and protect a new order that holds the promise of convincing potential competitors that they need not aspire to a greater role or pursue a more aggressive posture to protect their legitimate interests … we must maintain the mechanisms for deterring potential competitors from even aspiring to a larger regional or global role. An effective reconstitution capability is important here, since it implies that a potential rival could not hope to quickly or easily gain a predominant military position in the world. (New York Times 1992)

Within a decade, the George W. Bush administration was reiterating a similar imperial impulse in the equally infamous September 2002 National Security Strategy paper (Porter 2013: 8). The USA was determined to prevent the emergence of any competitive rival, viewing its lone superpower power status as the best way to protect Washington's interests. Bearing in mind the circumstances that led to the first and second world wars, the American leadership saw comprehensive military dominance as the best guarantee against a catastrophic global conflict with a hostile rival (ibid.; Mearsheimer 2014a). In the *Tragedy of Great Power Politics*, Mearsheimer (2014a) cogently explains the strategic rationale behind the USA's age-old commitment to geopolitical primacy:

> The more powerful a state is relative to its competitors, the less likely
> its survival will be at risk. No country in the Western Hemisphere,
> for example, would dare attack the United States, because it is so
> much stronger than any of its neighbors ... any state that achieves
> regional hegemony will want to make sure that no other great power
> achieves a similar position, freeing that counterpart to roam into its
> neighborhood ... the best way to survive in international anarchy is to
> be the sole regional hegemon.

To jealously guard its global position became a deeply ingrained strategic imperative, which, despite numerous strategic and economic setbacks over the years, persisted into the second decade of the twenty-first century, with the Pentagon's 2012 Defense Strategic Review stubbornly emphasizing the necessity for the USA to check the ambitions of potential rivals in key regions, namely the western Pacific and the Persian Gulf, to preserve the country's global leadership into in the new century. As American's top military leader, Chairman of the Joint Chiefs of Staff Martin Dempsey (2014), bluntly put it: 'Ultimately, the United States must continue to underwrite the international order'. But the wars in Afghanistan (2001–14) and Iraq (2003–11) were disastrous, exhausting America's strategic resolve. As one strategist aptly describes, 'America's strength is now strained to the point that it lacks the surplus reserve of power to respond to the contingent emergencies that its current course may produce' (Porter 2013:12). The Bush administration tried very hard to downplay the direct economic costs of those interventions, especially as the American people, and much of the world, began to condemn the tragic humanitarian costs of the two conflicts. The Bush administration's naive democracy-promotion project in the Middle East, through the barrel of a gun, created a dangerous political vacuum in Iraq, which gave birth to sectarian strife and the collapse of basic services for tens of millions of people. It also fuelled greater anti-American animosity in the region, empowering religious extremist groups, namely the al-Qaeda (AQ) franchise, which capitalized on the situation by conducting full-scale insurgency operations against American troops and their allies across the region. The war in Iraq, in particular, was condemned by much of the world as an exercise in imperial hubris, which was based on false intelligence (Saddam had no nuclear weapons, and there was no evidence to suggest he had an alliance with Taliban and AQ elements, as the Bush administration erroneously claimed), opposed by the large majority of the members of the United Nations, and partially driven by the desire to secure the world's richest hydrocarbon reserves. In *The Three Trillion Dollar War: The True Cost of the Iraq Conflict*, Joseph E. Stiglitz, Nobel Prize-winner in economics in 2001, and Linda J. Bilmes, senior lecturer in public policy at Harvard University, showed how the Bush administration's misadventures in the Middle East placed a colossal economic burden on the American economy. The two scholars estimate that the total accounting costs of the second Gulf War could reach as much as US$3 trillion – a figure which they later claimed to be 'too low' if additional economic costs such as the treatment, compensation and rehabilitation of war veterans were taken into consideration. The opportunity costs of the wars in Iraq and Afghanistan, which precipitated a devastating increase in global oil prices at the expense of both developing and industrialized nations, could be even more sobering. Far from serving as a viable economic stimulus to the American economy, which suffered from the 'dot-com bubble' burst in 2000, the war expenditures dramatically increased Washington's debt, worsened its dependence on external financing (from countries like China), deprived it of necessary funds to invest in more productive sectors at home and abroad, and undermined the country's long-term economic productivity. The reputational costs of the Bush administration's unilateral wars were equally, if not more, devastating, both in the short and the longer run. By the mid-2000s, Washington was confronting an alarming decline in its soft power, as China began to eclipse the USA in terms of approval ratings among Asia-Pacific countries, including long-time US allies such as Australia. According to a 2005 poll by Australia's Lowy Institute, a leading security think tank, 57 per cent of Australians perceived America's policies as a potential threat (to international security), with barely more than half of the population expressing positive feelings towards the USA. Meanwhile, nearly 70 per cent of Australians expressed positive feelings about China, whose leaders were warmly welcomed in the country (Kurlantzick 2007: 4).

In the long run, however, America's unilateral interventions, and brazen contempt for international law, encouraged emerging powers such as Russia and China to adopt a similar brand of coercive unilateralism and bellicosity in their own backyards, beginning with Moscow's invasion of Georgia in 2008, which was primarily a counter-manoeuvre against NATO's eastward expansion into the post-Soviet space and an attempt to reassert Russian primacy in eastern Europe and Central Asia. In the following years, China would also step up its territorial brinkmanship in the South and East China Seas, rekindling age-old maritime disputes after decades of promising economic integration in Asia (see Chapter 3). The Bush administration's naked display of imperial hubris shattered any illusion (and pretence to any form) of a rule-based international order after the end of the Cold War, facilitating the return of classical geopolitics (cynical interstate competition) to a supposedly post-imperial era of economic globalization.

The end of the first decade of the twenty-first century went hand in hand with a dramatic reconfiguration of the balance of power between Washington and its chief rivals. The 2007/08 Great Recession, in particular, exposed the vulnerabilities of Western economies, especially the Anglo-Saxon model of neoliberal economics. It undermined America's long-held image as a beacon of economic vitality, and accelerated the ability of newly rising powers such as China, which managed to maintain robust growth rates in the post-crisis period, to catch up. The seismic shift in the global balance of power encouraged renewed geopolitical assertiveness among Washington's rivals, exacerbated by an upsurge of popular nationalism in China and across East Asia. All of a sudden, the gradual emergence of a multipolar order, with the USA no longer viewed as the unrivalled omnipotent superpower, saw an explosion of conflicts across multiple theatres, shattering earlier hopes of a more stable, balanced post-American international system in the twenty-first century. The world entered a new age of uncertainty, defined by American strategic retrenchment and a rising tide of nationalism among emerging powers, particularly

China. Soon, the world had to contend with a more assertive and highly ambitious Chinese leader, Xi Jinping, who sought nothing less than parity between Beijing and Washington – and promised to restore China to its historical glory.

American retrenchment

Fresh into office, the Obama administration promised a new chapter in America's relations with the rest of the world. After eight years of devastating wars and unilateral interventions under the Bush administration, Obama represented a much-welcomed breath of fresh air. From Cairo to Berlin, he was heralded as an enlightened leader, promising to roll back Washington's military footprint in the Middle East, end the nuclear arms race among great powers, and endorse rule-based multilateralism as the primary driver of interstate relations. It all sounded dreamy, almost impossible, but the world was ready to fall for Obama's eloquence and unique charm. To the world's astonishment, Obama extended his hand to America's chief rivals, namely Russia and China. Washington enthusiastically pushed for a 'reset' in its bilateral relations with Moscow, hoping to transform a decade-long cold peace into a strategic partnership. This was followed by high-stakes negotiations over missile defence systems in Europe and proposed caps on the two powers' nuclear arsenals. As for China, the Obama administration tirelessly institutionalized bilateral strategic and defence dialogues with Beijing's top leaders. Describing China as the USA's most important bilateral relationship in the twenty-first century, the Obama administration purportedly laid down the foundations of a so-called 'G-2' – a condominium of the world's leading powers, jointly overseeing global governance in the new century. By more forcefully engaging Beijing, Washington sought to express its recognition of China's rise as a global power and deepen its stake in maintaining the existing international order. There were distinct similarities and differences with the previous administrations, though. Based on both personal conviction and strategic exigencies, Obama sought to avoid the coercive unilateralism of the Bush administration but, as Stephen Walt (2014) describes, he reverted back to key elements of the Clinton administration's grand strategy:

Both Obama and Clinton were committed to maintaining U.S. 'global leadership.' Both favored spreading democracy where possible, but turned a blind eye toward various dictatorships when circumstances seemed to require it. Both sought to engage a rising China, while hedging against a future rivalry. (Obama did more of the latter, of course, because there is now more to hedge against.) But most importantly, both Clinton and Obama were highly risk-averse regarding the use of American military power.

The new Nixon In retrospect, Obama's foreign policy approach eerily resembles the Nixon administration's in the early 1970s. While Obama had to overcome the devastating strategic and humanitarian legacy of the Bush administration, Nixon, in turn, came into power after years of domestic political polarization and strategic overstretch due to the Vietnam War, which heavily undermined the fiscal and ideological pillars of Washington. Recognizing the deep unpopularity of external military interventions and the unsustainable (economic) burden of maintaining American geopolitical primacy, Nixon saw the combination of retrenchment and realpolitik as the only viable strategy. Pre-emptive interventions and relentless unilateralism, based on purely ideological grounds, were out of question. On the one hand, Nixon pushed regional allies, from western Europe to the Pahlavi monarchy in Iran and post-war Japan, to shoulder greater responsibility for their own security amid Soviet expansionism. This went hand in hand with Nixon's fateful decision to end Washington's role in bankrolling the global fixed exchange regime, which became almost impossible in an era of stagflation. On the other hand, Nixon explored an unholy alliance with communist China, under Chairman Mao, to isolate the Soviet Union. In many ways, the so-called 'Nixon doctrine' was both necessary and largely successful in turning the Cold War in favour of the USA. Amid stubborn economic downturn, the Obama administration has sought to follow in the footsteps of the Nixon doctrine by astutely revisiting American military commitments in Eurasia, encouraging regional allies to bear greater responsibility for their own security, pursuing a leaner and meaner American military, and, perhaps above all, exploring a strategic accommodation with rival states such as Russia, China and Iran. Both Nixon and Obama recognized the inherent dangers of pursuing unfettered geopolitical primacy: strategic overstretch as the hegemonic power confronts the impossible task of defending and dominating an ever-expanding domain; free-riding by allies and strategic partners, which neglect domestic defence and shun international obligations under the security umbrella of the dominant power; and the lingering temptation to engage in pre-emptive wars in order to prevent the emergence of any powerful rival (Porter 2013).

Stuck in the Middle East Upon its assumption of power, one of the major promises of the Obama administration was to end the wars in the Middle East. Although committed to capturing Osama Bin Laden and neutralizing the threat from the AQ franchise, Obama sought to extricate American troops from the quagmire of Iraq and Afghanistan. But decoupling from the region proved to be almost impossible, despite Washington's repeated promise to rebalance its focus towards promising regions such as East Asia (see Chapter 3). In the Middle East, Obama struggled with the reverberations of the 2010/11 Arab uprisings, which led to the downfall of a number of American allies, namely Ben Ali (Tunisia), Hosni Mubarak (Egypt) and Ali Abdullah Saleh (Yemen), while threatening the rule of Arab sheikhdoms in the Persian Gulf. The uprisings in non-allied states such as Libya and Syria proved an even greater source of headache. In Libya, the Obama administration, on the pretext of implementing a Responsibility to Protect (R2P) mission to prevent mass atrocities at the hands of Mu'ammer Gaddafi's army, supported NATO-led military operations (2011), which helped the rebel groups to topple the regime. The result was the collapse of the state apparatus in Libya, a civil war among competing factions, and the proliferation of militias and radical Islamists groups, which exploited the power vacuum in the oil-rich country. Within a year, American ambassador to Libya Christopher Stevens was murdered by a radical Islamist group, underscoring the depth of the security crisis in the North African country. In Syria, where the majority Sunni population demanded political reforms and democratic accountability, the Obama administration confronted a proxy war against Russia and Iran, which stood by the Assad regime amid an intensifying revolutionary upheaval in a country that used to be the heartbeat of Arab nationalism. Unwilling to trigger a broader conflict with Moscow and Tehran, the Obama administration shunned military intervention and large-scale armed support for rebel groups, which began to mostly rely on the Sunni powers of Saudi Arabia, Qatar and Turkey to topple the Alawite regime in Damascus. As the civil war in Syria intensified, AQ-affiliated groups such as the al-Nusra Front, which managed to capture several oilfields and allegedly received logistical and financial support from supporters across the Arabian peninsula and beyond, gained the strategic upper hand – contributing to the inflow of radical Islamist groups into the Syrian theatre at the expense of moderate rebel groups, which failed to gain full-fledged support from Washington and other Western powers. By 2013, the Obama administration was confronting a new powerful extremist group, the Islamic State of Iraq and Syria (ISIS), which managed to conquer vast territories on Syria's eastern borders, paving the way for an all-out invasion of Baghdad under a Shia government. At this point, Syria and Sunni-dominated regions of Iraq transformed into a haven for extremism, arguably representing a greater threat than the AQ central command in the early 2000s. Beyond the Arab uprisings, however, the Obama administration also grappled with the Arab–Israeli conflict, hoping to restart negotiations between Israel and the Palestinian Authority (PA) on a two-state solution. But Israel's right-wing government under Benjamin Netanyahu refused to consider much-needed concessions, including on the issue of illegal settlements in the West Bank and the relaxation of the blockade on Gaza. The Palestinian side, meanwhile, struggled to form a unified government, with the Fatah and Hamas parties separated in ideological and geographical terms, and oscillated between pursuing full-fledged nation-state status at the UN, on one hand, and (hopelessly) negotiating with the Israeli government on a two-state solution, on the other. Facing domestic pressure from pro-Israeli interest groups and legislators, Obama's efforts ultimately fell short. No wonder his approval ratings dropped dramatically over the years, rivalling the Bush administration's dismal numbers, as Arab and non-Arab nations (Turkey and Iran) lamented Washington's record on, among other things, the Israeli–Palestinian conflict and the deeply unpopular drone wars across the greater Middle East, which were expanded under the Obama administration's watch (Harris 2012).

The Iranian nuclear programme represented another major concern in the Middle East. As a student of realpolitik – namely, the non-ideological pursuit of national interest on purely pragmatic grounds – Obama took the diplomatic leap of faith to engage the Iranian leadership like no other American administration in recent memory. After all, Obama was in no mood for a devastating war with Iran over the latter's controversial nuclear policy. By progressively downplaying the threat of war, and relying on diplomatic measures to address the Iranian nuclear issue, the Obama administration managed to institutionalize bilateral negotiations with Tehran, paving the way for a new chapter in Iran–US relations. If anything, Obama could count on growing support among the American people in his quest for a diplomatic compromise with Iran. According to a 2014 World Public Opinion survey, conducted by the University of Maryland's School of Public Policy and the Program for Public Consultation, 61 per cent of the American public supported a nuclear deal with Iran, whereby Tehran would benefit from sanctions relief in exchange for limiting its enrichment capacity and accepting a more robust inspection regime. The same number of people also supported some kind of tactical collaboration between the USA and Iran against Sunni extremist groups in Iraq, namely the Islamic State, which has undermined the territorial integrity of post-Saddam Iraq and created a new haven for international terror. A larger majority supported more confidence-building measures between Washington and Tehran, hoping to see more normalized bilateral relations after three decades of outright animosity. And according to a Gallup Poll (in Jones 2014), Americans see China – no longer Iran – as the USA's greatest enemy. The economic stakes were also high. According to a report (2014) by the National Iranian American Council (NIAC), 'Losing billions: the cost of Iran sanctions to the US economy', stringent sanctions against Iran have cost the US economy up to US$135 billion in forgone export revenues and hundreds of thousands of jobs in terms of employment opportunities. As for the Rouhani administration, the reformist Iranian government that was elected in mid-2013, its best hope of overcoming

Iran's economic conundrum, and turning the country into a viable emerging market, was to end Western sanctions against Tehran. In short, Obama found someone with whom he could work. Both Obama and Rouhani were aware of the limits of their diplomatic overtures. To speak of a new era of strategic partnership between the two countries was premature, if not geopolitically naive. Yet the aim of both sides was to reduce unnecessary tensions, explore potential avenues for limited cooperation, and deal with common challenges such as religious extremism in the Middle East. The Rouhani administration also did not rule out deeper economic engagement with Washington, as Tehran aimed to recover from years of devastating sanctions and economic isolation. The Obama administration recognized the fact that Iran is an influential country, which has considerable sway from Afghanistan to Iraq and Lebanon. But given the depth of the sectarian and economic challenges across the Middle East, no single power could overcome the wave of frustration, conflict and crises which has gripped the region for much of the modern age. Both Iran and the USA shared some common interests in stabilizing the region, while outright enmity between the two powers would only deepen uncertainty and conflict. The proliferation of extremist groups across the porous borders of Iraq and Syria, which culminated in the establishment of the Islamic State under the leadership of Abu Bakr al-Baghdadi, represented one of the biggest challenges to Iran's national security in years. Both Washington and Tehran shared an interest in ensuring the territorial integrity of post-Saddam Iraq and preventing the emergence of a hub of terror at the heart of the Middle East. The prerequisite to a neither-friends-nor-foes relationship between Iran and the USA, however, was the conclusion of nuclear talks, which culminated in the the Joint Comprehensive Plan of Action (JCPA) framework agreement, announced in Lausanne, Switzerland, in April 2015, after days of gruelling eleventh-hour haggling between Tehran and the major world powers led by the United States. It remains to be seen, however, whether Obama can overcome domestic opposition in the US Congress to fully implement the final comprehensive deal with Iran. Obama achieved an even more straightforward diplomatic success with respect to Cuba. After Obama's historic meeting with Raul Castro in April 2015 in Panama, Washington and Havana moved ahead with normalizing their diplomatic and trade relations (Davis and Archibold 2015).

New world disorder

A closer look, however, reveals how Obama's diplomatic achievements with respect to Cuba and Iran were overshadowed by a flurry of geopolitical tremors across the world. Not to mention, in operational terms, his foreign policy was also not significantly different from his predecessors'. Also, his attempts at correcting the past mistakes of the Bush administration, and recalibrating the USA's relations with the rest of the world, faced significant opposition at home, especially among hawkish elements within a Republican-dominated Congress as well as influential figures within his own political party, such as Senator Robert Menendez, former chairman of the Senate Committee on Foreign Affairs. Obama sought to sustain American global leadership without carrying the bulk of the burden of policing the international order. More importantly, the new American administration inherited a fairly similar foreign policy establishment, and there was not a significant reshuffle in the overall bureaucratic apparatus, which has guided Washington's post-Cold War foreign policy (Glennon 2014). Following the English legal scholar Walter Bagehot's theory of 'double government', Michael Glennon (ibid.: 1) argues, 'National security policy in the United States has remained largely constant from the Bush Administration to the Obama Administration,' especially when one looks at the Central Intelligence Agency's (CIA) key programmes and counter-terrorism operations, drone wars across the Middle East, and cyber attacks and covert operations against Iran's nuclear programme, among others. Beyond the Middle East, the Obama administration confronted new challenges across the world. In early 2014, Ukraine, long viewed as a buffer state between the West and Russia, experienced a popular revolution, which led to the collapse of the Viktor Yanukovych government, largely seen as a pro-Kremlin administration. But instead of ushering in a period of stability and democratic competition, the upheaval in Ukraine opened up a geopolitical floodgate, paving the way for Russia to annex Crimea and extend varying forms of logistical and financial support to pro-Russian rebels in eastern regions of the country (Galeotti 2014a, 2014b). The Putin administration had to act swiftly, and consider drastic measures such as facilitating the partition of Ukraine along ethnic-geographical lines, before a new pro-Western government in Ukraine laid down the foundations for eventual membership of the NATO alliance and the European Union (EU). Moscow saw the developments in Ukraine as a repetition of a previous crisis in Georgia, when a pro-Western government, under Prime Minister Mikheil Saakashvili, openly sought membership of NATO, which would have effectively brought the Western military alliance to Russia's doorstep. Putin's assertive policy in eastern Europe reflected a lingering sense of betrayal in Moscow, which, on the heels of the end of the Cold War, apparently negotiated (and secured) an agreement, albeit informally, with Washington on the non-expansion of NATO into eastern Europe, including former members of the Soviet Union (Sarotte 2014; Mearsheimer 2014b). Beyond geopolitical calculations, Moscow was also concerned about the creation of a prosperous, democratic Ukraine, which could rekindle and motivate anti-autocratic movements in Russia and across the post-Soviet space; Moscow had every reason to thwart a successful democratic transition in Ukraine, preferring a weak, dependent regime on its Western frontier (Meek 2014). Amid a low-intensity civil war in Ukraine, which set off alarm bells across eastern Europe, Washington and Moscow were locked into a second Cold War, with sanctions and recriminations poisoning bilateral ties. With the USA and the European Union (EU) coordinating succeeding rounds of sanctions, targeting Russia's key economic sectors and constraining Moscow's access to financial markets in Europe, the Obama administration also accused Moscow of violating the 1987 Intermediate-Range Nuclear Forces Treaty, which was designed to curb the nuclear ambitions of the Cold War's leading protagonists. NATO has also accused Russia of engaging in military provocations in eastern Europe, with Russian jet fighters apparently violating NATO members' airspace, while a Russian submarine entered Swedish waters without permission (Groll 2014; Brattberg and Tracz 2014). In East Asia, China bitterly opposed the Obama administration's Pivot to Asia (P2A) policy, dismissing it as a thinly veiled containment strategy against a re-emerging Asian power. Amid a rising tide of territorial nationalism, maritime disputes in Asia reached dangerous levels under the Obama administration's watch, as China relentlessly pushed the limits of its claims across the western Pacific.

The dynamic duo The post-Cold War period has seen a dramatic reversal in Sino-Russia power relations, with Moscow increasingly eclipsed by Beijing's growing economic might. China's demographic encroachment on Russia's Siberian borders has also served as a serious source of concern, especially given Russia's demographic decline and limited investments in its Far Eastern regions (*Economist* 2013a). For years, Russia prevaricated on negotiating large-scale energy deals with China, refused to export advanced military technology, and blocked Chinese investments in Russia's strategic energy sectors (4). Fears of China's growing conventional military capabilities have also influenced Russia's calculations on the issue of nuclear arms reduction. In fact, some of Russia's tactical nuclear weapons are pointed at China (*Economist* 2014c). But the two powers have sought to overcome their strategic differences and bitter historical memories. Jointly opposing what they see as predatory American hegemony, Russia and China have upgraded their strategic partnership with a whole host of new energy, defence and trading agreements, which are set to solidify Sino-Russian bilateral relations. In fact, Xi chose Moscow as his first foreign destination upon assuming power. Both Putin and Xi have painstakingly sought to downplay their historical enmities and contemporary strategic differences. In international fora such as the UN Security Council, both sides have either coordinated their positions or, at the very least, refused to openly criticize each other, no matter how controversial the issue (e.g. Russia's annexation of Crimea) (Johnson 2014a; Rozman 2014). After a decade of booming hydrocarbon revenues, Russia has accelerated its military modernization programme (Gvosdev 2014), allocating a growing proportion of its GDP to defence spending (see Figure 2.1). Much to the consternation of the West, Putin, after years of hesitance, has also pushed ahead with selling advanced S-300 and S-400 missile defence

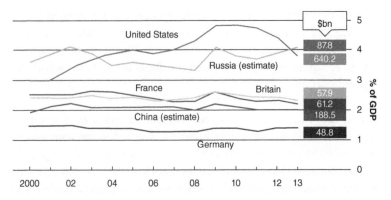

2.1 Russia's growing defence spending (*source: Economist* (2014c); Stockholm International Peace Research Institute).

systems to Iran and China, respectively (Putz 2015). The Sino-Russian tandem, anchored by a shared interest in pushing back against Western influence in the post-Soviet space and East Asia, represents an increasingly formidable opposition to American hegemony on the Eurasian landmass.

The Obama administration confronted a global geopolitical conundrum, eloquently captured by Zbigniew Brzezinski (in Rothkopf 2014), when he argued: 'I would even say that this is historically unprecedented, in the sense that simultaneously huge swaths of global territory are dominated by populist unrest, anger, and effective loss of state control'. The relative decline of American power, and the Obama administration's ambivalence about the use of force, encouraged an explosion of discontent and the realization of violent impulses among disenfranchised communities and/or irredentist powers across the world. As Michael J. Mazarr (2014), Professor of National Security Strategy at the National War College, aptly puts it: 'Today, the world's major security risks stem from the wrath of societies or groups that feel alienated or left behind by the emerging liberal order. Moving forward, most security threats will issue from a wounded people determined to overcome perceived humiliations and recapture their self-worth.' China's territorial assertiveness across the western Pacific, however, represented a particularly difficult geopolitical challenge.

After three decades of entente with Washington, the leadership in Beijing began to flex its muscles. And unlike any of Washington's strategic rivals, China possessed sufficient economic and military prowess to carve out a new regional order in its own image. China's new assertiveness was more than just an opportunistic exploitation of American vulnerability. It was the expression of a tectonic shift in the country's self-identity. Following G. W. F. Hegel's conception of the flow of human history, Francis Fukuyama (1992: xx) correctly saw how relations among states could largely be defined by a struggle for recognition: 'The struggle for recognition provides us with insight into the nature of international politics ... Nationalism, a modern yet not-fully-rational form of recognition, has been the vehicle for the struggle for recognition over the past hundred years, and the source of this [the twentieth] century's most intense conflicts.' The end of the Cold War saw the collapse of communist ideology as the main rival of Western democratic capitalism. Far from ushering in a new era of peaceful coexistence, however, the post-Cold War era saw the explosion of nationalist sentiments, not only among peripheral states but also among rising powers such as China. Rather than trade and economic interdependence, ideational struggles began to define the twenty-first century. The trend became more poignant in the case of China, colouring Beijing relations with its neighbours and the USA.

The tide of nationalism

Deng was hardly a true believer in capitalism, and he had no ideological commitment to the growing tide of neoliberalism, which took over the Western world, under the Reagan and Thatcher administrations, from the early 1980s onwards. Instead, he was primarily concerned with China's national development. After three decades of relentless economic growth, Japan, Taiwan, South Korea and much of the Western world managed to leap ahead of China. The Maoist era saw the reorganization of China's economy along socialist lines, with the state becoming the ultimate arbiter of economic decision-making and activity. In both rural and urban areas, under collective agricultural brigades and work units, labour was attached to the means of production, with the state ensuring a synchronized relationship between production and consumption patterns. By abolishing small capitalist enterprises and the family labour system, Maoist economic reforms marked a decisive departure with China's feudal past. The USSR served as a crucial source of financial, logistical and technological aid, thanks to Mao Zedong's incessant efforts to ensure maximum support from Moscow, particularly under Stalin. Under Mao's watch, China saw significant improvements in health, education and basic welfare of citizens. There was also a huge focus on heavy industries, the centrepiece of which were the SOEs, which accounted for almost 80 per cent of non-agricultural output, employing as many as 70 million people by the 1980s (Walker and Buck 2007). But China's developmental gains were overshadowed by the socio-political upheavals of the Maoist era, the inherent inefficiencies of command economy, and the failure to achieve rapid economic growth on a sustained basis, especially when compared to the developmental state regimes in neighbouring Japan, South Korea and Taiwan. Deng sought to correct the excesses of the Maoist era by reintroducing markets into the Chinese economy. The first stage of Deng's reforms (1978–92) saw the revival of key features of the Chinese economy during the Qing dynasty, when a strong state oversaw a thriving tapestry of small capitalist enterprises, commercialized agriculture and a family labour system (Andreas 2010). But the 1989 pro-democracy protests, in Beijing and 132 other cities across China, severely tested Deng's ability to maintain the CCP's grip on power. The ferocious debates over how the state should respond to the protesters created huge rifts within the Chinese leadership, and raised the possibility of military intervention by armed elements opposed to a bloody crackdown (Shirk 2008; Chang 2014a). After failed attempts at conciliation with the protesters, the regime saw the possibility of democratic revolution and/or protracted civil war amid defections within the PLA. In response, Deng purged the reformists/moderate voices, namely Party General Secretary Zhao Ziyang and General Xu Qinxian, and opted for a violent crackdown (Chang 2014a). The lesson was clear: Deng's (first stage of) economic reforms – with a focus on decollectivizing rural agriculture, unleashing small-scale entrepreneurial institutions, and establishing export-oriented SEZs – backfired. The introduction of market forces into the economy created major dislocations within Chinese society. The first stage of reforms saw the introduction of a household responsibility system, the abolition of the right to strike (1982), the lifting of restrictions on private firms (1987), the 1986 Land Management Law (revised in 1988) that allowed long-term leasing of state lands, the 1988 bankruptcy law that terminated the permanent employment guarantee for workers, and the Provisional Land Use Taxation Act and the Urban Planning Law of 1989 that paved the way for the emergence of a new class of rentiers and property speculators in China's megacities (Walker and Buck 2007). A decade of rapid economic growth resulted in the empowerment of a new, energetic middle class, which began to demand greater participation in the determination of China's political life. University students and the urban intelligentsia expected political reforms to go hand in hand with greater economic liberalization. A significant proportion of the population also lamented the immanent uncertainties brought about by an increasingly market-driven economy: a rise in inequality, spikes in inflation as the economy overheated in the 1986–88 period, a reduction in state welfare (or the smashing of Mao's 'Iron Rice Bowl'), partial privatization of SOEs (contracting out public enterprises and/ or divisions within to private cadres), and relaxation of price controls and state planning, among other things (Andreas 2008, 2010, 2012; Walker and Buck 2007). A combination of rising expectations, especially among the urban populace, and relative insecurity, due to the vagaries of market reforms, provided the structural underpinning of the social upheavals in the late 1980s (Andreas 2008, 2010). Prior to Deng's reforms, China was among the most egalitarian societies on earth. Three decades of rapid economic growth – increasingly driven by capitalist relations of production rather than simple marketization of a command economy – led to a massive explosion in inequality: the country's Gini coefficient (a measure of income inequality) increased from 0.30 in 1978 to 0.47–0.5 in 2009, making China among the most unequal societies on earth (Jacques 2012: 195). Joshua Kurlantzick (2009) thoughtfully captures the socio-political impact of Deng's reforms, when he argues: 'After Deng's willful smashing of the "iron rice bowl" – the Maoist era social welfare system – nothing was put in its place. Ordinary Chinese were left to fend for themselves in a society in which hospitals turn away patients who do not show up with cash, and parents with no money cannot enroll their children in a school.' Yet Deng refused to return to the discredited model of command economy prevalent in the Maoist days. He was determined to push the boundaries of China's economic modernization, bringing about 'Socialism with Chinese characteristics' – and what his protégé Jiang Zemin would later call 'socialist market economy' – based on a symbiotic relationship between single-party rule and market-driven capital accumulation, so long as it aided the country's industrial drive. But he was also determined to maintain the CCP's monopoly on political power. The early 1990s saw the second stage of economic liberalization, which witnessed a more decisive transformation of China's state-dominated economy into a fully fledged capitalist system – primarily anchored by profit maximization and productive efficiency (Andreas 2008). American sociologist Joel Andreas observes the emergence of a dynamic 'state capitalism' in China after three decades of economic reforms:

> There is no longer a socialist sector and virtually all enterprises that employ more than a handful of people, whether they are publicly or privately owned, now operate according to capitalist principles ... That the current configuration of power in China may appropriately be called a capitalist state is confirmed by the government's strong support for the expansion of the capitalist sector ... Capitalist encroachment on the family labour sector and the relentless displacement of small enterprises by larger ones is fundamentally market-driven, but it is also state policy.

The new ideological glue Grappling with the socio-political fallout of continued market reforms, Deng saw the potential of popular nationalism as a new ideology to bind the Chinese nation under the CCP's tutelage. As Deng's reforms took the whole nation through a 'valley of tears', brought about by the immensely disorienting nature of market reforms, nationalism could serve as a useful tool to maintain the coherence of the Chinese body politic. In an essay for the *New Left Review*, Benedict Anderson (2001) characterizes the Chinese post-

Cold War outburst of popular nationalism as a largely state-driven initiative: 'The contradictions between popular nationalism and official nationalism, which are so strikingly evident on the mainland [China] today, are ... not unique ... [But] China's sheer size, vast population, and a government, which, having effectively abandoned the socialism that once justified its dictatorship, shows every sign of turning to official nationalism for renewed legitimation of its rule.' Pioneering scholars on Chinese nationalism such as Suisheng Zhao (1998) describe how Chinese nationalism in the 1990s was 'constructed and enacted from the top', to counter the 'rapid decay' of communist ideology in the post-Cold War era, which presented a huge source of legitimacy crisis. The new form of nationalism espoused by the CCP was more focused on a self-serving version of patriotism (*aiguozhuyi*), essentially loyalty to the regime, rather than classical nationalism (*minzuzhuyi*), a sense of belongingness to the nation).[1] The bloody crackdown against pro-democracy protests in 1989 may have instilled fear among the populace and reformist factions, but it did little to enhance the CCP's legitimacy. As Zhao (1998: 287) explains:

> The patriotic education campaign was a state-led nationalist movement, which redefined the legitimacy of the post-Tiananmen leadership in a way that would permit the Communist Party's rule to continue on the basis of a non-Communist ideology. Patriotism was thus used to bolster CCP power in a country that was portrayed as besieged and embattled. The dependence on patriotism to build support for the government and the patriotic education campaign by the Communist propagandists were directly responsible for the nationalistic sentiment of the Chinese people in the mid-1990s.

In *Never Forget National Humiliation: Historical Memory in Chinese Politics and Foreign Relations*, Zheng Wang (2013a: 115) builds on Zhao's earlier work by explaining how *the* patriotic education campaign was a precursor of a 'major shift in Beijing's identity politics', which has proved to be 'one of the most important maneuvers the party has conducted for its survival in the post-Tiananmen and post-Cold

---

[1] For an interesting take on the CCP's deliberate and manipulative conflation of classical nationalism with loyalty to the regime, see Lu (2014a).

War eras'. Ruoxi Du, an academic based at the University of Kansas (n.d.: 5), explained the emergence of state-led popular nationalism as not only a strategic response to the CCP's international isolation after its violent suppression of the 1989 protests, which precipitated arms embargoes by Western powers, but also a strategy designed to re-establish 'Chinese people's political beliefs, loyalty to the communist state, and morality among the populace'. The CCP was driven by both short-term as well as long-term political considerations.

Perils of capitalism China's capitalist evolution, which took an accelerated form in the post-Cold War era, brought about an increasingly complex array of internal contradictions, which presented renewed challenges to the CCP's putative monopoly of power. (Although the CCP had to accommodate new political forces into its party-bureaucratic apparatus in order to cope with the increasingly amorphous, multifarious nature of power in a burgeoning capitalist system.) The privatization of SOEs led to massive layoffs, with as many as 60 million employees losing their jobs, while land-grabbing – often perpetrated by local party officials in cahoots with real estate developers, representing a classic case of accumulation by dispossession – in rural areas led to the displacement of as many as 40 million farmers. No wonder, as official figures admit, 'mass incidents' – spontaneous protests by aggrieved citizens, from migrant labourers to dispossessed farmers – jumped from 9,000 in 1993 to almost 90,000 in 2006 (Andreas 2012).

The violent crackdown on pro-democracy protesters in 1989, which precipitated defections within both the civilian and military leadership, strengthened the hands of hardline elements, especially within the PLA, who saw themselves as the saviours of the regime amid what seemed like an impending revolution. Recognizing the vulnerability of the CCP, the legitimacy of which was severely undercut by the bloody suppression of a largely peaceful pro-democracy movement, Deng and his successors more consciously sought to secure unflinching loyalty from the PLA, which, by now, demanded more political representation in the state apparatus and an increased defence budget for military modernization.

In a pioneering study on civil–military relations in China, Nan Li, Associate Professor at the US Naval War College, discussed how Deng's successors had to revolutionize China's long tradition of 'subjective control', whereby the paramount leaders, Mao and Deng, leveraged their credentials as the founding fathers of the communist regime to exercise personal control over the PLA. Belonging to the second generation of the Chinese leadership, Deng's successors had neither comparable revolutionary credentials nor any direct experience of military affairs. As a result, the Jiang and Hu administrations sought to introduce 'objective control' over the PLA, giving the armed forces more institutional autonomy and fiscal benefits in exchange for non-intervention in domestic political affairs. They painstakingly tried to facilitate the professionalization of the PLA and establish the supremacy of the civilian leadership (Nan 2010). As Nan (ibid.: 22) explains:

> The old party–army symbiosis, based on personal relationships, may have been characterized by political infighting among political-military factions, but in times of crisis, such as the Korean War and the 1979 war with Vietnam, it enabled charismatic political-military leaders like Mao and Deng to make quick decisions without much institutional hindrance. Since then, the institutionalization of civil–military boundaries that began under Deng has made it increasingly difficult for the new generations of uncharismatic technocrats like Jiang and Hu to do so.

Other scholars have taken an alarming view of the implications of the Tiananmen massacre on civil–military relations in China, and the growing rifts between the civilian leaders and their military counterparts in the last two decades. Gordon Chang (2014a), author of *The Coming Collapse of China*, argues that an additional challenge to the CCP was the growing tensions between the civilian and military leadership, which intensified after Deng's death in the mid-1990s: 'The unity between civilian and military leaders changed when Deng passed from the scene. Neither of his two immediate successors, Jiang Zemin and Hu Jintao, served a day in uniform. Moreover, Jiang and Hu had little contact with the officer corps prior to assuming power.' The extent of the PLA's direct influence on the CCP's decision-making process continues to be a subject of debate among specialists,[2] but it is clear that the armed forces were able to prove their indispensability to the maintenance and survival of the embattled regime. The Tiananmen massacre reinforced the CCP's lingering fixation with stability, inspiring a firm commitment to maintain an aura of leadership unity before the public. Keeping in mind the vicious civil wars of the early twentieth century, which almost led to the disintegration of the Chinese body politic, the CCP stepped up its efforts to prevent the eruption of large-scale, regime-threatening protests in the future. This led to the establishment of a gigantic internal security apparatus, equipped with an elaborate network of real-time surveillance to pre-emptively suppress any expression of discontent within civil society, which enjoys a larger budget than the country's armed forces (Shirk 2008; Jacques 2012; Chang 2014a).

A new paramount leader

The year 2013 saw the emergence of a new Chinese leader, Xi Jinping, who, beginning in late 2012, managed to swiftly assert control over all important pillars of the Chinese political system, namely the CCP, the state and the Central Military Commission (CMC). His predecessors, Jiang Zemin and Hu Jintao, were hand-picked by Deng Xiaoping, but never managed to achieve a comparable stature to either Mao or Deng. Both the Hu and Jiang administrations painstakingly maintained a tenuous balance among competing factions at the upper echelons of the Chinese political system, and at times struggled to introduce much-needed reforms to China's foreign and domestic policies owing to their lack of sufficient political capital. They were primarily bureaucrats, whose authority was underwritten by the collective support of the relevant power brokers in the regime – and the blessing of the late Deng. The transition from Jiang to Hu was also complicated by factional jostling. There were concerns as to the implications of Jiang's decision to hold on to the leadership of the CMC

---

[2] Based on the author's exchanges with Robert Sutter, professor of practice of international affairs at the Elliott School of George Washington University, during the latter's lecture at the University of the Philippines, Quezon City, on 9 June 2014.

two years into Hu's administration, which began in 2002. For some scholars, Jiang sought to maintain influence by denying Hu outright consolidation of power. While Jiang is considered as the leader of the so-called Shanghai faction/clique, which is known for its pro-market advocacies and amicable ties with the business sector, Hu represented a more centrist faction composed of communist youth leaders from humble socio-economic backgrounds, who rose to power owing to their sheer diligence and commitment to the egalitarian principles of the CCP (Shirk 2008; Nan 2010; Jacques 2012).

The selection of Xi Jinping as China's top political leader was the product of 'consociational' decision-making among the members of the Central Politburo Standing Committee of the Communist Party (PSC), the elite steering committee of the Chinese political system. It was the first transition of its kind in the communist regime's history. In many ways, Xi was a 'consensus candidate', who was acceptable to competing factions within the Chinese leadership. Dubbed as a 'princeling', Xi hailed from a prominent background: his late father, Xi Zhongxun, fighting side by side Mao and Deng, was among the founding members of the communist regime; Zhongxun later became a major proponent of economic reforms and a respected reformist leader within the CCP, known for his political moderation and personal integrity – a valuable source of political capital for his son. Xi Jinping's wife, Peng Liyuan, is a prominent singer and one of the most recognizable artists in China. As the dean of the People's Liberation Army Art Academy, she holds a civilian rank equivalent to major general. Xi's experience as an aide to Geng Biao, secretary general of the CMC and minister of national defence in the late 1970s and early 1980s, provided him with valuable connections and influence within the PLA. Throughout his career in government, he maintained strong ties with the military, once declaring, 'To meet the Army's needs, nothing is excessive' (Osnos 2014). Unsurprisingly, his rise to the top of the Chinese political system coincided with accelerated modernization of the PLA's equipment and a rise in their salaries and subsidies. But Xi was also an economic reformer. Following in the footsteps of his late father, he played an important role in the economic liberalization of China, overseeing economic boom in the prosperous provinces of Fujian and Zhejiang. But he was more than just an economic manager; Xi gained national prominence for his tough anti-corruption initiatives in Zhejiang, where he solidified his reputation as a sincere, decisive leader willing to confront unruly practices in an era of relentless economic growth. Resembling a philosopher-king, in the mould of ancient Confucian scholars at the service of the Chinese state, Xi authored two books, in 2006 and 2007 respectively – *Work on Real Things, Walk at the Forefront* and *New Thoughts from the Yangtze* – sketching out his distinct theory of how to combine the invisible hand of the market with the macro-strategic guidance of the CCP, so that the two hands can collectively function in a 'unified, mutually complementary and coordinated' manner (Martin and Cohen 2014; Osnos 2014). In Zhejiang (2002–07), he supported private enterprises by significantly reducing bureaucratic red tape, bringing the number of items requiring government approval from around three thousand to as little as eight hundred, and gleefully presided over the increasing contribution of the private sector to economic growth. At the same time, he defended the SOEs (against growing calls for privatization) by arguing that they could be reformed, subjected to market competition, and turned into competitive enterprises (and national champions) in an increasingly market-driven environment. He also argued about the necessity for a strong, decisive leader, even within a collective leadership system. The 'number one' should serve as 'the personification of the Party Committee and the government', Xi argued, and skilfully aggregate the interests and views of varying factions into a coherent whole (ibid.).

Consolidating power Overall, Xi was an ambitious and well-rounded leader, who maintained cordial ties with his superiors and successfully avoided scandals and confrontation with other officials. These factors made him a highly attractive candidate to succeed Hu, with the leadership transition process beginning in earnest in late 2012. True to form, he began consolidating power as soon as he took over the key organs of the Chinese political system in early 2013, placing himself at the centre of all important decision-making processes, reorganizing the bureaucracy to enhance his personal control. From early 2013 to early 2014, he began presiding over newly created and/or important state organs such as the National Security Commission, the Central Leading Group for Comprehensively Deepening Reforms, the Leading Small Groups (LSM) on foreign and security affairs as well as the Taiwan Affair, and a new group tasked with overseeing military reform. Xi has also established the State Security Committee (SSC), which allows him to personally supervise and streamline the civilian and military aspects of China's foreign and domestic security policy. The SSC, which is largely China's version of the USA's National Security Council (NSC), could also serve as a crisis management body, especially as Beijing's territorial spats with neighbouring states and geopolitical tensions with the USA intensify (see Chapter 3). Traditionally, the Chinese premier (the number two in the state) is tasked with overseeing economic affairs, but Xi could not resist outshining his deputy, Li Keqiang (protégé of Hu Jintao), by also chairing leading groups on financial and economic affairs, and prominently featuring in major state gatherings (e.g. the National People's Congress) on economic reforms and budgetary debates (Glosserman and Roy 2014).

Xi confidently presented himself as a synthesis of Mao's revolutionary leadership and Deng's pragmatic wisdom. He sought to carve out a legacy in China's history by promoting the slogan 'China Dream' as his overarching vision for the country. He was committed to making China prosperous and powerful enough to realize the dreams and aspirations of 1.3 billion people, ranging from the disenfranchised migrants and farmers to ambitious urban dwellers and consumerist middle classes. Inheriting a myriad of socio-economic and political challenges, China's new leader realized the importance of a decisive campaign to restructure the country's economic and political system. This was by no means an easy task, requiring, from Xi's point of view, an end to China's two-decade-long system of consociational leadership in favour of a new paramount leader, who wields sufficient bureaucratic power to overhaul the Chinese body politic. Xi had to launch a new economic revolution as well as a decisive campaign against corruption. The survival of the CCP was at stake. And if Xi wanted to guarantee his place in the exalted list of greatest leaders in China's history, he had to shepherd the country to the next stage of development. There was no turning back.

The economic conundrum China had largely exhausted the old model of export-oriented, labour-intensive industrialization, which was anchored by massive environmental degradation, perilous explosion of debt within the financial markets, repressive practices in the labour markets, and overcapacity in key sectors such as infrastructure and real estate. Deng's economic reforms had run their course. As Western markets entered a period of economic downturn after the Great Recession, China had to switch to a more sustainable development model, based on domestic consumption, services, research and development (R&D), and high-end manufacturing. In a country where the government has obsessively pursued at least 8 per cent economic growth per year, believing this is the safest rate of expansion necessary for the absorption of China's gigantic workforce and satisfaction of the citizenry, Beijing was desperate to avoid an economic contraction in the late 2000s. Its US$586 billion stimulus programme, underwritten by massive infrastructure projects and monetary easing, reinforced already worsening imbalances within the Chinese economy. In the late 1990s, the banking system was already struggling with one of the highest rates of non-performing loans on earth, which stood at between 30 and 50 per cent (Walker and Buck 2007). From 2008 to 2011, the state-dominated banking system churned out around US$4 trillion in new credit, dramatically increasingly overall liquidity (US$10 trillion) in the Chinese economy, outshining the world's largest economy, the USA (US$8 trillion). Given the lucrative nature of the real estate sector, much of the newly injected money went into a construction boom that saw, in 2010, almost 800 million square feet of real estate sold in China – more than in the rest of the world combined (Sharma 2012: 24).

While the public debt stood at relatively healthy levels (30 per cent of GDP), private debt reached as much as 130 per cent of GDP, a dangerously high level for an emerging economy like China. If China's 'shadow banking sector' – that is to say, lending practices that are off the official books and involve loan transfers among corporations and depositors, with banks primarily serving as intermediaries – is taken into consideration, the country's debt-to-GDP ratio would explode to almost 200 per cent (ibid.: 26). The Chinese banking sector faced a perilous systemic threat, mirroring the Wall Street bust in 2007/08, while inflation and real estate prices reached dangerously high levels – off the charts for developing countries (ibid.). Beijing's counter-cyclical measures in the late 2000s also led to inflationary spikes, which deeply affected the Chinese citizenry. In 2009/10, inflation rates increased by more than tenfold, while housing prices in major cities in 2009, thanks to the frantic expansion in the real estate sector, began to significantly outstrip the spending power of middle-class families. The urban unemployment rate, heavily affected by the decline in export markets and short-term adjustments in the economy, reached the highest level since 1980 (Ross 2012). More worryingly for Beijing, China faced one of the most serious street riots since the founding of the communist regime in 1949, when 70,000 people confronted law enforcement personnel in Shishou, in Hubei Province, which raised the prospect of widespread social instability across the country (ibid.). The advent of the 2010/11 Arab uprisings, which led to the swift, dramatic downfall of several autocrats across North Africa and the Middle East, exacerbated Beijing's sense of vulnerability. In 2011, the village of Wukan, in Guandong Province, saw an outright popular uprising against corrupt, abusive officials, which led to the expulsion of the village committee and the introduction of democratic elections (Al Jazeera 2013). It was a bold expression of the rising aspirations and sense of dignity among China's populace.

China has also been struggling with a major environmental crisis. It is home to sixteen out of the twenty most polluted cities on earth, with only 1 per cent of its urban population breathing safe air by EU standards. Its poor environmental record cost up to 3.5 per cent of its GDP in 2012, according to the Chinese government; in the late 1990s, according to the World Bank, the figure stood at between 3.5 and 8 per cent of its GDP (Thompson 2013). Water scarcity is another source of constant and growing worry for Chinese authorities. Home to almost one fifth of the world's population, China is host to only 7 per cent of the planet's fresh water. In the past six decades, about 27,000 rivers have vanished in China (Khan 2014). China has also been struggling with a huge 'water divide' between the largely arid north and the fertile south. More than 75 per cent of China's fresh water is concentrated in the south, forcing the government to consider draconian measures such as the Mao-era grand engineering project, which is set to transfer 45 billion cubic metres of water from prosperous southern provinces to the historically neglected regions of the north. Such artificial mega-projects could not only entail unforeseeable environmental costs, but could also fuel a growing schism between the prosperous farmers and urban dwellers in the south, on the one hand, and their fellow citizens in the north, on the other (ibid.). In fact, China has already been locked in water-related disputes with its neighbours: with China contemplating multiple, upstream hydropower projects on the Mekong river, from the Don Sahong project to the much larger Xayaburi dam farther upstream, resource-related disputes between Beijing and its ASEAN neighbours are set to intensify in the coming decades (Johnson 2014b). Since 2008, the country has also been grappling with a series of food safety scandals, provoking ever-diminishing public trust in the ability and political will of Chinese authorities to ensure safe and clean production as well as distribution of agricultural and food commodities. Massive urbanization has gone hand in hand with a growing fragmentation of the country's food supply chains. As Thomas Thompson (2012) explains:

> The growing distance from the farm to the dinner table that has come with China's rapid urbanization also presents problems. Because the country lacks an integrated chain of refrigerated trucks, warehouses, and retail space, contamination has been on the rise. It does not help that China's food supply system is highly fragmented. The country has approximately 500,000 registered food production companies, of which 80 percent are small food workshops with fewer than ten employees. Then there are the 200 million farmers who ship directly to the market with little documentation.

The second economic revolution By the time Xi came to power, the imbalances within the Chinese economy had been exacerbated, just as the country's GDP growth, after decades of double-digit expansion, slowed down to under 8 per cent. In 2007, China's GDP grew by as much as 14 per cent. By 2014, the GDP growth rate had halved, standing at just above 7 per cent; as the *Economist* (2014c) put it, the rapid catch-up by emerging markets such as China, accelerating since the late 1990s, could go down as a historical aberration in economic convergence:

> Over the past 15 years the currents that take people from such hinterlands of poverty to the broad open reaches of wealth have been flowing at an unprecedented rate. When adjusted for living costs, output per person in the emerging world almost doubled between 2000 and 2009; the average annual rate of growth over that decade was 7.6%, 4.5 percentage points higher than the rate seen in rich countries ... [the period] changed perceptions regarding just what is possible. But [it] also deceived people into thinking broad convergence is the natural way of things. It looks like the world is now being reminded that catching up is hard to do.

China had to contend with both a real estate bubble and ballooning debt among local governments. There was now little room for another stimulus package, while anaemic growth in Western economies limited the opportunity to accelerate exports to make up for domestic vulnerabilities. Local government units (e.g., provincial, prefectural, municipal, etc.) had accumulated a staggering US$1.8 trillion in debt. A credit crunch became unavoidable if Beijing sought to deleverage the financial sector (Feigenbaum and Ma 2013). The government had to boost consumer demand and enhance the contribution of the services sector at the expense of export-oriented industries and the real estate sector. But the eventual losers of such political transition had managed to establish formidable interest groups, within and outside the CCP, forcing the Xi administration to carefully calibrate economic reforms so as to prevent a political backlash and a socially destabilizing meltdown in traditional engines of growth. The bigger challenge, perhaps, was chronic corruption, as officials exploited their privileges to advance personal business interests amid rapid economic expansion. High-ranking officials and well-connected CCP members were among the biggest beneficiaries of the privatization – partial or comprehensive – of SOEs by optimizing schemes such as management buyouts (MBOs), which allowed them to become major shareholders in the previously collectivized enterprises. Having limited capital of their own, the former managers of work units and SOEs enjoyed access to massive borrowing from state-dominated banks. Intent on achieving maximum growth targets for promotional purposes, the local government officials, meanwhile, developed extraordinarily cosy relationship with the business sector. To attract investments, facilitate large-scale projects and gain access to capital, the local government units mortgaged state-owned lands, facilitated the repression of labour rights to enhance the profits of domestic industries, and oversaw the coercive appropriation of land from ordinary citizens and farmers. Corruption and bribery served as grist to the mill of large-scale capital accumulation, which primarily benefited big, well-connected businesses and government officials. Even within the country's armed forces, a growing number of high-ranking officials in the PLA became accustomed to corrupt practices, having been embroiled in a wide range of legal and quasi-legal business activities. Some estimates suggest that, from 1990, about eighteen thousand corrupt officials were responsible for siphoning as much as US$120 billion out of the country, a figure that is equivalent to the country's education budget from 1978 to 1998 (Huang 2013).

The Xi administration confronted a toxic combination of systemic corruption and structural economic imbalances, which collectively posed a threat to the legitimacy of the communist regime. As Yasheng Huang, a prominent economist at the Massachusetts Institute of Technology, argues, the corruption issue in China represents a matter of life and death for the CCP: 'When the economy is growing, people are willing to put up with some graft. When it is not, the same level of corruption is intolerable. If China continues with its political status quo, conflicts are likely to escalate sharply, and the pace of capital flight from the country, already on the rise due to declining confidence in China's economic and political future, will accelerate.'

Under Xi Jingping's watch, China witnessed an unprecedented anti-corruption crackdown. Under the aegis of the Central Commission for Discipline Inspection (CCDI), China's main anti-corruption body, up to 182,000 officials faced varying forms of disciplinary punishments (Xinhua 2014). Declaring war on 'flies' (low-to-medium-level corrupt officials) and 'tigers' (powerful corrupt officials), Xi placed restrictions on, among other things, luxurious banquets, exchange of expensive gifts, and construction of new government buildings. What initially looked like a 'cosmetic' reform to enhance the CCP's image gradually turned into a sweeping purge of high-profile individuals and a significant downturn in the demand for luxury products. The two biggest victims of Xi's measures were Bo Xilai, the former party chief of Chongqing and a charismatic neo-Maoist figure, and his patron, Zhou Yongkang, the former internal security tsar and member of China's top decision-making organ, the PSC. Through the anti-corruption crackdown, Xi placed himself in a position to target opponents on both sides of the political spectrum. On the one hand, he sought to rein in the growing influence of the New Left, neo-Maoist officials such as Bo Xilai, who wanted to revive the traditional emphasis on ideological purity and egalitarian economic policies with considerable success. As Wang Hui, an academic based in Beijing's Tsinghua University, argues, the New Left trend was particularly threatening to the regime's largely neoliberal economic reforms, which suffered a huge blow during the 2007/08 Great Recession:

> In Chongqing there was more emphasis than in some other places on redistribution, justice and equality, and because the province was already highly industrialised, state-owned enterprises were important to its model. Chongqing's experiment with inexpensive rented housing, its experiment with land trading certificates, its strategy of encouraging enterprises to go global: all these, under the rubric 'the state sector progresses, the private sector progresses,' contributed to society's debate ... The Chongqing experiment, launched in 2007, coincided with the global financial crisis, which made a new generation feel less confident of the benefits of free-market ideology. (Hui 2012)

The populist appeal of the New Left's policies was a potentially powerful challenge to Xi's power. In late 2013, after the Third Plenum (a four-day gathering of the top leaders), the Xi administration agreed that the markets should play a more 'decisive' role in the country's economy, with fewer restrictions on investments, more transparent fiscal policies, and more liberalized property rights for farmers, among other measures (4). Xi was in no mood for the neo-Maoist rhetoric from potential challengers such as Bo Xilai, who had few qualms about expressing their ambition for China's top office. In the minds of China's top leaders, the country was simply too integrated with and dependent on international markets to fully abandon its neoliberal economic reforms, as New Left populist rhetoric and projects implied. Xi was by no means a pro-market ideologue, however. And there were indications that he could also be fixing his sights on the patronage network of the Shanghai faction led by Jiang Zemin (Chang 2014b).

Back to the future Styling himself as the new Mao, Xi revived the mid-twentieth-century Maoist tradition of show trials, which involve the public humiliation of purged officials and prominent dissidents (Hayoun 2014). He also reintroduced Maoist practices such as the so-called 'self-criticism sessions', where top officials are forced to openly admit their faults, real or imaginary, as a form of ideological purification – and a reassertion of their commitment to serve the Chinese people (Martin and Cohen 2014). Evan Osnosa (2014), author of *Age of Ambition: Chasing Fortune, Truth, and Faith in the New China*, dramatically captures Xi's emerging cult of personality à la Mao Zedong:

> a quarter of the way through his ten-year term, he has emerged as the most authoritarian leader since Chairman Mao ... In the spirit of Mao's Little Red Book, publishers have produced eight volumes of Xi's speeches and writings; the most recent, titled 'The Remarks of Xi Jinping,' dissects his utterances, ranks his favorite phrases, and explains his cultural references. A study of the People's Daily found that, by his second anniversary in office, Xi was appearing in the paper more than twice as often as his predecessor at the same point. He stars in a series of cartoons aimed at young people, beginning with 'How to Make a Leader,' which describes him, despite his family pedigree, as a symbol of meritocracy – 'one of the secrets of the China miracle.' ... In January [2015], the Ministry of Defense released oil paintings depicting him in heroic poses; thousands of art students applying to the Beijing University of Technology had been judged on their ability to sketch his likeness. The Beijing Evening News reported that one applicant admired the President so much that 'she had to work hard to stop her hands from trembling.'

To enhance his image as a leader of the Chinese people, Xi went so far as dining, with few bodyguards and limited publicity, in a comfort food restaurant among ordinary citizens. In December 2013, Xi visited a popular state-owned chain, specializing in northern Chinese comfort food, in western Beijing, where he 'walked up to the counter and ordered six steamed pork and scallion buns, pig liver stew, and a plate of mustard leaf, for which he paid – with his own two hands, no less – $3.40' (Fish and Gao 2014). The story immediately went viral on China's main social networking platforms such as SinaWeibo (China's Twitter), inspiring outright admiration for what ordinary citizens saw as a sincere, down-to-earth leader (ibid.). As Isaac Stone Fish and Helen Gao (ibid.) write, Xi managed to pull off a highly successful publicity stunt with utmost finesse: 'Unlike similar stunts by Xi's predecessors and other high-ranking Chinese officials, Xi's visit seemed more authentic. Instead of the usual entourage of other authorities, state media, and bodyguards, Xi brought only two men with him, and he looked at ease as he sat and ate his food in public.'

It is precisely the combination of humility (before public eyes) and steadfastness (before officials) which has enhanced Xi's image among the populace. In mid-2014, as the anti-corruption efforts began to reach their peak and provoke divisions and criticism within the political classes, Xi passionately proclaimed, 'In my struggle against corruption, I don't care about life or death, or ruining my reputation', re-emphasizing his commitment to cleanse the CCP of the vestiges of corruption (Chang 2014b). On the eve of the 110th anniversary of Deng Xiaoping's birth, the Chinese government aired, in prime time, a forty-eight-episode biographical TV series, which dramatized the life of the late leader of China, who oversaw the breathtaking transformation of an isolated regime, under Mao, into a global economic powerhouse. Conveniently, the series covered only the first eight years of Deng's rise to power, from 1976 to 1984, avoiding the contentious politics ahead of and during the 1989 Tiananmen Square massacre. Attending a symposium on Deng's legacy at the Great Hall of the People in Beijing, just next to the Tiananmen Square, Xi lavished praise on his 'outstanding leadership', which allowed China to once again 'stand like a giant' after decades of economic boom. Describing Deng as 'great creator of an era, a great figure', Xi exclaimed: 'The contribution by Comrade Deng Xiaoping not only changed the historic destiny of the Chinese people but also changed the course of the world's history' (Al Jazeera 2014a). Leaving no doubt as to the political rationale behind the high-profile release of the TV series, the Xinhua news agency, the official media of the state, declared, 'To reignite a nation, Xi carries Deng's torch' (ibid.). There are even serious discussions over the possibility that Xi may stay in power well beyond his original decade-long tenure. As Wily Lam (2015), a leading China expert based in Hong Kong, explains:

> Xi's desire to rule for longer than a decade is best evidenced by his refusal to publicly groom potential successors. In China, leaders are often classified by their generation. Xi, a member of the fifth generation of leadership – a reference to cadres born in the 1950s – has failed to groom potential successors from the sixth or seventh generation ... If Xi were following the CCP's tradition of injecting new blood into the ruling elite, he should by late 2015 promote a few dozen seventh-generation officials to ministers and vice ministers. However, only one seventh-generation cadre – Shanghai Vice Mayor Shi Guanghui (born 1970) – has attained the rank of vice minister since Xi came to office in November 2012. It seems very unlikely that he'll elevate many more this year. Xi seems poised to break another unwritten rule.

It is still too early to say whether Xi will end up as another Deng, who will take China to the next stage of development, or, alternatively, become China's Gorbachev, tearing apart the communist regime in pursuit of ambitious reforms, which will unleash unforeseen forces that will ultimately spell the end of the CCP's rule. What is clear, however, is that Xi relishes China's global influence and seeks a greater voice on the international stage. Arguably, Xi sees foreign affairs as a great opportunity to enhance his political capital at home, as he struggles to overhaul the Chinese economy, rein in uncontrolled corruption, and carve out his own legacy. China's massive stock market crash in mid-2015 – forcing the government to impose draconian economic measures to arrest panic, and go so far as devaluing its currency to reflate a flagging economy – only reinforced Xi's acute economic dilemma at home (Heydarian 2015d). Under his watch, China has hardened its position on issues that it considers its 'core national interest', with troubling implications for not only the quasi-autonomous peoples on the peripheries of the Sino-sphere – especially Xinjiang, Hong Kong and Taiwan – but also the broader East Asian region. Weaker neighbouring countries, which have been locked in bitter maritime disputes with Asia's pre-eminent indigenous power, have anxiously watched the emergence of a distinctly nationalist leader in Xi Jinping, who has comfortably thrown Beijing's weight around and openly expressed his commitment to return China to its historical position of primacy in Asia. Driven by a fierce sense of popular nationalism, China's quest for national glory, backed by an increasingly sophisticated military, has contributed to a dangerous territorial escalation across the western Pacific, particularly in the South China Sea.

3 | WAR AT SEA: FROM THE MOTHERLAND TO THE BLUE SOIL

> There are both things in international law: the principle of territorial integrity and right to self-determination.
>
> Vladimir Putin

> When there is no enemy within, the enemies outside cannot hurt you.
>
> Winston Churchill

Viewing China as America's sole global peer, Xi confidently advocated an era of 'new great power relationship' with Washington. But this has not stopped Beijing from challenging, in general, the liberal international order, and, in particular, American hegemony in East Asia. His drive for political supremacy at home is predicated on his 'China Dream' vision, motivated by a centuries-old quest to restore China's grandeur, which was punctured by the colonial incursions of, first, Western powers and, later, Japan, from the nineteenth century up until the end of the Second World War. For the Chinese leadership, especially Xi, China is not a rising power per se, but simply returning to its rightful historical stature (Wang 2013b). As Chinese academic Zheng Wang (ibid.) explains:

> After suffering a humiliating decline in national strength and status, the Chinese people are unwavering in their commitment to return China to its natural state of glory, thereby achieving the Chinese Dream. However, China has never clearly stated what the criteria and measurements are to determine the realization of rejuvenation … whereas the American Dream emphasizes individuals attaining personal enrichment and success, the Chinese Dream is a collective undertaking that calls upon Chinese citizens to make personal sacrifices in order to serve the greater, national good.

The problem, however, is that this drive for national dignity has come with a tinge of aggrieved nationalism, which is beginning to threaten the fabric of regional integration in Asia – and a decades-long entente between Washington and Beijing. In early 2013, Xi left little doubt as to his commitment to defend China's territorial claims and national dignity, fervently declaring: 'No foreign country should ever nurse hopes that we will bargain over our core national interests ... Nor should they nurse hopes that we will swallow the bitter fruit of harm to our country's sovereignty, security and development interests' (Buckley 2013). For the Chinese leadership, contentious issues such as Xinjiang, Tibet and Taiwan – and increasingly the disputed territories in the western Pacific – fall under the 'core interests' category, which means they are non-negotiables that justify military intervention if and when necessary.

While Deng Xiaoping managed to establish a détente with the USA, the Jiang and Hu administrations, in turn, experimented with the prospects of 'strategic partnership' with the USA, particularly under the Clinton and Bush administrations. Under the Xi administration, however, Sino-American relations have moved closer to what can be considered 'competitive codependence', which denotes a complex state of economic interdependence persisting hand in hand with overt geopolitical rivalry. And beyond the Sino-American equation, neighbouring countries such as Japan, Vietnam and the Philippines have been increasingly alarmed by the territorial assertiveness of the Xi Jinping administration.

Economic codependence

According to some estimates, Chinese outbound investment in the USA rose from just under US$1 billion before the 2007/08 Great Recession to US$14 billion in 2013 (Shih 2014). This marked a dramatic reversal in the flow of FDIs between the two countries, as China began to invest more in the USA than the other way around. China's holdings of US treasuries (low interest, long-term government bonds) also soared to US$1.317 in 2013, according to the US Treasury Department (Katz 2014a). Bilateral trade, meanwhile, stood at almost US$600 billion in 2012, with China enjoying a record-high US$298 billion trade surplus (Office of the United States Trade Representative 2014). In 2013, China, responsible for US$3.87 trillion in exports and imports with the rest of the world, became the world's biggest trading nation, overtaking the USA, the total trade volume of which stood at US$3.82 trillion (Bloomberg 2013). On the surface, this might give an impression that China is in the driving seat, which partially explains growing exuberance among the Chinese leadership in recent years. In reality, however, China continues to depend on the USA as a major export market as well as an investment destination. A substantial portion of China's US$3.66 trillion foreign exchange reserves is in US dollars; the Chinese yuan, or renminbi (RMB), beginning in 1994, was also pegged to the US dollar, although the yuan experienced, under a 'managed float' system, gradual appreciation from 2005 onwards (Picardo 2014). So, Beijing has a direct interest in the stability of the US economy, which, in turn, influences the value and attractiveness of the US dollar as the world's reserve currency. It will take some time before China substantially reduces its dependence on exports to Western markets; displacing the US dollar as the global reserve currency will also require, among other things, China to make its own currency fully convertible and liberalize its capital markets, which carries significant risks for China's economic stability. This is precisely why a decades-long plan, beginning in the late 1980s, to make China's currency fully convertible has repeatedly failed to materialize (Aitken 2014).

Reflecting on the 1997/98 AFC, which was primarily sparked by the speculative movement of portfolio investments after the liberalization of financial markets in a number of South-East Asian countries, Chinese officials are extremely uneasy about the prospect of a similar financial meltdown at home. As Roger Aitken (ibid.), a finance expert, explains in *Forbes* magazine: 'Chinese policy makers fear that a nationwide liberalisation of capital and currency controls would spark a cash exodus. Indeed, according to a recent Hurun report a whopping 44% of Chinese individuals holding over RMB10m in their name have plans to emigrate. Also of particular concern are hot money flows, whereby money is invested to reap short-term profits on interest rate differences between countries.' Above all, one could argue that China has been among the biggest – if not the primary

– beneficiaries of the liberal international order in the last three decades: the USA's hegemony provided a semblance of stability in the global economy, allowing China to turbocharge its industrialization by gaining unprecedented access to advanced technology, foreign capital and lucrative consumer markets. Economic experts such as Niall Ferguson and Moritz Schularick went so far as to coin the term 'Chimerica' to underline the depth of economic symbiosis between China and America: 'Before the 2008 financial crisis, this was a marriage of opposites. China saved, exported and lent. America consumed, imported and borrowed. For a few heady years, the odd couple were happy together. Not only did the Chinese savings "glut" lower the cost of capital; the glut of Chinese workers also reduced the cost of labor' (Ferguson and Schularick 2013).

Recasting globalization Economic codependence, however, has not stopped the Chinese leadership from pursuing a separate agenda outside the existing architecture of global governance. After all, the BWS system continues to be dominated by the West, which enjoys disproportionately high levels of decision-making powers within the World Bank and the IMF. The USA's share of IMF voting rights is about 16.8 per cent, which gives the country a de facto veto power in the organization. As the world's second-largest economy, accounting for 16.1 per cent of global GDP, China's share of voting rights in the IMF stands at only 3.8 per cent; the IMF, by a controversial tradition, also continues to be headed by Europeans. Efforts at mild readjustment in voting rights of member countries have failed to materialize, because of the unwillingness of the US Congress to ratify an agreement to increase the voting powers of emerging economies such as China (Talley 2014). Among many emerging powers, especially China, there is growing frustration with the existing institutions of global governance, which continue to fail to reflect the shifting poles of economic power of recent decades. Far from harmonizing interstate relations, growing economic interdependence has introduced new areas of competition between status quo and rising powers. Reflecting on the increasing fragility of the post-Cold War order, and growing Sino-American tensions, Henry Kissinger (2014) explains:

The concept of order that has underpinned the modern era is in crisis
... The international order thus faces a paradox: Its prosperity is
dependent on the success of globalization, but the process produces
a political reaction that often works counter to its aspirations ... The
penalty for failing will be not so much a major war between states
(though in some regions this remains possible) as an evolution into
spheres of influence identified with particular domestic structures
and forms of governance. For the Xi administration, and many of its
nationalist supporters, China's recent success is largely a reflection
of its national resilience and determination, rather than the goodwill
and benevolence of the U.S. Thus, China has every reason to doubt
American intentions and challenge the latter's global hegemony in
defense of its own national interest.

China's positive experience of economic globalization, under the
auspices of American hegemony, failed to eliminate long-standing
suspicions as regards Washington. As influential Chinese opinion-
makers such as Ni Feng, the deputy director of the Chinese Academy
of Social Sciences' Institute of American Studies, bluntly put it, 'the
United States realizes that it needs China's help on many regional and
global issues', but it is also 'worried about a more powerful China',
therefore it will resort to 'multiple means to delay its development
and to remake China with U.S. values' (Nathan and Scobell 2012).
It is precisely these suspicions which have encouraged the Xi
administration to build on earlier efforts to enhance China's influence
in the international system, at the expense of America. There continues
to be a zero-sum understanding of great power relations. As American
political scientists Andrew Nathan and Andrew Scobell, authors of
China's Search for Security, explain: 'In the Chinese view, Washington's
slow rapprochement with Beijing [beginning in the 1970s] was not born
of idealism and generosity; instead, it was pursued so that the United
States could profit from China's economic opening by squeezing
profits from U.S. investments, consuming cheap Chinese goods, and
borrowing money to support the U.S. trade and fiscal deficits. While
busy feasting at the Chinese table, U.S. strategists overlooked the risk
of China's rise until the late 1990s' (ibid.). In fact, as early as 2005,
Joshua-Cooper Ramo (2005: 2–3) observed:

China's rise is already reshaping the international order by introducing a new physics of development and power ... China is in the process of building the greatest asymmetric superpower the world has ever seen ... marking a path for other nations around the world who are trying to figure out not simply how to develop their countries but also how to fit into the international order in a way that allows them to be truly independent, to protect their way of life and political choices in a world with a single massively powerful centre of gravity.

A decade after Ramo coined the term 'Beijing Consensus' – that is to say, China's pragmatic, non-ideological approach to international relations, which directly contradicts the doctrinaire foundations of the liberal international order – China represented not only a source of ideational challenge. Beyond representing an alternative model of development and a pragmatic partner in international affairs for poorer nations, China, under Xi Jinping, was now in a position to accelerate its efforts at reshaping its regional environment and the broader architecture of global governance to its taste. For optimists, this marked the beginning of the end for American hegemony, facilitating the establishment of a more balanced, multipolar order in international affairs. For China's critics, however, this raised the possibility of 'Finlandization' – the progressive inclusion of neighbouring states in China's sphere of deference, forcing weaker states to defer to China on key strategic issues at the expense of their national sovereignty – in China's immediate neighbourhood (e.g. Central Asia, South-East Asia and the Korean peninsula) and global peripheries, especially African and Latin American countries that have to come to heavily depend on China's cash and goodwill.

The Beijing Consensus

China has utilized multiple avenues to challenge the existing international order, without necessarily seeking to overturn it: China recognizes that the BWS is not entirely antithetical to its interests – and that it is essential to sustaining a measure of stability in the international system. China shuns any abrupt change in the existing order, since this could undermine international trade and pose new security challenges to the country. It is the Western domination of the BWS – rather than its existence and functions – which is the main source of concern to Beijing. What China seeks is the creation of new spaces to flex its muscle and deepen its influence – in turn, giving it more leverage to enhance its position within the BWS. As liberal international relations theorist John Ikenberry (2011) aptly puts it:

> The struggle over international order today is not about fundamental principles. China and other emerging great powers do not want to contest the basic rules and principles of the liberal international order; they wish to gain more authority and leadership within it … [Since they] have all become more prosperous and capable by operating inside the existing international order … Their economic success and growing influence are tied to the liberal internationalist organization of world politics, and they have deep interests in preserving that system.

For Ikenberry, the current international liberal order provides a solid structure of payoffs, ultimately encouraging compliance and cooperation rather than great power confrontation and hegemonic wars. In terms of carrots, the liberal international order provides a set of relatively stable, predictable and transparent institutional mechanisms to facilitate trade, cooperation and conflict resolution, especially among major powers. The cost of confronting or directly challenging the current order is simply too much: isolation, backlash from both emerging and established powers, trade disruption, and military confrontation with an alliance of status quo powers. Exercising its increasingly sophisticated 'convening power', China has served as a primary force behind the establishment of new cooperative networks that fall outside the American sphere of influence. China's founding of pan-regional, intergovernmental platforms such as the SCO and the Conference on Interaction and Confidence Building Measures in Asia (CICA), which deny the USA and Japan regular membership, has allowed Beijing to consolidate its influence in Central Asia and strengthen its strategic partnership with non-Western powers such as Russia, Iran and Turkey. During the fourth summit of the CICA, Xi Jinping boldly called for member states to 'innovate [their] security cooperation' and establish 'new regional security cooperation architecture', warning the USA against interfering in Asian affairs

(CBS News 2014). His statements were eerily reminiscent of Imperial Japan's calls, in the early twentieth century, for an 'Asia for Asians', which effectively meant the eviction of Western powers from the region in favour of a new Asian superpower. On a global level, China has stepped up its strategic partnership with the emerging powers of India, Russia, Brazil and South Africa, among others. No longer just a catchy acronym, originally coined by Goldman Sachs to assist institutional investors in exploring new opportunities in the rapidly growing developing countries, the BRIC grouping (Brazil, Russia, India and China) began holding regular summits in the aftermath of the 2007/08 Great Recession, culminating in the establishment of the New Development Bank (NDB) and the Contingent Reserve Arrangement (CRA) in 2014. (To expand their geographical representation, they became the BRICS by admitting South Africa into their group in 2011.) The NDB is patterned after the national development banks of Brazil and China, which have been responsible for large-scale loans to developing countries in need of capital and technical expertise in the realm of sustainable development. To give teeth to their newly created financial institutions, the BRICS pledged an initial amount of US$100 billion to the NDB and the CRA.

These newly established institutions are relatively small in comparison to the IMF, which holds around US$800 billion in its coffers, and the World Bank, which lends as much as US$60 billion annually (Matlack 2014). Over time, however, the NDB and the CRA are poised to expand in terms of their budget and capabilities, thanks to the large pool of currency reserves (more than US$5 trillion) and skilled development experts from the BRICS – which collectively represent 46 per cent of the world population, and have a combined GDP that rivals that of the USA and the EU – as well as other emerging powers such as Mexico, Indonesia, Turkey and Iran that might consider following suit in the future. In economic terms, China easily dwarfs other emerging powers, since its GDP and currency reserves are larger than those of the other BRICS members combined. No wonder China shouldered a huge portion (US$41 billion) of the CRA's budget. This huge economic disparity (between China and other member states) gives Beijing tremendous leverage in shaping

the institutions that are mainly composed of emerging powers and/
or developing countries. Despite stiff resistance from India, China
managed to win the argument on where to base the headquarters of
the NDB. Given Beijing's long-term hopes of transforming Shanghai
into the world's financial centre, it came as no surprise that the
booming, cosmopolitan city is poised to host the NDB's headquarters.
The BRICS, and other similar platforms of global governance, allows
China to challenge the financial supremacy of the US dollar by
facilitating the expanded usage of alternative currencies to conduct
trade among developing countries. The US dollar's privileged status
as the global reserve currency is under pressure. For instance, its share
in global foreign exchange holdings declined from 55 per cent in 2001
to 33 per cent in 2013 (Hallinan 2014). With China emerging as the
top trading nation in the world, a growing number of countries have
begun to conduct their trade in alternative currencies such as the
yuan. Western sanctions on oil-exporting countries such as Iran (over
its nuclear programme) and Russia (over its intervention in Ukraine)
have encouraged them to move away from the US dollar. On its own,
China has already emerged as one of the largest sources of soft loans
and development aid in the world. From 2001 to 2011, China's
development assistance pledges increased from US$1.7 billion to
US$189.3 billion, with (resource-rich) Latin American and African
countries as the biggest beneficiaries. China's cumulative pledges in
foreign development assistance (FDA), from 2011 to 2011, reached
almost US$700 billion (Wolf et al. 2013: xiii–xv). For instance, in
Latin America, Washington's backyard, China has emerged as the
main creditor to a whole host of leftist governments. Since 2005,
China is estimated to have committed nearly US$100 billion to the
region, with oil-rich Venezuela absorbing about half of it. In 2013,
China agreed to swap about 90 per cent of Ecuador's oil for financing
about 60 per cent of the troubled South American nation's budget
shortfall (Picq 2014). In South-East Asia, Indonesia, Malaysia and
Thailand were the top recipients (Wolf et al.: 50). During the 2013
Asia-Pacific Economic Cooperation Summit (APEC), Xi Jinping
upped the ante by promoting the proposed establishment of a US$50
billion Asian Infrastructure Investment Bank (AIIB), which is set to

rival the America/Japan-dominated Asian Development Bank (ADB), headquartered in Manila. The AIIB could serve as the backbone of China's 'Maritime Silk Road' initiative, which seeks to integrate South-East Asia into an evolving global trading regime, a 'New Silk Road' powered by Beijing's booming economy. By offering large-scale financial incentives (AIIB), upgrading alternative regional platforms (CICA) and establishing new global institutions (NDB), the Xi administration will be in a position to gradually carve out a new zone of deference in East Asia at the expense of the USA and its regional allies. And there are growing reasons to worry about a more aggressive Chinese foreign policy under the Xi Jinping administration, which has taken a tough position on contentious issues at home and abroad.

Consolidating the motherland

In Xinjiang, historically a Muslim-majority province on the western frontiers of China, inter-ethnic tensions and the number of insurgency movements have increased. Suffering from cultural repression, political oppression and economic marginalization, the Uighur population has become increasingly restless, fuelling a deepening cycle of violence, which has been exacerbated by the CCP's heavy-handed crackdown on any form of dissent. For decades, the Uighur population resisted what they saw as Han Chinese colonization of a distinct Turkic-Muslim nation, which enjoyed a brief period of independence (as the East Turkestan Republic) in the early twentieth century. Reporting from Xinjiang, Nick Holdstock (2008) explained the repressive atmosphere, which has enraged the Uighur population:

Restrictions have been placed on how and where Uighurs can worship. Mosques must be registered with the state; imams require government approval and have to attend political meetings; Uighurs who work in state-run institutions (a school, hospital or post office) are not supposed to display any signs of faith – fasting and praying during Ramadan are specially discouraged. At school Uighur children are taught that religion is mere superstition. These measures are resented, and economic recession, which began in the 1990s, when many state-owned factories and businesses were closed as part of nationwide economic reforms, has of course made things worse.

After decades of relentless exploitation of the region's mineral resources by Beijing and the massive migration of Han Chinese people to the Muslim-majority region, which later was named the Xinjiang Uighur Autonomous Region, the animosity of the Uighur population – suffering from high rates of unemployment and poverty – towards migrants from mainland China intensified, culminating in violent clashes between Uighur and Han residents in the regional capital city of Urumqi in mid-2009, which led to the death of 184 people and injury to hundreds more (ibid.). Beijing responded by ramping up security measures and accelerating investments in the troubled region, to no avail. The combination of uneven economic development, intensifying repression of Uighur cultural practices, and a brutal crackdown on even peaceful calls for political reform further radicalized the local population (Palmer 2014). Instead of instituting genuine reforms to appease the Uighur population, Beijing authorities have automatically put the blame on insurgency groups such as the East Turkestan Islamic Movement (ETIM) for any flare-up in violence. The emergence of the Xi administration, which confidently promised greater prosperity and security to the Chinese people under its watch, coincided with a spike in varying forms of terrorist attacks against innocent civilians across China, from Kunming to Beijing, which could be, as Chinese authorities adamantly insist, related to the deteriorating security situation in Xinjiang. In October 2013, three ethnic Uighurs in an SUV ploughed through tourists in Beijing's Tiananmen Square. Then, in March 2014, a group of knife-wielding attackers assaulted innocent civilians in a train station in Kunming, the capital of the south-western province of Yunnan; this was followed by deadly terrorist attacks in Xinjiang in May (Rauhala 2014). In July 2014, a terrorist attack against Han Chinese residents killed almost one hundred people in the north-western province, followed by the murder of an imam (an Islamic religious leader) close to the government (ibid.). True to form, Xi responded by (hyperbolically) calling for 'walls made of copper and steel' and 'nets spread from the earth to the sky' to hunt down the 'terrorists' behind these attacks, signalling a more comprehensive counter-terrorism operation in the restive province

(*Economist* 2014d). It did not take long before prominent, moderate voices such as Ilham Tohti, an Uighur economist known for his non-violent advocacy of political reform, were also silenced and sentenced to life imprisonment – burning the last bridges between the CCP and Uighur civil society (Wong 2014). Despite its image as an idyllic place, the Tibet Autonomous Region has also been rocked by growing expressions of discontent among the Tibetan minority. Since 2011, according to some estimates, on average a single Tibetan has resorted to self-immolation to protest against Chinese cultural and political repression (Al Jazeera 2015). As Isabel Hilton, author of *The Search for Panchen Lama*, explains (2015), 'Since 2008, restrictions on religious practice and on lay freedom of expression have grown. This has served only to make stronger the sense of nationhood that the Chinese occupation has forged in this scattered and disparate people.' Factors such as 'resource extraction and inward migration ... facilitate the marginalisation of Tibetans in Tibet, and the settlement of nomads in bleak, regimented villages' and embody and exacerbate the ongoing state of oppression (ibid.). Both the Uighur and the Tibetans gradually lost political autonomy in the immediate aftermath of the Second World War, when Chinese troops quashed any hopes for self-rule among these non-Han populations, and Mao Zedong and his successors sought to bring 'modernization' to China's peripheries. The upsurge in anti-government sentiment among the Uighur and Tibetan population has coincided with growing anti-Beijing protests in Hong Kong and Taiwan, as the Xi administration tightens its grip on the two prosperous Chinese-majority polities outside the mainland territory. The Chinese leadership has stepped up its efforts, as mandated by the country's constitution, to fulfil the 'great task of reunifying the motherland' and defending the 'sacred territory of the People's Republic of China' (Tsoi 2014). And Beijing has not shied away from using its economic prowess to achieve its political goals. Thanks to the sheer size of its booming economy, China has become central to the economic survival of Hong Kong and Taiwan, which played a crucial role in the modernization of mainland China in the late twentieth century. This shift in the balance of economic power has strengthened China's influence and empowered hardliners in Beijing, who oppose any genuine form of democracy in Hong Kong and any expression of independence in Taiwan. In 2013, merchandise trade with mainland China (US$502 billion) accounted for more than 50 per cent of Hong Kong's total trade. The Mainland and Hong Kong Closer Economic Partnership Arrangement (CEPA), a bilateral free-trade arrangement, allowed Beijing to cement its economic influence over the city-state (ibid.). Hong Kong has also become increasingly reliant on China in terms of its energy and water consumption. The city-state gets more than 70 per cent of its water (originating from the Dongjiang river in neighbouring Guandong Province), over half of its electricity and more than 90 per cent of its vegetables and fresh meat from mainland China (Law 2014). Major cities in China have begun to overshadow Hong Kong, which could lose its prime position as the financial hub of East Asia in the coming decades. Hong Kong's GDP (US$261 billion) has already been overtaken by Shanghai's (US$354 billion) and Beijing's ($US317 billion), with the southern cities of Guangzhou and Shenzhen, according to some estimates, poised to overtake Hong Kong in terms of GDP by around 2017 (Lu 2014b). For decades, Hong Kong's superb infrastructure, sophisticated labour force and long tradition of rule of law and political freedom has allowed it to stay ahead of the pack. But as China chips away at the autonomy of the city-state, it has become increasingly difficult for Hong Kong to maintain its competitive edge, especially vis-à-vis booming, cosmopolitan cities such as Shanghai (ibid.). From July to September 2012, Hong Kong was engulfed by growing protests – involving 120,000 participants at their peak – against Beijing's plans to introduce patriotic education into the primary and secondary schooling curriculum of Hong Kong residents (Tsoi 2014).

Anti-Beijing protests reached a new high on 1 July 2014, marking the anniversary of Hong Kong's return to mainland China after a century under British control, when perhaps as many as 510,000 residents joined the 'Occupy Central' movement in calling for Chinese authorities to honour their earlier pledge to introduce universal suffrage and democratic elections by 2017 in Hong Kong. The extraordinarily high number of participants in the demonstrations was triggered by a 10 June White Paper, issued by the Chinese leadership, which claimed, among other things, that Beijing exercised 'comprehensive jurisdiction' over Hong Kong, which effectively meant China will ensure that the city-state's leadership is 'loyal' and 'patriotic' to the 'one country' principle rather than the 'two systems' pledges of Beijing (Richardson 2014; Allen-Ebrahimian 2014). There were growing concerns that Beijing was abandoning the 'One China, Two Systems' policy, unwilling to honour its earlier pledge to respect the political autonomy of the former British colony, as provided in the Basic Law (Hong Kong's quasi-constitution), which has served as a global financial powerhouse and a gateway to the booming Chinese market for decades. By September, the Chinese leadership made it plainly clear that there were no democratic reforms on the horizon, and that Beijing will be firmly in control of the process of selecting Hong Kong's chief executive: voters in the city-state will have little role in determining the future candidates, who will have to be selected and screened by a nominating committee, loyal to Beijing, before running for office (Fish 2014). To put things into perspective, the Basic Law itself was relatively flexible in wording and open to varying interpretations. As Dianna Mendoza,[1] an expert on Hong Kong politics, explains:

> The Basic Law stipulated that universal suffrage could be instituted as early as 2007 for both the Chief Executive (CE) and the Legislative Council. But the relevant provisions clearly grant Beijing the ultimate right to decide on the pace and scope of changes after 2007. For instance, any amendments to the status quo can be made after 2007 … and will be subject to the National People's Congress approval, especially the CE selection. Other relevant provisions contain vague statements (subject to Beijing's interpretation) like 'in accordance to the principle of gradual and orderly progress' and 'in the light of HKSAR's actual situation'.

As Isaac Fish (2014) explains, the Chinese authorities are worried that democratic elections in Hong Kong will bring to power

---

[1]   Interview with the author, 17 October 2014.

a popular leader, who will call for more political autonomy, if not total independence. More worryingly, Beijing could also face growing demands by major cities across China for more democratic rights if Hong Kong were allowed to conduct fully democratic elections in 2017:

> Better for Beijing to prevent fair elections now – that's far easier than deposing a popularly elected leader or managing an independence movement ... If Beijing allowed Hong Kongers universal suffrage, it would be more difficult to argue that other parts of China did not deserve it. Already, there are grumblings in the nearby region of Macau, whose roughly 600,000 citizens enjoy a similar amount of freedom to those in Hong Kong. If a similar movement emerged on the Mainland, this would be far more worrying for the CCP.

The ongoing convulsions in Hong Kong, which culminated in weeks-long protests in late September and continued well into October, have served as a chilling warning to Taiwanese citizens, who have become increasingly uneasy with the prospect of (eventual) reunification with mainland China. After all, events in Hong Kong serve as a litmus test of how China treats special autonomous regions, which were promised greater political freedom as part of a 'One China, Two Systems' model. Pro-independence and pro-democratic movements in Taiwan became worried about the prospect of a growing Chinese economic stranglehold on the tiny democratic island. In 2013, 40 per cent of Taiwan's exports (US$121 billion) were destined for China (plus Hong Kong and Macau). In mid-2010, China and Taiwan signed the Economic Cooperation Framework Agreement (ECFA), patterned after the CEPA, which further integrated Taiwan into the larger Chinese economic realm (Tsoi 2014). Things came to head in 2014, when a group of students occupied (18 March–10 April) the Taiwanese parliament to oppose the lack of transparency in the ongoing negotiations over the Cross Strait Services Trade Agreement (CSSTA), which, according to some critics, could serve as an additional Trojan horse for full Chinese economic domination of Taiwan (G. Smith 2014). The students' audacious act gave birth to the so-called 'Sunflower Movement', which managed to gain widespread support among the Taiwanese youth and inspire huge protests; soon, it morphed into a large-scale opposition to the ruling Kuomintang Party, which, under Taiwanese president Ma Ying-jeou, cultivated cosy political and economic ties with Beijing. Growing solidarity between protesters in Hong Kong and Taiwan further rattled the Chinese authorities, who have, in turn, tried to suppress the development of robust civil society networks among protest leaders. There was, however, little indication that the Xi Jinping administration was considering any meaningful concession to the blossoming pro-democracy movements in Taiwan and Hong Kong. Worried by China's expanding shadow, a growing proportion of residents of Hong Kong and Taiwan have turned their hearts and minds from Beijing – reinforcing micro-nationalist sentiments on the peripheries of the Sino-sphere. According to a mid-2014 poll by the National Chengchi University, on the issue of Taiwanese identity, as many as 60 per cent of the respondents identified themselves as (exclusively) Taiwanese, with only 33 per cent seeing themselves as both Chinese and Taiwanese. Back in 2008, when a pro-Beijing government came to power after more than a decade of perilous cross-straits tensions due to the rise of pro-independence sentiments in the island nation, only 48 per cent of those polled identified themselves as (exclusively) Taiwanese, while up to 43 per cent expressed their attachment to both Taiwan and China. A similar trend has taken place in Hong Kong, with a June 2014 poll, released by the University of Hong Kong's public opinion programme, showing that 67 per cent of the respondents identified themselves as primarily 'Hong Kongers', compared to less than 50 per cent of the respondents who participated in a similar poll almost a decade earlier (Tsoi 2014).

Age of assertiveness But China's ambitions go far beyond consolidating its grip on Greater China. Simultaneously, China has pursued political domination over (often rebellious) autonomous regions on its peripheries as well as territorial claims in the highly strategic, contested waters of the South China Sea. From Latin American to Africa, China has emerged as a major strategic player, but now it is seemingly interested in securing primacy within its own neighbourhood. And far from a violent break with the past, Xi Jinping's territorial assertiveness is a reflection of a deeper transformation of China's strategic position and its evolving territorial calculation. As geopolitical expert Robert Kaplan (2010) observes: 'Empires rarely come about by design; they grow organically. As states become stronger, they cultivate new needs and – this may seem counterintuitive – apprehensions that force them to expand in various forms ... China today is consolidating its land borders and beginning to turn outward ... Thanks to this favorable situation on land, China is now free to work at building a great navy ... China is not so self-confident. Still an insecure sea power, it thinks about the ocean territorially.' Unlike Western status quo powers in history – from the Netherlands to Britain and the USA, which were largely committed to freedom of navigation across major sea routes to maintain their ascendancy in the global trading landscape – China, in contrast, has shown greater interest in treating what are largely seen as international waters, specifically the South China Sea, as the extension of its land-based territory. Driven by a combination of economic interests and nationalistic fervour, Beijing has begun to assert de facto – if not de jure – domination over its adjacent waters.

For the Chinese leadership, looking tough in the near-abroad, particularly on sensitive territorial issues that resonate with the broader Chinese population, has become a domestic political imperative; meanwhile, the Chinese military has been successfully translating the country's economic wealth into military muscle, and there are no institutionalized regional mechanisms to compel China to peacefully channel its rising territorial assertiveness. Back in the late 1990s, Bzrezinski (1998: 153) accurately saw the dangerous combination of rapid economic integration and deeply nationalistic-mercantilist mindsets among Asia nation-states: 'Although surpassing Europe in economic development, Asia is singularly deficient in regional political development. It lacks the cooperative multilateral structures that so dominate the European political landscape and that dilute, absorb, and contain Europe's more traditional territorial, ethnic, and national conflicts ... Asia is today the seat of the world's greatest concentration of rising and recently awakened mass nationalisms ...' Since 2009, China has stepped up its military operations in adjacent waters, from the South China Sea to the East China Sea, intimidating neighbouring countries – and key US allies – like Vietnam, the Philippines and Japan.

A confident Beijing has spared few punches to assert its antiquated and notorious 'nine-dash line' doctrine, which grants China, albeit symbolically, 'inherent sovereignty' over practically everything in the energy-rich South China Sea (SCS) basin. Beginning in 2010, China also stepped up its claims over the Senkaku islands (*Diaoyu* to the Chinese) in the East China Sea, which have been under Japanese administration for decades – and among Imperial Japan's spoils of war after its decisive defeat of the Qing Dynasty in the late-nineteenth-century Sino-Japanese naval battles. Communist China began to claw back the territories, real and imaginary, lost by its dynastic predecessors in the previous centuries. History was back with a vengeance, largely thanks to the post-Cold War Chinese Patriotic Education, which instilled a strong sense of aggrieved nationalism among China's populace. By now, China had also achieved – or was in the process of bolstering – the capability to act upon its historical claims. As the nineteenth-century German philosopher G. W. F. Hegel saw it, extended periods of peace tend to inspire complacency and apathy among peoples, as individuals take the existing political order – and its underlying network of values and privileges – for granted in a relentless pursuit of particularistic interests.[2] Interstate diplomacy becomes an extension of domestic narrow interests. Soon, conflicts – arising from the absence of diplomatic creativity and political conviction – become the only way of rekindling age-old commitments to more universalist notions of community and nationhood. As the First World War, which came on the heels of decades-long economic integration among European powers, demonstrates, the shift from economic interdependence to total war could be abrupt and devastating.

After a long period of peace in Asia, which underpinned an unprecedented expansion in intra-regional economic interdependence, old ideologies such as communism have lost their appeal. Democracy, in turn, is largely interpreted as a ritualistic exercise of voting for a collection of identical leaders with no discernible vision. Capitalism

[2]   See, for instance, Žižek (2013).

became the common variable among Asian countries. Amid an ideological vacuum in Asia, popular nationalism gained traction among the masses as well as the political leaders. More and more countries began to shift their attention to traditional notions of territorial integrity and historic rights – rekindling old-fashioned debates on the ownership of international waterways (Johnson 2014c).

No wonder important figures warned against the grim prospects of interstate confrontation and regional conflagration amid an unprecedented period of popular nationalism across Asia. 'This year marks the centenary of World War I. Britain and Germany were highly (inter)dependent economically. They were the largest trade partners (to each other), but the war did break out,' exclaimed Japan's prime minister Shinzo Abe during the 2014 World Economic Forum in Davos. 'What I would call a military encounter between Japan and China would deal great damage to both countries. Its regional and global impact would be extremely large' (Asahi Shimbun 2014).

From afar, intensified disputes over maritime features and resources in the western Pacific seem unreasonable and disproportionately risky. Some observers see nothing but a struggle over a bunch of worthless rocks in the middle of the maritime wilderness. Millions of people across Asia, however, regard themselves as participants in a highly emotionally charged struggle for national identity and pride. This should come as no surprise since the very concept of nation-state is itself largely a social construct – a functional outcome of industrial capitalism and European colonialism in recent centuries – that derives its energy from and sustains its immanent logic based on actual, material disputes over symbolically important elements, which give coherence and meaning to the collective memories and lives of peoples across the region. After decades of prosperity, many Asian nations have vigorously embraced the preservation of their territorial integrity as a self-reaffirming ritual of national glory. And this is precisely where pitched battles over a seemingly worthless bunch of rocks come into the picture. A closer look, however, also reveals the interplay of strategic, economic and legal dynamics in collectively shaping the trajectory of the maritime disputes in the East and South China Seas.

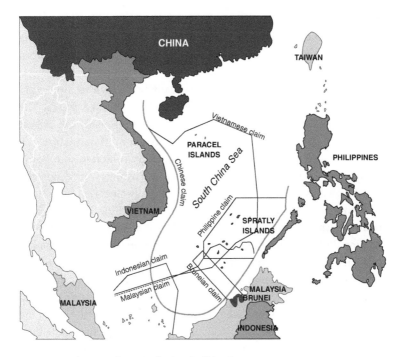

3.1 Overlapping claims in the South China Sea.

The anatomy of a crisis

Today, the South China Sea increasingly resembles a maritime battlefield, hosting a growing number of military garrisons, naval fortifications and adjacent military exercises by contesting parties. Historically, there were five ways to acquire territory: through cessation (when one party gives up its claims over a territory under a formal agreement, usually after a decisive military defeat), occupation of previously 'empty land' (*terra nullius*), prescription (the acquiescence and gradual recognition by the other of one's rule over a territory), accretion (expansion of existing territory through, say, land reclamation), and conquest (the brutal subjugation and forcible acquisition of rights over a territory). Since China's sweeping claims overlap with those of other South-East Asian countries, some of which are heavily resisting what they see as creeping Chinese invasion of their territorial integrity, the case at hand represents neither one of prescription nor of cessation. Some of the features claimed by China are already occupied by the troops and citizens of other claimant states, so obviously not all are empty lands (Hayton 2014b). So the fear is that the South China Sea disputes will basically boil down to a question of conquest and artificial expansion of already occupied features. The militarization of the South China Sea disputes is arguably the biggest challenge to regional security, threatening freedom of navigation in a global artery of trade, where an estimated US$5 trillion in ship-borne trade passes every year. It involves disputes where everyone claims the moral high ground, but hardly anyone, especially China, is completely innocent or capable of providing incontrovertible proof and/or demonstration of sovereignty over all of their claims. Neither are the ongoing disputes new, nor is there any valid mono-causal explanation for their persistence and intensification over time. China's 'historical' claim to disputed features across the South China Sea is primarily based on Beijing's supposed 'discovery' of a group of (uninhabited) rocks, atolls, sandbars and a few islands (i.e. Thitu and Itu Aba) in the Spratlys as far back as 23–220 AD, during the Han dynasty; more than a thousand years later, during the Middle Ages, the maritime trade-savvy Ming dynasty supposedly further consolidated China's claim over the area.[3] The Chinese people, however, were hardly the only ones exploring the South China Sea basin; people from archipelagic South-East Asian countries such as the Philippines (*Badjaos*), Indonesia (*Orang Laut* from the Riau islands) and Malaysia (*Bajaus*) were also actively fishing in the South China Sea for centuries (ibid.). But arguably it was only in the early twentieth century that Beijing – along with other claimant countries like the Philippines[4] – sought to formalize its claims (see Table 3.1).

---

[3] See, for instance, China Oceanic Information Network, Historical Evidence to Support China's Sovereignty over Nansha Islands, www.coi.gov.cn/scs/article/2.htm.

[4] In 1933, Filipino senator Isabelo de los Reyes asked the USA, the colonial ruler in the Philippines, to claim islands in the Spratlys, while four years later the Philippine interior secretary Elpidio Quirino reportedly filed similar claims with the US government. See, for instance, Bonnet (2004).

TABLE 3.1 Early-twentieth-century assertions of sovereignty in the South China Sea

Date	Statement of claim
1907	Japanese explorers such as Nishizawa Yoshiji laid claim to the *Pratas* group of islands in the South China Sea, asserting that he discovered these uninhabited features and they now belonged to him, prompting outrage from Chinese authorities in Canton (Guangzhou) and an anti-Japanese boycott in China. Two years later, on 12 October 1909, the viceroy of Canton and the Japanese consul struck a deal, leading to the Japanese exit from the *Pratas* in exchange for 130,000 silver dollars.
1914	Publication of the *New Geographical Atlas of the Republic of China*, drafted by private cartographer Hu Jinjie, included the *Pratas* and *Paracels* as part of Chinese territory.
1935	A Chinese government committee began placing names on contested features, translating or transliterating[a] earlier British names derived from colonial-era explorers like Richard Spratly, who named islands he spotted in 1843 in the South China Sea after himself.
1936	Members of the China Geography Society, particularly one of its founders, Bai Meichu, began drawing expansive 'maps of national humiliation'. In particular, the publication of the *New China Construction Atlas* included a 'U-shaped line' enveloping much of the South China Sea, which covered as far south as the James Shoal.
1947	Chinese authorities moved the name 'Nansha' southwards in their maps to cover the Spratly chain of islands; the Republic of China's top defence, security and naval officials agreed that China's claims covered everything within the 'U-shaped line', but precise maritime boundaries would be left to negotiation.
1953	The new communist leaders in China reduced the eleven-dash-line to a 'nine-dash-line' to provide room for compromise over the Tonkin Gulf with communist Vietnam.

Source: Hayton (2014a, b).

a As Bill Hayton (2014a) explains: 'For instance, Spratly Island became Si-ba-la-tuo, the Chinese transliteration of the English name, while in the Paracels, Antelope Reef became Líng yang, which happens to be the Chinese word for antelope, while the Scarborough Shoal was first transliterated as Si ge ba luo in 1935 before being changed to Min'zhu Jiao (Democracy Reef) by the Republic of China in 1947, then again revised to Huangyan (Yellow Rock) by its communist successor in 1983.'

Although the maritime disputes in the South China Sea technically involve six countries (Brunei, Malaysia, the Philippines, Vietnam, Taiwan and China), the fiercest clashes have been between China, on one hand, and Vietnam and the Philippines, on the other. Malaysia and China long maintained mutual non-confrontational posturing in the

South China Sea, while Brunei is a non-active claimant state. Taiwan, which controls the biggest island in the Spratlys, is not considered as a sovereign state, with China treating not only Taiwan but also Taipei-controlled features in the South China Sea (the Pratas group of islands and Itu Aba) as part of Greater China. So despite their overlapping claims (see Figure 3.1), the six countries have adopted different strategies, facing a dissimilar matrix of challenges and opportunities. Nonetheless, in recent decades we have seen growing global concern over these disputes. In the post-Cold War period, in particular, the South China Sea spats have been exacerbated by the intersection of several trends: the strategic vacuum resulting from the USA's withdrawal from its major military bases in the Philippines in 1992; the dramatic rise of China as a global power in the last decade, feeding its political ambitions as well as naval capabilities; the discovery of (and speculation over) sizeable amounts of hydrocarbon reserves in the South China Sea amid rapid industrialization across the region; the emergence of popular nationalism as a bedrock of the Chinese national psyche (as well as in South-East Asian claimant countries, especially Vietnam) at a time when communism has lost its ideological resonance in an increasingly market-oriented environment; intra-bureaucratic jostling, and political demagoguery over territorial issues by different governments in East Asia (see Chapter 4), especially during sensitive electoral cycles or leadership transition periods; and regional allies testing America's military commitment by taking an increasingly tough stance against China's perceived rising maritime threat (see Chapters 4 and 5). ASEAN, as an engine of integration in South-East Asia and beyond, could potentially play a decisive role by containing tensions between China and regional claimant states, and advancing legal measures to regulate the behaviour of conflicting parties (see Chapter 6). But there has been a perceptible fracture within ASEAN itself with China's and the USA's regional allies taking divergent positions over the organization's responsibility and approach to resolving ongoing disputes. There is also no consensus among claimant states on the utility and substance of international law and dispute settlement, particularly under the aegis of the United Nations Convention on the Law of the Sea (UNCLOS).

A power vacuum While China's claims are age-old, its assertiveness in the South China Sea is much more recent. China's behaviour has been largely shaped by balance-of-power considerations, no matter how entitled it has felt to ownership over a vast expanse of waters and contested features in the area. Throughout the 1970s and 1980s, China managed to expand its control across the South China Sea, primarily at the expense of Vietnam. China's territorial expansion was undertaken with considerable sensitivity to the regional balance of power. First, China exploited the Vietnam War to wrest control of South Vietnam-controlled features in the South China Sea, culminating in the 1974 clashes over the Crescent group of islands on the western tip of the Paracels. The USA, battered by the war in Vietnam, was in no position to aid its South Vietnamese ally in the South China Sea. From the perspective of China, taking control of the area was extremely important, because of the lingering fear that North Vietnam and its powerful treaty ally, the Soviet Union, could use the Paracel chain of islands as a platform to launch attacks on mainland China. By 1980, China had consolidated its control over the Paracels in the northern portion of the South China Sea, imposing, among other things, up to four danger zones between the southern Chinese province of Hainan and the Paracels, forcing international airlines to seek clearance from Chinese authorities before passing over the area – recognizing Beijing's de facto control. Next, it moved to expand its claims across the Spratly chain of islands, deploying the PLA navy across the southern portions of the South China Sea for exploratory missions. By the mid-1980s, Sino-Soviet tensions had begun to cool down, with the Soviet Union sending mixed signals on the extent of its commitment to its mutual defence treaty with Vietnam, which was invaded by China in 1979. By 1987, China had made the decision to establish a permanent physical presence in the Spratly chain of islands, with Fiery Cross Reef identified as a promising location for establishing an observation station. China and Vietnam stepped up their patrols and construction activities across the South China Sea, culminating in the 1988 naval battle over the Johnson South Reef in the Spratlys, which led to huge casualties on Vietnam's part (Garver 1992).

Throughout the Cold War, however, China was extremely careful to avoid clashes with ASEAN members such as the Philippines and Malaysia, which maintained relatively cordial ties with Beijing. As for the Philippines, it benefited from the American security umbrella, most evident in the large US military bases in Subic and Clark on the eastern tip of the South China Sea. Deng Xiaoping was also intent on revitalizing Beijing's ties with ASEAN and the broader region, so he was interested in avoiding maritime conflicts as much as possible. (Communist Vietnam, meanwhile, was relatively isolated in the region, after its military takeover of South Vietnam and invasion of Cambodia in 1978. As Deng correctly foresaw it, China lost little diplomatic support in the region by taking on communist Vietnam in the South China Sea.) The Sino-American entente, and the relatively stable ties between Beijing and ASEAN during Deng's rule, seemingly created sufficient strategic confidence in East Asia to justify the closure of American bases in the Philippines. The end of the Cold War encouraged nationalist circles in the Philippines to call for the termination of American military bases in the country. In Washington, there was also growing confidence that the demise of the USSR provided enough 'peace dividend' to downgrade America's military footprint in places such as the Philippines. But as soon as large-scale American bases in South-East Asia were gone, in 1992, China expanded its area-wide operations across the Spratly chain of islands, culminating in the 1995 Mischief Reef incident, when Beijing and Manila squared off over the ownership of the contested feature. Clearly, China's behaviour has proved sensitive to balance-of-power configurations. In the late 2000s, China would once again step up its territorial claims across the South China Sea, encouraged by the relative decline of the USA after a decade of military adventurism in the Middle East and a devastating economic blow in 2007/08. China's growing assertiveness in the western Pacific reflects its broader and evolving security doctrine. Aware of its conventional military inferiority vis-à-vis US naval power, China has rapidly upgraded its asymmetric anti-access/area denial (A2/AD) capabilities, while bolstering blue-water capabilities. The People's Liberation Army Navy (PLAN) now boasts an aircraft carrier, highlighting China's emphasis on greater investment in naval rather than land-based military capabilities – marking a decisive shift in the country's strategic calculus. The South China Sea's proximity to the mainland makes it a natural area for Chinese naval projection. China is deepening its presence in the area by expanding its nuclear submarine fleet and developing a second-strike nuclear capability, with its naval base in Hainan serving as a pivotal forward-deployment platform. There is also a greater strategic prize at stake: dominating the region gives China control of one of the world's busiest sea lines of communication (SLOCs) – rendering Japan and Korea vulnerable to any blockade – but it also enables Beijing to further its goal of transforming China into the prime Pacific power. Not to mention that dominating the South China Sea would make it more difficult for the USA to prevent a coercive reunification of mainland China and Taiwan by Beijing. Ideally, China's territorial ambitions should have been tempered by regional institutions such as ASEAN, which has sought to preserve maritime stability and enhance economic integration by harmonizing relations among member states as well as the great powers.

The institutional deficit By Asian standards, ASEAN is a fairly developed regional institutional organization designed to facilitate economic integration and security cooperation in South-East Asia and beyond. Since the formation of the regional organization in 1967 – partially inspired by the desire to avoid all-out military conflict (*Konfrontasi*) among competing archipelagic states, especially Malaysia and Indonesia, in South-East Asia – none of the member states have waged full-scale war against each other. Influential members within ASEAN, namely Indonesia, have also played an important role in mediating interstate disputes such as the Thailand–Cambodia border conflict, which almost triggered a large-scale military confrontation in 2011 but was eventually submitted for international arbitration (Kesavapany 2011). Intent on playing a balancing role between competing powers, ASEAN has also played an important role in establishing varying platforms, particularly the ARF, for constructive strategic-security dialogue among a wide range of external powers such as China, Russia, India, Japan and the USA. The aim is to prevent another Cold War in the region, and 'socialize' great powers' behaviour in accordance with ASEAN's founding principles and norms. However, it goes without saying that ASEAN is fundamentally a super-national organization that fosters soft regionalism, focusing on confidence-building and preventive diplomacy rather than conflict resolution/management. There is no transference of national sovereignty from individual member states to a central bureaucracy à la European Union (EU), so important decision-making processes are always driven by a painstaking series of interstate negotiations under the rubric of regional solidarity. As veteran ASEAN expert Muthiah Alagappa (2015) explains: 'The foremost priority for ASEAN national leaders in the foreseeable future will be making strong nations and states at home to preserve their hold on power. Regional community building will be lower priority and likely to succeed only when it can contribute to or does not hinder realization of the primary national objectives of incumbent leaders.' ASEAN works as a platform for incubating common regional principles and facilitating sustained economic integration among member countries. Unlike in NATO, member states are not bound by the principle of collective security, and South-East Asian countries are free to cultivate security ties with a diverse range of external partners. Unlike in the EU, where a central bureaucracy was in charge of facilitating sectorial integration and establishing a common market, economic integration within ASEAN has been primarily driven by the private sector, especially the MNCs, which have sought to enhance their economies of scale in South-East Asia by developing an expanding network of production across the region – optimizing price differentials in factors of production and availability of advanced (soft and hard) infrastructure. ASEAN's standards of membership have been primarily driven by geographic considerations: the inclusion of Indochinese states such as Vietnam, Cambodia, Myanmar and Laos, which technically fall within South-East Asia's geographical boundaries, was driven by the hope of enhancing regional solidarity and overcoming Cold War divisions, but there were no strict political and economic qualifications for membership. This explains why the regional body is composed of a very diverse collection of member states in terms of their political regimes, economic development and strategic outlook. ASEAN has neither compliance-enforcement mechanisms, nor a cache of developmental aid, which could be used as leverage to influence the behaviour and institutional make-up of member states. Diplomacy is its primary instrument of persuasion. ASEAN has struggled to address hard security issues, and has been plagued by internal divisions. On the South China Sea issue, for instance, members have taken varying positions. Laos and Cambodia have been sympathetic to China; Malaysia and Indonesia have cautioned against Washington's meddling; Thailand, Myanmar and Singapore took a more neutral stance; and Vietnam and the Philippines, wary of balance-of-power considerations, called for more decisive US policy on the issue. ASEAN may have achieved considerable success in the realm of economic integration and trade facilitation, but hard security issues continue to expose its fundamental weaknesses. These realities have allowed China to conduct its diplomatic tango with considerable ease. Two decades of charm offensive and rapid economic growth allowed China to deepen its presence among South-East Asian countries, especially in the realm of investment and economics. As the second-largest – soon to be biggest – economy in the world, China represents a key market for many resource-exporting countries in the region, from Burma and Indonesia to the Philippines and Malaysia. Moreover, China is a major source of concessional loans, cheap and affordable technology and favourable investment opportunities. China's growing middle class is also becoming a major boon for the regional tourism industry. With China becoming involved in strategic infrastructural development schemes – from railways to highways – Beijing has become central to the national development of its southern neighbours (Kurlantzick 2007; Mendoza and Heydarian 2012). Conscious of its economic influence, China has become more confident in pushing its political agenda. Despite growing regional interdependence – from industrial vertical integration to intra-regional complementary trade – China holds immense leverage over its neighbours. No wonder, then, that the Philippine president Benigno Aquino's 2011 visit to China – amid an intensifying territorial stand-off with China – ended up as a high-profile courtship for US$60 billion in bilateral trade and investments. The primacy of economic considerations has allowed China to shape the geopolitical architecture of the region. No wonder leading ASEAN experts such as Barry Desker have lamented: 'The ability of external parties to shape the positions of ASEAN members on regional issues such as the competing maritime claims in the South China Sea could undermine efforts to create an agreed ASEAN view. As China exerts its influence on ASEAN members to prevent any decisions which could affect its preference for bilateral negotiations, it will be increasingly difficult to reach an ASEAN consensus' (Desker 2015). Although many analysts tend to adopt a dichotomous understanding of China's foreign policy in South-East Asia, either bilateralist or multilateralist, in reality China is using a sophisticated bi-multilateralist approach. Under this doctrine, China tends to use multilateralism as a component of its charm-offensive strategy, but it simultaneously utilizes bilateral ties in order to reinforce, if not impose, its interests. Given China's huge economic clout, its investment prowess and its wide network of socio-political connections – especially with Chinese communities across South-East Asia – it has been very savvy in influencing its smaller neighbours, constraining their room for manoeuvre.

Since 2010, ASEAN has come under tremendous pressure to rein in growing territorial tensions among conflicting parties in the South China Sea, especially China, Vietnam and the Philippines. Operating on the principles of consensus and consultation, the regional body has lacked the necessary coherence, mandate and institutional teeth to enforce its principles of multilateralism and non-use of force regarding issues related to territorial maritime disputes. To be sure, ASEAN has achieved some progress in dealing with the ongoing territorial conflicts. Recognizing the gravity of the intensifying maritime disputes, the ASEAN summits in Vietnam (2010) and Indonesia (2011) attained perceptible successes on (i) recognizing the deleterious impact of ongoing disputes on regional security and (ii) the necessity to develop appropriate multilateral mechanisms to contain China's territorial assertiveness, regulate the behaviour of all claimant states according to the principles of international law, and peacefully resolve the disputes. In 2012, however, Cambodia's – largely seen as a key Chinese ally in South-East Asia – chairmanship of ASEAN undercut earlier institutional and multilateral gains. During the 2012 ASEAN Ministerial Meeting (AMM) in July, Cambodia blocked the inclusion of the ongoing disputes in the final communiqué, provoking uproar among regional states such as the Philippines and Vietnam. The two latter ASEAN members desperately hoped for a diplomatic breakthrough for the development of a legally binding regional code of conduct to complement the merely symbolic 2002 ASEAN-China Declaration on Conduct of Parties in the South China Sea. As a result, ASEAN failed for the first time in the grouping's history to arrive at a consensus to issue a communiqué, calling the very relevance and internal coherence of the organization into question. Months of rising diplomatic tensions followed between the Philippines and Cambodia, with other ASEAN members such as Indonesia – the region's informal leader – desperately trying to rescue the organization from internal disintegration. While Cambodia was accused of doing China's bidding, the Philippines and Vietnam were criticized for playing an overly aggressive card towards China over the territorial disputes. As strategic partners of the United States, Vietnam and the Philippines were also accused of pushing ASEAN towards confrontation with China (the region's biggest trading partner), while attempting to realign ASEAN with an essentially US-led regional order. Just months after the AMM, China, which prefers a predominantly bilateral approach to resolving disputes with its weaker individual neighbours, informally thanked Cambodia for its stand by providing more than US$500 million in soft loans and grants, with Beijing describing Cambodia as its 'most trustworthy friend', and expressing its 'high appreciation for the part played by Cambodia as the chair of ASEAN to maintain good cooperation between China and ASEAN' (*Reuters* 2012). China's manoeuvre vis-à-vis Cambodia represented a naked expression of the country's economic statecraft, utilizing financial incentives to gain strategic goals. It also contradicted the long-held Chinese contention that its approach to foreign aid was based on a no-strings-attached principle. Encouraged by Cambodia's intransigence, China refused to negotiate on any binding code of conduct (CoC)in the South China Sea, contrary to an earlier agreement with ASEAN in 2011. Alarmed by China's 'hijacking' of ASEAN,

the Philippines and Vietnam, meanwhile, deepened their military relations with the USA and stepped up their diplomatic pressure on China
and Cambodia. During the ASEAN summit in late 2012, Cambodia's
prime minister, Hun Sen, again blocked the inclusion of the maritime
disputes in the formal summit agenda, (falsely) claiming that there was
a 'consensus' among member states to exclude maritime conflicts. His
actions prompted a swift rebuke by Philippine's President Aquino, who
launched a formal protest against the motion, arguing there was no
such consensus and that the issue was too integral to regional security
to be excluded from this year's discussions. 'Among the principles that
the ASEAN community has pledged to abide by is that of centrality ...
Prevailing tensions in the area stand to impact regional peace and stability', Aquino stated in his formal intervention during the ASEAN+3
Summit. 'We reiterate our call on all parties concerned to avoid the
threat or use of force, and to adhere to universally recognized principles
of international law in settling disputes ... because respect for the rule
of law remains the great equalizer in the relations among nations [espe-
cially between China and the Philippines]' (Porcalla 2012). Aquino's
intervention was notably backed by certain claimant and non-claimant
states in attendance, including Brunei, Singapore, Vietnam, Malaysia,
Indonesia and Japan. The Philippine delegation could not hide its frustration, with Aquino – through multiple interventions – seeking the
diplomatic support of (potential or actual) sympathetic states such as
the USA, Japan, India and Australia. Most importantly, Aquino urged
greater commitment by the USA to the resolution of the territorial disputes in the South China Sea. 'Each one of our nations has a stake
in the stability of Southeast Asia. The U.S. understands this and, for
this reason, has chosen to work with us to ensure the peace and continuous advancement of our region,' Aquino stated during the summit.
'The ASEAN route is not the only route for us.' The whole episode
provoked panic among ASEAN's founding members, prompting Singapore, Malaysia, Thailand and Indonesia to step up their efforts to
break the diplomatic impasse and secure the integrity of the regional
organization (Emmerson 2012). When ASEAN fell into disarray after
the fiasco in Phnom Penh, influential and older group members such
as Singapore, Malaysia, Thailand and Indonesia played a crucial role

in salvaging the organization from diplomatic implosion. In particular, Indonesia's proactive mediation efforts, including shuttle diplomacy between rival states, resulted in 'Six-Point Principles' which called for (i) a peaceful, diplomatic resolution of the disputes in accordance with prior agreed-upon principles and (ii) the development of a regional code of conduct for the South China Sea. But the negotiation of a CoC and implementation of a 'freeze' in provocative manoeuvres by claimant countries such as China remained painfully elusive (see Chapter 6).

Legal ambiguity[5] The South China Sea conundrum is also the product of conflicting legal interpretations. To begin with, there is a disjunction between domestic legal regimes and prevailing international legal principles. Countries such as the Philippines and Vietnam have tried to align domestic legislation with international conventions. In 2009, the Philippines passed the Philippine Archipelagic baselines law, while in mid-2012 Vietnam's National Assembly unanimously passed a new Law of the Sea, which came into effect on 1 January 2013 (Tofani 2013). In contrast, China has embedded its controversial maritime claims in its constitutional framework, ranging from its 'Anti-secession Law' on Taiwan aimed at curtailing any declaration of independence by the island nation to a series of local – particularly the 1993 Fishery Law by Hainan authorities, which underwent a series of amendments in 2012 and 2014 – and national legislations, particularly the 2004 National Maritime Law, which aims to bolster China's claimed jurisdiction across much of the South China Sea (Shirk 2008; Fravel 2014).

---

[5] Analysis under this section was partly aided by a series of consultations with US-based legal experts from 1 to 19 December 2014, when the author was able to exchange views with Professor Anthony C. Arend (Georgetown University), Professor John Norton Moore and Professor Myron H. Nordquist (Virginia University), Professor Mathew Waxman (Columbia University), Professor James Hsiung (New York University), and several Law of the Sea experts at the United Nations (UN) and the Asia-Pacific Center for Security Studies (APCSS), among others, as well as exchanges with European and Asian Law of the Sea experts during the International Law of the Sea Conference in Hanoi Law University, on 23/24 March 2015.

The UNCLOS could – and, many would argue, should – serve as a platform for resolving territorial disputes in the region.[6] But China and South-East Asian countries have adopted divergent interpretations of certain provisions of the convention. There is no consensus on the 'regime of islands' (Art. 121), which seeks to clarify the nature of contested features in the South China Sea, and their corresponding jurisdictional implications and maritime entitlements. As legal experts such as Yann-huei Song (2010) point out: 'Different applications or interpretations of Article 121 [of UNCLOS] have also become one of the main sources of maritime disputes between the countries concerned.' According to the UNCLOS, naturally formed islands, which are capable of supporting human life, can generate up to 200 nautical miles of exclusive economic zone (EEZ), while high-tide elevation rocks, which can't support human habitation, can generate only 12 nautical miles of territorial sea. South-East Asian claimants such as the Philippines look at the majority of features in the South China Sea as either uninhabitable low-tide elevations, which can't be occupied and claimed, or rocks, which can't generate beyond 12 nautical miles of territorial sea. Adopting a more liberal interpretation of the UNCLOS's Article 121, China is said to have argued that many (Chinese) occupied/claimed features in the South China Sea are high-tide elevations, which can generate territorial waters of up to 12 nautical miles, as well as islands that can project their own 200 nautical miles of EEZ. Such an interpretation would effectively allow Beijing to project far-reaching claims from varying South China Sea features under its control, covering oil- and gas-rich areas as far south as the vicinity of Indonesia's Natuna islands as well as the Philippine-claimed

---

[6] The *Nicaragua v. Colombia* arbitration case, which was concluded on 19 November 2012, is considered by some scholars as a possible precedent or a useful case for assessing the possible utility of international law in dealing with the South China Sea disputes, particularly because the determination of the nature of disputed features (Art. 121) was a major component of the International Court of Justice's adjudication of the dispute. For instance, see Rothwell (2013). Other scholars, however, contend that the South China Sea disputes are sui generis, mainly because of China's unprecedented decision to cite (vaguely defined) 'historical rights/waters' as a basis to justify its sweeping claims.

Reed Bank, which is largely viewed as the biggest possible source of hydrocarbon riches for the South-East Asian country in the coming decades (see Chapter 4). Moreover, China has also been artificially transforming rudimentary features (e.g., reefs, atolls, sandbars, low-tide elevations and other forms of submerged features) into quasi-islands by installing relatively large-scale structures for civilian and military accommodations (see Chapters 4 and 6). China seems determined to turn features under its control, and well beyond its EEZ,[7] into de facto habitable islands.[8] In short, divergent characterizations of the features under contestation carry significant legal and jurisdictional implications.[9] As Robert Beckman, Professor of Law at the National University of Singapore, points out (2014): 'Under international law, a claim to sovereignty can only be made to offshore features that … [are a] naturally formed area of land, surrounded by water, which is above water at high tide. Low-tide elevations or submerged features cannot be subject to appropriation.'[10] Figure 3.2. provides a more detailed description of maritime entitlements under the UNCLOS.

[7] Under UNCLOS (Part V), Article 56 (b)(i) grants coastal states the right of 'establishment and use of artificial islands, installations and structures' within its EEZ.

[8] Some scholars have doubted whether the Chinese strategy of placing a population and advanced infrastructure on a contested feature would work, keeping in mind the *Ukraine v. Romania* dispute over the Snake Island in the Black Sea, where the International Court of Justice (ICJ), in its 3 February 2009 judgement, largely favoured Romania despite the fact that the disputed feature hosted a small Ukrainian population, with Kiev arguing that it had established significant infrastructure in the area to support active and continued habitation. See Song (2010).

[9] This is precisely why countries like the Philippines contend that third-party arbitration is a necessary means to resolve maritime delimitation concerns, because disputing parties can't even agree on the nature of features under contestation.

[10] Low-tide elevations can, however, be used as a base-point if situated within 12 nautical miles of the base-point of another rock/island under a coastal state's control. Specifically, Article 13 of UNCLOS (Part II) states: 'Where a low-tide elevation is situated wholly or partly at a distance not exceeding the breadth of the territorial sea from the mainland or an island, the low-water line on that elevation may be used as the baseline for measuring the breadth of the territorial sea.'

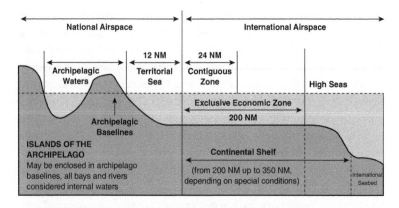

3.2 Maritime entitlements under UNCLOS. Within the territorial sea, the coastal state has almost total territorial jurisdiction, though it should respect the right of innocent passage of foreign vessels, provided this is not prejudicial to its interest (see Art. 17–32, Part II). In the contiguous zone, the coastal state can prevent infringement of its customs, fiscal, immigration or sanitary laws and regulations within its territory or territorial sea; and punish infringement of the above laws and regulations committed within its territory or territorial sea (Art. 33, Part II). Within the exclusive economic zone, the state has, among other things, sovereign rights for the purpose of exploring and exploiting, conserving and managing the natural resources, whether living or non-living, of the waters superjacent to the seabed and of the seabed and its subsoil, and with regard to other activities for the economic exploitation and exploration of the zone, such as the production of energy from the water, currents and winds (Art. 56, Part V). Regarding issues of overlapping claims within the EEZ, Article 59 (Part V) of UNCLOS states: 'the conflict should be resolved on the basis of equity and in the light of all the relevant circumstances, taking into account the respective importance of the interests involved to the parties as well as to the international community as a whole'. The high seas are beyond the jurisdiction of any sovereign coastal state.

South-East Asian countries such as the Philippines, under a 2011 'zone of peace, freedom, friendship and cooperation' (ZPFFC) initiative, contend that only portions of the South China Sea are subject to conflicting territorial claims. So a resolution of the disputes demands a precise segmentation of the South China Sea into contested and uncontested areas. Beijing, on the other hand, claims the whole nine-dash line (see Figure 3.2.), which could effectively render the entire South China Sea a Chinese lake. This is a big problem, because it allows China to claim areas already within the Philippines' jurisdiction (Bensurto 2011). The problem is that extralegal initiatives, either through bilateral or regional mechanisms, have failed to bear fruit, further deepening suspicion towards China. In 2002, China and members of ASEAN signed the Declaration of Conduct (DOC), which emphasizes peaceful, multilateral and rule-based resolution of conflicting claims in the South China Sea in accordance with established regional and international principles. Crucially, the DOC encourages the claimant states to 'undertake to resolve their territorial and jurisdictional disputes by peaceful means, without resorting to the threat or use of force', and 'exercise self-restraint in the conduct of activities that would complicate or escalate disputes and affect peace and stability' by 'refraining from action of inhabiting on the presently uninhabited islands, reefs, shoals, cays, and other features and to handle their differences in a constructive manner'.[11] But the non-binding declaration leaves no mechanism for monitoring and enforcing its implementation. This is where a legally binding code of conduct (CoC) was needed. The problem, however, is that China has continuously dragged its feet on negotiating any binding document, which may tie its hands in the South China Sea. For instance, almost a decade after the signing of a DOC, which was supposed to act as a precursor to a more binding agreement, ASEAN and China agreed to negotiate the guidelines of a CoC in 2011. By 2012, however, China was refusing to follow through, with its regional ally, Cambodia, going so far as to totally block discussions over the issue. In late 2013, during a Senior Officials Meeting in Suzhou, there were signs that the two sides were about to break the deadlock, with China and ASEAN agreeing to continue negotiations over the guidelines of the CoC in 2014. The following year, however, China refused to discuss the CoC,

[11] See the DOC on the ASEAN website, www.asean.org/asean/external-relations/china/item/declaration-on-the-conduct-of-parties-in-the-south-china-sea.

calling instead for clarification on the implementation of the DOC. Time and again, China cautioned against rushing the negotiation of a CoC, just when ASEAN countries were hopeful of expediting the process of hammering out a legally binding document. Clearly, China was not interested in any legally binding document that would tie its hands and limit its room for manoeuvre in the South China Sea. China simply utilized the mirage of negotiations to ward off its critics in ASEAN and avoid complete alienation of its neighbours (Severino 2013; Dizon 2014). On the other hand, the 2005 Joint Marine Seismic Undertaking (JMSU), signed by the Philippines, Vietnam and China, was a novel attempt at transforming the issue into a potential source of cooperation. However, the JMSU agreement, which involved the Philippine National Oil Company (PNOC), PetroVietnam and the China National Offshore Oil Corporation (CNOOC), was later on mired in controversy (see Chapter 4). Whenever there is a quasi-legal vacuum, marked by the absence of clear and defined legal regimes, political forces take over.

The inflection point One could trace the roots of the recent upsurge in territorial disputes to the year 2009, the deadline for claimant states to clarify their extended continental shelves under the auspices of the UN. In May 2009, Malaysia and Vietnam, despite vigorous Chinese opposition, proceeded with their joint submission to the UN Commission on the Limits of the Continental Shelf (CLCS), extending their territorial claims well beyond the EEZ. Other South-East Asian claimant states, the Philippines and Brunei, refused to join, fearing a diplomatic backlash from China, which opposed the internationalization of the territorial disputes. China responded by submitting a *Note Verbale*, which argued that Malaysia and Vietnam's submissions infringed upon Beijing's territorial rights. In addition, China also forwarded a controversial map, with a 'nine-dash line', encompassing almost the entire South China Sea. This represented a significant diplomatic escalation in the disputes. Moreover, after the expiration of the JMSU in June 2008, the Philippines and Vietnam decided to proceed with the unilateral exploration of areas which previously fell under a joint-exploration scheme with China. Having no significant offshore energy exploration and drilling capabilities of their own, Vietnam and the Philippines relied on multinational and foreign-owned energy companies to extract valuable hydrocarbon resources in the South China Sea. In Beijing's view, the other claimant states were engaging in provocative actions, which undermined previous bilateral and regional agreements on how to manage the South China Sea disputes. It did not take long for China to decide to sabotage efforts by the Philippines and Vietnam to develop offshore hydrocarbon resources in the disputed waters. By early 2011, reports suggested that there were at least five incidents involving, among other things, Chinese surveillance vessels harassing Philippine energy exploration activities in the Reed Bank, which falls within Manila's EEZ (International Crisis Group 2012b). Table 3.2 highlights the key incidents in 2011 alone, which underlined growing tensions after years of relative calm in the area.

TABLE 3.2 Major incidents in the South China Sea in 2011

Date	Incident
February 2011	Philippines accuses a Chinese frigate of making warning shots against a Filipino boat near Jackson Atoll.
May 2011	Vietnam accuses China of severing the seismic survey cables of oil exploration vessel *Binh Minh 02*.
9 June 2011	Vietnam accuses China of harassing a ship conducting seismic surveys within its EEZ and continental shelf in the South China Sea.
4 March 2011	The Philippines files a formal complaint against China over the harassment of its energy survey ship near the Reed Bank.
27 March 2011	Vietnam accuses three Chinese patrol boats of harassing and damaging the equipment of a Vietnamese ship conducting oil exploration in the South China Sea.

Source: Reuters; Deutsche Welle.

In many ways, there is nothing unique about China's sweeping territorial claims across the western Pacific. Back in the seventeenth century, rising powers such as England tried to extend their territorial jurisdiction way beyond their coastlines, directly contradicting the position of the reigning maritime superpower of the time, the Netherlands, which argued that the high seas were the common heritage of all mankind. In 'The Open Sea' (1609), Dutch jurist Hugo Grotius argued in favour of freedom of navigation across the high seas, believing 'Every nation is free to travel to every other nation, and to trade with it' (Johnson 2014c). Obviously, the Dutch had a direct interest in ensuring unimpeded navigation across international waters, particularly the North Sea, since they represented the pre-eminent maritime power, which desperately wanted to break out of its geographical isolation as a tiny continental European nation off the North Sea. In 'The Closed Sea' (1635), an explicit rejoinder to Grotius' work, John Selden, a prominent British lawyer famed for his massive legalistic treatise and acquisition of an exquisite map of the Ming dynasty in China, argued 'That the Sea, by the Law of Nature, or Nations, is not common to all men, but capable of private Dominion or proprieties, as well as the Land ... that the dominion of the British sea, or that which encompasses the isle of Great Britain, is, and ever has been, a part or appendant of the empire of that island ... The King of Great Britain is Lord of the Sea flowing about, as an inseparable and perpetual Appendant of the British Empire' (ibid.). In effect, Selden, much to the delight of King Charles I, put forward a legalistic justification for ambitious kingdoms, especially rising powers that were unsatisfied with the naval dominance of a rival state, to significantly extend their land-based jurisdiction far into the high seas. Thanks to the Glorious Revolution, which saw the Dutch take over the British crown, Selden's home country had to eventually abandon his argument. Over the succeeding centuries, Britain would come to replace the Netherlands as the leading maritime trading power, hence its growing interest in preserving freedom of navigation on the high seas. But Selden's views provided a perfect inspiration for contemporary China to justify its sweeping claims across the western Pacific. As Keith Johnson (ibid.) explains: 'This all matters today, because like a zombie Selden's ideas are clawing their way out of the grave thanks to China. Its appropriation of many of the same legal arguments that Selden made for King Charles to wield against the Dutch are now being turned against Beijing's neighbors in the western Pacific – and against the United States.'

Much of the region, as well as external powers such as the USA and the EU, reject China's treatment of international waters as its 'blue territory'. China's interpretation of the EEZ – echoing Selden's notion of 'Closed Sea' – is at odds with other claimant states in the region. On multiple occasions, Chinese officials (military and civilian) have argued that it has the legal right to impose restrictions on the freedom of navigation of foreign armed forces within its EEZ. Andrew S. Erickson and Emily de La Bruyere of the United States Naval War College explain (2014): 'The PRC government actively and loudly opposes the presence of foreign surveillance ships, particularly those of the U.S., in its own claimed EEZ. In a string of incidents since 2001 – including the highly publicized March 2001, March 2009, and May 2009 confrontations with the USN ships *Bowditch*, *Victorious*, and *Impeccable* – Chinese vessels and aircraft have harassed American surveillance ships operating, legally, in China's EEZ.' Although the USA is not a party to the UNCLOS – largely because of the refusal of the US Congress to subject American naval operations to legal restrictions – it has, in actuality, respected (albeit self-servingly) freedom of navigation in international waters and allowed foreign military vessels (including China's) to conduct surveillance and research operations (SROs) within its 200 nautical miles of EEZ. Curiously, China's own 1998 EEZ and Continental Shelf Act is largely consistent with the conventional interpretation of EEZ under UNCLOS, which, as Beckman (2014) explains, is 'a functional maritime zone prescribed by UNCLOS in which the coastal State enjoys "sovereign rights" for the purpose of exploring, exploiting, conserving and managing the natural resources in and under the water, as well as rights with regard to other activities for the economic exploitation and exploration of the zone'. The EEZ does not, however, accord full territorial rights to a coastal state. As Beckman put its, 'In the EEZ, other states (including states who are not parties to UNCLOS) enjoy the freedoms of navigation and overflight and of the laying of submarine cables and pipelines, and other internationally lawful uses of the sea relating to these freedoms. These include uses associated with the operation of ships, aircraft and submarine cable and pipelines.'

Aware of the weaknesses of its sweeping territorial claims, however, China astutely maintained strategic ambiguity regarding its territorial positions and legal interpretations – further complicating the ongoing disputes. The 'nine-dash-line' itself is particularly vague on its exact coordinates and the nature of China's claims.[12] In its pronouncements, China, supposedly with 'abundant historical and legal evidence', has claimed 'indisputable sovereignty over the islands in the South China Sea and the adjacent waters, and enjoys sovereign rights and jurisdiction over the relevant waters as well as the seabed and subsoil thereof' (Gupta 2014). So, is China laying claim to all features in the South China Sea, or, more maximally, also the surrounding waters? John Lee (2014: 5), adjunct professor at Sydney University, succinctly captures the ambiguities of China's territorial claims:

> On the one hand, subsequent *notes verbales* regarding the submission suggest that China only claims islands and their adjacent waters, which it refers to as its 'territorial sea,' with islands entitled to exclusive economic zones (EEZs) and continental shelves in accordance with UNCLOS provisions – regions far less extensive than that indicated by the nine-dashed line. Yet, in the same submission, Beijing argued that 'China's sovereignty and related rights and jurisdiction in the South China Sea are supported by abundant historical and legal evidence,' seemingly introducing the 'historic waters' argument into the claim. Indeed, Beijing has asserted several times that UNCLOS 'does not restrain or deny a country's right which is formed in history,' suggesting that its 'historic waters' rationale exists outside the boundaries of current international law and UNCLOS provisions.

There at least three possible interpretations of the nine-dash-line: first, the maximalist interpretation treats almost the entirety of the South China Sea, including all enclosed features, as practically an internal lake; secondly, an intermediate interpretation, which treats all features and their surrounding (territorial) waters as part of China's territory; and lastly, a minimalist interpretation, which grants China

---

[12] For instance, see the US State Department's Bureau of Oceans and International Environmental and Scientific Affairs 5 December 2014 report on China's nine-dash-line claims, entitled 'Limits in the seas', www.state. gov/documents/organization/234936.pdf.

rights to all fisheries – and perhaps also hydrocarbon resources – across the contested waters, well beyond the territorial waters of individual claimant states. The maximalist interpretation would represent a direct challenge to freedom of navigation in and flight over the South China Sea, since it gives China absolute right over the entire contested area. This is crucial, because the USA treats freedom of navigation as a 'national interest'. American global hegemony is largely anchored by the US Navy's 'all-domain access' across all important waterways. The intermediate interpretation clashes with the claims of other littoral states, which also lay claim to disputed features in the Spratlys and Paracels chain of islands, but does not necessarily clash with American interests in the area. The minimalist definition, however, may provide some room for workable compromise and legal justification, since it ultimately implies joint development and exploitation of resources across the waters. In a highly controversial article, Gupta (2014) made a distinction between 'historical waters' (more in tune with a maximalist interpretation) and 'historical waters' (more in tune with a minimalist interpretation), arguing in favour of the legal validity of the latter:

> Fishing rights and related activities in semi-enclosed seas can assume a character other than being practiced exclusively. Article 123 of the [UNCLOS] (which pertains to semi-enclosed seas) however enjoins all bordering coastal states to cooperate in the exercise of their rights with regard to the conservation, exploration and exploitation of the living resources of the sea. Article 62 of [UNCLOS] (which relates to EEZs), meantime, enjoins the coastal state to give others access to the surplus of the allowable catch in its own EEZ. Read together, they provide a bias – and basis – toward admitting the non-exclusive and non-exclusionary exercise of traditional fisheries rights in semi-enclosed seas such as the South China Sea ... so long as China practices such activities on a non-exclusive basis and desists from enforcing non-conforming rights that exceed those listed in Article 123, such as resource development/marine scientific research, the nine-dash line as a perimeter of exercise and enforcement of China's sovereign rights and jurisdiction of traditional/historic fishing activities in the South China Sea is not inconsistent with international law.

Whenever China engages in a provocative action, which ostensibly violates regional agreements and international law, it tends to resort to a multitude of legal explanations to justify its move. As Chito Santa Romana, a China analyst and a long-time journalist based in Beijing, explains: 'China's claims are anchored on several legal doctrines in international law: "historical rights" based on prior discovery of the islands and reefs in the South China Sea, "inter-temporal doctrine" for its nine-dash-line (that is to say, its nine-dash-line preceded UNCLOS by several decades), and "effective occupation" over the islands, reefs and shoals that are currently occupied by China. There is an intense debate in the international legal community over these doctrines ...'[13] Within the legal community, there is a spirited debate as to whether China's concept of historical rights is relevant in the South China Sea; to begin with, the UNCLOS is applicable to disputes which have a sovereignty-related dimension. For instance, Alexander Proelss, a leading German legal scholar, argues:

> From a theoretical perspective, I think that the concept of historic rights (i) is accepted under international law, and (ii) may refer to both exclusive usage rights and title to territory ... As far as sovereignty issues are concerned, the UNCLOS does not establish a self-contained regime. Quite the opposite, the Convention does not contain any rules and principles applicable to the establishment of sovereignty over territory, which is why general international law must be applied in this respect. This should also be taken into account with regard to the South China Sea. In light of the aforementioned, I consider historic rights as a specific occurrence of either customary title to territory or customary title to exclusive usage rights.

As Bill Hayton (2014a), author of *The South China Sea: The Struggle for Power in Asia*, revealingly explains, China's expansive territorial claims, particularly its 'nine-dash-line' doctrine, are a product of an early-twentieth-century cartographic nationalism, which emerged in response to the crumbling and eventual collapse of the Qing dynasty:

---

[13] Interview with the author, 30 July 2014.

Chinese geographers such as Bai Meichu, one of the founders of
the China Geography Society, began to draw maps to show the
public how much territory had been torn away from China by the
imperialists. These 'maps of national humiliation' assumed that
China's rightful territory included every former vassal that had once
offered tribute to a Chinese emperor. They included the Korean
peninsula, large areas of Russia, Central Asia, the Himalayas and
many parts of Southeast Asia. Lines were drawn on these maps
to contrast the vast domains of former empires with the country's
shrunken state. Fatefully, after the official Chinese committee had
renamed the islands in the South China Sea in 1935, one of these
lines was drawn around the Sea. This is what is now called the
'U-shaped' or '9-dash' line encompassing 80 per cent of the Sea
and all the islands within it. That cartographical accident, based
on misreadings of Southeast Asian history, is the basis for China's
current claim of sovereignty.

For Professor Proelss,[14] China will face an uphill battle to demonstrate historic rights[15] over contested waters, since it will have to provide
evidence of acquiescence by other states (to its sweeping claims) as well
as continuous and effective occupation. For him, justifying its claims,
particularly the 'nine-dash-line' doctrine, will be extremely difficult:

> While I think that historic rights could, in theory, be invoked also
> in order to demonstrate title to territory (and not only in respect of
> exclusive usage rights such as, e.g. historic fishing rights), I do not
> believe that China will manage to provide the necessary evidence
> concerning all territorial features and marine areas. Furthermore, it is
> not possible to draw a boundary line in a unilateral manner. Finally, it
> will be challenging for China to demonstrate that it has continuously
> exercised effective control over the features concerned from time
> immemorial, accompanied by acquiescence from other States ... China
> will only be able to exercise sovereignty over those features which are
> entitled for being claimed as forming part of territory (islands, but in

[14] Interview with author, 26 March 2015.
[15] For a detailed defence of China's historical rights claims see Talmon and
Jia (2014); also Gao and Jia (2013).

my opinion not low-tide elevations) at all, and with regard to which China is able to provide the evidence necessary in order to demonstrate that it has continuously exercised effective control over the features concerned from time immemorial, accompanied by acquiescence from other States. Only as far as these requirements are met will China be entitled to claim EEZ and continental shelf areas, provided that the features concerned are to be qualified as islands and not as rocks in terms of Art. 121 (3) UNCLOS.

Other legal experts such as Professor John Norton Moore,[16] a former US ambassador for the Law of the Sea Convention, have been more sceptical with respect to the legal validity of China's nine-dash-line claims, viewing the UNCLOS as the ultimate reference point for assessing the legal dimensions of the South China Sea disputes. Many legal experts contend that China's 'nine-dash-line' doctrine, based on its unique and expansive concept of historical rights, has no place in the UNCLOS, which accommodates only historical rights-based claims to territory in near coastal waters and bays,[17] but not a claim to much if not all of international waterways such as the South China Sea. Maintaining that China's claims stand in contradiction to international law, some South-East Asian claimant states have progressively internationalized the disputes, with the Philippines subjecting its territorial claims – and, by extension, those of China – to compulsory third-party arbitration under the auspices of the UN. Nonetheless, many leading experts have expressed their reservations with respect to the effectiveness of any compulsory arbitration in the South China Sea, given China's outright opposition and contention that UNCLOS has no mandate to address disputes that are essentially sovereignty-related (see Chapter 4).

Energy security But there are more immediate economic considerations influencing China's geopolitical manoeuvring in the South China Sea, including its growing stake in the global commodities trade

[16] Based on exchanges with the author, 2 December 2014.
[17] The UNCLOS refers to historic rights concerning bays (Art. 10 (6)) and maritime delimitation (Art. 15).

and the necessity of securing natural resources to continue economic expansion. Energy security is a key Chinese national priority, making the South China Sea important in light of two developments: growing volatility in energy markets partly as a result of instability in the Middle East as well as China's rapid development of its offshore drilling and downstream technological capabilities. The South China Sea potentially hosts one of the world's richest reservoirs of hydrocarbon resources, and China increasingly views its claims in the area as part of its energy security agenda. In terms of proven and probable reserves of oil and gas, the US Energy Information Administration (EIA) estimates the entire South China Sea holds as much as 11 billion barrels of oil and 190 trillion cubic feet of natural gas. Crucially, the bulk of those projected undiscovered hydrocarbon deposits lies specifically within the Reed Bank and surrounding areas. Citing a US Geological Survey, the EIA estimates 'between 0.8 and 5.4 (mean 2.5) billion barrels of oil and between 7.6 and 55.1 (mean 25.5) trillion cubic feet (TCF) of natural gas in undiscovered resources' are in the contested north-east end of the 'South China Sea, encompassing areas of the contested Spratly islands and the Reed Bank'[18] (see Figure 3.3). Unsurprisingly, major national and international oil companies have also joined the fray, intent on exploring and exploiting the hydrocarbon riches of the South China Sea. Table 3.3 provides key details about the area of operation and estimated oil and gas production, as well as contracts held by national and foreign firms, which have sought to tap the oil and gas riches in the contested waters. Though China's estimates of hydrocarbon reserves in the South China Sea have been largely contradicted by more credible sources, Beijing's exploration schemes in the area have continued apace. By early 2015, Beijing boasted about discovery of the Lingshui 17-2 gas field, which is located about 150 kilometres south of China's southernmost province of Hainan. According to a January 2015 report by the China Petroleum and Chemical Industry Federation, a third of China's offshore oil and gas reserves are in the South China Sea, roughly 11 per cent of the country's total hydrocarbon reserves (Yu 2015).

---

[18] See the EIA website, www.eia.gov/countries/regions-topics.cfm?fips=scs.

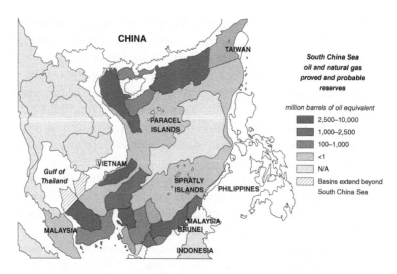

3.3 Hydrocarbon reserves in the South China Sea (*source*: EIA).

Aside from the (confirmed and speculated) hydrocarbon riches of the South China Sea, there is also the concern over the safe passage of fossil fuels across the contested waters. More than 80 per cent of China's oil imports pass through the Indian Ocean and the South China Sea, making the country extremely vulnerable to any disruption on the high seas. China is particularly worried by the possibility of hostile states sabotaging the flow of hydrocarbon products in international waters, which could severely undermine the country's economic stability – with dire socio-political ramifications at home. More specifically, China is concerned by 'chokepoints' from the Persian Gulf to the Indian Ocean and the Malacca Strait. After all, the USA enjoys considerable naval presence in the Persian Gulf and across international waters; India has a growing military presence on the Andaman and Nicobar islands in the Indian Ocean; and American strategic partners such as Singapore and Indonesia surround the Malacca Strait, with Australia not far away. In present conditions, a coordinated sabotage of China's hydrocarbon imports by the USA and its partners remains an inconceivable outcome, but Chinese strategic planners have painfully explored

TABLE 3.3 Hydrocarbon exploration and production in the South China Sea

Country	Oil[a] 1000 barrels/day	Natural gas billion cubic feet	Major exploration and production areas	National oil companies	Foreign firms
Brunei	120	400	Baram Delta	PetroleumBRUNEI	BHP Billiton, ConocoPhillips, Hess Corporations, Kulezyk Oil Ventures, Mitsubishi Corporation, Murphy Oil, PETRONAS, Polyard Petroleum, QAF Brunei, Shell, Total
China	150	600	Pearl River Mouth Basin Qiongdongnan Basin	CNOOC Sinopec CNPC	BG Group, BP, Chevron, ConocoPhillips, Eni, ExxonMobil, Husky, Newfield, Shell, Total
Indonesia	60	200	Natuna Basin	PT Pertamina (Persero)	PetroChina, Chevron, CNPC, ConocoPhillips, Eni, ExxonMobil, Husky, KUFPEC, PETRONAS, Santos, Statoil, Total
Malaysia	500	1,800	Sabah Sarawak Malay Basin (w/ Thailand)	PETRONAS	Lundin, BHP Billiton, ConocoPhillips, ExxonMobil, Hess, KUFPEC, MDC O&G, Murphy Oil, Newfield, Nippon, Petrofac, Roc Oil, Shell, Talisman Energy
Philippines	25	100	Palawan Basin	PNOC	ExxonMobil, Shell
Thailand	–	–	Gulf of Thailand Malay Basin (w/ Malaysia)	PTTEP	BG Group, Chevron, Shell
Vietnam	300	300	Cuu Long Basin Nam Con Son Basin	Petro Vietnam	KNOC, ConocoPhillips, Geopetrol, Prenier Oil, PTTEP, Santos, SK Corp, Total, Zurubezhneft

Sources: EIA, *Oil & Gas Journal*, IHS, CNOOC, PFC Energy.
a Oil production includes lease condensate.

various contingencies, which underline Beijing's growing sense of vulnerability (Kaplan 2010).

Rising geopolitical tensions between China, on one hand, and the USA and its Asian allies, on the other, has simply reinforced Beijing's bid to explore varying means to enhance its energy security. As Li (2010) explains:

> Hu [Jintao] has been particularly concerned about China's newly emerging national interests in terms of energy security ... [As early as November 2003] Hu, as the new CCP general secretary, advanced the concept of oil security, and stressed the need to develop a new energy-development strategy from a 'strategic overall height' to achieve national energy security. Because the South China Sea has potentially rich deposits of fossil fuels and natural gas and straddles major sea-lanes through the Strait of Malacca into the Indian Ocean, Hu seems to favor particularly the development of the South Sea Fleet.

China's growing concerns with energy security are also a natural byproduct of the rapid expansion in its hydrocarbon imports, which are necessary to feed its rapidly growing economy. Beginning in 1993, China became a net oil importer country, but it was in the first decade of the twenty-first century that China's hydrocarbon imports exploded to unprecedented levels, partly driven by a decline in domestic production capacity, which encouraged the Hu administration to pay closer attention to energy security and more proactively explore opportunities to enhance the country's access to hydrocarbon resources (Tang 2006). Between 2000 and 2008, China's rapidly expanding energy needs accounted for about 51 per cent of the growth in world energy demand, consuming 43 per cent of the world's coal, 10 per cent of its oil and 19 per cent of its hydroelectric power (Kennedy 2010).

Domestically, China has rapidly expanded its renewable energy capacity, while compelling industries to employ more energy-intensive technology. Externally, China has stepped up its energy exploration activities in the South China Sea. It protects its energy surveillance vessels and oil rigs by an expanding flotilla of paramilitary forces, which are supported by a burgeoning network of civilian and military structures built across the disputed waters (see Chapter 4). From South-East Asia to western Europe, China has also established a so-called 'string of pearls' by purchasing stakes in and/or developing major ports, enhancing its position as regards global maritime routes and exploring alternative routes for its energy imports. So far, China has fallen short of developing any overseas naval presence comparable to American forward deployment outposts in Japan, Guam and Hawaii. The Chinese leaders have astutely calculated that establishing fully fledged naval bases abroad, especially along strategic waters such as the Indian Ocean, would be unnecessarily costly and strategically provocative. Nonetheless, what caught the attention of Western and Indian strategists, in particular, was China's lead role in development and/or negotiation of basing agreements in Gwadar (Pakistan), the Seychelles, Chittagong (Bangladesh) and Hambantota (Sri Lanka), increasing Beijing's strategic footprint across the Indian Ocean. As naval strategists James Holmes and Toshi Yoshihara (2012), authors of *Red Star over the Pacific: China's Rise and the Challenge to U.S. Maritime Strategy*, explain: 'Beijing is negotiating agreements that grant Chinese vessels the right to call at ports like Gwadar, Hambantota, and Chittagong to rest, refuel, and perhaps refit ... our best guess is that China is laying the foundations for a hypothetical build-up of hard naval power while debating the wisdom of such an expensive, arduous, potentially hazardous course of action ... the port facilities under development in the Indian Ocean boast infrastructure that is "clearly adequate" for military use should Beijing see the need.'

In many ways, China is simply following in the footsteps of the USA. After consolidating its continental borders, the USA began, in the nineteenth century, to develop a global strategic presence by first establishing naval supremacy in adjacent waters (i.e. the Caribbean), then gradually expanding throughout the Pacific waters, with the Philippines, in the early twentieth century, serving as Washington's forward deployment base in East Asia. In his groundbreaking work *The Influence of Sea Power upon History: 1660–1783*, the American naval strategist Alfred Thayer Mahan (1840–1914) argued that the British Empire's strength was anchored by its ability to command the high seas. Although it was not the dominant continental power, especially in terms of land-based warfare capabilities, Britain managed to become the most consequential power of its time. It achieved this by maintaining a powerful fleet capable of dominating sea lines of communication at the expense of rivals. Britain was able to protect its merchant vessels and preserve international trade, which was central to its imperial economy. In contrast to other prominent geo-strategists such as Halford Mackinder, who emphasized the importance of continental power and the strategic centrality of the Heartland (the Eurasian landmass stretching from eastern Europe to northern China), Mahan underlined the importance of naval power in determining geopolitical ascendancy. His works shaped the military strategy of not only the USA, but also rising powers such as Wilhelmite Germany and Imperial Japan. His ideas served as the driving inspiration for an expansionist naval strategy among the leading powers of the early twentieth century. Today, with Beijing managing to successfully consolidate its position as a continental power, there are concerns that Chinese naval strategies seem to have eagerly adopted Mahanian lessons to pursue Chinese global supremacy (Holmes 2011; Kaplan 2013). With a growing number of pundits speaking of a '1914 moment' in Asia (Nye 2014), there are growing debates on whether today's China is following Wilhelmite Germany, the then dominant continental power in Europe, which played a crucial role in triggering the First World War when it sought to match Britain's naval capabilities. As China seeks to counter the USA's naval supremacy in the Pacific, there are growing fears of a major showdown between the region's two dominant powers. James Holmes (2014) provides a useful comparison between the naval strategies of Imperial Germany and today's China:

> China promises to be a far more formidable seafaring state than [Wilhelmite] Germany ever was, with leadership that's just as mercurial … While China accepts Mahan's general logic of sea power – indeed, this long-dead American navalist commands virtual rock-star status there – it reversed the German pattern of naval development. PLA officers and weaponeers focused first on asymmetric weaponry, then turned their energies to symmetrical, blue-water platforms such as aircraft carriers, guided-missile destroyers, and amphibious transports.

Fisheries The South China Sea is often likened to the Persian Gulf, a conflict-prone area that represents one of the world's most critical sea lines of communication (SLOCs) – and a massive source of hydrocarbon resources. But the South China Sea happens to be, first and foremost, extremely rich in fisheries resources, a key source of livelihood for tens of millions of people residing in the coastal regions of East Asia. Forty per cent of the world's tuna, for instance, is born in these contested waters, home to the world's most biodiverse marine life (Hachigian 2015). This makes the South China Sea arguably an even more economically significant and resource-diverse SLOC than the Persian Gulf. Beijing has repeatedly sought to portray Chinese fishermen straddling the South China Sea as private citizens, acting on their own volition, trying to make a living in areas where China has 'inherent and indisputable sovereignty'. But there are signs that at least some of these Chinese fishermen are state-sponsored actors, which, in the form of maritime militia forces, stand at the forefront of Beijing's territorial posturing in the South China Sea. Under the so-called 'cabbage strategy', Chinese fishermen-cum-militia represent the outer layer of a multi-tier Chinese maritime offensive, part of the broader people's war for asserting China's national interest in the seas, with the PLA navy standing as the innermost core and paramilitary vessels as the intermediate layer. When other claimant countries confront and/or apprehend Chinese fishermen/militia, they face the risk of retribution from the other two layers, with the implicit threat of eventual PLA navy intervention representing the last stage in a prospective chain of escalation. As Erickson and Kennedy (2015) explain, the fishermen-cum-militia represent an integral part of China's territorial ambitions in adjacent waters:

> drawing on the world's largest fishing fleet, China is also strengthening its maritime militia, a dual-hatted force of specially registered fishing vessels with fisherman–soldier crews. Portions of these coastal militias are organized by local military and government officials along the nation's many ports, providing China with small tactical units designed to execute specific missions in support of the country's more professional military and maritime interests. China has had maritime militias dating back to the 1950s, but they have increased

in importance as Xi has sought a more active presence in the South China Sea ... All together, China's navy, local law enforcement, Coast Guard, and maritime militias are making the country a great maritime power, indeed ... Working in greater numbers and capable of reaching shallower waters, trawlers operated cheaply by Tanmen [the Village Maritime Militia Company, in Hainan] and other militias sometimes prove more efficient than larger, more professional resupply vessels. Smaller craft can simultaneously resupply multiple stations instead of fuel-thirsty helicopters or scarce dedicated supply ships. Fishing vessels also draw much less attention politically than navy or coast guard vessels ... Such maritime militia activities are growing along China's southern coast; with cities and counties in Guangdong, Fujian, and Guangxi Provinces all experimenting with and strengthening paramilitaries under close supervision of local party, government, and military officials.

China has reportedly installed a home-grown Beidou satellite system on more than fifty thousand Chinese fishing boats, allowing the Chinese fishermen to call in support whenever they face any threats from other claimant states. With overfishing thinning out stocks in near waters, Chinese fishermen have ventured farther into the high seas and well into the EEZ of other claimant countries such as the Philippines. China's per-capita fish consumption (35.1 kilograms) has reached astronomical levels, twice the global average (18.9 kilograms). Local government units, particularly Hainan, have proactively encouraged their fishermen to venture deep into the South China Sea, as far as 670 miles to the south, while providing fuel subsidies (US$320–US$480 per day) for larger vessels and up to US$322,500 in renovation grants for the large boats of major fishing companies (Ruwitch 2014). Hainan's current and former governors, Liu Cigui (former State Oceanic Administration Director) and Luo Baoming (First Director of Hainan's National Defence Mobilization Committee) respectively, have played a critical role in enhancing China's ongoing efforts to dominate contested waters and features in the South China Sea, with the Hainan government allocating US$4.5 million to the cause in 2013 (Erickson and Kennedy 2015).

With the rapid deterioration of marine and fisheries resources in the area, largely thanks to large-scale illegal fishing (mostly by Chinese vessels), the impetus for locking up depleting resources in the South China Sea has reached new heights. In early 2015, China finalized a comprehensive fisheries survey across the South China Sea, reflecting its growing concern over the livelihood of millions of Chinese fisherfolk, who depend on unimpeded access to large-scale marine resources. China's most recent survey suggests between 73 million and 172 million tons of mesopelagic fishery reserves in the contested areas (Xinhua 2015a). In the absence of democratic elections, the Chinese Communist Party (CCP) primarily relies on its economic performance to generate legitimacy and prevent social upheavals. So clearly there are domestic political considerations behind China's resource-motivated move into the South China Sea, aside from the widely reported necessity to appease hardline nationalist constituencies in military and civilian circles. With the world's largest coastguard fleet, dwarfing those of all neighbouring countries combined, China will be in an increasingly powerful position to push its interests in adjacent waters by using civilian law enforcement agencies, backed by fishermen-cum-militia forces, rather than conventional military forces. This will give China enough space to keep the ongoing spats in adjacent waters just below a specific threshold of violence, which could activate existing military commitments between Washington and its Asian treaty allies such as the Philippines and Japan. Confident about the efficacy of its existing strategy, which primarily relies on militia and paramilitary patrol forces, China has expanded its patrol vessels fleet by 25 per cent in the last three years, building as many as sixty patrol vessels in 2014 (Perlez 2015a).

Interest groups In recent decades, particularly under Hu Jintao and Jiang Zemin, one of the most challenging aspects of the territorial disputes in the South China Sea has been the highly fragmented nature of the Chinese maritime bureaucracy, involving eleven ministerial-level government agencies, which, in turn, oversaw five law enforcement agencies. Dubbed as the 'five dragons contending for the sea', China Marine Surveillance (CMS), the Border Control Department (BCD), the Fisheries Law Enforcement Command (FLEC), the General

Administration of Customs, and the Maritime Safety Administration
(MSA) jostled for influence over China's territorial claims in the South
China Sea, with each agency pursuing its own bureaucratic interests
and strategic vision in the disputed waters. On a macro-level, leading
law enforcement agencies, particularly the CMS and the FLEC, had
to contend with other major actors in shaping Beijing's policy in the
South China Sea: namely, the provincial government in Hainan (and
to a certain degree also those in Guangdong and Guangxi), which
has a direct stake in the rich marine resources in the disputed waters,
the PLA navy (South Sea Fleet), which has vociferously lobbied
for increased defence spending and an expanded strategic presence
across the western Pacific in recent decades, and the Chinese Foreign
Ministry, which has largely sought to prevent a diplomatic breakdown
with rival claimant states (International Crisis Group 2012b; Ruwitch
2014; Nan 2010; Erickson and Collins 2013).

No wonder other claimant states have questioned whether China has
had any standard, unified policy on its territorial claims. This presented
two key problems for the region: (a) with multiple competing actors
shaping China's territorial policies, the risk of unintended clashes
and rogue activities by hardline elements progressively increased; and
(b) the Chinese Foreign Ministry gradually lost its long-privileged
position as the main diplomatic bridge between Beijing and its worried
neighbours, which began to doubt whether Chinese diplomats
carried the necessary mandate to negotiate any lasting solution to
the brewing maritime disputes in the South China Sea. The region
confronted the spectre of a powerful but internally fragmented China.
For some countries in the region, it was time for the USA to step in.
And Washington did exactly that, with the Obama administration's
highly touted Pivot to Asia (P2A) policy reflecting its determination to
rebalance its strategic orientation towards East Asia. Deeply worried
about China's territorial designs, the Philippines, perhaps more than
any country, warmly welcomed a greater American strategic footprint
in the region.

4 | BETWEEN AN EAGLE AND A DRAGON: THE TRAGEDY OF SMALL-POWER POLITICS

> Sentimentalism and emotionalism should not play a part in international relations ... As Filipinos, we must look out for ourselves, because no one else will. That is the essence of our independence.
>
> Claro M. Recto, 17 April 1951

> Here is a land in which a few are spectacularly rich while the masses remain abjectly poor. ... Here is a land consecrated to democracy but run by an entrenched plutocracy.
>
> Beningo Aquino Jr, July 1968

> I would rather have a country run like hell by Filipinos than one run like heaven by the Americans.
>
> Manuel Quezon, president of the Philippine Commonwealth (1935–44)

After eight years of foreign policy misadventure under the Bush administration, President Barack Obama promised a new era in America's relationship with the rest of the world. Initially, his approach to international affairs was more about decoupling from the legacy of the previous administration than shaping a brave new world. Resetting relations with the Muslim world, especially the Middle East, was at the heart of Obama's emerging strategy. In operational terms, ending the grinding wars in Iraq and Afghanistan became the centrepiece of Washington's new foreign policy doctrine. No degree of public diplomacy, despite Obama's eloquence, could have concealed the ubiquity of American boots straddling the region – a great source of animosity among the Muslim world's population towards Washington. Even more profoundly, ending the conflicts was about redressing America's strategic overreach. The fiscal and humanitarian burden of the two wars became politically untenable for much of the American public, especially in the aftermath of the 2007/08 Great Recession. Now it was time to refocus on the home front. It soon became clear that much of Obama's inclination towards disengaging from the Middle East had to do with his growing desire to tap economic opportunities in the booming markets of the Pacific Rim and check China's rising maritime assertiveness in the area. Under the Bush administration, there was a palpable feeling that the USA had abandoned Asia to the whims of emerging powers such as China, which had become the leading trading partner of much of the Pacific region, including Australia, Japan and ASEAN. It was time, then, to 'rebalance' the strategic landscape by reinserting Washington into the centre of Asia-Pacific affairs. Across Asia, perhaps no allied country was as desperately in need – and wholeheartedly appreciative – of American military assistance as the Philippines. Fearful of China's expanding designs across the South China Sea, the leadership in Manila solicited greater external support, most especially from the USA. Washington has been, by far, the Philippines' most important strategic security partner. Some Filipino intellectuals would go so far as arguing that Washington has virtually acted as the sole guarantor of the South-East Asian nation's security.[1] China's ascent as an Asian powerhouse, coupled with the relative decline of the USA, threatened to reconfigure this equation, as Manila, beginning in the mid-2000s, tried to diversify its external relations and adopt an equi-balancing approach to its relations with Beijing and Washington. But China's growing maritime assertiveness in the late 2000s gradually unravelled the two decades of its relatively successful charm offensive across Asia. By now, Manila was once again moving into Washington's strategic orbit, with the maritime dispute in the East and South China Seas gradually transforming into a broader Sino-American rivalry for primacy in Asia.

A history of dependency

In many ways, the modern Philippine nation-state was formed under American colonial patronage. It was the USA which introduced modern infrastructure, universal education and institutions of electoral

[1]   Interview with Walden Bello, 15 December 2011; September 2012.

democracy to the country. Throughout its three centuries of rule over the Philippines, Spain – which mostly oversaw the administration of the island nation through its viceroy in Mexico – was a largely neglectful colonial master. There was not much effort to lay down the foundations of a modern state; Madrid was more interested in expropriating natural resources, exporting its religion and exploiting the labour power and geostrategic position of the Philippines, which served as a major trading hub in the Pacific – connecting the New World with (the Ming and Qing dynasties of) China. It was an exclusionary form of colonization, which left much of the indigenous population illiterate, without much access to public goods. And much of the domestic economy was dominated by a landed class, which made little efforts to industrialize a backward, agricultural nation (Anderson 1987, 1997).

But the late-nineteenth-century transition from Spanish to American rule instilled a deep sense of betrayal among Filipino nationalists, who made the fatal mistake of welcoming American military assistance to topple their Spanish colonizers. The Filipinos mistook American opportunism for a benign expression of solidarity against colonial Spain, which sold the Philippine islands – along with other colonies in the Americas and the Pacific – to Washington under the 1898 Treaty of Paris. After successfully consolidating its dominance in the western hemisphere – eradicating the Spanish Empire's foothold in Latin America, finally fulfilling the precepts of the Monroe Doctrine – the USA began to expand its strategic horizons, seeking new opportunities in East Asia. The Philippines served as a crucial step towards fulfilling Washington's vision of Pacific supremacy (Bello 2010). By conquering the Philippines, the newly rising power was in a strong position to compete for enormous market opportunities in Asia. It did not take long before the indigenous nationalist movement clashed with Washington, giving birth to the Philippine–American War (1899–1902), claiming the lives of more than half a million Filipinos (Fallows 1987). Equipped with modern technology and a powerful navy, the USA managed to overcome indigenous resistance and expand the operational boundaries of the Philippines deep into the Muslim-dominated islands in the south. After quashing the revolutionary forces, Washington introduced a relatively benign form of colonization, which relied on public services, co-optation of the Spanish-era elite (the cacique), and the development of modern electoral institutions. After living for centuries under Spain's shadow, the indigenous population was now ruled by a significantly more capable and ubiquitous foreign power, which was interested in creating a showcase colony in Asia. As Neil Sheehan (1989: 131) explains, the USA had to invent a new form of colonialism, because it faced profound domestic and ideological opposition to European-style colonialism:

> Having overt colonies was not acceptable to the American political conscience. Americans were convinced that their imperial system did not victimize foreign peoples. 'Enlightened self-interest' was the sole national egotism to which Americans would admit ... Americans perceived their order as a new and benevolent form of international guidance. It was thought to be neither exploitative, like the [nineteenth-century-] style colonialism of the European empires, nor destructive of personal freedom and other worthy human values, like the totalitarianism of the Soviet Union and China and their Communist allies. Instead of formal colonies, the [USA] sought local governments amenable to American wishes and, where possible, subject to indirect control from behind the scenes. Washington wanted native regimes that would act as surrogates for American power. The goals were to achieve the sway over allies and dependencies which every imperial nation needs to work its will in world affairs without the structure of old-fashioned colonialism.

The American colonial project was founded upon an astute combination of continuity and change: Washington was firmly at the centre of a state-building process, cultivating the Spanish-era mestizo-class political elite and empowering a growing portion of the indigenous population. The Filipino elite combined Spanish indolence and corruption with American efficiency and pragmatism. The Philippines gradually transformed into a crude reflection of the American political system, thanks to what one could term 'participatory colonization', with the domestic elite and much of the upwardly mobile sections of society relishing the patronage of a foreign power. In the words of Benedict Anderson (1987):

Americans installed, by stages, a political regime, modelled on their own, which turned out, perhaps to their own surprise, to be perfectly adapted to the crystallising oligarchy's needs ... the prominent collaborator oligarch Manuel Roxas became in 1946 the independent Philippines' first President. Before his death in 1948 he had achieved the following triumphs: amnesty for all 'political prisoners' (mainly those held on charges of collaboration); an agreement permitting the US to retain control of its bases in the Philippines for 99 years, as well as a US–Philippines Military Assistance Pact; and the amending of the Commonwealth Constitution of 1935 to give Americans 'parity' access to the economic resources of the 'independent' Philippines (and, of course, the oligarchy's continuing access to the protected American market).

Instead of a confident, self-reliant nation, the product of America's colonial project was a dependent, insecure nation, which eternally struggled to establish for itself an authentic vision of national development and autonomy. As Filipino national hero Benigno Aquino Jr (1968) memorably wrote: 'Almost half a century of American rule bequeathed to the Asian Filipino a trauma by making him uncomfortably American in outlook, values and tastes. What was left was a people without soul ... Filipinos are bewildered about their identity. They are an Asian people not Asian in the eyes of their fellow Asians and not Western in the eyes of the West.'

The Philippines was never able to establish the kind of popular nationalism which gripped neighbouring nations, from China and Vietnam to South Korea and Japan. Successive waves of nationalist leaders, from Andres Bonifiacio in the nineteenth century to Claro M. Recto in the twentieth century, were never able to mobilize the indigenous population in the same manner that, say, Japan's Meiji Restoration, Sun Yat-sen (and Mao Zedong) in China, Sukarno in Indonesia, and Ho Chi Minh in Vietnam were able to do. Ironically, it was Jose Rizal (the iconic Filipino thinker) and the broader late-nineteenth-century indigenous independence movement in the Philippines which served as a huge source of inspiration for nationalist leaders across Asia (Mishra 2013). Arguably, the brave Visayan chieftain Lapu-Lapu was the first East Asian warrior to defeat a major

Western commander, Ferdinand Magellan, in the Battle of Mactan in 1521. But the modern-day Philippines largely outsourced its national security to its last colonial master, which bequeathed formal independence to the Philippines in 1946. As James Fallows (1987) cogently put it:

> America prevented the Filipinos from consummating their rebellion against Spain. In 1898 the United States intervened to fight the Spanish and then turned around and fought the Filipino nationalists, too. It was a brutal guerrilla war, in which some half million Filipino soldiers and civilians died … But American rule seemed only to intensify the Filipino sense of dependence … in immeasurable, intangible ways. [American patronage] seems to have eroded confidence even further, leaving Filipinos to believe that they are not really responsible for their country's fate.

After its formal independence, the Philippines continued to rely on the American security umbrella. In exchange, the Philippines served as a loyal partner. Throughout the twentieth century, Filipinos fought side by side with Americans against, first, Imperial Japan, then North Korea and communist China in the Korean War (1950–53), and North Vietnamese forces and the Vietcong in the Vietnam War (1959–75). After the Cold War, Filipino troops also joined the 'Coalition of Willing' forces, which toppled Iraq's Saddam Hussein in 2003. From the early twentieth century up until the end of the Cold War, the US military served as the backbone of Philippine national security. Less charitable critics would go so far as to dismiss the Philippines as essentially an American protectorate. The South-East Asian country's dependence on American goodwill was largely due to the folly of the Philippine state-formation process, rather than, say, some Orientalist cultural malady. Unlike many of its neighbours, particularly the 'developmental state' regimes in South Korea, Singapore, Thailand and Taiwan, the Philippines repeatedly fell short of (i) developing state autonomy vis-à-vis the predatory political elite and (ii) enhancing executive capacity, particularly in terms of nurturing an independent, patriotic and competent bureaucracy, which could transcend the self-serving and short-sighted calculations of elected officials, many of whom hailed from the traditional oligarchy that deeply cherished American patronage (Quilop 2006).

An evolving security environment Though the Philippines gained formal independence, a series of agreements such as the US–Philippines Military Assistance Pact (1947), the Military Bases Agreement (1947) and the mutual defence treaty (MDT) of 1951 ensured that the USA would stand as the de facto guarantor of the Philippines' territorial integrity (Bello et al. 1982; Bello 2005). Throughout the Cold War, the Philippine–US alliance was anchored by the MDT in particular, which obliges both parties to come to each other's aid in the event of conflict with a third party. Article IV of the MDT states: 'Each Party recognizes that an armed attack in the Pacific Area on either of the Parties would be dangerous to its own peace and safety and declares that it would act to meet the common dangers in accordance with *its constitutional processes* [author's own emphasis] …'. Article V, in turn, states: 'an armed attack on either of the Parties is deemed to include an armed attack on the metropolitan territory of either of the Parties, or on *the island territories under its jurisdiction in the Pacific or on its armed forces, public vessels or aircraft in the Pacific* [author's own emphasis]'. The agreement, in accordance with Article VIII of the MDT, 'shall remain in force indefinitely. Either Party may terminate it one year after notice has been given to the other Party.' The MDT served as the overarching document, which facilitated all major bilateral defence and strategic agreements, including the establishment of American bases in the country throughout the Cold War period. But with the collapse of the USSR in 1991, there was an upsurge of nationalist sentiments, with leading legislators calling for an end to American bases in the Philippines. On the one hand, American military installations in the country were seen as a potential target for foreign enemies, exposing the Philippines to unnecessary danger. On the other hand, the decisive defeat of communism – long seen as a major threat to Philippine democracy – created a sense of complacency among Filipino leaders. On Washington's part, economic considerations were also in play. Not only was the USA increasingly uncomfortable about maintaining its expensive bases in the Philippines, but its bases in Subic and Clark were also severely affected by the 1991 Mount Pinatubo volcano eruption. By 1992, the Philippines had terminated the US military presence in the country, without significant opposition from the USA, which was unwilling to offer more than US$203 million in annual aid for an extended lease on the 60,000-acre Subic base – the principal ship-repair installation in East Asia (Sanger 1991). But the removal of American bases immediately left a regional power vacuum, which China sought to fill. Then, in 1995, the Philippines faced a potential armed conflict with China after it discovered that the Mischief Reef in the South China Sea – formerly controlled by the Philippines – had been taken over by Chinese forces, who later on detained Filipino fishermen straddling areas claimed by China, the Philippines and Vietnam. The Philippines also discovered that China was building a military compound on this atoll. In turn, this led to increased tensions between China and the Philippines. Unsurprisingly, in response to China's increasing military assertiveness, a vulnerable Philippines invited the Americans back. The 1998 Visiting Forces Agreement (VFA), the bilateral agreement signed between the United States and the Philippine government, allowed for a substantial US military presence in the country. For the USA, the VFA was part of a broader security framework that allowed the United States to retain its geostrategic supremacy in the Asia-Pacific region (Lourdes 2006).

The tragic events of 9/11 provided the pretext for the United States to expand its regional presence under the banner of 'war on terror' (Achariya and Achariya 2007). In December 2001, the Philippines became part of Operation Enduring Freedom – the Philippines thus becoming an ally in this global war. Members of Special Operations Command Pacific (SOCPAC) were deployed to support these operations in early 2002. At that time, the *New York Times* described this mission as the 'the largest single deployment of American military might outside Afghanistan to fight terrorists since the Sept. 11 attack' (Schmitt 2002). The US military quickly moved towards re-establishing a permanent troop presence in Mindanao, offering logistical and intelligence support to the Philippine military against such groups as the Moro Islamic Liberation Front (MILF), the Moro National Liberation Front (MNLF), the Abu Sayyaf Group

(ASG) and the al-Qaeda regional offshoot, Jemaah Islamiya (JI). In 2003, the Department of Defense announced that the Philippines and the United States would engage in a combined operation against the ASG, raising speculation that the US forces were now potentially directly participating in combat operations on Filipino soil. The operation involved sending 350 US special operations personnel to work with Philippine soldiers, who were logistically backed up by 750 Americans in regional headquarters in Mindanao. While the Philippines had initially invited the US military back as a form of deterrence against Chinese incursion into disputed territories, now there were concerns that the Philippines was becoming a training ground for both US military counter-insurgency operations and mercenary private contractors. Blackwater's spokeswoman, Anne Tyrrell, announced in 2007 that '[w]e are no longer pursuing a facility in the Philippines', referring to the vacated Subic Bay base. However, in 2009, American investigative journalist Wayne Madsen alleged that Blackwater subsidiary Satelles Solutions was using a 'five-acre facility in the former United States naval base [Subic] to train operatives for secret US-backed military operations in Iraq, Afghanistan and other hot spots' (Papa 2009). Despite the Subic Authority's outright rejection of Madsen's report, the Philippine National Police, under growing pressure from the media and people, launched an investigation to determine its veracity. However, the 2010 elections overshadowed the Blackwater issue, and it faded from the limelight. Intermittently, various legislators and nationalist quarters called for a review of the VFA. For instance, Senator Loren Legarda, a prominent Filipino politician, declared: 'We are mandated to review the VFA and to consider this in the light of the numerous calls for action on reported inequities and legal questions characterizing the agreement' (Mendez 2010). Over the years, the Philippine military has expressed support for the VFA and review process, in order to advance the security interests of both nations while improving the Philippines' own capacity to thwart terrorist threats.

The diplomatic card Throughout the 1990s, the Philippines tried to rely on diplomatic means, bilateral and also under the aegis of

ASEAN, to deal with Chinese threats against its territorial claims in the South China Sea. In fact, throughout the latter decades of the twentieth century, the Philippines and China managed to maintain robust diplomatic relations, with their top officials and heads of states making frequent bilateral visits (see Table 4.1).

TABLE 4.1 Philippine–China bilateral visits by heads of state/government (1975–2007)

Date	Official visit
June 1975	Filipino president Ferdinand Marcos visits China
November 1996	Chinese president Jiang Zemin visits the Philippines
May 2000	Filipino president Joseph Estrada visits China
November 2001	Filipino president Gloria Arroyo visits China
September 2004	Filipino president Gloria Arroyo visits China
April 2005	Chinese president Hu Jintao visits the Philippines
January 2007	Chinese premier Wen Jiabao visits the Philippines

Source: Mendoza and Heydarian (2012).

Like many of its neighbours, the Philippines welcomed greater engagement with China throughout the 1970s, with bilateral ties largely stable throughout the reign of Deng Xiaping, Jiang Zemin and much of the Hu Jintao administration. Nonetheless, cognizant of the immense power asymmetry between itself and China, the Philippines tried to leverage multilateral platforms to manage its territorial disputes with Beijing. 'The Philippines primarily employed the "ASEAN strategy" to manage its territorial disputes with China,' observed Herman Kraft,[2] former director of the Institute for Strategic and Developmental Studies (ISDS), a leading regional think tank based in Manila. Instead of using power politics and involving the USA directly in the dispute, the Philippines, under the Fidel Ramos administration (1992–98), sought to use collective bargaining – in cooperation with other ASEAN member countries – to temper and tame China's efforts at consolidating its territorial claims. The Philippines also engaged China on a bilateral basis. During the Joseph

[2] Interview with the author in December 2011 at the University of the Philippines Diliman, Political Science department.

Estrada presidency (1998–2001) and the first few years of President Gloria Macapagal Arroyo, there were few bilateral agreements. But Philippine–China relations reached their zenith in the following years. The year 2004 marked a decisive point. The crucial juncture in Philippine–China relations came at the height of the insurgency in Iraq and the Global War on Terrorism (GWOT). In that year, an extremist group in Iraq took a Filipino worker hostage. In exchange for his release, the Iraqi militants demanded that Filipino troops leave Iraq. The subsequent withdrawal of the Filipino forces, under growing pressure from the Filipino public, adversely affected US–Philippines relations. The Bush administration's uncompromising slogan 'you are either with us or against us' meant that the Philippine actions led to a decrease in US military and economic assistance. In response, Filipino policy-makers began knocking on China's door. President Arroyo's state visit to Beijing signalled a new relationship between the two countries. In November, defence ministers from both sides signed a Memorandum of Understanding on Defence Cooperation. To sweeten the deal, China proposed greater military exchanges and offered RMB10 million in non-lethal military assistance, which was followed by RMB20 million in military equipment (Morada 2006). On the economic front, China–Philippines trade increased from US$17.6 billion in 2005 to US$23.4 in 2006 and US$30.6 billion in 2007 (Mendoza and Heydarian 2012). China was poised to become the Philippines' largest trading partner. Figure 4.1 and Table 4.2 show the Philippines' top trading partners in 2013.

China dramatically improved political ties with the Philippines, expanding its role in key economic sectors such as telecommunications and transport. As part of the ASEAN Regional Forum (ARF) and as a strong supporter of many ASEAN–China cooperation schemes, the Philippines became an important regional player in accommodating China's growing influence in the region. From China's vantage point, its growing ties with the Philippines were part of its broader regional strategy of expanding its economic dominance and diminishing the prospects of a sustained and strong US-led regional coalition bent on containing its rise (Mendoza and Heydarian 2012). At some point, even Washington was impressed by China's efforts to gain the goodwill of its neighbours.

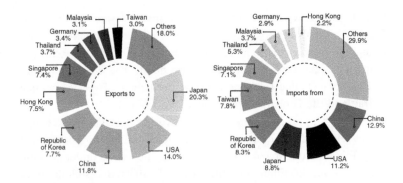

4.1 The Philippines' top trading partners in 2013.

TABLE 4.2 The Philippines' top trading partners in 2013

Trading Partner	Imports	Exports	Total Trade
Japan	5.2	11.4	16.6
China	8.0	6.6	14.6
Hong Kong, China[a]	1.3	4.4	5.7
USA	6.7	7.8	14.5

Source: Global Trade Atlas using Philippine statistics. Philippines and US data may diverge slightly due to different counting methods.

a Hong Kong is a special administrative region of China but a separate economic entity and customs territory.

In a cable entitled 'More on Hu Jintao's visit to the Philippines', the American embassy in Manila expressed a largely positive assessment of the Chinese president's 2005 visit to the Philippines:

> President Hu's charm offensive in Manila does not appear significantly different from that in other ASEAN capitals. Better and broader bilateral ties advance regional interests, as other ASEAN members have also discovered. However, the conservative Philippine defense establishment – whose doctrine, equipment, and training are all US-based – will be cautious so as not to jeopardize its close relationship with the United States military, especially as it undertakes (with US help) fundamental restructuring and continues to combat

multiple terrorist threats. [Philippine] Foreign Secretary Romulo's upcoming visit to Washington offers a timely opportunity further to discuss the evolving PRC role in Asia and Philippine perceptions of long-term Chinese goals. (Cable 05MANILA2174)

The USA was also broadly optimistic vis-à-vis Philippine–China efforts to de-escalate their territorial tensions in the South China Sea. In a 2006 cable entitled 'Joint seismic survey in South China Sea makes progress', the American embassy in Manila cautiously welcomed the 2005 JMSU agreement as a timely confidence-building measure among disputing parties:

The first phase of a joint seismic survey for hydrocarbon deposits undertaken by the national oil companies of the Philippines, China, and Vietnam in an 143,000 square kilometer zone of the South China Sea is near completion. After its partners conducted a 'reconnaissance' survey of the entire zone, the Philippine National Oil Corporation is now interpreting the initial survey data, which it expects to finish by the end of the year. Promising areas identified in the first phase will be surveyed again more closely in the second phase. If viable deposits are ultimately found, a new agreement would be needed to cover any joint development, which Philippine sources predicted would be reserved for the three national oil companies. The joint seismic survey offers a good model for potential subsequent cooperation on exploration and exploitation, and fits neatly with Philippine goals of increased interaction between ASEAN and China and the promotion of confidence building measures. The true test of the cooperative spirit, however, will come when the parties may contemplate extraction.

Astonishingly, through its subtle and sophisticated diplomacy, China was seemingly able to portray its charm offensive towards the Philippines as largely benign and non-threatening, even to the USA. The Philippine–China diplomatic honeymoon, however, didn't last long.

A new leadership The 2010 election of Benigno Aquino III ushered in a new foreign policy orientation in the Philippines. But changes came on a gradual basis, as one crisis after the other undermined bilateral relations. The son of two leading Filipino political figures, Aquino promised transformative change in the country's domestic and foreign policies. Early in office, the Aquino administration's foreign policy seemingly mirrored that of other weaker regional powers caught between the USA and China. But over time, Aquino's strong anti-corruption agenda began to have an impact on bilateral relations with China. Aquino was not only rejecting his corrupt predecessor, Gloria Arroyo, but also her foreign partners such as China, which also became embroiled in corruption scandals. After all, Chinese overseas companies – mostly tied to the government – are notorious for corruption: according to the Bribe Payers Index, which measures a country's willingness to engage in bribery to win contracts, China ranks among the most corrupt countries in the world. Towards the end of the Arroyo administration (2001–10), corruption scandals were embroiling Chinese companies which won major infrastructure contracts with the Philippine government. The most prominent case, currently used by the Aquino administration as grounds for imprisoning former president Arroyo, is the 'NBN-ZTE scandal', implicating a Chinese telecommunications company (ZTE), which received a contract to build the National Broadband Network (NBN). After whistleblowers exposed the anomalies in the contract, with allegations of kidnappings and charges of extortion thrown into public discussions, the whole deal was cancelled – to China's dismay and embarrassment. But other challenges followed. The Filipino public suspected that the Arroyo administration may have treasonously compromised the Philippines territorial integrity in the JMSU agreement, potentially even agreeing to joint development in areas not claimed by China (International Crisis Group 2012b). The JMSU expired in 2008, with progressive-nationalist groups filing a case at the Supreme Court of the Philippines on the grounds that the agreement violated the National Economy and Patrimony provisions of the 1987 Constitution. According to Article XII, Section 2 of the National Economy and Patrimony provisions: 'The exploration, development, and utilization of natural resources shall be under the full control and supervision of the State ... The State shall protect the nation's marine wealth in its archipelagic waters, territorial sea, and exclusive economic zone, and reserve its use and enjoyment exclusively to Filipino citizens.' Moreover, there was also a huge concern over lack of transparency and consultation: Section 10 of the JMSU, which imposes secrecy and compels parties to withhold information about the agreement for an extended period, violated Philippine legal provisions on ensuring transparency in government contracts as well as the constitutional provision on the obligation of the executive branch to 'notify Congress with every contract entered into within 30 days from its execution' (Colmenares 2008).

Early in office, Aquino faced two major incidents that tested his country's relations with China. The first was the Manila hostage crisis in August, in which eight Hong Kong nationals died and nine others were injured. The tragedy quickly evolved into a diplomatic crisis. Hong Kong accused the Philippine government of gross mismanagement of the hostage negotiations, and China issued a travel warning. The Philippine government's diplomatic efforts in the aftermath of the crisis bordered on 'tiptoeing' around China, which sided with the Hong Kong authorities, who demanded compensation and an apology from Aquino. Manila oscillated between appeasement and self-vindication. But Aquino clearly caved in on another issue, when under Chinese pressure he turned down an invitation to attend the Nobel Peace Prize ceremony honouring Chinese dissident Li Xiaobo. In so doing, the Philippines joined a group of autocratic economic-political allies of China that also boycotted the ceremony out of solidarity with Beijing. In response, the Chinese government expressed its deep appreciation for Manila's display of support. Chinese ambassador to Manila Liu Jianchao said, 'I appreciate the understanding shown by the Philippine government of the Chinese people and the Chinese government' (GMA News 2010).

America steps in In the meantime, the South China Sea disputes were heating up (see Chapter 3). As China stepped up its territorial posturing in the South China Sea, the Aquino administration began to seriously rethink its foreign policy and reach out to Washington. There was also a growing worry among American policy-makers over the possibility that China would leverage its economic prowess to force neighbouring countries to choose between Beijijng and Washington. In one diplomatic cable, the US ambassador to Beijing, Clark T. Randt, wrote, 'Perceived threats to China's security posed by Japan's participation in missile defense or by future high-tech US military technologies might cause tomorrow's Chinese leaders to change their assessment and to exert economic pressures on US allies like Thailand or the Philippines to choose between Beijing and Washington.'[3] In another cable, entitled 'Stomp around and carry a small stick: China's new "global assertiveness",' the American embassy in Beijing shared a growing worry over China's diplomatic behaviour vis-à-vis other powers, as well as its actual behaviour vis-à-vis territorial disputes with neighbouring countries:

> The harsh (per usual) PRC [People's Republic of China] reaction to the recent U.S. announcement of arms sales to Taiwan and President Obama's intention to meet with the Dalai Lama has focused Chinese domestic attention on a phenomenon already observed (and criticized) abroad: China's muscle-flexing, triumphalism and assertiveness in its diplomacy. Foreign diplomats note that China is making no friends with its newly pugnacious attitude, but the popular assessment of China's stance, personified by the nationalistic, jingoistic and Chinese Communist Party-affiliated newspaper Global Times (Huanqiu Shibao), is 'it's about time'. (Cable 10BEIJING383)

In the cable, American diplomats shared how 'numerous third-country diplomats, in their conversations with the U.S. embassy staff in Beijing, have complained that dealing with China has become more difficult in the past year'. More specifically, the cable notes that 'Europeans have been the most vocal in their criticism', while 'Indian and Japanese ambassadors voiced similar complaints'. The cable also mentioned the rise of 'ultra-nationalism' in the country and jingoistic rhetoric among the Chinese media – further exacerbating territorial tensions with neighbouring countries. The USA began to view China as a real source of threat to the regional order and its bilateral alliances, with China's growing territorial assertiveness in the South China Sea serving as a key point of contention. During the ARF meeting in July,

[3] See Cable 09BEIJING22_a, entitled 'LOOKING AT THE NEXT 30 YEARS OF THE U.S.–CHINA RELATIONSHIP', at the Wikileaks website, www.wikileaks.org/plusd/cables/09BEIJING22_a.html.

ASEAN again challenged China's territorial claim to the South China Sea. With the United States focused on freedom of navigation in the South China Seas, Secretary of State Hillary Clinton affirmed that '[l]egitimate claims to maritime space in the South China Sea should be derived solely from legitimate claims to land features'. In other words, China's territorial claims were 'invalid' because no Chinese live on these atolls. She offered to help create a binding code of conduct in the region. After more than a decade of diplomatic finesse, China's response was swift and brusque. Chinese foreign minister Yang Jiechi accused ASEAN members of conniving with the United States to corner China. According to the *Washington Post*, the Chinese minister allegedly shot back, 'China is a big country and other countries are small countries, and that's just a fact' (Pomfret 2010). The message to ASEAN countries was clear: China is no longer just a rising power, but considers itself the regional power and will not tolerate any diplomatic offensive by its smaller neighbours. As a major claimant in the South China Sea dispute, the Philippines took careful note. While in New York (September 2010), President Aquino and President Obama held sideline discussions during the second US–ASEAN leaders meeting on maintaining regional stability, which included the territorial disputes with China. Later, during the US–ASEAN meeting, President Aquino raised the Spratly issue. After expressing strong support for Secretary Clinton's remarks in July which called for 'collaborative diplomatic processes', he voiced concern over China's growing military manoeuvring in the disputed areas. He felt this was best met by a united front should China decide to settle the issue through aggressive means. In response, the Chinese embassy in the Philippines said it would not comment until the dust over the hostage crisis incident settled. Prior to the meeting, ASEAN leaders had hoped to draft a joint statement to 'oppose the use or threat of force by any claimant attempting to enforce disputed claims in the SCS [South China Sea]'. The final statement merely 'reaffirmed the importance of regional peace and stability' and invoked international law as a method of resolving disputes. Later, during the 2011 Asia-Pacific Economic Cooperation (APEC) meeting, China refused to alter its position on the issue – another indication of its new assertive face.

Raising the stakes

Depending on one's ideological bent, America's so-called 'Pivot to Asia' could be interpreted in varying ways. However, one thing that is increasingly clear is that the Obama administration has been intent on reasserting America's strategic centrality in the Asia-Pacific. The USA never left Asia, but it failed to catch up with a dramatic shift in the balance of power. For the Obama administration, the Eurasian theatre increasingly represented more of a distraction than a core interest. Against this strategic backdrop, the so-called 'Pivot to Asia' policy was conceptualized. Officially, Obama launched the new policy during his address in late 2011 before the Australian parliament, where he promised to reinforce Washington's strategic footprint in the Asia-Pacific and underline his country's commitment to remaining an anchor of stability and prosperity:

> Our new focus on this region reflects a fundamental truth – the
> United States has been, and always will be, a Pacific nation ... Here,
> we see the future. As the world's fastest-growing region – and home
> to more than half the global economy – the Asia Pacific is critical to
> achieving my highest priority, and that's creating jobs and opportunity
> for the American people ... As President, I have, therefore, made
> a deliberate and strategic decision – as a Pacific nation, the United
> States will play a larger and long-term role in shaping this region and
> its future, by upholding core principles and in close partnership with
> our allies and friends ... We will keep our commitments ... we will
> constantly strengthen our capabilities to meet the needs of the 21st
> century. Our enduring interests in the region demand our enduring
> presence in the region.[4]

Secretary of State Hillary Clinton further articulated the Pivot to Asia policy in a 2011 piece for *Foreign Policy*, entitled 'America's Pacific century', arguing America's centrality to the stability and prosperity of the Asia-Pacific region:

---

[4] The complete speech is available at the White House website, www.
   whitehouse.gov/the-press-office/2011/11/17/remarks-president-obama-
   australian-parliament.

The Asia-Pacific has become a key driver of global politics ... At a time when the region is building a more mature security and economic architecture to promote stability and prosperity, U.S. commitment there is essential. It will help build that architecture and pay dividends for continued American leadership well into this century, just as our post-World War II commitment to building a comprehensive and lasting transatlantic network of institutions and relationships has paid off many times over – and continues to do so ... Harnessing Asia's growth and dynamism is central to American economic and strategic interests and a key priority for President Obama ... The region is eager for our leadership and our business – perhaps more so than at any time in modern history.

In a follow-up article in mid-2012, she reflected on Washington's growing interest in the maritime disputes in the South China Sea, stating: 'The South China Sea connects many of the nations of the Asia-Pacific, some of which have competing claims on its waters and islands. Half the world's merchant tonnage flows through the South China Sea, so the stakes for maritime security and freedom of navigation are high' (Clinton 2012). But the P2A raised concerns over a Thucydides trap, pertaining to the possibility of a great-power clash as a result of weaker allies dragging their strategic patrons into their own disputes. As prominent American Sinologist Robert Ross (2012) points out:

The decision to pursue the pivot was based on the premise that a newly emboldened China was challenging U.S. interests and undermining regional stability simply because it could – that is, because its growing military power made aggressive diplomacy easier and more attractive than in the past ... The new U.S. policy unnecessarily compounds Beijing's insecurities and will only feed China's aggressiveness, undermine regional stability, and decrease the possibility of cooperation between Beijing and Washington ... By threatening China and challenging its sovereignty claims over symbolic territories, Washington has encouraged Chinese leaders to believe that only by adopting belligerent policies will a rising China be able to guarantee its security. Herein lies the great irony of the pivot: a strategy that was meant to check a rising China has sparked its combativeness and damaged its faith in cooperation.

The P2A raised expectations among allies that America would stand by them as they struggled against creeping Chinese expansionism in the South China Sea. And this was certainly true in the case of the Philippines.

Taking on China

Two years into office, Aquino faced a major foreign policy crisis, threatening an armed conflict with China. In April 2012, the Philippines summoned China's ambassador to Manila after a dangerous stand-off between a Philippine navy vessel (*Gregorio Del Pilar*) and two Chinese paramilitary vessels in the Scarborough Shoal ('Huangyan Island' to the Chinese and 'Panatag Shoal' to the Filipinos), which has been contested by both Manila and Beijing (see Figure 4.2). Since 2010, the shoal, a triangle-shaped grouping of rocky islets and reefs covering around 150 square kilometres, had fallen under the municipal jurisdiction of the northern town of Masinloc (200 kilometres away) on the Philippine archipelago. In terms of distance, it is situated about 125 nautical miles from the nearest Philippine coastline, well within the country's 200-nautical-mile EEZ.

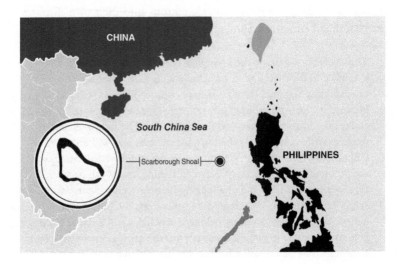

4.2 Scarborough Shoal.

In 1978, Filipino strongman Ferdinand Marcos pushed ahead with Presidential Decree no. 1596, which sought to provide a legal basis for the Philippines' claims over nearby features, hydrocarbon and fisheries resources in the South China Sea, particularly the Spratly chain of islands (Kalayaan to Filipinos). The Marcos administration argued that 'much of the [claimed] area is part of the continental margin of the Philippine archipelago ... these areas do not legally belong to any state or nation but, by reason of history, indispensable need, and effective occupation and control established in accordance with international law, such areas must now be deemed to belong and subject to the sovereignty of the Philippines'. Cognizant of (dormant) claims by neighbouring countries such as China, the Philippines argued that 'while other states have laid claims to some of these areas, their claims have lapsed by abandonment and can not prevail over that of the Philippines on legal, historical, and equitable grounds'. A brilliant strategist, Marcos also moved ahead with establishing an airstrip on Thitu Island (Pag-Asa to Filipinos), correctly anticipating the growing importance of (and willingness of claimant states to up the ante over) the contested features in the coming decades. He knew that down the road legal proclamations alone would not be enough to protect the Philippines' claims in the middle of a maritime wilderness. But the Philippines' claims in the area were much older. In the early twentieth century, during the American occupation of the South-East Asian country, various Filipino officials prodded Washington to protect and reiterate the Philippines' claim over adjacent waters, the underlying resources and features, particularly the Spratlys and Scarborough Shoal, in the South China Sea. The Philippines claims that it has exercised continuous and effective sovereignty[5] over the Scarborough Shoal for over a century, dating back to the Spanish colonial era and augmented during the Cold War, when American

---

[5]   The *U.S. v. Netherlands* dispute over the Island of Palmas (or Miangas), which was resolved (4 April 1928) in favour of the party which exercised continuous and effective sovereignty, has set out a key basis for adjudicating conflicting claims over maritime features. Subsequent cases involving Clipperton Island (1931) and the Minquiers and Ecrehos group of islands (1953) were resolved in similar fashion. See, for instance, Esposo (2013).

naval forces, with Manila's consent, used the area to stage military exercises.[6] In contrast, China's nearest coastline is 472 nautical miles away, with Beijing failing to exercise any discernible form of occupation over the Scarborough Shoal in modern times. The shoal, however, falls within China's notorious 'nine-dash-line' doctrine. But as leading maritime experts such as Jay Batongbacal,[7] an expert on international law at the University of the Philippines, argue, China's claims over the Scarborough Shoal have little basis in modern international law:

China has no real historical claims to the South China Sea (SCS), and nothing in modern international law supports it. [For much of recent history] China had always been ambivalent and unable to explain the 9 dashed lines, and even in diplomatic conferences such as all the negotiations for the Law of the Sea Convention which took place from 1950s–1980s, it never claimed 'historic fact' as a basis for the 9 dashed lines, and it never claimed the waters as under its complete sovereignty until recently. The SCS has always been a shared maritime space between the [ASEAN] region and the world, and China never had any exclusive historical rights of any kind to any maritime resources or uses. Its reference to 'historical facts' and 'historic rights' is absolutely contrived and not supported by its previous statements or actions. It is only now that China is attempting to reshape reality and revise history to make it appear that it has exercised exclusive historic rights to the vast area of the SCS.

The Scarborough Shoal crisis was provoked by the Philippines' decision to use the *Gregorio Del Pilar*, a warship, to arrest Chinese fishermen in the area. From Manila's standpoint, the Chinese fishermen, who went to the area without getting permission from Filipino authorities, were engaged in 'illegal' exploitation of the Philippines' marine resources. Normally, countries use their coastguard forces to undertake law-enforcement-related operations. By using its conventional naval forces, the Philippines provided a perfect excuse for China to dispatch a growing number of paramilitary forces to

[6] For an excellent overview of the Philippines' claim to Scarborough Shoal, see Batongbacal (2014).
[7] Interview with the author, 14 July 2014.

the area, effectively placing the Filipino warship under siege.[8] The stand-off between Filipino and Chinese forces continued for almost two months, until the deadlock was broken by a desperate diplomatic gamble by the Philippines. Confrontation with China was unthinkable. The Philippines' acute military weakness is a reflection of many factors, including an excessive strategic orientation towards internal threats such as insurgency and terrorism, chronic underinvestment in military modernization, high levels of official corruption in military procurements, and a heavy strategic reliance on treaty allies such as the USA. Unlike its predecessors, particularly those of Jimmy Carter and Bill Clinton, the Obama administration refused to clarify whether the 1951 US–Philippine MDT covered disputed Pacific features – and Filipino troops stationed in the area – such as the Scarborough Shoal. Historically, Washington has maintained that the MDT covers 'Philippines armed forces, public vessels or aircraft' in the South China Sea. The Obama administration, in contrast, has refused to clarify whether Washington will come to the Philippines' aid if armed clashes erupt between Manila and Beijing in the South China Sea (Malig 2012; Calonzo 2014). This has had a profoundly chilling strategic effect on the Philippines. Since the Aquino administration failed to solicit American military backing during the Scarborough Shoal crisis, it had little choice but to find a diplomatic compromise with China in order to prevent an escalation into armed confrontation.[9]

A diplomatic disaster Rising diplomatic tensions with China led to divisions inside the Philippine ruling establishment, a widening

---

[8]   It is not yet fully clear whether the Filipino warship was acting under the direction of higher authorities, the defence and foreign ministries or the presidential office. There were suspicions that it was a unilateral decision on behalf of the vessel's captain to arrest Chinese fishermen, instead of waiting for the Philippine Coast Guard (PCG) to dispatch its forces to the area. Filipino officials also made the argument that the Gregorio Del Pilar was coincidentally patrolling in the vicinity of the Scarborough Shoal, so instead of waiting for the PCG, the vessel's captain felt compelled to act as soon as it detected what it viewed as a violation of Philippine territorial integrity.

[9]   The author confirmed this in conversations, specifically in late 2014, with diplomats who had direct knowledge of the circumstances of Philippine–US exchanges during the Scarborough Shoal crisis.

and potentially destabilizing rift that almost split President Benigno Aquino's administration. While Aquino publicly took a hard line in response to Beijing's perceived provocations in the South China Sea, he also sanctioned 'back-door' diplomacy with China in a bid to maintain crucial bilateral trade and investment ties. While Aquino publicly condemned Chinese aggression over the Scarborough Shoal, he apparently secretly sanctioned a junior senator, Antonio Trillanes, to pursue a parallel track of back-door diplomacy with Beijing.[10] Although the president, according to the Philippines' 1987 Constitution, has the final say over Philippine foreign policy, the Department of Foreign Affairs (DFA) is functionally the main institutional arbiter of external relations. Up until then, Philippines' South China Sea policy was largely handled by the energetic and sometimes controversial foreign affairs secretary Albert Del Rosario. He was praised domestically by increasingly nationalistic constituencies for his vigorous attempts to rally international support against China's rising assertiveness in the South China Sea. Del Rosario also emerged as one of the more determined regional players, alongside leaders in Tokyo and Singapore, to welcome the larger American strategic footprint in Asia. Owing to the outsized significance of Sino-Filipino relations, DFA's control over China policy would be challenged by competing interest groups, including highly influential business corporations with interests in China, estimated at about US$2.5 billion, who supported Trillanes' back-door diplomacy initiative. The gambit became public, with some commentators claiming the diplomatically inexperienced Trillanes fell unwittingly into a Chinese trap. There were concerns that Beijing exploited the junior legislator's budding political ambitions by using him to divide the Philippine leadership, assert greater control over the contested Scarborough Shoal, and isolate the purportedly pro-US faction within the DFA. Chinese officials apparently convinced Trillanes they were willing to

---

[10] The gambit was reportedly initiated with little or no consultation with Foreign Secretary Albert Del Rosario – although other sources say that Del Rosario was in the cabinet meeting while Aquino was talking with Trillanes on the phone in loudspeaker mode – and without consultations with then Senate president Juan Ponce Enrile. See Heydarian (2012b).

withdraw their vessels from the disputed maritime territory around
Scarborough Shoal in exchange for a reciprocal move by Manila. US
senior envoy for East Asian and Pacific Affairs Kurt Campbell had
earlier suggested to both the DFA and China making a simultaneous
withdrawal to de-escalate tensions and avoid militarization of the
disputed area. Trillanes boasted soon after in the local press about
his role in 'easing tensions' and 'avoiding war', bringing the back-
channel talks into the public eye. Manila's withdrawal, however,
was met by China removing only some of its naval ships, then later
consolidating its hold over the disputed shoal (Rodis 2012; Nanning
2013). Beijing has since fortified its position around the shoal with a
growing number of paramilitary and surveillance vessels. In July 2012,
China sought to strengthen its position in the area by upgrading the
administrative status of the nearby Sansha island, and demonstrated a
willingness to defend the contested outpost through subsequent naval
manoeuvres in the vicinity. The Scarborough Shoal area has since
for all practical purposes been off limits to even Filipino fishermen
and once-probing media. Critics of the Trillanes-led deal claim that
as a result the Philippines has lost whatever measure of control it
previously exercised over the shoal and its surrounding lagoon through
its secretly negotiated withdrawal. They note that China has even
refused to honour the reported mutually agreed fishing ban to preserve
the shoal area's fragile ecosystem. The fallout reverberated through
the Philippines' domestic politics, pitting China hawks against China
doves. For his part, Trillanes reportedly practically accused Del Rosario
of treason for his dealings with the USA and antagonism towards
China, charges the Aquino administration, the foreign secretary and
his supporters strongly refuted and dismissed (Severino 2012). As
the former Philippine ambassador to Washington, Del Rosario was
a major force behind the revitalization of Philippine–US strategic
ties, including through several hat-in-hand trips to Washington. In
criticizing DFA policy, Trillanes claimed that most Filipinos are
uninterested in the Scarborough Shoal issue and would prefer instead
to have cordial relations with China. The Trillanes camp also implied
a conflict of interest on Del Rosario's part by pointing out he used to
work with Filipino magnate Manny Pangilinan, chairman of Philex

Petroleum, which is a key player in the exploitation of oil and gas in
disputed South China Sea territories. They publicly questioned Del
Rosario's 'impartiality' in dealing with China, insinuating a conflict
of interest between his public and past private roles. The Del Rosario
camp dismissed such accusations as baseless, with the Filipino foreign
secretary blaming China's intransigence as the reason behind the
Scarborough Shoal crisis. In a recent interview, Del Rosario revealed
that in 'the case of Scarborough Shoal, we had over 50 bilateral
engagements with them [China] and that did not work because ...
every bilateral meeting you have with China, unfortunately, [leads
to their saying] to you, "We have indisputable sovereignty over the
entire South China Sea"'. The war of words and Aquino's apparent
secret diplomacy outside of DFA channels reportedly prompted Del
Rosario to consider resigning his post in protest. Trillanes reportedly
called for Manuel Roxas, the newly appointed interior secretary and
anointed successor of Aquino, to replace Del Rosario should he step
down. On the other side of the political divide, Senate president
Enrile rushed to Del Rosario's defence. Enrile accused Trillanes of
not only bypassing normal parliamentary procedures in pursuit of
the back-door gambit (protocol required notifying Senate president),
but also of serving as a Chinese 'fifth column'. Citing information
provided by the Philippine ambassador to China Sonya Brady, Enrile
claimed that Trillanes held talks with top Chinese officials on at least
sixteen occasions. Enrile also insinuated that Trillanes' 'treason'
allegations against Del Rosario, including accusations that the foreign
secretary aimed to create a 'war event' to justify boosting US military
ties, were motivated by his Chinese contacts. Enrile himself was later
accused of treason for revealing confidential diplomatic notes in an
open Senate session. The antagonistic rhetoric and intra-government
rifts put Aquino in a tight political spot. In a bid to stem the political
damage, Aquino asked both Del Rosario and Trillanes to stop
making public statements on the issue (Rodis 2012; Diola 2015).
'Senator Trillanes has the best interest of the country in mind ... I can
categorically say the secretary of foreign affairs enjoys the trust and
confidence of the President,' presidential spokesman Edwin Lacierda
said diplomatically. Aquino publicly denied Trillanes' claim that he

was quietly appointed as a special envoy to China, saying instead he merely responded positively to Trillanes' suggestion of exploratory talks to ease tensions with China ahead of a trip he planned to make to China in May 2012, which was sponsored by Filipino-Chinese business executives (Ubac 2012a). Philippine industrialists and businessmen looked to Trillanes to smooth relations after Beijing imposed obstacles to bilateral trade and travel in the wake of the Scarborough Shoal stand-off. In a press interview, Trillanes said he was approached by the Federation of Filipino Chinese Chambers of Commerce and Industry to play a mediating role. Lucio Tan, the Filipino-Chinese owner of Philippine Airlines with business interests in China, even sponsored his first-class trip to Beijing, Trillanes said in the interview.

The economic stakes involved in falling foul of China are huge. In 2011, the two countries agreed to expand their bilateral trade to US$60 billion by 2016, which if achieved would transform mainland China alone into the Philippines' biggest export market. Leading Filipino entrepreneurs with interests in China's booming real estate and retail sectors have banked heavily on their growing foreign investments there. Chinese visitors to the Philippines, meanwhile, were the fourth-largest source of tourist revenues in 2011. Beijing has also been a growing source of badly needed foreign direct investment, with China-financed projects across the Philippines worth nearly US$8 billion by some estimates. Despite concerns about corruption and transparency, China is still considered a key source of concessional loans, primarily in the area of infrastructure development, a core component of Aquino's economic agenda. In this light, Aquino's apparent approval of Trillanes' back-channel diplomacy was an attempt to balance competing interests and appease Beijing while not backing away publicly from his tough rhetoric on defending the country's territorial integrity. The Scarborough Shoal crisis further poisoned bilateral relations when China resorted to punitive economic sanctions, from non-tariff barriers on Filipino agricultural exports to the issuance of travel advisories for Chinese citizens planning to visit the Philippines. Hardline elements within China pushed for more extensive sanctions to punish the Philippines (Cayabyab 2012; Corr and Tacujan 2013; Wolf et al. 2013).

Collapse in talks Aside from the fact that the back-door diplomatic efforts failed to secure the Philippines' interest in retaining a measure of control over the Scarborough Shoal, the Aquino administration was also snubbed by President Hu Jintao, effectively terminating hopes for high-level talks to ease bilateral differences. On 5 September 2012 Philippine president Benigno Aquino issued Administrative Order 29, which officially renames the South China Sea the West Philippine Sea on national maps. After making the executive order, he notably failed days later to meet Chinese president Hu Jintao on the sidelines of the Asia-Pacific Economic Cooperation (APEC) meeting held in Russia. The controversial order aimed to firm up Manila's claims to disputed features within its EEZ. Aquino justified the action by saying 'it is important to clarify which portions we claim as ours versus the entirety of the South China Sea'. The move was also interpreted as a quasi-legal manoeuvre to compel the USA to stand by the Philippines militarily over the Scarborough Shoal and other contested features claimed by Manila. At the same time, he expressed hopes for 'a dialog [with China] where we can have a heart-to-heart talk and share our thoughts in total honesty and openness'. China's Foreign Ministry swiftly dismissed the order, saying in a statement that 'China claims indisputable sovereignty over islands in the South China Sea'. It invoked Beijing's wide-ranging nine-dash map of its claimed territories over the maritime area, those claims including areas within the Philippines' 200-mile EEZ (Ubac 2012b). Running out of diplomatic options, Aquino tasked Interior Secretary Roxas to meet (21 September 2012) China's next leader, Xi Jingping, as a special envoy. Xi and Roxas were both heads of the ruling parties in Beijing, the CCP, and Manila, the Liberal Party, and anointed successors by the sitting presidents. But the Xi–Roxas exchanges failed to achieve any major breakthrough. 'I conveyed to vice president Xi [that] talk is better than no talk. So the fact that we are talking at the highest levels, the fact that messages are reliably conveyed, I think it's a good foundation,' Roxas said in a news briefing after the meeting. 'I think given the situation at least we are talking again with senior officials of the People's Republic of China, so that's a nice start,' Aquino added. The diplomatic niceties partly helped to ease bilateral tensions while China's leadership transition unfolded, but the pitched struggle between competing factions with divergent views towards China inside Aquino's administration remained wholly unresolved. Infighting became a serious concern within the Philippine ruling establishment. Earlier hopes that a leadership transition in China would help to ease tensions in the South China Sea faded as Beijing carved out a more assertive position in the contested waters.

The construction game In a move that promised to raise regional tensions, China stepped up construction work in contested territories in the South China Sea. In late September 2012, Beijing announced plans to accelerate the building of Sansha city, a newly formed administrative unit on Yongxing Island, internationally known as Woody Island, in the disputed Paracels archipelago. The city will oversee Beijing's administration of the Paracel islands, Macclesfield Bank, Scarborough Shoal and other assorted reefs, sandbanks and some two hundred small uninhabited islets and their surrounding waters in the contested Spratly islands. The People's Liberation Army (PLA) announced – without supplying detailed plans – the intention to build a military garrison at Sansha, a move that threatens greater militarization of the south. China's US$3 million construction plan included seven road projects with a total length of 5 kilometres, an inter-island transportation network with docking facilities, and a desalination unit with a 1,000-cubic-meter capacity to ensure freshwater supplies for the city's estimated 3,500 permanent inhabitants. Sansha city was upgraded to prefecture level on 24 July 2012 amid a naval stand-off with the Philippines over control of the adjacent Scarborough Shoal. China's announced building plans agitated the Philippines, which controls Thitu Island, one of the biggest features in the Spratly chain of islands, as well as Vietnam, which lays claim to the Paracel chain of islands. Both countries lodged official complaints against Sansha's upgraded status in mid-2012. In response, Manila summoned a senior Chinese diplomat to protest formally against growing construction activities in areas Philippine officials have consistently argued fall within their country's exclusive economic zone (EEZ). The complaint came soon after Philippine military officials spotted a number of Chinese vessels in the area, ranging from a salvage and research ship to cargo boats

unloading construction materials and building posts on Iroquois Bank
in the vicinity of the Spratly islands, just 125 nautical miles off the
coast of the Philippines' southern island of Palawan. Manila also raised
its voice against China's expressed plans to plant a 'mega oil rig' in the
area, raising the possibility of Chinese oil depots and installations near
Philippine shores. China is also reportedly planning to build an airstrip
at Subi Reef, just next to Philippine-controlled Thitu Island. The 3.7-
kilometre-wide contested reef housed two living quarters for Chinese
troops, two four-storey buildings and a large radar dome. The Armed
Forces of the Philippines (AFP) responded by deploying 800 marines
to Palawan, an island close to contested areas in the South China
Sea. 'These two battalions which arrived recently will be augmenting
protection of our islands. We are just on a defensive posture and are
ensuring the defense of our islands. It is better to defend than retake
islands once other claimants occupy them,' said Lieutenant General
Juancho Sabban, head of the AFP's Western Command, making veiled
reference to Mischief Reef, which China seized from the Philippines by
force in 1995. To bolster coordination and command over deployed
forces, the Philippines opened a new Marine Brigade headquarters
in nearby Palawan. 'Every time we take periodic pictures of all the
islands in the Spratlys, we notice some changes, we observe changes
in structures,' Sabban said, referring to recent Chinese construction
at Sansha. At the same time, the Philippines also said that it might
consider firing on Chinese surveillance drones that enter areas it claims
in the South China Sea. Yang Yujun, an official with China's Defence
Ministry, confirmed plans to use unmanned drones to monitor activity
in disputed areas of the South China Sea, including the Scarborough
Shoal, the Spratly islands and their adjacent waters. Yang asserted
China's 'indisputable sovereignty' over those areas in announcing
its use of drones (Agence France Presse 2012; Xinhua 2012). For
almost two decades, the Philippines watched anxiously as China has
fortified its claims in the South China Sea. In 1995, just three years
after the closure of US bases in the Philippines, China seized control
of Mischief Reef from Philippine forces. Soon thereafter, China built
structures resembling military installations on the reef, though Beijing
claimed at the time they were shelters for fishermen.

The Philippines is perhaps the only country that has failed to make any significant improvements to its structures in the nine islands and reefs it directly controls in the Spratly islands. Malaysia, another claimant state, has built spas and diving resorts on the Layang-Layang Reef, which it controls. China and Vietnam have built fortifications, watchtowers, lighthouses, airstrips and even buildings powered by solar panels in their respective areas of control. Most Philippine structures in the area date back to the 1960s and 1970s and are poorly maintained and deteriorating, diminishing the operational capacity as well as the morale of Philippine forces stationed in the area. Philippine officials cite their commitment to the 2002 conduct agreement as a reason for their lagging investment in maintaining and improving structures in the Spratly islands. As a relative latecomer, China has sought to catch up with some of its South-East Asian neighbours, which have managed to establish airstrips and various installations on disputed features in the Spratly chain of islands. Figure 4.3 shows the outposts

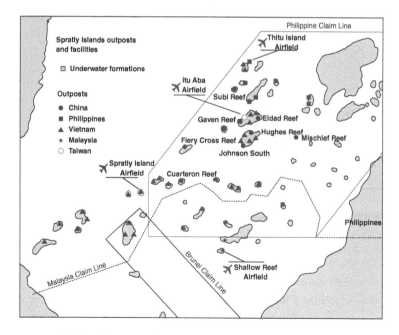

4.3 Islands and outposts of competing claimant states in the Spratlys.

and facilities of various claimant states, with Vietnam (21) leading in the number of features under its occupation, while the Philippines (9) and Taiwan (1) have occupied the biggest features, Thitu Island and Itu Aba respectively. There are an estimated 97 features (e.g., islands, rocks, caysand reefs) in the area, with at least 41 of them already occupied (Tordesillas 2014).

Commentators have pointed towards a lack of strategic foresight on the part of the Philippines, as the AFP has focused more on internal threats caused by various insurgencies across the country. As Roilo Golez,[11] the Philippines' former National Security Adviser, laments:

> The AFP concentrated too much on internal security and this was understandable during the 1980s and the early 1990s with the combined threat of the [communist] and the Mindanao secessionists. But the security environment changed in the 1990s. The leadership should have seen China's move towards the South China Sea, specifically our EEZ, with the Mischief Reef incident in 1995 up to 1999, with the initial grab then the construction of concrete structures there. Congress enacted the AFP Modernization Act in 1993, which included the AFP Modernization Trust Fund. P7.8 billion was supposed to go to that fund from the sale in the 1990s of Fort Bonifacio but this did not happen. ... [T]his fund is [still] missing ... Nothing was achieved by way of minimum deterrence during the 1990s and 2000s ... Planning was dominated by internal defence officers. The defence and security leadership looked inward and ignored the China threat in spite of the warnings.

China's build-up could serve as a foundation for fortifications that enable large-scale future military deployments, with Sansha city serving as the core location for coordinating operations across the South China Sea. But Filipino officials, for a long time, ignored the strategic significance of China's construction activities. Golez explains:[12] 'The problem with some so-called military analysts is that they measure territorial importance almost in number of square kilometers and ask, why quarrel over small rocks in the middle of the ocean. They seem

---

[11] Interview with the author, 29 August 2014.
[12] Ibid.

to ignore the strategic value of a string of rocks and reefs and shoals that are convertible into potent military stations to control the vast sea around them.'

The gloves are off During his late-2012 address at the UN General Assembly in New York, Philippine foreign secretary Albert Del Rosario made an emphatic speech to rally global support for his country's rule-of-law position vis-à-vis China over ongoing territorial disputes in the South China Sea. 'Today my country faces its most serious challenge to the security of its maritime domain and integrity of its national territory, as well as its effective protection of its marine environment,' said Del Rosario. 'The UN Convention on the Law of the Sea has never been more relevant than it is today, all States must respect their obligations to settle their maritime disputes by peaceful means, without threats or use of force under UNCLOS.' In a veiled criticism of China's growing assertiveness, he called for a 'rule-based approach' to avoid weaker countries being forced to accept that 'might is right'. His speech was a clear appeal for greater international intervention while portraying the Philippines as a responsible member of the international community – and not just an instrument of America's Pivot to Asia to contain China (Tagala 2012). The Philippines continued its diplomatic offensive, taking advantage of its hosting of the third ASEAN Maritime Forum (AMF) in 2012, which brought together leading experts as well as high-level representatives from across the Pacific. The forum provided a crucial platform for Manila to refocus ASEAN efforts on the issue of maritime security, emphasizing the need for regional solidarity and increased cooperation. Manila had earlier failed to win sufficient support for its diplomatic proposals, especially regarding a binding regional code of conduct (CoC) for the South China Sea, during both the 2011 ASEAN Regional Forum (ARF) in Indonesia and the 2012 ASEAN Ministerial Meeting (AMM) in Cambodia, where Phnom Penh – allegedly under Beijing's influence – blocked even the inclusion of the ongoing disputes in the South China Sea in the final communiqué.

With the fate of a regional CoC in limbo and growing concerns over strategic rifts within ASEAN, the Philippines was desperate to inject some life back into its diplomatic efforts and steer a more unified regional approach. On 3 October, the Philippines hosted the third AMF, a confab that assembled senior foreign ministry officials from across South-East Asia for a three-day event focused on interrelated maritime issues such as maritime connectivity, the marine environment, sea piracy, search and rescue at sea, fisheries, and maritime security. The forum built on the conclusions of the 6th East Asia Summit, where EAS leaders underscored the importance of maritime cooperation and security. Aside from being the region's primary forum for the discussion of maritime issues, the year's AMF was also the first Expanded ASEAN Maritime Forum (EAMF), which brought together all eighteen members of the broader pan-regional East Asia Summit. Significantly, the Chinese Foreign Ministry refused to divulge the identity of its representatives ahead of the forum, while there were hints that the Japanese representatives would attempt to discuss the ongoing dispute with China over the Senkaku islands in the East China Sea. Filipino officials were straightforward about their objectives for the forum. 'The Philippines would like to positively engage our partners to discuss cross-cutting maritime issues and explore ways and means to enhance activities aimed at bolstering maritime security and cooperation in East Asia,' said Foreign Affairs Assistant Secretary Raul Hernandez. Simultaneously, the Philippines expressed its desire to open sensitive discussions with the Chinese and Americans while rallying support from both ASEAN members and varying strategic partners across the Pacific for a more concrete security architecture to oversee ongoing territorial disputes. The Philippines thus sought to put ongoing disputes under the spotlight in a bid to build urgency around the need for a more binding CoC. It also highlighted 'freedom of navigation' issues related to the disputes. Back in 2010, during the ASEAN Regional Forum (ARF) in Hanoi, the USA showed favour towards Vietnam and the Philippines, when it indirectly chastised China's growing assertiveness in the South China Sea and identified 'freedom of navigation' as a national interest, carving out a place for it at the centre of ongoing territorial disputes in the South China Sea. Ahead of the forum, US Secretary of State Hillary Clinton expressed Washington's support for the objectives and format of the event by stating, 'All 18 East Asia Summit states have been invited for in-depth discussions on how to improve safety on the region's waterways, combat piracy, protect the environment, and we are encouraged by the recent informal dialogue between ASEAN and China as they work toward a comprehensive code of conduct for the South China Sea as a means to prevent future tension in the region.' To underscore the forum's importance in the eyes of the Filipino leadership, Vice-President Jejomar Binay was also in attendance. In his keynote speech, he couched his statements in the more benign language of regional maritime cooperation by emphasizing the need to rein in growing NTS (Non-Traditional Security) challenges while ensuring the steady flow of energy shipments across vital regional sea lanes. He also underscored the AMF's utility as a platform for continuous maritime strategic cooperation. 'It is therefore of vital importance to secure sea lanes communication and continue combating piracy to ensure freedom and safety of navigation in the seas of Southeast Asia,' Binay said. 'Without duplicating the work of relevant ASEAN bodies, the ASEAN Maritime Forum should be institutionalized as the comprehensive and cooperative platform for strategic engagement.' Owing to the sensitivity of the issues on the agenda, potential areas of cooperation among member countries were initially discussed behind closed doors. The chairman's statement from the third AMF, however, raised two significant points: (1) participants' emphasis on respecting international law, including the 1982 United Nations Convention on the Law of the Sea (UNCLOS) and the 2002 ASEAN Declaration on the Conduct of Parties in the South China Sea (DOC), as well as the grouping's recent Six Point Principles on the South China Sea; and (2) the participants' recognition of the critical role of sharing information and best practices. On the first day of the forum, the Philippines put forward a proposal for a regional information-sharing system to supposedly protect South-East Asia's waters against a whole range of 'threats', including drug trafficking, gun smuggling, human trafficking, illegal fishing and weather disturbances. According to the proposal, the system would 'provide timely, relevant and material information to appropriate action agencies to enable them to combat non-traditional security threats at sea'. To avoid controversy and ensure engagement among participants with conflicting positions, the proposal's wording was intentionally vague. In particular, it failed to specify the mechanics of 'information-sharing' and omitted any mention of territorial disputes in the South China Sea. The Philippines managed through diplomacy to return the issue of maritime security and the need for cooperation back to the centre of regional official discussions (Agence France Presse 2013).

The legal weapon In early 2013, the Philippines (under Article 287 and Annexe VII of the UNCLOS) initiated court proceedings,[13] filing Notification and Statement of Claim against Beijing's sweeping claims and assertive behaviour in the South China Sea. The aim was to (indirectly) reinforce Manila's claim to a number of features within its 200-nautical-mile exclusive economic zone (EEZ) by directly questioning the legality of China's historical claims in the South China Sea on the basis of international law, specifically the provisions of the UNCLOS. The UNCLOS, which came into effect in the immediate aftermath of the end of the Cold War, provided new sets of principles to guide maritime sovereignty claims, determine maritime delimitation issues and steer a rules-based resolution of territorial disputes. As a signatory to the UNCLOS, all key claimant states in the South China Sea are expected to play by the existing rules of the game. (Although Washington is not a signatory to the UNCLOS, thanks to the intransigence of a hardline minority in the US Senate, it has observed the principles of UNCLOS in actual policy.) Table 4.3 highlights key developments in the arbitration proceedings.

---

[13] An arbitral tribunal at The Hague oversees the case, while the Permanent Court of Arbitration (PCA) serves as its registry. The arbitral tribunal (under Art. 3 of UNCLOS Annex VII) is composed of a five-member panel, the Philippines nominating Rudiger Wolfrum, the president of the International Tribunal on the Law of the Sea (ITLOS) appointing three members of the panel, plus Stanislav Polack, who was nominated by the head of ITLOS (under Annex VII) in light of China's refusal to nominate a panel member. The arbitral tribunal is independent of both PCA and ITLOS. Owing to concerns over conflict of interest, one of the judges, Chris Pinto, was replaced by Thomas Mensah, who later became the president of the tribunal.

TABLE 4.3 Key developments in the *Philippines* v. *China* South China Sea arbitration

Date	Arbitration proceedings
23 January 2013	Philippines filed Notification and Statement of Claim (NSC) in the South China Sea
19 February 2013	China formally rejected the Philippines' NSC, a position it reiterated on 1 August 2013
11 July 2013	The arbitration panel met at the Peace Palace in The Hague
30 March 2014	The Philippines submitted a 4,000-page *Memorial*
15 December 2014	China failed to submit a counter-memorial
16 March 2015	The Philippines submitted a 3,000-page supplemental memorial
15 June 2015	Deadline for China to respond

Source: Batongbacal (2015).

But China boycotted the entire proceedings. Although China is a signatory to the UNCLOS, having ratified the convention in 2006, it has refused to subject its territorial claims to third-party arbitration, as expressed in a 2006 written statement to the UN secretary general, in which it opted out (under Article 287 of UNCLOS) of compulsory arbitration with respect to issues concerning 'maritime delimitation, territory and military activities'. Article 9 of UNCLOS Annexe VII, however, does not prevent the arbitration proceedings from moving forward in the event of one party's refusal to participate (Batongbacal 2015). But China's refusal to engage in the arbitration process could ultimately undermine the Philippines' legal strategy. As Batongbacal[14] explains:

> There is really no precedent for a case where one party has absolutely refused to participate from the very beginning. Even the case of *Nicaragua* v. *US*, wherein the US did not recognise the jurisdiction of the International Court of Justice, had the US contesting jurisdiction in the preliminary phase of the proceedings; also, the ICJ deemed that it was seized of jurisdiction because of certain technicalities in the terms of the US withdrawal from jurisdiction. Philippine claims to the Spratly Island chain are sound, on the basis of effective occupation, and its claims to the maritime areas around them are likewise credible on the basis of modern international law.

[14] Interview with the author, 21 July 2015.

By pushing ahead with the arbitration, the Philippines hoped to rally the international community behind its own cause, portraying China as a legal pariah. In spite of China's refusal to participate in the proceedings, the Philippines believed that the arbitration could still be pursued. Since China is party to UNCLOS, the Philippine government contends that Annexe VII of UNCLOS grants the UN arbitral tribunal in The Hague jurisdiction to pursue the arbitration.

This was by no means an easy choice. On one hand, filing the case risked permanent estrangement with China, the total collapse of bilateral ties, and the increased probability of economic sanctions as well as military confrontation in the South China Sea. Even if the Philippines manages to get a favourable verdict, there would be no existing 'enforcement mechanism' to ensure China respects the outcome of the arbitration. The Philippines' legal complaint further heightened bilateral tensions with China, which, in turn, hardened its position on any ASEAN-mediated diplomatic solution to the dispute, namely on the issues of (a) establishing a legally binding CoC and (b) freezing construction activities and maritime patrols across disputed waters. Arguably, the Philippines' unprecedented decision to take China to court over the ongoing territorial disputes has had a negative impact on bilateral trade and investment relations, with Beijing seemingly withholding large-scale investments from the South-East Asian country. While China stands as a leading source of capital and affordable technology for developing countries around the world, the Philippines, quite astonishingly, has made more direct investments in China than the other way around. According to the Chinese ambassador, Zhao Jianhua, the Philippines has been a recipient of less than 2 per cent of China's total outbound investments, which have amounted to US$90 billion in recent years (Agence France Presse 2014a). By some accounts, the Philippines is deliberately excluded from China's ambitious Maritime Silk Road initiative, a multibillion-dollar infrastructure development bonanza to be funded by China across the ASEAN area (Browne 2014). With the exception of the Philippines, China is the top trading partner of almost all East Asian economies. More importantly, there is hardly any sustained, formal high-level dialogue between the two countries, especially above ambassadorial level. Since Xi Jinping's ascent to power, the Philippines is yet to host the Chinese president, premier or even foreign minister. While China has worked on confidence-building measures with Vietnam and Japan, the Philippines is yet to negotiate a single hotline with its Chinese counterparts. In short, diplomatic ties have been frozen amid the arbitration showdown. Moreover, as Batongbacal[15] argues, there is a possibility that the Philippines will receive an unfavourable verdict: 'The problem, however, is that Philippines' actions since the 1970s have not been very consistent in terms of consolidating our sovereignty and jurisdiction over the area. If the Philippines were to litigate sovereignty over the islands, the outcome would not be certain because we are looking at over forty years of activities, some good, some bad, for the determination of sovereignty and jurisdiction.'

Shortly before the 15 December deadline to submit its counter-memorial to the arbitral tribunal, China released (7 December) a position paper, which forwarded three major arguments: first, the arbitration body has no jurisdiction over the Philippines' complaint, which fundamentally concerns questions of sovereignty; secondly, China has 'indisputable and inherent sovereignty' over the disputed features in the South China Sea, since its 'historical rights' transcend the jurisdiction of the UNCLOS; and lastly, the Philippines has violated prior agreements, both bilateral and multilateral, by initiating compulsory arbitration over the South China Sea disputes. The Philippines, however, maintains that on the contrary it is China which has violated prior agreements, particularly the 2002 DOC, which explicitly discourages competing parties from unilaterally altering the status quo in disputed areas. In recent years, China has expanded construction activities in both the Paracel and Spratly islands, widened its paramilitary patrols across disputed waters and coercively challenged the Philippines' claims in the Scarborough Shoal (2012) and the Second Thomas Shoal (since mid-2013). To skirt around the issue of sovereignty, which transcends the jurisdiction of the arbitral tribunal, the Philippines astutely framed its case as one that concerns (i) the determination of the validity of China's claims based on the provisions of the UNCLOS; (ii) the determination of the nature of

15 Ibid.

the disputed features (Article 121), specifically whether they can be appropriated, as well as generate their own territorial waters; and (iii) the claiming that China has been coercively preventing the Philippines from rightfully exploiting marine and hydrocarbon resources within its EEZ. In fact, the Philippines maintains that China's occupation of numerous features within its EEZ, Johnson South, McKennan, Cuarteron, Subi, Fiery Cross, Gavenand Mischief reefs, and Scarborough Shoal, is illegal (Batongbacal 2015). Legal experts such as Alexander Proelss[16] are doubtful whether the arbitral tribunal will exercise jurisdiction over the case, a decision that should come three to six months after the 15 June 2015 deadline for China to respond to the Philippines' supplemental memorial:

> Concerning jurisdiction in the *Philippines* v. *China* arbitration, the tribunal will have to (1) deal with the declaration submitted by China in terms of Art. 298 UNCLOS, and (2) answer the question raised by China of whether Part XV UNCLOS (including the question of whether the tribunal is competent to decide on its jurisdiction under Art. 288 (4)) is at all applicable. My prediction is that taking into account that many of the arguments raised by the Philippines at least indirectly affect the question of sovereignty over some of the territorial features in the marine area concerned (notwithstanding contrary statements submitted by the Philippines), the tribunal might be forced to deny its jurisdiction over some of the claims invoked by the Philippines. In my opinion, the initiation of compulsory arbitration by the Philippines thus carries the risk that China's position might be more advantageous following the arbitration than prior to it. At the same time, should the tribunal come to the conclusion that it has jurisdiction over the majority of claims, China will be forced to clarify the legal status of its 'nine-dash-line'. Other coastal states in the area which have disputes with China over marine areas and features in the SCS are therefore recommended to carefully study the outcome of the *Philippines* v. *China* arbitration concerning jurisdiction. Ultimately, I think compulsory arbitration will turn out to be one tool in the quest for resolving the disputes in the SCS, but certainly not the only one.

---

[16] Interview with the author, 26 March 2015, Hanoi.

Beyond sovereignty claims, the very credibility of international law is also at stake. As Columbia University professor Matthew C. Waxman (2014) succinctly puts it, 'For the UNCLOS system – as a body of rules and binding dispute settlement mechanisms – prominence and credibility are at stake. A decision that the arbitral panel has jurisdiction' could put the arbitration body at risk of 'being ignored, derided and marginalized by the biggest player in the region'. In the end, there may be no clear winners in the legal battle.

Nudging up the crisis In late 2012, China pushed ahead with an announcement that Chinese patrol vessels would, beginning in 2013, 'intercept and board' any foreign vessels in areas over which it claims sovereignty in the South China Sea, representing the gravest threat yet to freedom of navigation in an area crucial to global trade. Adding to the tensions, Beijing also issued new passports for its citizens which bear an official Chinese map that incorporates all contested territories in the South China Sea. In mid-2013, tensions between China and the Philippines once again spiked as the two sides jostled for control over another contested feature. Nearly one year after Chinese paramilitary forces and the Philippine navy squared off precariously over the contested Scarborough Shoal, the Second Thomas Shoal (known as 'Ren'ai' in China and 'Ayungin' in the Philippines) emerged as a new regional flashpoint. The newly contested shoal is 168 kilometres off the Philippine western island of Palawan and almost 965 kilometres from the nearest Chinese port. It has been under the de facto control of Philippine forces for over a decade, with Manila arguing that the shoal is well within its 200-nautical-mile exclusive economic zone (EEZ). Beijing has repeatedly referred to Manila's claims over the island and reefs in the area as 'illegal occupations'. To mark Manila's claim, a small contingent of Filipino marines has been perched on a rusty hospital ship (BRP *Sierra Madre*) that ran aground on the coral reef in 1999. By late May 2013, a Chinese flotilla, including a naval frigate, surrounded the small contingent of Filipino marines, raising accusations that Beijing intentionally blocked their access to supplies. In response, Manila dispatched a new contingent of marines with fresh supplies of fuel, food and water. On 21 June 2013 Beijing referred to

Manila's occupation of the shoal as 'illegal'. On 15 July 2013, the Philippine Foreign Ministry issued an eight-point statement, claiming China's provocations had made it 'impossible' to continue bilateral negotiations on their territorial disputes. China's Foreign Ministry fired back the next day, saying it was 'dissatisfied' over Manila's 'closure of the door to dialogue'. For the Philippines, maintaining control over the Second Thomas Shoal is not only a question of preserving territorial integrity (Baruah 2014). The shoal also serves as a critical gateway to the currently Philippine-controlled Reed Bank, situated 80 nautical miles from Palawan and estimated to possess among the largest reserves of untapped oil and gas in the western Pacific. Crucially, the bulk of projected undiscovered hydrocarbon deposits lies specifically within the Reed Bank and surrounding areas. In 1976, the Philippines started exploration and development activities in the Reed Bank area, complementing the nearby Shell-operated Malampaya Natural Gas Field, which is responsible for 40–50 per cent of power generation for the industrializing northern island of Luzon. With the natural gas facility set to exhaust its 2.7 trillion cubic feet of reserves in the next decade, Reed Bank is viewed by Manila as crucial to the nation's future energy security. The Philippines currently imports around 40 per cent of its energy needs, which are fast growing with recent strong economic growth. Lacking sophisticated technology and sufficient capital, the Philippines has historically relied on foreign companies to develop its offshore hydrocarbon resources. For Reed Bank, Manila enlisted the support of the US-based Sterling Energy in 2002 and the UK-based Forum Energy in 2005. The Recto Bank concession, or SC-72, has so far been composed of three drilled wells located at the south-west end of the complex. Since 2008, Forum Energy has been joined by Monte Oro Resources & Energy Inc., forming an Anglo-Filipino consortium to manage the concession. Forum Energy holds a 70 per cent stake in SC-72. A subsequent 2D and 3D seismic interpretation study was conducted by Weatherford Petroleum consultants and revealed that the Sampaguita Field within the concession area contained 5.5 TCF (trillion cubic feet) of prospective in-place gas resources and 2.6 TCF of contingent in-place gas resources, plus possible gas-associated condensates. Forum Energy's own estimates put the gas field's gross reserves at over 11 TCF, dwarfing the size of the now semi-exhausted Malampaya. In short, the Reed Bank is a viable and potentially game-changing hydrocarbon reservoir close to both China and the Philippines in the South China Sea (Energy Information Agency n.d.). The previous Gloria Macapagal-Arroyo administration (2001–10) – allegedly swayed by Chinese economic sweeteners such as big-ticket infrastructural and investment pledges – agreed to slow the development of Reed Bank and join the JMSU (2005–08), which sought the joint exploration of hydrocarbon resources in the contested waters. Arroyo's agreement, however, was shunned by the incumbent Benigno Aquino administration, which since taking office in mid-2010 has pushed for the immediate development of the Reed Bank and protection of what Manila deems as its rightful claim to the area. Since then, Manila has claimed that Chinese paramilitary vessels have actively sabotaged oil exploration activities in the area. In late 2011, for example, Philippine navy chief Vice-Admiral Alexander Pama reported an 'accidental collision' in which a Philippine navy gunboat (PS-74) allegedly fended off a Chinese mother ship escorting up to twenty-five smaller boats. This confrontation presaged the month-long stand-off in 2012 over the Scarborough Shoal, over which China has since asserted virtual control. Philippine energy companies have raised similar alarms. 'If Chinese gunboats appear on the horizon, then there could be delays as those rigs and survey ships are owned by other countries,' said Manny Pangilinan, chairman of Philex Petroleum Corp., the majority owner of Forum Energy, in mid-2012. By January 2013, citing territorial disputes with China, Forum Energy delayed plans to drill two new wells in SC-72 until 2015. In March 2015, however, the company again cited the ongoing disputes as a reason to postpone any drilling activity in the area (GMA News 2015).

Courting American boots Sensing the rapidly deteriorating situation, Aquino pushed for tighter security ties with the USA. By September 2013, the Philippines had provisionally agreed to allow a stronger US military presence on its soil, as tensions mounted with China over contested territories in the South China Sea. The proposed agreement provided a framework for the semi-permanent 'rotational' stationing of

American troops and military hardware in the Philippines, representing potential strategic ballast to the USA's efforts to counterbalance China's influence in the region. Beginning in July 2013, after a series of bilateral talks throughout 2011 and 2012, Manila and Washington engaged in several rounds of intensive negotiations over a new strategic arrangement between the two treaty allies. Since the closure of US military bases in the Philippines in 1992, the two countries have been bound by the 1998 Visiting Forces Agreement (VFA), which allows for the stationing on a rotational basis of a limited number of US troops in the Philippines. Under the VFA, US troops provided logistical, intelligence and alleged operational support to the armed forces of the Philippines' ongoing campaign in the country's southernmost regions against Islamic rebels, including the al-Qaeda-affiliated ASG. In light of the Philippines' struggle to build a minimum deterrence capability against external threats, including China, the US agreement was expected to potentially allow Filipino troops to use American hardware currently stationed at Philippine bases. The agreement was advertised, especially by the Aquino administration, as a potential game-changer in the ongoing regional competition over disputed features in the South China Sea by boosting the Philippines' ability to more decisively defend its claims and hedge against further Chinese territorial assertiveness. The Philippines and the USA have held annual joint military exercises, with most recent manoeuvres taking place near contested areas in the South China Sea. The proposed agreement was meant to send an even stronger message to China about the USA's commitment to maintaining stability in the maritime area. On at least four occasions, the USA has communicated in varying degrees its willingness to come to the Philippines' aid in the event of a confrontation in the South China Sea, couched in terms of Washington's commitment to maintain 'freedom of navigation' in the area. During the Jimmy Carter administration, then US Secretary of State Cyrus Vance clarified that the treaty covered both 'an attack against the metropolitan territory of the Philippines as well as an attack on Philippine forces in the Pacific Area'. Even in the post-Cold War period, when US bases in the Philippines were closed amid the dissolution of the Soviet Union's naval threat, the Bill Clinton administration asserted 'the South China Sea to be part of the Pacific

Area' (Malig 2012). At the time, Manila may have read the statement to mean that an attack on Philippine troops in the South China Sea would compel an American response. Despite Washington's increased military support to the Philippines, the latter was largely treated by the George W. Bush administration as an instrument for the broader strategy of containing Islamic extremists. Under Bush, there was no significant US aid for or investment in improving the Philippines' minimum deterrence capabilities against external threats. Rather, US-backed counter-terrorism operations merely reinforced the Philippines' domestic-oriented security doctrine, which was primarily focused on confronting local insurgent groups on the southern island of Mindanao and communist-related groups spread throughout the country. The Philippines' post-Cold War constitutional restriction on the establishment of permanent foreign bases on local soil also served as an obstacle to a fully fledged realignment of US forces in the region, with the likes of Singapore and Australia taking the initiative to welcome a stronger US military presence ahead of treaty allies such as the Philippines. Confronting a significantly more powerful and suddenly more assertive China, the Philippines was in significant need of US aid. Figure 4.4 details US military assistance to the Philippines in recent years.

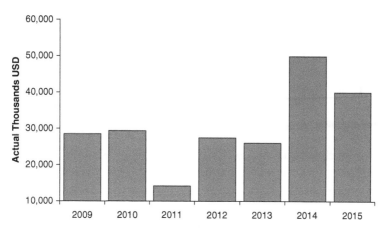

4.4 US military assistance to the Philippines (2009–15) (*source*: US State Department).

By mid-2013, the USA had begun to sharpen its tone towards China's assertiveness in the South China Sea. This was most evident in its response to China's push into Philippine-controlled features such as the Second Thomas Shoal, which saw Washington explicitly criticize any unilateral seizure of contested territories in the South China Sea. It provided a pretext for the USA's more vigorous push for a bolstered military presence in the Philippines. After an initial round of bilateral negotiations in July 2013 over a new basing agreement, US Secretary of Defense Chuck Hagel made a high-profile visit to Manila in late August 2013, meeting Philippine president Benigno Aquino as well as defence secretary Voltaire Gazmin. 'The United States does not seek permanent bases in the Philippines – that would represent a return to an outdated Cold War mentality,' Hagel said after meeting Aquino. 'We are using a new model of military-to-military cooperation befitting two great allies and friends.' In exchange for allowing a greater US military presence in the Philippines, Hagel said Washington would help in 'building a modern military' as well as sharing 'what we've [the USA] learned with our Filipino allies'. When pressed on how China would be likely to respond to the proposed agreement, Hagel stated that the region could not meet its economic potential 'without stability, without security' – a thinly veiled jab at China's supposed contribution to regional insecurity. Shortly before Hagel's visit, the two country's military chiefs, General Emmanuel Bautista and General Martin Dempsey, signed a joint statement in Washington affirming both sides' commitment to the 1951 MDT. Hagel's visit was meant to iron out differences and prepare the ground for forthcoming negotiations in Washington to finalize the new 'rotational' basing agreement. The USA pushed for a twenty-year rotational presence agreement, provoking legal debates over its constitutionality (Mogato 2013).

A small diplomatic window Irked by Philippine–US moves to deepen their military alliance, and simmering tensions over Manila's decision to take Beijing to court, China abruptly rescinded its invitation to Aquino to visit the 10th Association of Southeast Asian Nations–China Economic Expo held in Nanning in September of 2013[17], raising

---

[17] http://www.chinaexhibition.com/trade_events/3427-CAEXPO_2013_-_The_10th_China-ASEAN_Expo.html.

new concerns over already deteriorating Philippine–China bilateral relations. The 10th CAEXPO in Nanning – where the Philippines was the 'country of honour' – represented a perfect opportunity to break the ice in bilateral relations, a unique opportunity for Aquino to meet his Chinese counterparts, whether President Xi Jinping or Premier Li Keqiang. Manila acknowledged that the establishment of a more robust US military presence in the Philippines would take time to scale up; meanwhile, China's boycott of the Philippines' arbitration efforts also dampened the prospects of a swift, favourable ruling. Expansive bilateral trade and investment relations between China and the Philippines also served as impetus for reviving bilateral diplomatic ties and avoiding confrontation. However, earlier hopes that Aquino's presence at CAEXPO would put business interests ahead of security imperatives were dashed by his rescinded invitation to the event. 'If the President will come to the CAEXPO, I am sure he can attract more Chinese investments into the Philippines and sell more Philippine products over there,' the Philippine Chamber of Commerce and Industry's president, Miguel Varela, said in late August 2013, emphasizing how Aquino's visit to China was seen as a crucial step towards promoting the interests of Filipino industrialists and businessmen interested in China. 'This is a great opportunity for us to promote the Philippines not just to the Chinese but to the rest of the world.' Aquino's own statements, however, suggested that the planned visit would have gone beyond mere economic diplomacy. There was a clear effort to initiate high-level talks on the sidelines of the event, paving the way for a reopening of bilateral diplomatic channels. To downplay expectations of a major diplomatic breakthrough, Aquino decided to limit his trip to a single day, citing his wish not to 'overstay' his welcome. So when China, mainly in reaction to Hagel's push for a twenty-year rotational military presence in the Philippines, and shortly after his tense exchanges with Chinese officials over rising tensions in the South China Sea, rescinded its invitation to Aquino and subsequently denied that it had earlier sought his presence, it signalled to many analysts a hardening of Beijing's position. A commentary by China's state media agency Xinhua summed up the reason for withdrawing Aquino's invitation, effectively accusing the Philippines of diplomatic duplicity: 'On the one hand, the Philippines [has] referred the dispute in the South China Sea to a United Nations tribunal for arbitration ... [while] pursuing a "hard-line" approach by begging [for] military help from the United States and even Japan' (Liming 2013). The situation was further complicated when Filipino officials claimed that Chinese officials made 'subsequent concerns and conditions to the President's attendance'. The cancellation of Aquino's visit was thus touted by officials as a decision to 'stand firm in the defense of the country's national interest'. Subsequent reports suggested that Chinese officials made Aquino's visit conditional on the Philippines withdrawing its UNCLOS case at The Hague and pulling out its troops and grounded vessel at the contested Second Thomas Shoal – conditions to which Manila would never agree. Adding fuel to the fire, Philippine defence secretary Voltaire Gazmin, citing aerial photos taken by Philippine armed forces, reported the presence of Chinese coastguard ships and about thirty concrete blocks around the Scarborough Shoal. Describing the move as a 'prelude to construction', Gazmin characterized Chinese actions as a glaring violation of the 2002 Declaration on the Conduct of Parties in the South China Sea, which discouraged disputing states from (forcibly) occupying contested features in the area. 'First rocks, then a pile driver, then a foundation ... When you get back again, if you don't survey, there will be a garrison,' Gazmin warned during his testimony to the Philippine Congress, where he pushed for more legislative support for boosting the military's deterrence capabilities and seeking more external military support. 'The important thing is we put men there, so this can be prevented ... [But] we don't have the capability to do that at the moment.' The depth of the diplomatic crisis was evident when the Philippine Department of Foreign Affairs recalled its top representative to China, Ambassador Erlinda Basilio, for a special consultation over the brewing crisis related to China's decision to apparently lay up to seventy-five concrete blocks in the Scarborough Shoal's vicinity. Filipino officials feared that China was moving closer to consolidating its hold on the contested feature, similar to how it won control of the Mischief Reef in the Spratly islands after its seizure by Chinese forces in 1995 (Ten Kate 2013; Magkilat 2013).

Obama's no-show After weeks of intense build-up for US president Barack Obama's Asian tour in October 2013, when many expected the American leader to make a strong pitch for a bigger US strategic footprint in the region, an untimely and bitter deadlock in Washington forced the cancellation of his trip. Amid the first federal government shutdown since the Clinton administration, the White House first announced Obama's decision to skip state visits to Malaysia and the Philippines. Later high-profile visits to Indonesia for the Asia-Pacific Economic Cooperation summit (APEC) and Brunei for the Association of Southeast Asian Nations Summit (ASEAN) were also nixed. While various Asian partners politely expressed their appreciation of Obama's domestic priorities, there was a palpable sense of absence. Given lingering anxieties over US commitment to the region amid oncoming steep defence budget cuts and the continued focus on crises in the Middle East as a policy priority, many Asian allies had hoped Obama would use his Asia trip to shore up support and signal deeper engagement. 'While politically we understand the reason for the president's decision, of course it is disappointing for all those involved,' a Bruneian foreign ministry official said on condition of anonymity. 'I'm sure people looked forward to the pageantry of a presidential visit.' Among the region's most vocal and proactive strategic players, Singapore prime minister Lee Hsien Loong was uncharacteristically straightforward in his assessment: 'America has to continue to be engaged in this region because it plays a very important role which no other country can replace, not China, not Japan, not any other power.' Obama's absence in the major Asian gatherings reinforced two fundamental perceptions among allies and adversaries alike. First, it signalled their relative secondary status in Obama's strategic calculus. Secondly, and perhaps more importantly, the shutdown crisis laid bare the downside of US democracy, exposing ugly ideological rifts and undermining the credibility of the country's state institutions. Considering also an anaemic economic recovery, many Asian allies now wonder whether the USA has the political or economic wherewithal to serve as an anchor of stability in the Asia-Pacific.

In the meantime, Obama reached out to strategic adversaries, ranging from his early June 2013 shirtsleeved summit with Chinese president Xi Jinping at the exclusive Sunnylands estate in California, to his historic late September phone call with Iranian president Hassan Rouhani in New York. In contrast, Obama was yet to visit Manila. While the Philippines held the world's highest favourable rating (at 85 per cent) towards the USA, according to a Pew Global Attitudes Project survey in 2013, it was also deeply dependent on American military support to confront security challenges on both its southern (Mindanao) and northern (South China Sea) fronts. Obama's scheduled visit to Manila was thus being touted as both a symbolic and a tangible expression of Washington's commitment to US–Philippines bilateral relations. Shortly ahead of his expected arrival, top Filipino officials expressed hopes that the US leader's visit would coincide with the signing of a new defence framework agreement, which, if passed into law, would allow for an expanded rotational US military presence on Philippine soil, specifically in the Clark and Subic bases. '[Obama's visit] is quite important because it endorses the value of our relationship,' Philippine foreign secretary Albert Del Rosario said during a budget hearing in the Philippine Congress in late September, reflecting the government's anticipation at the time. 'We're hoping to get the framework agreement by that time, but we'll see what happens.' Given growing concerns over the constitutionality of the new proposed strategic agreement with the USA, with the Philippine government insisting that it was a purely executive agreement that did not require Senate ratification, Filipino officials hoped that Obama's star power would sway the general public and disarm critics in the legislature and civil society. There was a strong sense of strategic urgency behind the agreement. The Philippines was locked in a bitter territorial dispute with China over areas of the South China Sea. In absence of high-level bilateral meetings, communication channels effectively collapsed. For Filipino officials, Obama's visit could have helped to ease that rising sense of vulnerability and dispelled doubts about Washington's commitment to its treaty ally's national security.

Obama's chief economic carrot is the twelve-nation Trans-Pacific Partnership (TPP) free trade agreement, which aspires to embrace one third of world trade and about 40 per cent of global gross domestic product while excluding China. After eighteen rounds of negotiations, however, key political issues concerning restrictions on government procurement, curtailment of consumer access to public services and imposition of more stringent intellectual property rights emerged as sticking points. Obama's trip would have provided an opportunity to personally lobby Asian states like Japan, Malaysia and Vietnam, all currently sitting on the fence, to sign up to the TPP. China has been pushing for an alternative economic bloc, the Comprehensive Economic Cooperation in East Asia. With Obama's absence at the 2013 Asian summits, Xi was in the limelight. He was the first foreign leader to deliver a speech at the Indonesian parliament, served as the keynote speaker at the APEC summit, and was set to visit Malaysia to deepen bilateral relations and defuse tensions over South China Sea disputes. Translating economic prowess into strategic influence, Xi presented plans for a US$50 billion Asian Infrastructure Bank – rivalling the US–Japan-led Asian Development Bank – to woo South-East Asian neighbours. Meanwhile, Chinese premier Li Keqiang utilized his country's boosted status to brush aside disputes in the South China Sea, snubbing the Philippines and emphasizing the necessity for prioritizing economic ties over intractable territorial issues. Despite efforts by the USA, Japan and Australia to bring the South China Sea disputes to the heart of the ASEAN summit's agenda, the meeting ended with no clear plan for or momentum towards developing a binding code of conduct for a peaceful, rule-based resolution of the South China Sea disputes. Many in Manila had hoped Obama's presence and advocacy would have brought the issue to the summit's fore. The Sino-American rivalry for full-spectrum ascendancy in the region resulted in a zero-sum dynamic. In that game, Obama's no-show in Asia was widely viewed as a major strategic setback for the USA and created a sudden sense of isolation among its strategic Asian allies (Romero 2013; Agence France Presse 2013).

Aquino recalibrates After months of diplomatic confrontation, Philippine president Benigno Aquino sought to re-engage China by dialling down bilateral tensions and promoting the language of dialogue and cooperation. Significantly, the move came in the wake of US president Barack Obama's cancellation of his scheduled tour of Asia. Downplaying local criticism of China's purported ambivalence towards reaching a multilateral resolution to the ongoing territorial disputes in the South China Sea, Aquino opted to welcome Beijing's agreement in principle to negotiate a binding code of conduct (CoC) through the Association of Southeast Asian Nations (ASEAN). Contradicting his own cabinet members, namely Secretary of Defence Voltaire Gazmin, Aquino vigorously denied earlier accusations that China had placed concrete blocks at the contested Scarborough Shoal, purportedly as a prelude to establishing military fortifications in the area. At the same time, his government was conditionally supporting negotiations between major Filipino and Chinese companies to jointly develop hydrocarbon resources in the Reed Bank. Obama's absence at the regional summits (i.e. ASEAN and APEC) added momentum to local calls for re-engagement with China. The fourth round of Philippines–US negotiations in early October 2013 aimed at expanding Washington's rotational military presence in the country failed to provide a major breakthrough, with top Filipino negotiators pointing to 'major gaps in the critical provisions' of the new proposed framework agreement. 'There's more work needed to be done on these provisions that will define this agreement. Both parties recognize that we have to work on them with more deliberation,' said Defence Undersecretary Pio Lorenzo Batino after the inconclusive round of talks. Foreign Affairs Assistant Secretary Carlos Sorreta, the spokesperson for the Philippine negotiating panel, also noted a lack of agreement over 'major details of the substantive issues', and the need to 'make sure that this agreement would be mutually beneficial'. Although the exact details of the then ongoing negotiations were unknown, with critics lambasting their lack of transparency and raising concerns about the constitutionality of the process, news reports suggested that disagreements centred on the nature and duration of 'pre-positioning' of US defence equipment and 'ownership' of the equipment to be pre-positioned and the proposed facilities to be installed by the USA at Clark and Subic. Questions over how American forces would specifically aid their Filipino counterparts in maritime defence activities in the South China Sea, the 'added-value' of a new agreement beyond the VFA, which already facilitates annual and sustained joint exercises, as well as what type of equipment may be leased to Filipino forces on a rotational basis have all apparently vexed the negotiatiors. Obama's scheduled, then cancelled, 11/12 October 2013 visit to Manila was supposed to iron out these substantial differences. With stalled negotiations on a new security deal with the USA and Obama's recent no-show in Manila, Aquino sought to explore alternative channels of cooperation with China.

Aquino was particularly encouraged by talks between the Philippine-owned Forum Energy and the Chinese state-owned oil company China National Offshore Oil Corporation over a joint-exploration venture in the hydrocarbon-rich Reed Bank. The negotiations provided Manila with an opportunity to reopen communication channels with Beijing and temporarily shelve sovereignty issues in order to pursue mutual economic interests – injecting a constructive atmosphere into bilateral relations which will be crucial to any future territorial agreement. With Washington driving a hard bargain on a new security pact, Aquino seemed increasingly keen to engage rather than confront Beijing (Cheng 2013; Philippine Daily Inquirer 2013; Gomez 2013).

Burning bridges China began 2014 by signalling its intent to consolidate contested territorial claims in the South China Sea. Authorities in the southern Chinese province of Hainan introduced an amended maritime regulation that requires foreign fishing-related vessels to secure the permission of local authorities before entering China's claimed maritime jurisdiction. The new regulation was passed by Hainan's People's Congress in November and came into effect on 1 January. According to the state-owned China News Service, foreign vessels could be apprehended and face up to 500,000 yuan (US$91,800) in fines if they failed to secure entry permission from the relevant and responsible government department before entering areas of the South China Sea. The new measure was the second amendment to a 1993 provincial Fishery Law and is in line with a 2004 national maritime law that is designed to enforce the country's jurisdiction over adjacent waters. Anticipating the potential diplomatic fallout of the new measure, Chinese authorities tried to downplay the impact of the regulation by emphasizing its primary role as a clarification of pre-existing maritime legislation. '[China] has the right and responsibility to regulate the relevant islands and reefs as well as non-biological resources,' Foreign Ministry spokeswoman Hua Chunying stated, justifying the legality of the new measure. 'For more than 30 years, China's relevant fisheries laws and regulations have been consistently implemented in a normal way and have never caused any tension.' Hua went on to portray the new measure as an environmental regulation to ensure the conservation and sustainability of maritime resources in the South China Sea: 'The goal is to strengthen the security of fisheries resources and to openly and reasonably utilize and protect fisheries resources'. Critics claim that the new regulation provides a quasi-legal cover for China's bid to enforce its sweeping claims across a huge swath of contested waters. Based on Hainan Department of Ocean and Fisheries documents released in 2011, the provincial authorities claim jurisdiction over more than half of the South China Sea, or 2 million square kilometres out of a total of nearly 3.5 million square kilometres.

Shortly after the new regulation came into effect, Vietnamese media outlets reported the confiscation on 3 January of a Vietnamese fishing vessel by Chinese law enforcement authorities. The Vietnamese government, which has been negotiating a 'joint development' scheme with China in the contested Paracel islands, remained silent on the issue. Neighbouring countries such as the Philippines and Taiwan, as well as the United States, however, criticized China for allegedly stoking tensions through the new legal measure. Philippine authorities, at least initially, were more calculated in their response. Raul Hernandez, spokesman for the country's Department of Foreign Affairs (DFA), politely expressed Manila's displeasure at not being properly informed about the implementation of the new regulation and subsequently sought further 'clarification' from Chinese authorities through its embassy in Beijing. The DFA's initially cautious response marked a notable departure from its more explicit criticism of similar Chinese measures in the past.

In recent months, President Benigno Aquino's administration has sought to reopen communication channels with China by toning down rhetoric and emphasizing common areas of interest and the importance of dialogue. The tactical decision made in late 2013 to revise Manila's strategy towards Beijing has been evident in Aquino's repeated calls for direct talks with the Chinese leadership, his cautious endorsement of China's decision to once again negotiate a binding code of conduct in the South China Sea, and his decision to explicitly contradict his own cabinet members by rejecting reports that China allegedly began to place concrete blocks at the hotly contested Scarborough Shoal. With Washington's backing on the issue, the Philippines has since stepped up its rhetoric, with Hernandez later referring to the new regulation as a 'gross violation of international law' that 'escalates tensions, unnecessarily complicates the situation in the South China Sea and threatens the peace and stability of the region'. Manila's statement echoed Washington's criticism of the new measure. 'China has not offered any explanation or basis under international law for these extensive maritime claims,' State Department spokeswoman Jen Psaki stated, underscoring Washington's continued commitment to freedom of navigation in international waters. 'Our long-standing position has been that all concerned parties should avoid any unilateral action that raises tensions and undermines the prospects for a diplomatic or other peaceful resolution of differences.' Some analysts have played down the geopolitical implications of the new measure by emphasizing the variability and arbitrary nature of its implementation. 'I think Hainan put it out to tell relevant countries we have such a regulation, but how we practice it depends on how bilateral relations are,' Shi Yinhong, Professor of International Relations at Renmin University in Beijing, told *Reuters*. 'If ties are good, the regulation may be loose. If not, we will practice it strictly, which means that you have to get approval from us [Chinese authorities] before entering.' China's new maritime regulation comes against the backdrop of rising territorial tensions, fuelled in large part by Beijing's late-November decision to impose an air defence identification zone (ADIZ) in the East China Sea, which covers territories claimed by both South Korea (Ieodo/Suyan rock) and Japan (Senkaku/Diaoyu islands). Washington and its allies swiftly challenged the new measure by conducting military exercises in the area while warning China against interrupting freedom of flight in the region (Mogato and Wee 2014; Fravel 2014). This was followed by Japan's vigorous efforts to rally regional support against China. In an indirect criticism of China's ADIZ, Tokyo and the ten-member Association of Southeast Asian Nations (ASEAN) expressed their common concern over 'freedom of over-flight and civil aviation safety' during the ASEAN–Japan Summit in mid-December. For South-East Asian states such as the Philippines and Vietnam, the bigger concern was and is China's possible imposition of an ADIZ in the South China Sea. Against this backdrop, the latest maritime regulation in Hainan was viewed as a fallback option for China – in the tentative absence of an ADIZ for the area – to embolden its territorial claims across the western Pacific and respond to US-led efforts to contain its regional influence (see Chapter 5).

The free fall Efforts at bridging bilateral differences with China failed to produce a breakthrough. The Philippines risked permanent estrangement with China by pressing ahead (30 March 2014) with its arbitration case before a United Nations arbitral tribunal in The Hague. With its latest legal manoeuvre, the Philippines tried to place maximum diplomatic pressure on China amid an intensifying territorial dispute in the South China Sea. China vehemently opposed the arbitration case, and argued against the 'internationalization' of what it deems to be essentially bilateral territorial disputes to be resolved outside a court of law. For more than a year, China repeatedly sought to discourage the Philippines from legally challenging what it considers to be its 'indisputable' and 'inherent' sovereignty over most features in the South China Sea. It reportedly even threatened the Philippines with sanctions and other punitive measures. Frustrated by the lack of development on the diplomatic front, Philippine president Benigno Aquino III effectively abandoned his earlier attempts at reviving bilateral channels of communication with top Chinese leaders. In early 2014, he compared China's territory-claiming efforts to those of 'Nazi Germany' and stressed the importance of refusing to appease Xi. During an exclusive interview with the *New York Times*, Aquino reportedly stated, with respect to China, 'You may have the might, but that does not necessarily make you right'. Outraged by Aquino's comments, China dismissed Aquino as an 'ignorant, amateurish' leader, who failed to appreciate the delicate art of conflict management and diplomacy. At this juncture, there was little goodwill left for reviving bilateral diplomatic channels (Bradsher 2014). Eager to avoid an embarrassing legal showdown, China reportedly offered certain 'carrots' such as investment and trade deals and mutual disengagement from contested features such as the Scarborough Shoal. In exchange, the Philippines was asked to postpone its arbitration efforts in The Hague. The Aquino administration reportedly convened (late January) a special cabinet meeting to discuss the offer, although Beijing denies having ever made it (Esmaquel 2014). Bearing in mind the Scarborough Shoal stand-off, and the failure to reach an effective and mutually satisfying diplomatic compromise, the Aquino administration turned down the reported Chinese offer. Against the backdrop of rising tensions between the Philippines and China, President Obama's 2014 trip (28/29 April) to Manila could not have been timelier. Bereft of any credible minimum deterrence capability, the Philippines sought deeper military cooperation with and commitment from its long-time ally, the United States. Shortly before Obama's arrival, the two countries signed a new security pact, the Enhanced Defense Cooperation Agreement (EDCA), which granted American troops rotational access to Philippine bases in Clark and Subic. In exchange, the Philippines is supposed to benefit from expanded joint military exercises and enhanced interoperability with the US military. The new agreement aimed to strengthen bilateral defence cooperation in both traditional and non-traditional security realms. While the latest agreement deepened the United States' strategic footprint in Asia, adding much-needed momentum to the Obama administration's P2A policy, the Philippines, in turn, was slightly alarmed by the lack of explicit American commitment to come to its rescue in the event of an armed showdown with China over disputed features of the South China Sea. In contrast, the Obama administration was explicit in its expression of military commitment to Japan over the Senkaku disputes in the East China Sea. A few days before his visit to Manila, Obama arrived in Japan, where he unequivocally declared Washington's commitment to Tokyo over the latter's maritime disputes with China: 'The policy of the United States is clear – the Senkaku islands are administered by Japan and therefore fall within the scope of ... the U.S.–Japan Treaty of Mutual Cooperation and Security' (*Reuters* 2014).

There are two key reasons why Japan has enjoyed more definitive American commitment than the Philippines. The first has to do with the substance and spirit of their MDTs with Washington. Article I of the US–Japan MDT declares that 'Japan grants, and the United States of America accepts, the right ... to dispose United States land, air and sea forces in and about Japan. Such forces may be utilized to contribute to the maintenance of international peace and security in the Far East and to the security of Japan against armed attack from without.' Unlike the Philippines, which gained formal independence, post-war Japan was stripped of its ability to wage war and develop offensive military capability, making it effectively an American protectorate. Of course, some analysts maintain that both the Japanese and Filipino MDTs with the USA carry a degree of uncertainty vis-à-vis the coverage of disputed territories in the western Pacific. But as Filipino historian Manuel Almario (2014) perceptively explains:

> [Under the US–Japan MDT], the United States is committed unconditionally to 'utilize' its forces for the security of Japan against 'armed attack from without.' On the other hand, there is no such guarantee of automatic defense by the United States in case of an armed attack on the Philippines from without ... There is no declaration that the US armed forces would be 'utilized to contribute to the security' of the Philippines, except to bind both parties to 'meet the common dangers' in accordance with their 'constitutional processes'. The 'constitutional processes' probably mean that the congresses of the two parties would have to consent to any action to be taken.

The second factor has to do with demonstration of continuous and effective occupation of the disputed features. In the last four decades, Japan has managed to demonstrate such a level of de facto sovereignty over the Senkaku islands, which fall under the administrative control of the Okinawa prefecture. The same, however, can't be said about Filipino-claimed features such as the Scarborough Shoal. American officials have repeatedly declared their government's neutrality vis-à-vis sovereignty claims in the South China Sea (Bello 2014). As former US Navy rear admiral Michael McDevitt (2013: 29–30) writes:

> At first glance, the disputes China has with the Philippines over Scarborough Shoal in the SCS [South China Sea] appear similar to the situation in the ECS [East China Sea] with Japan, because the U.S. is a treaty ally of the Philippines. Actually, however, the two situations are different. In the case of Scarborough Shoal, the Philippines did not have undisputed 'administrative control' prior to the 2012 confrontation over the islet. Second, the U.S. is not directly involved in the Scarborough Shoal dispute because its mutual defense treaty with the Philippines does not obligate Washington to take sides over sovereignty questions. However, the treaty does include language related to attacks on 'its [the Philippines'] armed forces, public vessels or aircraft in the Pacific.' In the unlikely event that China were to attack a Philippine naval or coast guard ship, Washington therefore could find itself in a difficult position regarding its willingness to live up to treaty obligations and its perceived reliability as a security provider in East Asia.

And there is nothing in the EDCA which resolves such uncertainty; at best, the new Filipino–American security agreement provided 'marginal advantages' for the Philippines, such as a more extensive rotational presence in and American military aid and joint exercises with its South-East Asian partner (Thayer 2014), and, at worst, may be in violation of constitutional restrictions on the establishment of foreign military bases on Philippine soil. Critics of the EDCA have demanded Senate deliberation on the defence agreement to ensure its constitutionality and compliance with the Philippines' national interest. During his visit, Obama disappointed his hosts when he refused to clarify whether the US armed forces would automatically come to the Philippines' rescue against China over disputed features.

Just a few days earlier in Japan, Obama had expressed his country's firm commitment to aid Japan if a conflict were to erupt over the disputed Senkaku islands in the East China Sea. Obama also made it very clear that the EDCA was not aimed at China, and he cautioned his allies against going to war over 'a bunch of rocks', reiterating that the USA was neutral with respect to the ownership of disputed territories in the South China Sea. He tried to encourage the Philippines to pursue a diplomatic compromise with China, since 'it is inevitable that China is going to be a dominant power in [the Asian] region' (Esquerra and Burgonio 2014; Orendain 2014). To make matters even more complicated, the EDCA's implementation has been hampered by a pending case at the Philippine Supreme Court, which is deliberating the constitutionality of the new security agreement. Since the EDCA is an executive agreement, and the Aquino administration is expected to step down in mid-2016, Washington will most likely try to renegotiate the agreement with the succeeding administration. In short, the EDCA (provocatively) signalled the Philippines' intent to contain China through an explicit alignment with the USA – but without any tangible gains in terms of deterrence.

Bilateral defence ties took another hit when a US serviceman was accused of murdering a Filipino transgender in Subic, rekindling old wounds vis-à-vis abuses suffered by locals at the hands of foreign troops stationed in the country during the Cold War. No wonder a growing number of nationalists and leftists groups began to call for the abolition of the VFA and the scrapping of the EDCA (Agence France Presse 2015a). Amid lingering uncertainty over American assistance, the Philippines sought greater support from other regional powers such as Japan. Along with China, Korea and much of South-East Asia, the Philippines bore the brunt of Japanese militarism during the Second World War, with countless Filipinos falling victim to Japanese cruelty and much of Manila devastated by war. But in a telling sign of the Philippines' growing current anxieties with China, Del Rosario, in a 2012 interview with the *Financial Times*, went so far as to openly support a rearmed Japan shorn of its pacifist Constitution: 'We are looking for balancing factors in the region, and Japan could be a significant balancing factor.' Japan welcomed the Philippines' open support for a greater regional role for Tokyo by offering its biggest-ever security-related package in the post-Second World War period:

ten cutters worth around US$12 million to be donated (or offered under soft loans) to the Philippine Coast Guard (Pilling and Landigin 2012). China's maritime assertiveness provided a new opening for Japan – and other middle powers – to assume a greater role in maintaining regional security. The South China Sea disputes were by now fully internationalized.

5 | THE MIDDLE POWERS: A GAME OF THRONES

The point in history at which we stand is full of promise and danger. The world will either move forward toward unity and widely shared prosperity – or it will move apart.

Franklin D. Roosevelt

Democracies are indeed slow to make war, but once embarked upon a martial venture are equally slow to make peace and reluctant to make a tolerable, rather than a vindictive, peace.

Rheinhold Neibuhr

Compared to its predecessor – primarily concerned with enlisting Asian countries' help in the GWOT and preoccupied with democracy promotion in the much-troubled Middle East – the Obama administration has shown more interest in re-engaging with Asia. It has focused much of its diplomatic energy and imagination on repairing, upgrading and elevating ties with Asian powers, while consistently demonstrating Washington's commitment to multilateralism and regional integration in Asia and the Pacific. In fact, Japan, China and South Korea were among Obama's first official foreign trips, signifying renewed US interest in this key region. The Obama administration has also acknowledged the growing significance of South-East Asian countries. To his credit, Obama has been proactive in his engagement with ASEAN, something that has been accomplished in part through the USA's signing of the Treaty of Amity and Cooperation; invigorating the US–ASEAN Leaders' Meeting; supporting ASEAN's constructive engagement with Burma; the opening of a permanent US mission in ASEAN; conducting ministerial meetings with Lower Mekong countries; supporting a 'regional' solution to the South China Sea conflict; and strongly engaging Indonesia while integrating it into the world's top intergovernmental decision-making body, the G20 (Heydarian 2010; Campbell and Ratner 2014).

Time and again, however, the P2A has raised more questions than answers, simultaneously creating expectations of cooperation (mainly for allies) and conflict (mainly for China), without fully clarifying the extent of American commitment to its allies. As former US Assistant Secretary of State for East Asian and Pacific Affairs Kurt Campbell (2009–13) and Ely Ratner, a research fellow at the Center for a New American Security, put it: 'Almost three years later, the Obama administration still confronts the persistent challenge of explaining the concept and delivering on its promise. But despite the intense scrutiny and short-term setbacks faced by the policy, there is little doubt that a major shift is well under way. And whether Washington wants it to or not, Asia will command more attention and resources from the United States, thanks to the region's growing prosperity and influence – and the enormous challenges the region poses' (Campbell and Ratner 2014).

There are two dimensions to America's P2A. First, it is a logical 'rebalancing' of America's global strategic-military commitments in light of a sober recognition of the country's overextension in the Eurasian region. This rebalancing gained its initial momentum with the US withdrawal from Iraq in 2011 and subsequent withdrawal from Afghanistan in 2014. It explains why the United States played a 'supporting role' rather than occupying centre stage during the Libyan military campaign in 2011. It also explains America's reluctance to take drastic action against the Syrian regime in late 2013 – amid allegations of the use of chemical weapons by the Assad regime against its own population, violating Obama's (self-imposed) red line – while mainly focusing on a diplomatic resolution of the Iranian nuclear conundrum. The US military build-up in the western Pacific will be facilitated by a redeployment of naval forces from the Atlantic theatre to the Pacific Command and an increased rotational military presence across the region, namely in Japan, Australia and Singapore. A refurbished forward-deployment base in Guam – in anticipation of proposed changes to the American military presence in Japan – underlined the new security architecture. The emerging network of primary allies will be bolstered by a string of secondary partners, which will further cement America's strategic leadership in Asia. Among the latter group are treaty allies such as Japan and the Philippines and strategic partners such as India and Vietnam, who share, in varying degrees, Washington's anxieties regarding China. The aim, as many Chinese strategists perceive, is to create a 'reversed Wall of China' – anchored by an 'Asian Arc of Democracy', composed of India, Japan, Australia and potentially even Indonesia and South Korea – to keep Beijing's ambitions in check. Secondly, it is a response to the growing importance of the Asia-Pacific region in both economic and strategic-military terms in the twenty-first century. As the region transforms into the centre of global economic output and productivity, America's embattled economy is in desperate need of growing export markets and trading partners to rejuvenate its shaky foundations.

In this sense, it is essentially a continuation, or resuscitation, of earlier attempts by the Clinton administration to enhance US economic presence in booming Asian markets. After all, the region hosts industrial giants such as Japan and China; 'newly industrializing countries' (NICs) such as South Korea, Hong Kong, Thailand, Singapore and Taiwan; booming emerging markets such as Indonesia, India, Vietnam and the Philippines; and vast investment opportunities in places such as Bangladesh and Myanmar. The Trans-Pacific Partnership Free Trade Agreement (TPP-FTA) represents the Obama administration's most explicit attempt at deepening the American economic footprint in the Asia-Pacific. The proposed TPP deal aims to further integrate economies across the Pacific Rim by, among other things, reducing barriers to foreign investments and dismantling state-dominated industries. Major US multinational companies will be among the biggest beneficiaries of the proposed trade agreement. Obviously, it is the strategic-security dimension of America's pivot which is most controversial. While the Clinton administration pushed for the accommodation of China as a 'strategic partner' and witnessed the drawdown of the US military presence in the Philippines, the Obama administration is instead increasingly concerned with 'constrainment' of China – preventing the emergence of China as a strategic competitor through the deployment of diplomatic, economic and military assets. The United States has been deepening its strategic presence in the region, expanding its bases in Australia, reasserting its commitment to forward-deployment bases in Japan and South Korea, upgrading facilities in Guam, reconcentrating US naval firepower (i.e. aircraft carriers), and extending its rotational presence across South-East Asia.

But the pivot is more of an evolving strategic disposition than a fixed and concrete element of a broader 'grand strategy' for the twenty-first century. It is a reflection of a seemingly declining power, the USA, which is catching up with the march of history after almost a decade of strategic fiasco on the part of the Bush administration. Washington has realized that its GWOT has brought it close to the brink of fiscal collapse and strategic overextension, allowing countries like China (and even Russia) to gain significant ground in Asia. Thus, the Obama administration is simply trying to reassert America's century-old foothold in the region, while hedging its bets against a rapidly rising China. But we no longer live in a world where select powers can treat the globe like a chessboard. In today's world, the USA is at best a stage master, a visionary leader capable of creating temporary coalitions and steering international cooperation in moments of crisis, and at worse a declining superpower desperately holding on to the inertia of its historical dominance, unwilling to cede influence to emerging powers and jealously guarding its military hegemony in key regions of the world. By and large, in our globalized world, the USA is influencing events on the ground without explicitly dictating the terms of action or unilaterally determining the course of history. America's P2A is an ongoing project that will require the growing cooperation of its allies to succeed, but allies and strategic partners also have their own ideas and (distinct) interests, with middle powers such as Japan and India seeking a greater role in shaping the Indo-Pacific order, while Australia, South Korea and Indonesia stubbornly pursue an equi-balancing strategy vis-à-vis China and the USA. Amid growing strategic uncertainty, all are hedging their bets. And it is this inherently indeterminate dynamic which is defining the post-American order in Asia.

The pivot and its discontents

Washington has said it intends to deploy 60 per cent of its surface ships to the region, amounting to six aircraft carriers and the majority of its submarines, littoral combat ships and destroyers. In 2012, Washington said that it had already reportedly deployed 60 per cent of its aircraft carrier battle groups and nuclear submarines to the region. The problem, however, is that the P2A policy's added-value is under question. As Ross (2012) explains:

> Washington has been devoting more resources to the region since at least 1997, when it first moved a submarine from Europe to Guam. The Clinton and George W. Bush administrations then deployed every type of major naval and air weapons system to Guam and Japan, cooperated with Singapore to build an aircraft carrier facility at the Changi Naval Base, and strengthened U.S. defense cooperation with Japan and the Philippines. The Bush administration assigned an additional aircraft carrier to the Pacific theater, and the Pentagon announced in 2005 that it would deploy 60 percent of U.S. submarines to Asia. Throughout the wars in Afghanistan and Iraq, military funding for the Pacific theater remained at high level.

In fact, as Robert Kaplan points out, as far back as October 2007 the US Navy expressed its willingness to have a sustained forward presence across the Asia-Pacific region, from the western Pacific to the Indian Ocean, representing 'a momentous shift in overall U.S. maritime strategy' (Kaplan 2010). America's Pivot to Asia is an evolutionary process, especially in the strategic-security realm, primarily because it is largely viewed as a reaction to China's economic dominance and growing military assertiveness in recent years. However, this view represents only half of the story, since the pivot is characterized by a constellation of dynamic 'threat perceptions' adopted by the USA, China and their respective allies and partners (Brookings 2012). One could say China is as much an architect of the so-called pivot as the USA. The pivot is a product of a strategic dialectic, which is viewed from diametrically opposing positions in Beijing and Washington: the more aggressive China is in expanding its naval capabilities and asserting its territorial claims, the more determined is the United

States to reassert and deepen its foothold in the region. From China's point of view, the US pivot is a provocative process, which in turn fuels Beijing's growing assertiveness, especially in territorial disputes in adjacent waters.

An often neglected element is how the US allies – from the Philippines to Vietnam and Japan – have been playing their own strategic games, simultaneously testing America's commitment to regional (or bilateral) security and China's ability to exercise self-restraint. Of course, on the other side of the fence you have China's quasi-satellite states in Indochina – namely Laos and Cambodia, and to a certain degree Myanmar (although Myanmar has begun to distance itself from China since the onset of its liberalization process).[1] Outside this theatre of strategic jostling, states such as Indonesia – the informal leader of ASEAN – are most interested in preventing a brewing Sino-American rivalry from turning into a direct confrontation, desperately trying to manage a region splintering along conflicting allegiances and competing national interests. Mindful of their tight economic relations with China, America's regional allies have touted the pivot as an attempt to improve regional security, tackle 'non-traditional security' (NTS) issues (e.g., piracy, terrorism, human trafficking, etc.), and enhance the minimum deterrence capability of less powerful countries like the Philippines. Crucially, there has been hardly any explicit reference to China as a motivating factor behind growing security cooperation between the United States and its regional allies. This is obviously an attempt to allay China's anxieties about the emergence of a US-led, regional effort to contain its rapid rise. However, facts on the ground belie such caution: Vietnam and the Philippines are clearly seeking American military assistance in the form of a greater rotational presence and/or joint military exercises, arms sales and

---

[1] In mid-2014, the author, on the sidelines of a high-profile experts' conference on the South China Sea disputes, had informal conversations with (former and serving) high-level diplomats from Myanmar, who consistently expressed their willingness to be more independent from China, a development that has been facilitated by the country's lessening dependence on China thanks to the once-reclusive junta's opening to foreign investors from Japan, Singapore, Thailand and the West and its assumption of ASEAN chairmanship in 2014.

increased military aid. Japan – facing renewed clashes with Beijing over disputed territories in the East China Sea – has sought the United States' explicit reiteration of its commitment to their mutual defense treaty. Both sides of the simmering conflict are fully aware that China's rise is at the centre of the pivot. Ironically, the whole pivot phenomenon is encouraging all stakeholders to take bolder positions vis-à-vis regional territorial conflicts, with Chinese leaders also intent on shoring up domestic popular support by taking a tougher stance towards neighbouring countries, using a combination of paramilitary elements (fishing boats and surveillance vessels), diplomatic-economic intimidation and threat of force to assert their territorial claims (see Chapter 3). The growing US military presence may have boosted the morale of allies such as the Philippines, but it also partly shifted the focus away from diplomacy and dialogue towards brinkmanship and competitive alliance-building, with middle powers such as Japan and India playing an increasingly important role in shaping the geopolitical showdown in the western Pacific.

Recent years have also seen an arms race in the region. The USA's recent big-ticket military sales to regional allies also underscore the degree to which the American industrial-military complex has been energized in the process. The US pivot is thus reinforcing a large and growing network of vested interests in the ongoing disputes. Among the biggest beneficiaries of recent US commitments is the Aerospace Industries Association (AIA), a massive trade group that includes top Pentagon suppliers such as Lockheed Martin Corp., Boeing and the Northrop Grumman Corp. Fred Downey, vice-president for national security at the AIA, recently said: '[The pivot] will result in growing opportunities for our industry to help equip our friends' (Wolf 2013). In the face of an anaemic economy and reeling from deepening fiscal woes, the Pentagon has wrestled with (proposed and actual) budget cuts. This has not only raised questions over the USA's capacity to rein in China's perceived expansionism and aid troubled allies but has also evoked deep worries about future profits among American arms suppliers. To buttress its expressed commitment to regional security and freedom of navigation in international waters and revive the domestic defence industry, Washington has stepped up its increasingly sophisticated military sales to the region. Between 2011 and 2013, the USA's worldwide military sales hovered above US$60 billion, with a US$6.9 billion acquisition deal with India in 2011 and US$13.7 billion in overall sales to Pacific partners in 2012. In 2013, new military acquisitions by US allies included, among other things, a US$5 billion Lockheed Martin radar-evading F-35 Joint Strike Fighter aircraft deal with Japan, a US$1.2 billion Northrop Grumman high-flying RQ-4 'Global Hawk' spy drone deal with South Korea, and a US$1.85 billion Lockheed Martin-led retrofitting of Taiwan's 145 F-16A/B fighters with advanced radars and electronic warfare suits (ibid.). The USA has also encouraged further self-reliance and interoperability among allied Asian nations, especially powerful regional players such as Japan, which has, since the end of the Second World War, acted as a pillar of an American-led order in East Asia, hosting large-scale American military bases, acting as a bulwark against communism throughout the Cold War, and providing financial and logistical support during the GWOT. The biggest losers in the US–China-driven escalation will likely be the political moderates who have called for a more sanguine, diplomatic resolution of the decades-long maritime disputes and deeper pan-regional economic integration. The overtly military aspects of the USA's pivot, however, vindicated hawks in Beijing, who consistently downplayed American reassurances of peaceful coexistence and an amicable global partnership. By rallying regional allies against China and equipping them with state-of-the-art military equipment, the US pivot risked intensifying Chinese anxieties while emboldening strategic partners such as the Philippines, Vietnam and Japan – and even India – to push Beijing into a corner (Desker 2012). But a US-driven arms race in the region, one that benefits Washington's military-industrial complex, could torpedo any chance of patient, peaceful diplomacy. As Justin Logan of the conservative think tank the Cato Institute explains (2013): 'Although American political leaders regularly deny it, the US military is working to contain China in the Asia-Pacific region. American military planners have developed a posture in Asia that is designed with the obvious purpose of putting China's seaborne commerce at risk ... The first problem with American strategy is that its "congagement" [containment and engagement] approach is built on contradictory policies.' The P2A became a counterproductive policy: While allies such as Japan and the Philippines lamented the supposed lack of actual (military) commitment by the USA, rivals such as China complain about a supposed US-led containment strategy, built on greater rotational presence in the region and military sales to allies. Ironically, the USA was simultaneously accused of making too little commitment to its allies, on one hand, and pushing too hard against China, on the other.

Mixed signals For the Obama administration, it was important to not only enhance the defensive capabilities of its allies and strategic partners, but also to reach out to China. It was an almost impossible balancing act to pull off. Efforts at deepening bilateral ties with China moved towards greater institutionalization during the Great Recession (2007/08) and gained pace after the announcement of the P2A (2011). In particular, 2013 was a big year for Sino-American bilateral diplomacy, with the world's two leading powers holding the fifth US–China Strategic and Economic Dialogue in Washington. At that meeting, both sides committed to a significant broadening of their bilateral relations. The US–China dialogue covered key bilateral issues, namely the promotion of an open and secure cyberspace, cooperation on the Korean peninsula crisis, coordination on anti-proliferation efforts vis-à-vis Iran, how to achieve a political settlement in Syria, various bilateral trade concerns, and joint support for enhancing global energy security and development. Crucially, the USA also emphasized the importance of maintaining strong military-to-military contacts with China, with the 9 July 2013 Strategic Security Dialogue covering sensitive bilateral issues such as cyber and maritime security as well as nuclear and missile defence policy. In order to enhance bilateral confidence-building measures, the two sides agreed to pursue a notification mechanism for major military activities and address the establishment of mutually acceptable rules of behaviour for air and maritime manoeuvres. Crucially, China agreed to attend the 2014 Rim of the Pacific (RIMPAC) naval exercise, the world's largest maritime warfare exercise, led by the US Pacific Command and held biennially with top traditional allies, to be held off Hawaii. For South-East Asian countries such as the Philippines and Vietnam, there was a palpable lack of priority – especially on the part of the USA – placed on the peaceful resolution of maritime disputes pitting weaker US allies against an increasingly powerful China. While the USA is expected to look beyond its East Asian strategic commitments when managing a bilateral relationship of global significance, America's allies warily watched the deepening interdependence between Washington and Beijing on a wide host of international issues, which collectively have overshadowed their territorial disputes with China. Moreover, the USA saw China's cooperation on North Korea and Iran as essential to its global anti-proliferation efforts. As a sign of good faith, China showed greater cooperation on isolating North Korea by closing a bank account belonging to North Korea's Foreign Trade Bank, while largely acquiescing to economic sanctions against Iran's nuclear programme and key economic sectors, which gained pace in 2013 (Bradsher and Cumming-Bruce 2013; Heydarian 2012f).

Beyond Washington's objective recognition of China's global importance, the personal dynamics between US president Barack Obama and Chinese president Xi Jingping also gave the relationship a boost. The two leaders got along well precisely because they built their political capital on charismatic leadership and staked their legacies on espousing a global vision for their respective countries. Obama's eagerness to find a sympathetic counterpart in Beijing was apparent in his decision to host a shirtsleeved summit with Xi at the exclusive Sunnylands estate in California in mid-2013. Washington's hope was that by skipping formalities and agenda-driven meetings there would be a greater degree of openness and 'personal touch'. Both sides were quick to herald the meeting as a success, with Xi saying the two sides had 'reached an important consensus' on developing 'a new type of [great power] relationship' that among other things would 'improve and develop bilateral military ties and push forward the construction of a new type of military relations'. Typically such personalized arrangements are reserved for top US allies, from British prime minister David Cameron's 2012 intimate sojourns with Obama to former president George W. Bush's Graceland meeting with Japanese prime minister Junichiro Koizumi in 2006 after the latter's historic support for the GWOT, including a prominent supporting role in post-invasion Iraq. Despite its genial exchanges with China's top leaders, the USA nevertheless sought to assuage its strategic Asian allies by rhetorically underscoring its commitment to an international law-based resolution of territorial disputes in the western Pacific (Chen 2013). 'The United States does not take a position on competing territorial claims over land features, but we have a strong and long-standing interest in the manner in which disputes in the South China Sea are addressed and in the conduct of the parties,' US Secretary of State John Kerry said at the ASEAN Regional Forum in mid-2013. Yet ASEAN – and its role in fostering inclusive security architecture in the Asia-Pacific – was hardly mentioned in the US–China bilateral exchanges. Kerry himself raised eyebrows among some Asian allies when, during his confirmation speech in the US Senate, he raised doubts as to whether Washington should use its military muscle to rein in Chinese territorial ambitions:

> I'm not convinced that increased military ramp-up is critical yet. I'm not convinced of that. That's something I'd want to look at very carefully when and if you folks confirm me and I can get in there and sort of dig into this a little deeper. But we have a lot more bases out there than any other nation in the world, including China today. We have a lot more forces out there than any other nation in the world, including China today. And we've just augmented the president's announcement in Australia with additional Marines. You know, the Chinese take a look at that and say, what's the United States doing? They trying to circle us? What's going on? And so, you know, every action has its reaction. It's the old – you know, it's not just the law of physics; it's the law of politics and diplomacy. I think we have to be thoughtful about, you know, sort of how we go forward. (Economy 2013)

No wonder many of Kerry's statements, as well as the Xi–Obama meeting, underscored how the two powers were – and see themselves as – the bedrock of the pan-regional order. In the meantime, China again agreed to negotiate a CoC with ASEAN, after convincing its ally, Cambodia, to block any discussion of the South China Sea disputes in 2012. It was a clever manoeuvre to silence critics and strengthen the momentum for greater US–China codependence without addressing the rising militarization of the South China Sea disputes. For Manila, Washington's occasional expressions of discontent over China's territorial ambitions, especially since the China–Philippines stand-off over the Scarborough Shoal in mid-2012 and subsequent tensions over the Second Thomas Shoal (see Chapter 3), were yet to be matched with actual commitments on the ground. American military aid to the Philippines has been consistently dwarfed by that given to non-allied nations such as Egypt – not to mention nuclear-armed Israel, which received several times more – which, since its peace agreement with Israel in 1979, doesn't face any serious external threat: between 1948 and 2011, the USA gave Egypt about US$71.6 billion in bilateral development and military aid, with annual military aid averaging about US$1.3 billion since 1987 (Plumer 2013). Quite naturally, among Asian allies like the Philippines and Japan, there were concerns that growing interdependence and diplomatic dynamism between the USA and China could affect Washington's resolve and its bilateral military commitments to defend its allies against Beijing's maritime posturing. Australian strategist Hugh White (2014), author of *The China Choice*, captures the hollow and inherently tenuous nature of the pivot when he argues:

> [The question is] whether America really [has been] willing to use 'all the elements of American power' to resist China's challenge to the regional status quo based on US leadership in Asia. This is, after all, precisely what the pivot is all about. And the pivot got into trouble almost as soon as it was announced when, early in 2012, Beijing set out to test it on the Scarborough Shoal. The pivot failed that test when Washington was not willing to support Manila in resisting China's takeover there ... Obama will only be able to preserve the status quo if he really can convince Beijing that he is willing to go to war with China rather than see the US step back from regional leadership ... America would not lose a war with China in the East China Sea, but America has no clear way of winning it and no sure way to control it and limit the risk of escalation ... Ultimately, the danger is that China is as serious about changing the status quo in Asia as America is about preserving it.

From China's point of view, the USA was (reluctantly) acknowledging China's growing geopolitical and economic importance. Beijing demanded a more equal relationship with Washington, implicitly suggesting that the latter should abandon its P2A policy – and support for allies amid ongoing maritime disputes – in favour of a more collaborative relationship. The Obama administration ended up disappointing both its allies and China: on the one hand, it sought to engage Beijing on the diplomatic front, ever more explicitly acknowledging the growing importance of Sino-American relations, while, at the same time, gradually buttressing the USA's military footprint in East Asia, but refusing to formally support its allies' (Japan and the Philippines) sovereignty claims against China. As Sinologists such as Ross (2012) explain, the pivot creates a 'lose-lose' outcome for the USA and its allies: 'The pivot has already damaged U.S. security interests, and the cost will only grow. If Washington continues down its current path, Chinese resistance to U.S. policies will inevitably increase … as China pushes back against the United States' growing presence on its borders and nationalist tension rises between China and U.S. security partners over disputed but inconsequential islands.'

Meanwhile, Obama's signature economic initiative, the TPP, repeatedly stumbled. In Japan, negotiations over the TPP were severely hampered by powerful domestic opposition to reduction of tariffs and other forms of trade barriers on the agriculture, beef and pork sectors as well as the automobile market. Other negotiating partners, particularly developing countries like Malaysia and Chile, expressed strong concerns over proposed provisions on protection of Intellectual Property Rights (IPR), which would give multinational companies (MNCs) tremendous power over critical sectors such as healthcare at the expense of consumers. State-dominated economies such as Vietnam were also concerned about the impact and scale of privatization. The late-2013 Wikileaks revelation of the controversial provisions of the TPP negotiations represented a PR coup, which further encouraged domestic opposition to the pan-regional trading agreement. The Obama administration also faced heavy opposition among its own ranks, with Democrat legislators, labour unions and progressive activists mobilizing against the TPP and opposing Obama's request for a 'Fast-Track Authority' to expedite finalization of the deal (Weisman 2015; Heydarian 2014c). All the while, China swiftly pushed ahead with major economic initiatives, particularly the AIIB and the Maritime Silk Road (see Introduction and Chapter 3). Interestingly, it was arguably the late Singaporean leader who encouraged the USA to push ahead with initiatives such as the TPP to preserve Washington's strategic relevance in the region. In a 2007 cable, entitled 'Lee Kuan Yew on Burma's "stupid" generals and the "gambler" Chen Shui-bian',[2] the Singaporean leader 'urged the United States to pursue more Free Trade Agreements to give the region options besides China', lest Beijing leverage its economic prowess to gain strategic concessions from neighbouring countries, particularly those in ASEAN. Amid growing uncertainties over the extent of American resolve and wherewithal to check Chinese territorial ambitions, regional powers such India, Japan, Australia and South Korea have stepped up to the challenge by trying to constrain China's maritime assertiveness and protect their own national interests. On the surface, these new players, all liberal democracies, are acting on behalf of an American-led regional order. But a more careful look suggests that even Washington's allies are no longer taking US hegemony for granted, recognizing the dramatic power shift represented by China's inexorable rise – and its maritime-territorial reverberations. No less than the USA's leading Asian ally, Japan – the linchpin of American hegemony in Asia – has been among the proactive middle powers seeking to shape the trajectory of the maritime disputes in the western Pacific.

Japan steps in

After its decisive defeat in the Second World War, Japan transformed, under the so-called Yoshida doctrine, into a de facto American protectorate. The country's political system and constitution are a legacy of post-war American occupation (1945–52), which aimed to transform a former rival into a key regional ally. The USA saw Japan as a bulwark against communism, as the USSR threatened Western hegemony in the region. In exchange for its subservience to Washington, Japan benefited from the American security umbrella,

---

[2] The cable can be found at the Wikileaks website, wikileaks.org/plusd/cables/07SINGAPORE1932_a.html.

economic aid and markets (Pyle 2008). This strategic bargain underpinned an American–Japanese dyad, which proved crucial to Washington's attempt to assert its hegemony in East Asia and maintain a broadly liberal order in the region. As a key element of the American-led hubs-and-spokes network of alliances in the Asia-Pacific theatre, Japan pulled off an impressive post-war economic recovery, once again emerging as the leading industrial power in the region. The second half of the twentieth century saw a broadly collaborative, mutually beneficial US–Japan alliance, which served as the anchor of the regional order. As eminent Japan expert Kenneth Pyle (2014) explains: 'Throughout the postwar period, Japan has occupied a uniquely subordinate position in the American world order. The result of unconditional surrender, occupation, and an imposed alliance, subordinate independence has compelled Japanese deference to American hegemony. The cost of such deference to national self-respect has been considerable.'

An economically ascendant Tokyo turbocharged industrialization across South-East Asia and later in China, while American bases – spread across Japan, South Korea and the Philippines – served as a tangible expression of Washington's geopolitical ascendancy in the region (ibid.). Benedict Anderson (1998) explains the symbiotic relationship between the two former rivals:

> Tokyo came late to the imperialist game ... Beginning with the acquisition of Taiwan in 1895, and the annexation of Korea in 1910, Japanese ruling élites sought ... a zone of hegemony equivalent to that of the United States in the Western hemisphere ... In the period of postwar recovery, the old ambitions did not disappear, but took an essentially economic form. Assured of its political and military dominance over Japan, and eager to make the Japanese economy a cornerstone of capitalist strength in Asia, Washington put no real obstacles in Tokyo's way ... Beginning in the Fifties, thanks to a series of war reparations agreements whereby Japan provided substantial funds to South-East Asian countries for the purchase of its manufactures ... [b]y the early Seventies, Japan became the single most important external investor in the region, both as extractor of natural resources (timber, oil and so on) and in industrial and infrastructural development.

Amid China's rise, however, Japan – battered by decades of economic stagnation and political paralysis – confronted an evolving regional security environment, which demanded a fundamental rethink of its foreign and security policy, which, for decades, was anchored by unremitting subservience to American strategic dictate. After years of a cosy relationship between Prime Minister Junichiro Koizumi (2001–06) and George W. Bush in the early 2000s, new political forces tried to reshape the China–Japan–USA strategic triangle. In 2009, the centre-left Democratic Party of Japan (DPJ), under the leadership of Yukio Hatoyama, managed to end the decades-long hegemony of the conservative Liberal Democratic Party (LDP). Amid much fanfare, Prime Minister Hatoyama (2009–10) promised to 'revisit' the Japan–US security alliance by seeking a close and equal relationship, while fostering cordial ties with China as part of a broader effort to establish an 'East Asian community' devoid of age-old rivalries (Hemmings 2010). In short, he sought to end six decades of strategic subservience to the USA and transform Japan into an independent force for stability and progress in the region. An equi-balancing policy vis-à-vis China and the USA was at the heart of Hatoyama's calculus. Barely a year into office, however, Hatoyama resigned, citing his failure to honour his campaign promises, especially his inability to implement the pending relocation of the American Futenma Marine Corps Air Base in Okinawa (McCurry 2010). Without Hatoyama, the DPJ struggled to maintain its already waning political mandate, with succeeding prime ministers constantly falling short of fulfilling Hatoyama's campaign promises. Japan was once again gripped by political paralysis. Hatoyama's hopes for an East Asian community, however, were dashed by renewed territorial tensions with China over the Senkaku (*Diaoyu* to the Chinese) islands in the East China Sea (see Figure 5.1).

On their own, the islands represent seemingly inconsequential islets scattered between Chinese and Japanese waters. But the tug-of-war over their ownership symbolized a seismic transformation in the regional balance of power: A rising China was intent on correcting historical mistakes by reasserting control over territories it had lost to Imperial Japan almost a century earlier, while a declining Japan

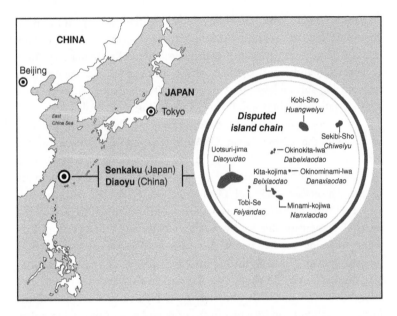

5.1 The Senkaku/Diaoyu islands in the East China Sea.

stubbornly defended its claims and refused to turn back the clock. Driven by an acute sense of aggrieved nationalism, China sought to redefine the regional landscape. The Senkaku islands, which for centuries fell within Imperial China's sphere of influence, were occupied by Imperial Japan in the late nineteenth century. The occupation of the islands was part of a larger phenomenon: the decline of the Qing dynasty, and the emergence of a new industrial power in Asia, Japan. After its decisive victory over Beijing in the 1884/85 naval wars (Holmes 2012, 2014a), Tokyo embarked on frantic territorial expansionism, acquiring Taiwan in 1895, annexing Korea in 1910, and later invading mainland China, beginning with the occupation of Manchuria (1931) and culminating in the 1937 Sino-Japanese War. As Australian scholar McCormack (2013) eloquently puts it, the occupation of Senkaku islands by Japan, which reacquired Okinawa and the Senkaku islands (from the USA) in 1972, epitomized China's humiliating defeats – at the hands of what

it had considered for centuries to be a vassal state – in the nineteenth
and twentieth centuries:

> 'Senkaku' is of course not to be compared to the vast domains
> that were then at stake in 'Manchuria,' but its importance far
> outweighs its barren and unpopulated rocks and focuses similarly
> passionate, uncompromising sentiment ... From China's viewpoint,
> a single line may be drawn from Ryukyu (1879), Senkaku/Diaoyu
> (1895), Taiwan (1895), to Dongbei or 'Manchuria' (1931) ...
> International law offered no system to which aggrieved colonial
> or semi-colonial countries could appeal and no such recourse was
> open to China – whether the Republic (whose capital moved from
> Nanjing to Taiwan in 1949) or the People's Republic (from 1949)
> – until the time it was actually shown, when the withdrawal of US
> forces from Okinawa became imminent and focused attention on
> what was and what was not 'Okinawa' and to whom it should be
> 'returned.'

For China, the defeat of Imperial Japan during the Second
World War should have been followed by the reversion of formerly
colonized features such as the Senkakus to their rightful owners,
Beijing. Instead, the post-war order rewarded, in China's view, former
colonial powers, with international law allowing a country such as
Japan – similar to some Western powers – to enjoy disproportionate
maritime and territorial privileges: in terms of ocean domains Japan
ranks among the top countries in the world, exerting control over a
maritime domain five times greater than that of China. Beijing viewed
Tokyo's control over the Senkaku islands as a fundamental reflection
of the inherently imbalanced nature of international law – a body of
principles and regulations which were formed amid China's decline
and outside its ancient (Sino-centric) worldview in the nineteenth and
twentieth centuries. In 1990, Japan's GDP represented 15 per cent
of total global economic output. By 2008 it had fallen to 10 per cent,
and was projected to decline to as little as 6 per cent in 2030. From
1990 to 2030, China's share is expected to explode from 2 to 25 per
cent. After the 2008 Great Financial Crisis, China replaced Japan
as the world's second-largest economy – ending almost six decades

of Japanese economic hegemony in Asia (ibid.). The battle over the Senkaku islands served as a concrete test of the balance of power between the two old rivals. The decades-long formula of 'shelving' sovereignty disputes, introduced by Zhou Enlai and Deng Xiaoping in the late twentieth century to facilitate Sino-Japanese economic ties, gradually fell apart (see Chapter 1).

The inflection point From 2010 onwards, a series of events completely undermined efforts by the DPJ – now bereft of Hatoyama's leadership – to upgrade relations with China. Territorial tensions flared up when the captain of a Chinese fishing vessel was apprehended by the Japanese Coast Guard near the Senkaku islands, provoking a diplomatic crisis, which saw Beijing vigorously pushing for the immediate release of the Chinese national by Japanese maritime authorities. China went so far as to leverage its rare earth exports – crucial to sophisticated industrial production – to resource-poor Japan, threatening a major shock to bilateral trade relations. Tokyo eventually relented, releasing the Chinese captain without pressing charges, but the Senkaku issue was by now a de facto flashpoint in the East China Sea. Hardliners on both sides seized the opportunity to up the ante, sidelining moderates, who tirelessly sought to place broader bilateral interests above ancient territorial disputes. Tokyo's firebrand mayor Shintaro Ishihara lambasted the DPJ and accused it of cowardice before China. To display his determination to defend Japan's territorial claims over the Senkakus – mostly owned by wealthy private citizens, who provided a veneer of plausible deniability by downplaying Japan's controversial exercise of sovereignty over the disputed features – Ishihara proposed purchasing the feature, placing it explicitly under the Japanese government's control. To prevent an outright diplomatic crisis, the DPJ government opted for what it saw as a lesser evil: the national government, instead of Tokyo's mayor, would purchase the islands, presenting this as a more preferable outcome to China, which vehemently opposed Ishihara's manoeuvre as an unacceptable, provocative action. The timing could not have been worse, as the nationalization of the Senkaku islands coincided with annual anti-Japanese, patriotic commemorations in China, while China's outgoing president, Hu Jintao, faced tremendous pressure (from his colleagues and successors) to send a strong message to Japan. What followed were large-scale anti-Japanese protests across Chinese cities, leading to the massive destruction of Japanese-owned properties, businesses and products in China. Few believe that the violent protests were not welcomed by the CCP, which tried to present the protests as a genuine expression of Chinese public sentiment. As Richard Katz (2013), an expert on Sino-Japanese economic relations, explains, the islands disputes threatened the interests of two extremely interlinked economies:

> many Chinese citizens boycotted Japanese products and took to the streets in anti-Japanese riots. This commotion, at times encouraged by the Chinese government, led the Japanese government to fear that Beijing might exploit Japan's reliance on China as an export market to squeeze Tokyo into making territorial concessions ... For several weeks in August and September [2012], Chinese protesters caused a ruckus, damaging Japanese-made cars, vandalizing stores selling Japanese products, and setting a Panasonic factory on fire. The police vacillated between encouraging and suppressing the riots, and some Chinese state media outlets listed Japanese brands to boycott. By the time the dust settled, Japanese firms operating in China had suffered about $120 million in property damage, and for a few months thereafter, sales of Japanese cars fell by approximately 40–50 percent.

China also stepped up its paramilitary patrols in the East China Sea, sending an ever-increasing number of vessels (and jet fighters) to the Senkaku islands' surrounding (territorial and contiguous) waters, provoking a massive counter-mobilization by Japanese maritime forces. Figure 5.2 shows the growing frequency of Chinese paramilitary patrols deployed into Japanese-claimed waters off the Senkaku islands from 2008 to 2015.

The two countries began sleepwalking into a military conflict. Japanese exports to and investments in China were also jeopardized; to maintain its market share in China's massive automobile market, Japanese car manufacturers had to introduce special insurance schemes

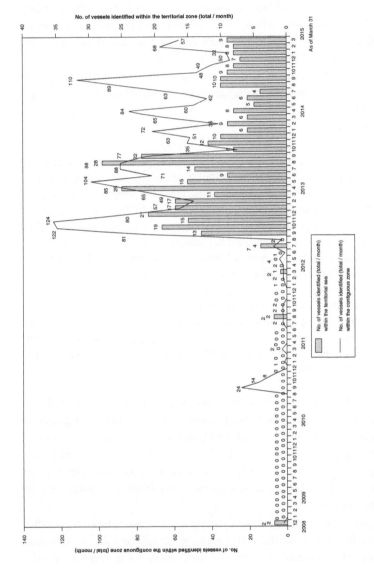

5.2 Chinese paramilitary patrols off the Senkaku islands, 2008–15 (*source:* Japanese Ministry of Foreign Affairs).

to cover anti-Japanese protests (Katz 2013; Chang 2013). Economic interdependence failed to stem bilateral disputes, as the struggle for national identity and territorial integrity dominated bilateral relations.[3] As Gordon Chang (2013) explains, Japan and China were now on the verge of delinking their economies, dangerously undermining their decades-long economic interdependence, which has served as a great incentive for stable bilateral relations:

> In 2013, trade volume between China and Japan dropped 5.1% from the year before. That followed a 3.9% fall in 2012. To put these figures into context, China's total trade was up 6.2% in 2012 and 7.6% last year while Japan's volume increased 1.0% in 2012 but was down 7.8% in 2013 ... Not surprisingly, investment between China and Japan has also taken a hit. Japanese direct investment in China dropped 4.3% last year even though overall foreign direct investment in China increased 5.3%. At the same time, China's direct investment in Japan fell 23.5% at a time when its overall outbound investment jumped 16.8% ... As Samuel Huntington noted in his landmark *The Clash of Civilizations and the Remaking of World Order*, 'high levels of economic interdependence' can be 'war-inducing' instead of 'peace-inducing' if 'states do not expect high levels of interdependence to continue.' ... When economies are pulling apart, nations perceive they have less interest in others' success. History, unfortunately, tells us what can then happen.

No longer seen as a viable, desirable alternative to the LDP, the DPJ – widely criticized for its perceived mishandling of the Fukushima nuclear meltdown in 2011, among other things – was poised for a massive defeat in the late-2012 parliamentary elections, which saw the return of nationalist prime minister Shinzo Abe, who briefly replaced Koizumi back in 2006. The new prime minister built on Hatoyama's vision of a more independent Japanese foreign policy. But he reversed earlier efforts at reaching out to China by more explicitly seeking US military assistance over the Senkaku islands and vigorously seeking the support of other Asian countries to rein in China's maritime

---

[3]   For an excellent overview of the domestic politics and ideational struggles behind the Sino-Japanese territorial stand-off see Smith (2015).

assertiveness. The territorial disputes empowered hardliners in both countries, placing two nationalistic leaders in power: Xi in China, and Abe in Japan. The world witnessed the commencement of a second round of Sino-Japanese rivalry in Asia, rekindling the dark memories of the Sino-Japanese series of conflicts in the late nineteenth and early twentieth centuries.

Reinventing Japan

After decades of self-imposed pacifism, Japan is beginning to carve out a new role in regional maritime affairs. Newly elected Japanese prime minister Shinzo Abe launched a charm offensive across the Pacific, with Australia, India, Indonesia, the Philippines and Vietnam among the countries Tokyo aimed to align against China's rising assertiveness. Abe vowed to revisit Japan's pacifist Constitution, recalibrate its security alliance with the United States, and steer the establishment of a so-called 'democratic security diamond', a proposed strategic alliance of like-minded Indo-Pacific countries that share similar anxieties about China's growing naval might. He aimed to inject Japan into the heart of the intensifying Pacific struggle between Beijing and Washington for regional maritime dominance. Under his watch, Japan broke with tradition by increasing its defence budget for the first time in eleven years, providing military aid to Cambodia and East Timor, and considering the sale of military equipment such as seaplanes and advanced Soryu submarines to strategic partners such as Australia. Abe represented a potentially game-changing leader in Japan's modern history. The Japanese government established new agencies such as the National Security Council, passed new legislation such as the secrecy law, and introduced a National Security Strategy to facilitate crisis management and address evolving security threats to Japan.[4] Abe sought to revive patriotism and national pride in Japanese society, while contemplating various means to augment Japan's development and acquisition of offensive military capabilities (Glosserman and Kang 2014). While Washington is traditionally the first foreign destination for newly elected Japanese leaders, the

---

[4] This section is partly based on exchanges between the author and high-level Japanese diplomats throughout 2014.

new Abe administration chose to prioritize southern partners in the Pacific on their international itineraries. In January 2013, Abe visited Indonesia, Thailand and Vietnam, while dispatching Deputy Prime Minister Taro Aso to Myanmar and Foreign Minister Fumio Kishida to Australia, Brunei, the Philippines and Singapore. South-East Asia has been a particular region of focus for Abe, because, as Japanese academic Satoru Nagao, explains: 'Japan is focusing on South-East Asia because there is a possibility that the region will become the most important theatre for the US–China power game ... If South-East Asian countries [wish] Japan to become a security provider, Japan will try to respond to such initiatives without necessarily compromising [its] national independence.'[5] There was also an economic momentum behind Abe's diplomatic pivot to South-East Asia. While Japan–China trade fell from 18.4 per cent of Tokyo's total exports in 2000 to 11.2 per cent in 2011, exports to the Association of Southeast Asian Nations' (ASEAN) Indonesia, Malaysia, the Philippines, Thailand, Singapore and Vietnam rose from 9.7 to 10.9 per cent over the same period, according to a report from the Japan Research Institute (Miller and Yokota 2013). South-East Asia represented a particularly important platform for Japan's reassertion of its historical economic hegemony in the region. Regional experts such as Malcolm Cook (2014) underscored the significance of this 'second wave' of the Japanese economic push into the ASEAN region, partly driven by growing concerns about over-concentration of Japanese FDI in China and continued reluctance to invest in other potentially huge markets such as India:

> It is common knowledge that the first major wave of Japanese FDI to Southeast Asia was central to the region's development success. Supply chains, production networks, export-oriented industrialization, exchange rate volatility, 'flying geese' and even ASEAN economic integration have all become focal points of the regional economic discussion in part due to the regional effects of the first wave of Japanese investments ... From 1985 to 1990, Japanese FDI increased five-fold to Malaysia, six-fold to Singapore and an

---

[5]   Interview with the author, 3 July 2014.

incredible 25-fold to Thailand, with Southeast Asia's share of total Japanese FDI outflows roughly doubling in this period. Japanese FDI to the region, centered on the electrical and electronics and the automobile industries, maintained this new and much higher level for a decade ... [In recent years] the tide has turned and Southeast Asian economies are benefitting from corporate Japan's growing concern over the overconcentration of overseas production in China ... The two major push factors for Japanese FDI into the region – Japan's demographic decline and the rising costs of business in China – are structural in nature, suggesting that this second wave will not crest and subside soon.

'Currently, the strategic environment in the Asia-Pacific region is going through a dynamic change,' Abe said in explaining his reasons for choosing South-East Asia as his first foreign destination. 'During this change, having closer relations with ASEAN countries contributes to the region's peace and stability and is in Japan's national interest.' Japan is at the forefront of large-scale industrial investments in liberalizing Myanmar, which is gradually emerging out of China's decades-long patronage through more engagement with the West. Japan's Sumitomo Corporation, Mitsubishi Corporation and Marubeni Corporation are set to take a 49 per cent stake in a US$12.6 billion Special Economic Zone (SEZ) situated at Yangon's Thilawa Port, and Japanese companies are heavily involved in other large-scale industrial developments in the country (Slodkowski 2013). Thailand, Japan's regional manufacturing hub with over eight thousand companies situated in the country, is also slated to benefit from a new wave of investments as more small and medium-sized manufacturers look to relocate outside of Japan (Pinijparakarn 2013). The moves came at a time when nationalistic protests and spiralling wages threatened and undermined Japan's interests in China. However, deeper geostrategic considerations were also driving Japan's southern pivot, which aims at revitalizing defence relations with old partners to rein in China's assertiveness.

One of the most explicit attempts by Abe to rally South-East Asian countries against China was during the Japan–ASEAN Summit in 2013, which took place shortly after China declared an ADIZ in the

East China Sea. During the meeting, Abe promised almost US$20 billion in Japanese trade and financial incentives, while aggressively lobbying South-East Asian countries to more vociferously criticize China's maritime assertiveness and calling for a joint Japan–ASEAN defence officials meeting. Eventually, the two sides agreed to release a joint statement, expressing their shared concern over threats to freedom of overflight and navigation in international waters, namely the South and East China Sea (Heydarian 2013g).

Towards a 'normal' Japan

In mid-2014, Japan took a fateful step towards becoming a 'normal' power by adopting the doctrine of 'collective self-defence', paving the way for Tokyo to play a more direct role in ensuring stability in international waters as well as in aiding allies in times of crisis. It took a combination of iron-willed leadership, under Abe, and deepening territorial disputes with China over the Senkaku islands in the East China Sea, to force Japan to take greater responsibility for its own national defence. Uncertainties over Washington's commitment to reining in China's territorial ambitions encouraged Japan to become more self-reliant. Washington welcomed Tokyo's decision to adopt a more flexible defence doctrine, facilitating broader efforts to upgrade US–Japanese bilateral defence guidelines, which were last revised back in 1997. Against the backdrop of a rapidly changing regional security environment, the aim is to create a more dynamic US–Japanese alliance, with Tokyo contributing more proportionately to regional stability in East Asia. After all, throughout the post-Cold War era, the USA has repeatedly sought to mitigate 'free-riding' by well-endowed allies, such as Japan. As expected, China was perturbed by the resurgence of its arch-rival, Japan. The Xi Jinping administration spared no efforts in denigrating its counterparts in Tokyo. Aware of lingering regional anxieties over Japan's early-twentieth-century imperial aggression, especially in South Korea, Beijing sought to convince the world that Japan was revisiting its militaristic past. During his high-profile mid-2014 visit to South Korea, amid much fanfare, Xi, in a speech at the prestigious Seoul National University, declared: 'In the first half of the 20th century, Japanese militarists carried out barbarous wars of aggression against China and Korea, swallowing Korea and occupying half of the Chinese mainland' (Al Jazeera 2014b). Any sober analysis, however, would suggest that the real bone of contention is an emerging Chinese–Japanese contest for regional leadership, as Washington gets more comfortable with playing the role of an offshore balancer. Gradually, bitter territorial disputes have seemingly rekindled a century-old rivalry for the soul of Asia.

Endurance of pacifism Japan's recent lurch towards a more proactive foreign policy, however, met stiff domestic resistance. Pacifism continues to be a cornerstone of Japan's national psyche, preventing the Abe administration – and its like-minded predecessors – from garnering sufficient public support as well as a legislative super-majority to amend Japan's Constitution. The tumultuous memories of the Second World War continue to cast a long shadow over Japanese society. But like any astute political leader, Abe has instead opted for reinterpreting existing provisions of the Japanese Constitution, striking a tenuous balance between Tokyo's evolving security calculus, on the one hand, and the pacifist spirit of the Constitution, which prohibits the country from using coercive means to settle international disputes, on the other. Far from introducing a new approach, however, Abe has simply followed in the footsteps of his predecessors, who did not shy away from reinterpreting Japan's Constitution to pursue specific political goals. After the Korean War (1950–53), the Japanese leadership reinterpreted Article 9 of the Japanese Constitution – particularly vis-à-vis prohibitions against developing a 'war potential' – to allow for the establishment of the Self Defence Forces (SDF), which purportedly served exclusively defensive objectives bereft of any aggressive operational capability to project power beyond Japan's immediate territories. By maintaining a minimalist doctrine of pacifism, Tokyo sought to justify the constitutionality of even nuclear weapons so long as they stayed within the ambit of 'minimum necessary level for self-defence'. Interestingly, Abe's own grandfather, Prime Minister Kishi Nobusuke, was responsible for a series of bureaucratic manoeuvres to influence and shape executive agencies, specifically the Cabinet Legislation Bureau

(CLB), in charge of operationalizing and safeguarding the pacifist provisions of the Japanese Constitution.

While politically motivated legal interpretations allowed Japan to develop one of the most capable armed forces in the world, the country has continuously struggled to play a consequential role in international security affairs. This was particularly acute during the early post-Cold War period, with Japan exercising minimal direct influence over a major crisis which affected Tokyo's national interests. During the first and second Gulf Wars, which imperilled Japan's energy security, Tokyo struggled to have any meaningful role in shaping military interventions in the Middle East. At best, Japan chiefly served as a source of funding and minuscule quasi-peacekeeping operations. No wonder ambitious, nationalist leaders have tried to push the legal boundaries, overcome bureaucratic obstacles and create more room for defence and foreign policy reformulations (Gupta 2014; Ackerman and Matsudaira 2014; Liff 2014; Akita 2014a). As eminent Japan expert Kenneth Pyle (2014) explains:

> The fact is, however, that because the Japanese Supreme Court has chosen to cede official interpretation of Article 9 of the constitution to the political process, this so-called no-war clause has always been the subject of controversy, reinterpretation, and political manipulation. Absent the ruling of an independent judiciary, official interpretation of Article 9 has been made by a bureaucratic agency attached to the Cabinet, the Cabinet Legal Bureau, which has been at critical times subject to the will of a strong prime minister and his foreign policy agenda ... In recent years, responding to the changing post–Cold War international structure, various administrations have steadily loosened all these self-binding policies (with the exception of the nuclear one, but even there the taboo on openly discussing it is gone). The relaxation of these self-binding policies has amounted to an incremental reinterpretation of what Article 9 allows ... Although not openly revealed, the recovery of a more autonomous foreign policy is fundamental to Abe's agenda.

The rise of China has also overshadowed Japan's defence capabilities. In 2000, Japan's defence budget was 60 per cent larger than

China's. By 2012, it was barely one third of China's. Japan's qualitative edge could also be in danger, with China placing ever-greater investments in cutting-edge military technology (De Koning and Lipscy 2013; Walton 2014). The Abe administration is determined to make Japan a more consequential power, reviving its economy as well as adopting a more proactive foreign policy. This would not only make the country more effective in safeguarding its territorial integrity against Chinese provocations, it would also allow Japan to make another run at regional leadership. For Abe, survival and prestige are two inextricably linked elements at the heart of his vision for Japan.

The battle for Asia As smaller Asian countries nervously watch Beijing's territorial brinkmanship in the western Pacific, the Abe administration has discovered a new opening for reasserting Japan's historical leadership. Japan's early-twentieth-century attempts at creating an 'Asia for Asians', under the so-called Greater East Asia Co-Prosperity Sphere, ended in a nightmare. Imperial Japan's desperate colonial rivalry with the West led to a devastating defeat and countless atrocities against fellow Asians. But the last decades of the twentieth century – more pronounced after the Plaza Accord of 1985 – saw the emergence of a benign, prosperous Japan as the chief engine of economic growth and industrialization across the region – commonly referred to as the flying-geese phenomenon – which precipitated an economic miracle in South-East Asia. Trade and economic diplomacy stood at the heart of Japan's influence in Asia. China's entry into global markets, however, progressively eclipsed Japan's economic dominance in the region. By the first decade of the twenty-first century, China would emerge as the key trading partner of almost all East Asian countries, with the notable exception of the Philippines. And unlike Japan, China faced no self-imposed restrictions on developing its military capabilities in tandem with a booming economy. Meanwhile, historical animosities encouraged South Korea, a US treaty ally, to not only flirt with China, but also to adopt a security doctrine which, in the words of strategist Edward Luttwak (2013), 'remains obsessed with an utterly unthreatening

Japan … purchasing air power to contend with imagined threats from Tokyo as opposed to the real ones just north of the demilitarized zone'.

This rapid shift in the regional balance of power – further accentuated by the 2007/08 Great Recession, which severely disrupted Western economies – may have played a key role in motivating more overt Chinese assertiveness in recent years. And the Abe administration is intent on reversing this trend by launching its own charm offensive across the Asia-Pacific region, courting like-minded South-East Asian states such as the Philippines and Vietnam as well as Pacific powers such as Australia and India, which share Japan's strategic anxieties regarding China. Upon his return to power in late 2012, Abe swiftly moved towards revitalizing Japan's influence in the region. By early 2013, Japan's top leaders were visiting South-East Asia and Australia, exploring large-scale investment opportunities and new strategic agreements. As mentioned above, while Prime Minister Abe visited Indonesia, Thailand and Vietnam, he dispatched Foreign Minister Fumio Kishida to Australia, Brunei, the Philippines and Singapore, and Deputy Prime Minister Taro Aso to Myanmar. Viewing India as a potential counterweight to China, and a huge untapped market for Japanese companies, the Abe administration also vociferously pushed for deeper bilateral ties with New Delhi. In less than two years, Abe would end up visiting forty-two nations, roaming across Asia, Africa and Latin America, pledging Japanese development assistance and trade – part of his global strategy of making Japan once again a relevant international player (Asahi Shumbun 2014). To support a more ambitious foreign policy, Abe also pushed ahead with a series of stimulus programmes and structural reforms to reflate Japan's flailing economy. As a result, Japan's stock markets have recovered from long-term stupor, while business confidence in the economy has been gradually restored. By managing to pull off a controversial reinterpretation of the Japanese Constitution, whereby Tokyo could deploy its armed forces 'if the country's existence, the lives of the people, their freedoms, and the right to seek happiness are feared to be profoundly threatened because of an armed attack on Japan or other countries', the Abe administration can more credibly present Japan as a serious counterweight to China. Legal experts Bruce Ackerman (Yale University) and Tokujin Matsudaira (Kanagawa University) cogently explain the immense ramifications of Abe's constitutional manoeuvre:

> [The reinterpretation would] authorize Japan to use force in defense of the United States or other close allies. Such preemptive attacks – including the authority to use the military to break embargos on oil or food so long as the 'right to seek happiness' is endangered – go far beyond the principles of self-defense authorized by Article 51 of the United Nations Charter, and erase Article Nine's emphatic renunciation of 'the threat or use of force.' ... Despite the extreme nature of the proposed revisions, Abe seems to be overcoming his coalition partner's resistance. While New Komeito may eliminate some of the broader reinterpretations as a face-saving measure, it may go along with a constitutional revolution by unconstitutional means – unless public opinion at home and abroad emphatically oppose the move. (Ackerman and Matsudaira 2014)

For the Abe administration, constraining China could come in the form of a network of informal alliances in the region, with the United States as the ultimate offshore balancer. Beyond revisiting Japan's pacifist Constitution, the Abe administration has eased restrictions on arms exports, paving the way for more robust defence cooperation with regional partners. By launching an arms procurement agency, Japan would be in a position to develop joint ventures in the realm of defence with partner countries. More capable partners such as Australia and India are set to benefit from sophisticated Japanese defence technology and joint-development ventures, while smaller countries such as Vietnam and the Philippines will benefit from Japanese assistance in terms of developing domain awareness and minimum deterrence capabilities within their maritime jurisdictions. China's actions, particularly its decision in 2014 to deploy Type 094 missile-capable submarines to the Yulin naval base on Hainan Island, have deepened the sense of urgency for greater defence cooperation between Japan and its partners. Overall, while China managed to progressively push its territorial claims to their fullest extent, it risked empowering a long-time rival, Japan, which showed unprecedented determination to serve as a regional counterweight under the Abe administration.

A new era?

While Xi Jinping's top priority is arguably the necessity to transform China into a knowledge-driven, high-productivity and consumption-based economy (see Chapters 2 and 3), Shinzo Abe is intent on reflating Japan's economy in order to support his ambitious foreign policy. For Xi, maintaining strong credentials on foreign policy issues is crucial to achieving sufficient political capital to push for much-needed and difficult reforms, which have been opposed by powerful lobby groups, from corrupt officials to export-oriented business. For Abe, getting Japan's economic house in order is key to reviving Japan's status as a major power in Asia and beyond. Despite Abe's efforts at reviving Japan's economic dynamism, however, the North-East Asian country is still struggling to gain a stable footing. The so-called Abenomics, composed of the three 'arrows' of reform, is still in the experimental stage, with the first two arrows (fiscal and monetary expansionary policies) injecting some energy into the country's stock markets and raising hopes of increased inflation and growth. But short-term gains have proved to be more tenuous than they initially seemed. On one hand, Abe's decision to push ahead with a highly controversial consumption tax hike (April 2014) led to a staggering 1.8 per cent GDP contraction in the second quarter of 2014 (Glosserman and Kang 2014). In fact, Abe failed to achieve macroeconomic targets, especially on GDP growth and inflation, for 2014. The Abe administration's initial decision to raise the consumption tax to 10 per cent by October 2015 raised serious concerns over an additional consumer spending shock, which could adversely impact GDP growth (see Figure 5.3). Back in 1997, Japan engaged in a similar policy, but the consumption tax increase undermined economic recovery and pushed the country back into recession (Krugman 2014; *Economist* 2014a). To offset the impact of the tax hike, the government introduced a US$51 billion fiscal expansionary policy, but the public infrastructure projects were

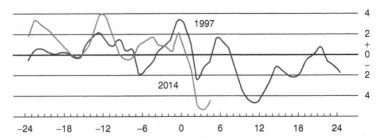

Number of months before and after April 1997 and 2014 consumption-tax increases

5.3 Japan's consumer spending (1997 versus 2014) (*source*: Oriental Economist Report; *Economist Intelligence Unit*).

hobbled by delays and worker shortage. With a debt-to-GDP ratio of 240 per cent, the Japanese government cannot repeatedly rely just on sustained fiscal expansionary policies (*Economist* 2014a). In late October 2014, the Bank of Japan (BoJ) stunned financial markets by introducing a new round of quantitative easing (QE), issuing more government bonds that will swell its monetary base to as much as US$712 billion. Many economic observers had ruled out any additional QE in 2014, not expecting more until 2015. By injecting more liquidity into the financial markets, the BoJ aims to increase inflation, encourage more business activity and notch up GDP growth. In the end, the stock markets reached their highest levels in seven years, but the BoJ admitted that the country would fall short of its 2014 targets: GDP growth for 2014 stood at around 0.5 per cent, while inflation hovered around 1 per cent (*Economist* 2014b).

Moreover, Abe's controversial actions, such as his visit (December 2013) to the Yasukuni shrine – home to fourteen Class-A war criminals and dedicated to 2.5 million soldiers who fought during the Japanese imperial era – have also negatively impacted confidence in the economy (see Figure 5.4), with the stock markets tumbling amid international outcry over the Japanese government's supposed display of historical revisionism and unwillingness to repent for the country's past crimes against humanity. On the eve of the seventieth anniversary of the end of the Second World War, with China, the

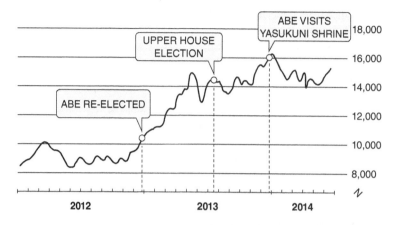

5.4 The impact of Abe's shrine visit on the Japanese stock markets (Nikkei) (*source*: Thomson Reuters; *Economist Intelligence Unit*).

Koreas and Russia expected to stage large-scale commemorations of the defeat of Axis powers, Abe has sought the advice of experts on drafting a new apology statement to reiterate Japan's remorse and potentially assuage aggrieved neighbours like China and South Korea. But it is far from clear how the Abe administration will sufficiently accommodate its neighbours, given the regular visits of his cabinet members to the shrine, and the spate of controversial statements by high-ranking Japanese officials – specifically, the denial or downplaying of the 'comfort women' issue and Japanese imperial forces' systemic aggression against ordinary citizens in neighbouring countries like China and South Korea – that reinforce a lingering perception that the new government in Japan embraces historical revisionism. Margarita Estévez-Abe (2014) succinctly captures the nationalist-conservative mood underpinning Abe's rise to power:

> Abe has stoked a patriotic fervor, promoting Japan as a 'beautiful country,' untainted by the ugly episodes in its past. In a sharp break from the country's postwar international posture – which, mindful of the transgressions of Japan's imperial era, emphasized humility and circumspection – Abe and his allies consistently express pride

in Japan's national strength and maintain that during the twentieth century, Japan behaved no worse than any other colonial power ... Abe has taken a different path this time around. Japan's relations with China and South Korea have deteriorated in recent years, but Abe nevertheless chose to visit the shrine last December, prompting predictable howls of outrage from Beijing and Seoul. The visit signaled that on matters both domestic and international, Abe has become much bolder. What remains unclear is the extent to which his popularity and political strength reflect a deep-seated shift among the Japanese public in favor of a more assertive, nationalist foreign policy – one that could prove a source of trouble as tensions in Asia rise to levels not seen in decades.

Amid continued economic uncertainty, from stagnant wages to massive youth underemployment, consumers have decided to cut back on their spending to cope with new tax increases (Glosserman and Kang 2014; *Economist* 2014a). With minimal improvements in the short run, Abe cannot take his political capital for granted. But as most economists would argue, it is the third arrow (structural reform) that is of greatest significance to Japan's medium- to long-term economic fortunes. But as Katz (2014b) explains, there are still limited indications of Abe taking on domestic interest groups to inject more competition, flexibility and openness into the agricultural and corporate sectors as well as the labour markets. Abe needs more success in the short run in order to generate maximum political capital to take on powerful lobby groups (e.g., rice producers, domestic companies, lifelong employees, etc.), which have benefited from the status quo. As Katz (ibid.) explains:

In the end, it is Abe's third arrow – structural reform – that will determine whether Japan can raise its long-term real growth rate from the 0.8 percent average prevailing since 1992 to the two percent the prime minister has promised. Even Japanese government economists admit that without reform, the country's long-term growth rate will never exceed around 0.5 to 1.0 percent. With the working-age population shrinking, the only way to generate more growth is to gain more productivity from each worker. Japan's GDP per hour worked lags behind the average for rich countries by 25 percent. Yet the erosion of human capital caused by the rise of irregular workers makes raising productivity even harder ... the lion's share of the economy is domestically oriented, and much of it is shielded from both international and domestic competition by domestic regulations and cartel-like business practices ... Abe certainly has the clout to take on these vested interests: he still enjoys an approval rating around 60 percent, and his party holds an overwhelming majority in parliament. Yet it seems impossible to find a single case in which the prime minister has truly challenged a powerful domestic constituency.

Reviving the Japanese economy is crucial to Abe's plans for building a more formidable Japanese defence capability – and transforming Japan into a more independent regional power. With no discernible turnaround in the country's economic trajectory, Abe has been circumspect in his defence-related plans: under his five-year plan, introduced in 2013, Japan's defence spending in 2014 increased by 0.8 per cent. Beyond 2014, Abe proposed about US$9 billion in extra spending up until 2018, amounting to a 16 per cent increase over the 2014 military budget. Since 2009, Japan's defence spending has decreased by 0.5 per cent, and in 2013 there was a 0.2 per cent contraction. In comparison, China and Russia have been spending more than 2 per cent of GDP on their military. (Given the lack of transparency in its defence sector, it is highly possible that China is spending well above the official figures.) China's defence budget in 2013 amounted to US$171 billion, increasing by about 7 per cent annually in the past decade. South Korea's per capita defence spending is 50 per cent higher than Japan's (Glosserman and Kang 2014). Above all, however, the major obstacle to Abe's vision of a powerful and independent Japan is the potently pacifist nature of Japanese public opinion, which has repeatedly rejected, in succeeding polls, any policy that could effectively 'remilitarize' Japan, neutering the pacifist Constitution by transforming the North-East Asian country into a military behemoth with an offensive, interventionist defence doctrine. Japan's ageing population has also presented a major demographic challenge, forcing the country to be more averse to military conflicts, which would endanger an already

shrinking working population (Glosserman 2014). Glosserman and
Kang (2014) sum up the Japanese public's extreme aversion to any
effective form of remilitarization, which may jeopardize the country's
post-war legacy of a peaceful rise anchored by economic prowess and
subtle diplomacy:

> The public remains fundamentally hostile toward an activist
> foreign policy and profoundly suspicious of any role for the
> military ... [More] Japanese oppose Abe's Yasukuni Shrine visits
> than support them; opinion polls consistently show that with the
> exception of environmental issues, few Japanese believe their
> country should play a regional role, and even fewer believe it
> should play a global role ... The persistent belief among some in
> Japan that the country needs to be 'more normal' and shoulder
> more responsibilities in the provision of international or regional
> security public goods is countered by an equally powerful and
> compelling belief among a larger group of Japanese that one of
> the most important contributions that their country can make in
> this endeavor is serving as an example of a resolute 'peace-seeking
> country.'

Despite his popularity, Abe has not managed to convince Japanese
society to shed its pacifist psyche.

The rise of others

China's territorial assertiveness has not only encouraged Japan
to reinvent its foreign policy, it has also strengthened strategic ties
between Tokyo and like-minded Pacific powers, particularly India and
Australia. While ongoing territorial disputes and historical animosities
have prevented a Japan–Korea alliance against China, with high-profile
diplomatic spats often colouring ties between the two North-East
Asian powers, Seoul has nevertheless also upgraded its defence ties
with fellow US allies like the Philippines, which have fiercely opposed
Beijing's territorial posturing in the South China Sea. South Korea
is not only locked in its own separate territorial disputes with China,
it is also increasingly concerned by the potentially negative impact of
the South China Sea disputes on its regional trade and the security of

its hydrocarbon imports, which mostly pass through contested waters claimed by China. All these middle powers, Japan, South Korea, Australia and India, share a common interest in the stability of the SLCs (Sea Lines of Communication) as well as a more responsible, self-restrained China, which has become a leading trading partner to all of them.

Asia's other behemoth Alarmed by China's posturing in the South China Sea, India, beginning in late 2012, waded more overtly into territorial disputes between China and South-East Asian nations in the South China Sea, a move that promised to raise tensions between New Delhi and Beijing. After decades of low-profile diplomacy in the Pacific, where it has been constantly overshadowed by the likes of the USA, Australia, China and Japan, an increasingly confident India gradually stepped up its engagement with the wider region and flexed its increasingly robust naval muscle in the process. India's booming trade with South-East Asian countries, paved by New Delhi's 'Look East' policy towards the region in response to a period of fast economic growth in the 1990s, gave a refurbished Indian navy more reasons to develop an expeditionary outlook and transcend its traditional areas of operation, principally in the Indian Ocean. Against the backdrop of rising rivalry between the USA and China, and Japan's resurgent foreign policy under a more hawkish new leadership, India's entry into the South China Sea drama promised to transform the Pacific theatre into an arena for a truly multipolar strategic battle for power and influence. Increasing economic and political integration between the Association of Southeast Asian Nations (ASEAN) and India has resulted in three significant interrelated trends, namely: first, an ASEAN–India economic symbiosis whereby both sides have emerged as new centres of economic growth and dynamism, creating tremendous potential for large-scale bilateral trade and institutionalized economic integration; secondly, a mutual strategic recognition of India's rising strategic relevance as a new pole of power; and lastly, growing convergence in threat perceptions vis-à-vis China in the South China Sea, particularly between New Delhi and claimant states such as Hanoi and Manila. No wonder New Delhi has consistently reiterated its commitment to freedom of navigation in the area. India's push into the western Pacific has gone hand in hand with a growing Chinese push into the Indian Ocean, setting off a maritime rivalry between the two Asian giants. C. Raja Mohan, a leading Indian strategist and author of *Samudra Manthan: Sino-Indian Rivalry in the Indo-Pacific*, cogently captures the evolving maritime rivalry between New Delhi and Beijing:

> With their growing and globalized economies, China and India are now dependent on the seas as never before in their history. Both are building large navies. Naval planners in Beijing and Delhi would like to project power way beyond their territorial waters to secure the increasingly dispersed interests of their nations. In both capitals, the traditional attachment to the ideology of 'non-alignment' is giving way, if slowly, to the recognition of the need to have the capacity to influence developments far from their shores. Naval leaders in both Beijing and Delhi would like to win access to facilities in critical locations and build special political relationships that will allow their incipient blue water navies to operate in far seas. As their maritime interests expand and their naval footprints overlap, there is new friction between China and India in the Pacific and Indian Oceans. (Mohan 2012)

A strategic watershed The year 2012 was decisive in India's policy towards the South China Sea. As a rising Asian power with broad trade and strategic interests across the globe, India could not afford to ignore the spiralling territorial conflicts. While New Delhi is not a direct party to the conflicts, it is heavily invested in crucial hydrocarbon projects in one of the most turbulent areas of the disputed waters, where Vietnamese and Chinese forces have occasionally squared off. Despite vehement Chinese opposition, Indian companies have ploughed resources into various exploratory energy projects off the coast of Vietnam. The Indian state-run Oil & Natural Gas Company (ONGC) has not only been a major shareholder in a joint offshore gas project with TNK Vietnam, it renewed (2012) a two-year joint-exploration project with Petro Vietnam. In mid-2014, the Indian energy company won another contract in Vietnam, this time without any competitive bidding, underscoring the budding strategic partnership between India and Vietnam (Chaudhury 2014). Moreover, as one of Indian's leading experts on China, Srikanth Kondapalli, succinctly put it: 'With 55 percent of Indian trade passing through South China Sea, this is "national interest" for India and hence its position on freedom of navigation.'[6] And as India aims to become a major economic power, its trade with a dynamic East Asian region is expected to accelerate in the coming decades. New Delhi's wade into the South China Sea was dramatized by an ominous warning (to China) from top Indian military officials: 'Not that we expect to be in those waters [South China Sea] very frequently, but when the requirement is there for situations where the country's interests are involved ... We will be required to go there and we are prepared for that,' Indian navy chief Admiral D. K. Joshi declared in December 2012 (Keck 2012).

Notwithstanding India's evolving and complex bilateral relations with China, and its usual reticence in confronting its Asian rival, Joshi's statement represented a watershed moment in defining New Delhi's future position towards China's rising assertiveness in the South China Sea – signalling a more ambitious Indian naval vision. Joshi's comments came on the heels of China's increasingly aggressive posture in the immediate aftermath of Beijing's highly sensitive leadership transition from Hu Jintao to Xi Jinping in early November 2012. Despite earlier hopes of a more amicable Chinese approach under Xi ahead of the November 2012 ASEAN summit in Phnom Penh, Beijing continued to press its advantage by encouraging Cambodia to block any unified regional measure on the maritime disputes. To consolidate its domestic position, the Xi-led new leadership also upped the ante by engaging in even more provocative measures, which not only spooked many South-East Asian states, especially claimants Vietnam and the Philippines, but also arguably encouraged greater Indian involvement in the issue. In November 2012, China published a new official map including South China Sea features that clearly fell within Vietnam's exclusive economic zone (EEZ). Moreover, provincial authorities on the southern Chinese island of Hainan announced new maritime regulations governing searching for and intercepting foreign vessels in

---

[6]   Interview with the author, 8 July 2014.

Beijing's claimed maritime territories in the area. The last straw for India was Vietnam's allegation that a number of Chinese paramilitary members harassed the Vietnamese *Binh Minh* 2 seismic survey vessel off the coast of Vietnam, where India's ONGC was operating. China's subsequent decision to issue new controversial passports, bearing a map that lays claim to all its disputed territories across Asia, including Indian-claimed areas in the Himalayas, also reportedly irked India. Joshi's controversial comments coincided with renewed Sino-Indian talks over disputed territories in the Himalayas, which sparked the 1962 India–China border war that China won and which has ever since embittered bilateral relations.

New assertiveness In December 2012, against the backdrop of more Chinese provocations, the ASEAN–India summit kicked off with a common goal of boosting bilateral trade and, more importantly, fostering maritime security. Judging by the statements of ASEAN leaders at the meeting, nearly all sought greater Indian involvement in the disputes. 'At this time of rising concerns about maritime issues, the need to maintain a high level of maritime security and freedom of navigation offers us [India and ASEAN] … an opportunity for enhanced cooperation,' Philippines vice-president Jejomar Binay stated, stimulating further Indian commitment to freedom of navigation in the South China Sea. Vietnamese prime minister Nguyen Tan Dung went one step farther by directly soliciting India's support to peacefully resolve the territorial disputes, based on agreed-upon regional and international principles. The summit significantly closed with a decision to upgrade bilateral relations from a 'dialogue partnership' to a 'strategic partnership', underscoring growing common interests vis-à-vis China. Both sides also agreed to raise bilateral trade to as much US$200 billion in the next decade. The summit's concluding document, announced as a 'common vision', expressed both sides' interests in ensuring maritime security in the South China Sea: 'We are committed to strengthening cooperation to ensure maritime security and freedom of navigation and safety of sea lanes of communication for unfettered movement of trade in accordance with international law, including UNCLOS' (Colvin 2012). In light of China's meteoric

rise, fuelling its appetite for energy resources and in tandem with
rapidly advancing naval capabilities, India has undergone strategic
soul-searching over the optimal way to deal with Beijing's growing
muscle. India is still heavily embroiled in territorial disputes with its
two major neighbours –with Pakistan over Kashmir and China in the
Himalayas (see Figure 5.5). And only in recent years has it started to
focus on developing its naval capabilities.

After a decade of robust economic growth, a more confident India
is finding it increasingly difficult to maintain a low-profile presence
in crucial regional and international spheres. In addition, India's
booming economy has also expanded its global strategic horizons,
with major Indian companies searching for raw materials, technology
and markets in new territories. Indian strategists have thus fixed
their gaze on developing a truly formidable navy to protect India's
emerging global interests, especially the safe and predictable flow of
strategic commodities from surrounding waters. In the last decade,

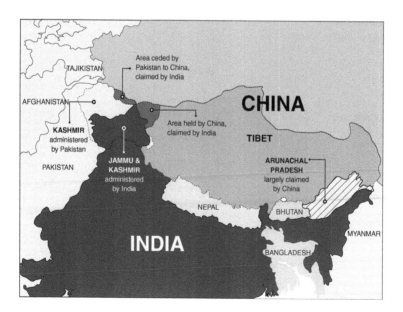

5.5 India's territorial disputes with China and Pakistan (*source: Economist*).

the Indian navy's share of total military expenditure has increased from 15 to 19 per cent (Jaishankar 2012). In the coming decade, the navy will be boosted by an armada of new acquisitions, including: two new aircraft carriers, at least three Kolkata-class destroyers, indigenously designed nuclear submarines, a Boeing P-8I Neptune maritime multi-mission aircraft, and advanced stealth frigates led by the *Sahyadri* and the *Satpura*. These acquisitions will place up to a total of 140 warships in India's service (Asia Defence News 2012). Surrounded by two rivals, Pakistan and China, India has accelerated its defence spending in order to enhance its deterrence capabilities, along the way emerging as the world's leading importer of military hardware (see Figure 5.6). For half a decade, India has been the world's leading importer of weapons, with a defence budget of US$46.8 billion (ranked seventh in the world). By 2020, the country is expected to overtake Japan, France and Britain in terms of defence spending. It is bolstering its airforce with a US$12 billion deal to buy as many as 126 Rafale fighter jets from France, while developing its ballistic missile capabilities, recently testing a missile with a range of 3,100 miles – comfortably placing much of China within its range (*Economist* 2013b).

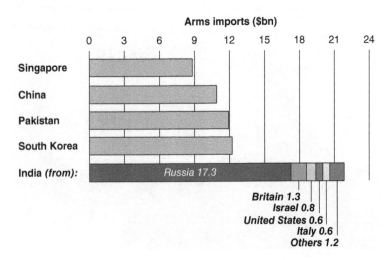

5.6 The world's biggest arms importers (*source: Economist* (2013b)).

TABLE 5.1 Comparison of military capabilities of Asia's four most populated countries

Active forces		Reserves	
India	1,325,000	India	1,155,000
China	2,285,000	China	510,000
Pakistan	642,000	Pakistan	na
Indonesia	395,000	Indonesia	400,000
Main battle tanks		Principal surface combatants	
India	3,274+	India	24
China	77,430+	China	77
Pakistan	2,411+	Pakistan	10
Indonesia	na	Indonesia	11
Combat capable aircraft		Strategic missiles	
India	870	India	24
China	1,903	China	77
Pakistan	423	Pakistan	10
Indonesia	69	Indonesia	11
Tactical submarines		Defence budget* $bn	
India	15	India	38.5
China	61	China	102
Pakistan	8	Pakistan	5.8
Indonesia	2	Indonesia	7.7

Source: ISS, *Military Balance*, 2012; *Economist* (2013b).
* Direct spending on armed forces only.

While India has maintained a considerable military edge over Pakistan, it has been overshadowed by China. The alliance between Pakistan and China has been a steady source of worry and annoyance for New Delhi, with Indian strategists constantly anticipating the ways by which Sino-Indian tensions could in turn affect the India–Pakistan equation. India has also been alarmed by China's growing presence across the Indian Ocean, from Myanmar to Bangladesh, Sri Lanka and Pakistan. In a dramatic display of its growing naval ambitions, Chinese warships managed to stage their first joint naval exercises with Iran in the Persian Gulf in 2014 (Erdbrink and Buckley 2014).

India largely treats the Indian Ocean as its natural backyard, but China has sought to challenge this in recent years. For naval experts such as James Holmes (2014b), India may actually hold the upper hand in the emerging maritime contest in the Indian Ocean for the foreseeable future:

> The Andaman and Nicobar Islands, for instance, stand athwart the western approaches to the Strait of Malacca. The Indian military can position surveillance assets and antiaccess forces along the island chains to deliberately compound the 'Malacca dilemma' of which China's leaders have spoken ... The Indian Navy has operated aircraft carriers for decades and will not face the steep learning curve the PLA Navy faces as it experiments with operating jets from floating air bases. If commanders leverage such niche advantages effectively, they can hope to outmatch a PLA operating far from home.

China views India's naval dominance in the Indian Ocean, over which the majority of China's hydrocarbon imports pass, as a source of (energy security) vulnerability, especially in the event that India – unilaterally or in coordination with other Pacific powers, particularly the USA – chooses to impose, in the middle of a large-scale conflict or diplomatic breakdown, a naval blockade on China's commodity imports passing through the area. In 1993, Zhao Nanqi (in Kaplan 2009), a high-level official at the PLA, proclaimed: 'We can no longer accept the Indian Ocean as an ocean only of the Indians,' while another prominent Chinese strategist, Zhang Ming, argued, 'India is perhaps China's most realistic strategic adversary ... Once India commands the Indian Ocean, it will not be satisfied with its position and will continuously seek to extend its influence, and its eastward strategy will have a particular impact on China.' As Kaplan (ibid.) explains, China and India have been locked into a competitive naval competition in the Indian Ocean: 'India has responded to China's building of a naval base in Gwadar by further developing one of its own, that in Karwar, India, south of Goa. Meanwhile [a Chinese naval analyst] has warned that the 244 islands that form India's Andaman and Nicobar archipelago could be used like a "metal chain" to block the western entrance to the Strait of Malacca, on which China so desperately depends.' Figure 5.7

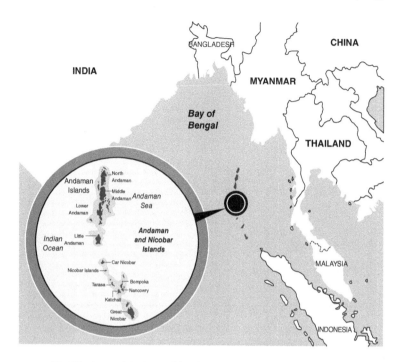

5.7 The Nicobar and Andaman islands

shows the strategic position of Nicobar and Andaman along SLOCs, resting on the intersection of the Indian Ocean and the western Pacific. Figure 5.8 shows China's so-called 'string of pearls' in the Indian Ocean.

The capability gap In the last decade, the Indian navy has intensified its joint exercises with major naval powers, especially the US Pacific Command, to enhance its operational readiness and interoperability with allies. Those enhanced ties may have been motivated in part by past Chinese provocations. But India is acutely aware of its relative weakness vis-à-vis China. And it has repeatedly sought to focus on common bilateral interests, trade and investment, and confidence-building mechanisms to manage territorial disputes and strategic differences. As J. Smith (2014) explains:

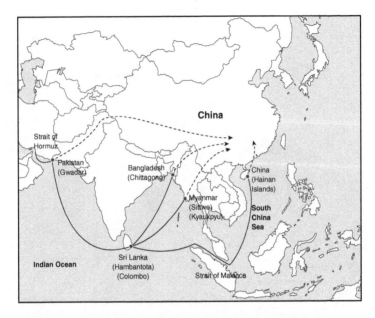

5.8 China's 'string of pearls' in the Indian Ocean (*source*: globalbalita. com/wp-content/uploads/2013/01/String-of-Pearls.4.jpg).

Bilateral trade expanded sixty-seven-fold from 1998 to 2012, and the Chinese and Indian armies held their first-ever joint military exercise in 2007, followed by two more in 2008 and 2013. They have periodically found common agendas on global issues of mutual interest like world trade talks, climate-change negotiations, the primacy of state sovereignty, and the need to reform global-governance institutions ... Most important, both capitals have shown a commitment to mitigating recurring tensions in the relationship. When crises do arise – as was the case when a Chinese border patrol intruded across the Line of Control for three weeks in April 2013 – they have responded with calm and patience to dissolve the crisis diplomatically. At the government-to-government level relations are, in a word, civil ... for the immediate future China will remain a distant peer, and this gap is matched by a major asymmetry in threat perception.

For good reasons, India treats China as a top security concern, though the latter is more focused on the USA and Japan as its leading strategic threats: in 2012, China's nominal GDP was four times bigger than that of India, while its military budget was three times larger. In human development terms, India's literacy rates are two-thirds those of China, while the proportion of its population living in poverty is almost twice as large (J. Smith 2014). Although India is expected to have a more favourable demographic trajectory in the coming decades, with its working population set to overshadow that of China, the real question is whether India can effectively invest in the human capital of its citizens and cope with its youth bulge (ibid.). This acute capability gap explains India's calibrated approach to China. In 2011, Chinese warships reportedly threatened an Indian navy vessel patrolling off the coast of Vietnam. At the time, New Delhi's response to the incident was subdued. In 2013, top Indian officials, intent on preventing a diplomatic crisis with China, repeatedly denied that Joshi's comments suggest Indian 'interference' in the South China Sea disputes. 'There are fundamental issues there that do not require India's intervention,' then external affairs minister Salman Kurshid stated with respect to South-East Asian maritime disputes during the ASEAN–India summit. '[These sovereignty issues] need to be resolved between the countries concerned.' Despite India's efforts to ramp up its military capabilities, with its defence spending expected to approach around US$130 billion by 2020 as part of a broader effort to close the conventional and nuclear gap with China, the South Asian powerhouse has still fallen short of establishing fully modern, self-sufficient and capable armed forces. As defence experts such as Harsh Pant (2014) explain:

> The Indian Army urgently needs new field artillery, with some reports even suggesting that it may not even have sufficient reserves to sustain a full-fledged war for 20 days. The Indian Air Force has repeatedly expressed concerns about the obsolescence of its ground-based air defense systems, the number of fighter aircraft due for retirement after completion of their technical life far exceeds the rate at which their replacements can be inducted in the IAF … The Indian Navy's depleting submarine fleet poses its own set of challenges with just 13 conventional diesel-electric submarines, 11 of which are 20–27 years old … Though in the mid-1990s, India was assured that indigenous content of weaponry would increase from 30 to 70 percent by 2005, the nation still continues to import more than 70 percent of its defense requirements from abroad.

Modifying India's global position For decades, especially after the Cold War, India followed a policy of non-alignment, avoiding an explicit tilt towards Washington or Beijing. But there are signs that things are beginning to change. And a change in India's leadership is playing a key role. Towards the end of its tenure, the Congress Party-led ruling coalition in India was battered by a combination of corruption scandals, rising inflation, a widening trade deficit and slowing economic growth, paving the way for the emergence of new political forces on the national stage. Amid a climate of political paralysis and economic uncertainty, the Indian electorate overwhelmingly voted (mid-2014) for Narendra Modi, whose parliamentary coalition achieved the country's biggest electoral victory in almost three decades (Macaskill and Krishnan 2014), giving the new government an extraordinarily high level of political capital. Modi hailed from the Hindu nationalist Bharatiya Janata Party (BJP), which successfully positioned itself as an alternative to the secular, centre-left Congress Party – the most dominant political party since the country's independence in the mid-twentieth century. After displaying his managerial prowess as the chief of the state of Gujarat (2002–14) for more than a decade, Modi came to be viewed as a no-nonsense, tough leader; he vowed to realize India's tremendous economic potential and protect its territorial integrity. 'I swear in the name of the soil that I will protect this country,' Modi declared, ahead of his rise to the top office in India, in a widely attended rally in Arunachal Pradesh, a highly contested eastern region of India, which is claimed by China. No longer attached to India's decades-long policy of 'non-alignment', a cornerstone of the Congress Party's foreign policy vision, Modi has instead called for a 'web of allies' to protect India's national interest (Mohan and Medcalf 2014). To match China's growing military might, he increased the country's defence spending by 15 per cent (Twining 2014). Leveraging India's image as Asia's (other) rising giant, Modi swiftly proceeded with upgrading New Delhi's bilateral ties with like-minded Asia-Pacific countries such as Australia, Vietnam and Japan. After all, they all share similar concerns about China's territorial assertiveness, which stretches from the Himalayas to the western Pacific. Modi was interested in exploring new avenues for strategic cooperation, establishing an informal alliance to check China's ambitions. For India's new leader, Japan represented a particularly enticing potential ally. Japan and India are widely hailed as the two largest and most powerful democracies in Asia, which can form a formidable counterweight to an autocratic China. Beyond the attractive symbolism of an India–China dyad (against China), Modi also cultivated very close relations with his similarly charismatic nationalist Japanese counterpart, Shinzo Abe. In many ways, the two share an ideological affinity: the belief in decisive leadership and the inherent threat posed by a rising China; the determination to restore their countries to a position of power and glory; and the commitment to steer their nations towards a new, prosperous future. No wonder there is a lot of good personal chemistry between the two leaders. On Twitter, Abe follows only three persons: Modi is one of them (Times of India 2014). Modi chose Tokyo as his first major foreign destination for a bilateral summit. During his high-profile meeting with Abe (early September 2014), the two engaged in high-stakes talks over a series of defence and trade agreements (Kondapalli 2014).

In economic terms, India represents a potentially lucrative consumer market and an increasingly attractive site for Japanese manufacturing investments. Amid growing anti-Japanese protests and newly imposed state regulations in China, Japanese companies are also seeking alternative investment opportunities in the broader Asian neighbourhood. In China, there are about 80,000 Japanese companies, compared to only 1,300–1,400 in India. There is obviously huge room for improvement (Takahashi and Katakey 2014). So far, the Abe administration has pledged about US$35 billion in investments, which would go a long way to deepening bilateral economic ties with India. Japan and India have also been exploring closer defence ties and a civilian nuclear agreement. Thanks to Japan's decision to relax restrictions on its arms exports, there have been talks over the potential export (or joint development of) Japan's amphibious aircraft US-2 to India. The two countries also stepped up their joint military exercises, with Japan expected to be a more regular participant at the annual India–USA 'Malabar' naval exercises, which are held in the Bay of Bengal. Under Modi's watch, Indian warships also made a highly symbolic port visit to Japan's Sasebo naval base near Nagasaki.

As Rajan Menon (2014a), one of the leading experts on India foreign policy notes: 'Keep an eye on Indo-Japanese security ties if you're looking for shifts. Change was in the air even before Modi's electoral victory ... Most Asian countries oppose Abe's plans for a more muscular defense policy; India welcomes it. Count on Modi to be especially enthusiastic.' In many ways, the stage was set for an Abe–Modi confab: from 2012 to 2013, Japan engaged in joint naval exercises with India; Japanese and Indian navies conducted joint exercises in the Japanese port of Sagami in 2012 and in the Indian city of Chennai the following year (Takahashi and Katakey 2014). Japan's defence minister visited New Delhi for close consultations in 2013, while Abe was the chief guest during India's Republic Day celebrations in January 2014 (Menon 2014a). Overall, there was a timely confluence of interests: concerns over China, on one hand, and expanding trade and investment opportunities, on the other, brought Japan and India closer than ever. Although neither of them is directly involved in the South China Sea disputes, both India and Japan have irked China by deepening their strategic and defence ties with countries such as Vietnam, which has sought support, especially military hardware and advanced coastguard vessels, from external powers in order to push back against Beijing's maritime ambitions in the region. Vietnam has become an important pivot state in ASEAN, striking dozens of defence and strategic agreements with all relevant Pacific powers in recent years (Kaplan 2014). While the late 1970s saw a Sino-American alliance of convenience to check Soviet–Vietnamese actions in South-East Asia, the late 2000s saw a Vietnamese–American tactical alliance to counter China's actions in the South China Sea (Vuving 2015).

Business first Alarmed by deepening India–Japan relations, Xi Jinping embarked on a crucial visit to India in late September 2014. The summit represented a historic opportunity for China's president to prevent further estrangement with India, dampen the prospects of a full-blown Japan–India alliance, and ease diplomatic tensions over border disputes in the Himalayas. During his visit, Xi displayed diplomatic acumen by seeking to enhance his personal rapport with India's new leader. Modi welcomed his guest by hosting a lavish traditional ceremony in his home state of Gujarat. China's two previous leaders were quintessentially bureaucratic, if not dull: Hu Jintao and Jiang Zemin usually conducted routine, formal visits abroad, and were nowhere as keen as Xi on visiting India so early into the term of a new prime minster in New Delhi. Xi, in contrast, indulged in bonhomie, immersing himself in the cultural festivities prepared by his Indian host. The intended message was clear: China was more of a peer than a threat to India. As for Modi, who aggressively sought Chinese investments during his tenure in Gujarat, pragmatism was the name of the game. Many experts would contend that Modi's nationalist rhetoric may not necessarily spill over into his actual policy-making, especially towards China. As Kondapalli explains:

> The BJP's election manifesto and the [Indian] president's speech in June to the joint sessions of the parliament indicate that so far it is modest in nature with no nationalist rhetoric explicit in the pronouncements or actions ... The formation of the foreign policy team – foreign minister Sushma Swaraj (who was the opposition leader before); deputy minister (General V. K. Singh, a former army chief and now in charge of overseas Indians); foreign secretary (Sujatha Singh, who continues from the previous government), National Security Adviser (Ajit Doval, who is considered to be an internal security expert with no significant foreign assignments but headed for a long time a think tank with a foreign policy focus) – indicates [the] immediate neighbourhood as the [main] focus [of the new government] ... Overall, there is no rupture with the past government's policies ... Overall on China, the Modi government is likely to continue a cautious policy initiated by the previous government, although [he] will strengthen conventional and nuclear deterrence against China. This is a long process and no spectacular results could be visible overnight.[7]

Modi wants Beijing to commit more capital and technology to the Indian economy. Despite its promising growth spurt since the early 1990s, when India opened up to global trade and reduced state intervention in the economy, New Delhi has struggled to unleash the

---

[7] Ibid.

country's economic potential. Most of the recent growth has been concentrated in the service sector, which has failed to provide well-paying jobs for the majority of the unemployed population, who lack the necessary skills and competencies to join the elite cadre of Indian professionals who have benefited from a boom in the Business Process Outsourcing (BPO) and Information Technology (IT) hubs in places like Bangalore and Mumbai. The manufacturing sector, which has been crucial to the rapid development of Asian tigers such as South Korea, Singapore, Taiwan and China in recent decades, has been responsible for a disproportionately small contribution to the Indian economy. In short, India has fallen short of creating inclusive growth, with a disproportionately large number of billionaires dominating an economy which has failed to improve the living conditions of hundreds of millions of citizens, who live beneath or close to the poverty line (Sharma 2012; Rodrik 2011). Modi was interested in attracting more Chinese investments in the Indian manufacturing sector, which holds the promise of providing meaningful employment to the legions of low-skilled Indian citizens who have struggled to make a living in the low-end services and agricultural sectors – the backbone of India's economy. Modi also sought greater Chinese investments in India's underdeveloped infrastructure; he knows that unless New Delhi upgrades and turbocharges its infrastructure development, it will struggle to attract large-scale FDIs. Modi also tried to explore avenues that could redress the highly lopsided bilateral trade with China. For a long time, India has been largely a source of basic commodities, while China has flooded the country with value-added manufacturing products. If India wants to stand a chance of closing its trade deficit with China, it should push for greater trade liberalization on the part of Beijing to allow large-scale exports of pharmaceuticals, agricultural products and IT services, among other more value-added products.

The Cold Peace endures At the end of Xi's trip, the two countries signed twelve different agreements in various fields. India managed to receive a Chinese pledge of US$20 billion in investments. This fell way short of earlier expectations (of US$100 billion and above) of Chinese investments in the country. Moreover, Xi's trip was overshadowed by troubling developments, with Indian sources accusing the PLA of engaging in provocative manoeuvres on the India–China disputed borders. There were reports of Chinese forces mobilizing within areas claimed by India ahead of Xi's visit, with another round of supposed 'incursions' taking place within forty-eight hours after the Chinese leader departed India (Medcalf 2014). New Delhi was alarmed by the possibility of PLA forces operating without the formal consent of Xi himself, who appeared to be interested in easing bilateral territorial tensions with India during his trip. But one can't discount the possibility of Xi seeking to send a clear signal to his Indian counterpart, who has more assertively sought to fortify India's position on the disputed borders. Intent on preventing fresh confrontations with Chinese forces, Modi's predecessors froze infrastructure development in Arunachal Pradesh. But Modi, upon assuming power, eased legal restrictions, including environmental regulations, on the construction and upgrade of (civilian and military) facilities close to the disputed areas. Modi's decision was described as a 'complete shift in strategic thinking' for India by one commentator. During his inauguration ceremony, Modi also dismayed Beijing by inviting Tibetan prime-minister-in-exile Lobsang Sangay. His government, during the visit of Chinese foreign minister Wang Yi to India shortly after Modi came to power, also insisted that China should respect 'One India' policy: that is to say, Beijing should stop abetting its ally, Pakistan, in seeking to regain or influence domestic politics in the disputed Kashmir region. Territorial disputes have been a major sticking point. Throughout Xi's visit, there was no tangible agreement on their territorial disputes along the Line of Actual Control (LAC). The two countries still lived in the shadow of their 1962 border war; it is clear that it would take a herculean effort by both sides to achieve a genuine compromise along the LAC. In the meantime, however, India will be continuously courted as a 'global swing state', given its rising importance as a largely independent pole of power, standing between China and a US-led network of alliances in the Indo-Pacific theatre. It is also clear that the Modi administration is gradually chipping away at a decades-long legacy of non-alignment and equi-distancing (from China and the USA) in favour of a more collaborative strategic partnership with like-minded states in the region. The once-budding US–Indian relations, which entered a critical stage when the G. W. Bush administration decided to provide civilian nuclear technology to New Delhi, have been undermined by diplomatic tensions in recent years, ranging from the US State Department's decision to impose a travel ban on Modi (owing to his alleged role in not preventing intercommunal riots in Gujarat in 2002, which led to the deaths of possibly thousands of Muslims), and the arrest of an Indian diplomat in the USA (over the treatment of her housekeeper), to trade disputes in the WTO and regulatory impediments to American investments in the Indian civilian nuclear sector, as well as Obama's perceived aloofness towards India, despite his unprecedented decision to openly endorse the South Asian country's permanent membership of the United Nations Security Council (Burns 2014; Chatterjee-Miller 2014).

The global swing state Once Modi was elected prime minister of India, however, the USA lifted its travel ban on him,[8] warmly welcoming the Indian leader as a crucial ally – and the leader of the world's largest democracy. During his visit to the USA in October 2014, Modi was welcomed like a rock star by legions of fans, mostly Indian-Americans, who have vigorously pushed for closer strategic ties between the two countries. 'We already have the foundation of a strong partnership,' Modi declared during his meeting with Obama. 'We now have to revive the momentum and ensure that we get the best out of it for our people and for the world' (Holland and Brunnstrom 2014). Much to the dismay of China, Obama and Modi, in their joint statement, agreed to, among other things, upgrade their joint naval exercises, and reiterated their shared interest in ensuring 'freedom of navigation and unimpeded movement of lawful shipping and commercial activity, in accordance with accepted principles of international law' (White House 2014). As Daniel Twining (2014) explains, Sino-Indian tensions provide a perfect opportunity for the USA and its allies to reach out to New Delhi in order to build pressure on an assertive China:

---

[8]   The travel ban was based on accusations that Modi was somehow complicit in the inter-ethnic riots in Gujarat in the early 2000s. See, for instance, Mishra (2012).

A China–India axis would tilt the balance of power against the United States, calling into question the future of its alliances with nations like Japan, and the ability of the U.S. to lead globally. By contrast, a U.S.–India partnership would make it more difficult for China to challenge American leadership in Asia and the world ... New Delhi is complicit in China's domestic insecurity by virtue of India's strong support for Tibet, including hosting its government-in-exile. In India, Xi was met by waves of pro-Tibetan protestors angry about China's crackdown there. For its part, China has stepped up claims to what it calls southern Tibet – otherwise known as the Indian state of Arunachal Pradesh. China also supports a Pakistani 'deep state' that has produced waves of terrorism against India, and endorses Pakistan's claim to Indian-controlled Kashmir ... New Delhi's approach to China will be influenced by America's approach. Modi has indicated his openness to a strategic alliance between the world's largest democracies ... if U.S. power and purpose appear resurgent, Washington will be a more attractive partner to New Delhi, reinforcing common interests ...

Hedging their bets, Japan and India are potential great powers. The former has been shackled by the negative legacy of its early-twentieth-century aggression and the US-imposed pacifist Constitution, which has transformed Tokyo into what many see as an American protectorate since the end of the Second World War. As Nagao explains:[9] 'Abe wants to change the Constitution and make Japan a "normal country" ... Despite the new "reinterpretation" [of the Constitution], there is still severely limited room for a Japanese military role abroad. For instance, Japan [still] cannot join a war like the Gulf War or Iraq War, etc. This means that Japan will still not become a "'normal country'". Abe will try to change Japan in the near future if he can keep working as Prime Minister. This is difficult to achieve even if Abe has been among the most popular leaders in Japan's history.' In the last two decades, India has managed to beat its traditional 2–3 per cent annual GDP growth, the so-called 'Hindu rate of growth' according to Indian economist Raj Krishna (Menon 2014b). Throughout the 1990s, the country sustained around 6 per cent annual GDP growth, soaring to

---

[9]   Interview with the author, 3 July 2014.

almost 9 per cent in the 2003–07 period, the golden age for emerging markets. By 2012, the growth declined to 6.5 per cent (ibid.; Sharma 2012). And the following years saw a significant deterioration in all major macroeconomic indicators, which convinced the electorate to vote out the ruling coalition under the Congress Party. India is struggling with its domestic contradictions, from its weak, antiquated bureaucracy, beset by corruption and inefficiency, to massive poverty and inequality, which have overshadowed positive gains in recent decades. A combination of acute developmental concerns at home and bureaucratic weaknesses could seriously hamper Modi's vision of a more consequential India on the global stage. Manjari Chatterjee-Miller (2014) cogently underlines the inherent vulnerabilities of the Indian foreign policy apparatus:

> India's foreign policy establishment is severely understaffed. Indian Foreign Service (IFS) officials admit they are constantly firefighting – that is, responding to immediate issues rather than strategizing about the future. Foreign diplomats have noticed the problem and claim that it hurts India's performance in negotiations and meetings … Quick expansion has led to the hiring of less able recruits without, for example, English-language skills … the lack of emphasis on strategic vision, which is one of the consequences of understaffing, can be addressed with the creation of a research wing. India's Ministry of External Affairs used to have a much-consulted 'historical division,' as officers refer to it, which focused on strategy. For example, it prepared India's case in the last border negotiations with China, in 1960. But the body has since disappeared.

For the foreseeable future, the imperatives of economic development (in the case of India) and revival (in the case of Japan) will continue to place serious limits on the ability of Modi and Abe to significantly alter their foreign policy.

The other guys

With Japan and India still grappling with a myriad of obstacles in realizing their full potential as great powers, more modestly equipped regional powers such as Australia, South Korea and Indonesia have begun to make their presence felt in the evolving Asian geopolitical landscape, particularly with respect to the ongoing maritime disputes in the western Pacific.

As a major naval power in the Asia-Pacific region, Australia has emerged as an increasingly influential player, with its leaders ever more explicitly emphasizing the importance of freedom of navigation in international waters and calling for a CoC in the South China Sea. In the middle of the twentieth century, Australia cruised out of the shadow of Great Britain, moving instead into a military alliance with the then rising superpower, the USA. Half a century later, Australia emerged as a key supplier of mineral resources to a booming China. By the twenty-first century, China was Australia's biggest trading partner, but the USA was its key security ally. As Sino-American rivalry intensified, Canberra confronted a daunting balancing act. As Carl Thayer,[10] a leading Australian strategist, explains:

Australia has a policy very similar to the declared policy of the USA but it is less vocal in expressing this in public ... Australia is mainly concerned about the adverse impact of territorial disputes on maritime security and safety and the consequent disruption of international trade. Australia firmly supports freedom of navigation and overflight, the non-threat and use of force, peaceful resolution of disputes, the role of international law, including the UNCLOS, the strict implementation of the DOC and the early conclusion of a Code of Conduct in the South China Sea. The [Tony] Abbott administration actively participates in the USA–Japan–Australia trilateral meeting and is very likely to join the quadrilateral USA–India–Japan–Australia security dialogue. At the same time Australia pushed engagement between the Australian Defence Force and the People's Liberation Army. Australia has even hosted small-scale exercises with the United States and China near Darwin aimed at HA/DR [humanitarian assistance/disaster relief] cooperation. [But] Australia [also] supports the United States on South China Sea issues and under Obama's rebalancing policy is making Australian naval, air and other defence [resources] available to an increasing number of US planes and ships on a rotational [non-permanent] basis.

[10] Interview with the author, 19 March 2015.

To make matters more complicated, recent polls suggest that a majority of Australians consider China as the country's best friend in Asia, ahead of Japan and South Korea; at the same time, about half of those polled said that China will be a military threat in two decades. Against the backdrop of mixed popular feeling towards China, Australia has adopted a hedging strategy, whereby it seeks to avoid complete estrangement with China by fostering greater economic and maintaining robust diplomatic engagement, while deepening military coordination with the USA in preparation for a possible major conflict in the Pacific. Under the US P2A strategy, Australia is not only set to host thousands of American troops, but it has, under the leadership of conservative prime minister Tony Abbott, signed (mid-2014) a new Force Posture agreement, which, in the words of Obama, 'will enhance the bilateral arrangements between [the US and Australian] militaries and give [them] additional reach' (Glenday 2014). Progressively, Australia has been locked into the USA's broader military strategy in the Pacific, which means Canberra will almost automatically be drawn into a conflict should the USA engage in an armed confrontation with China. Australia has progressively enhanced its military interoperability with the United States, with a growing focus on ensuring freedom of navigation in international waters. In 2013, during the biennial Talisman Saber, 8,000 Australians and 20,000 Americans participated in a twenty-two-day military exercise – spanning wide areas of Australia – that, according to the *Asahi Shimbun* newspaper, 'simulated war games against a fictitious enemy that one Australian defense expert identified as China' (Go 2013). Aside from the USA, Australia has also tightened its strategic ties with Japan, with Abe making a high-profile visit to Canberra in mid-2014, where he highlighted growing strategic affinity between the two US allies. Shortly after, the countries embarked on a potentially game-changing endeavour: the joint development and/ or purchase of Japan's prized Soryu submarine (Johnson 2014c). According to defence expert Kyle Mizokami (2014), Australia's acquisition of up to ten Soryu submarines from Japan has significant strategic implications: 'Japan's Soryu-class submarines are some of the most advanced diesel-electric submarines in the world ... China will be unhappy with the prospect of a Japan–Australia alliance, as well as ten more advanced, reliable submarines on the other side of the military balance.' Australia has also sought deeper strategic ties with India, with the Abbott administration striking a civilian nuclear deal with New Delhi (Pillalamarri 2014). The strategic implications are immense. Australia decided to provide uranium to a country (India) that has not signed up to the Non-Proliferation Treaty (NPT), which would allow India to divert a growing proportion of its limited uranium stockpile to its nuclear weapons programme at a time when China is expanding its nuclear arsenal. Raja Mohan and Rory Medcalf (2014), among leading strategists in India and Australia, respectively, have called for an even more robust alliance between the two countries:

> Australia and India have their own substantial capabilities, the benefits of their strategic geography close to vital sea-lanes, and most importantly, the potential to engage and mobilize a wide range of partners between them ... For Australia, such initiatives would fit well with Canberra's efforts to deepen Asian security partnerships alongside the U.S. alliance ... Moreover, a prominent role for Australia in Indo-Pacific coalitions that did not include the United States would confirm that its robust U.S. alliance is not an obstacle to prosecuting an independent foreign and security policy in the region. For India, the stakes are even higher. Building Indo-Pacific coalitions of middle powers could well become a critical element of a strategy to cope with the power shift in Asia and the uncertain evolution of U.S.–Chinese relations. This would help Delhi relieve the tension in its policy between seeking to balance a rising China, while avoiding an entangling alliance with the United States.

In contrast, South Korea has been more cautious in cultivating strategic ties with the likes of India and Japan. Booming economic ties and concerns over North Korea, which heavily relies on Beijing for its economic survival, have discouraged South Korea from taking a tough position on China. After all, South Korea seeks stable relations with China in order to keep North Korea at bay. Recognizing Seoul's strategic dilemma, and intent on weakening the USA–Korea–Japan trilateral alliance, Xi kicked off a high-profile state visit to South Korea in mid-2014, where he recalled their shared traumatic experience under Imperial Japan's aggression in the early twentieth century (Al Jazeera 2014b). China has sought to deepen the antagonism in the already frayed Japan–South Korea relations, while signalling Beijing's preference for deeper strategic engagement with Seoul at the expense of Pyongyang, which has, under the leadership of Kim Jung Un, adopted a more lukewarm approach towards China. Ferocious disagreements over historical animosities even prevented Abe from securing a summit with his South Korean counterpart, Park Geun-hye. In the end, it took tremendous diplomatic effort on the part of Washington just to bring the two North-East Asian leaders together for a trilateral summit in The Hague in early 2014. As Miller (2014) explains:

> The past year has seen little respite from the constant sniping and bitterness that has long characterized Japan–Korea relations. South Korea protests Japan's resurgent nationalism and its lack of contrition for the crimes Japan committed during its colonization of Korea in the first half of the twentieth century. Tokyo, meanwhile, complains of 'Korea fatigue,' noting that its repeated apologies and efforts to repair relations have met with sharp elbows and harsh rhetoric from Seoul … Seoul has also prodded Tokyo through controversial judicial decisions demanding that Japanese companies compensate South Korean citizens for conscripting their labor during the colonial period. In response, Japan has argued that these issues were legally resolved with the signing of the Japan–Korea treaty, which normalized ties in 1965.

The two countries have also been locked in a territorial stand-off over the Liancourt Rocks (*Dokdo* to South Korea, *Takeshima* to Japan), a group of islets in the East China Sea, which have been a source of great diplomatic irritation and increasingly emotional disputes between the two North-East Asian neighbours (Carpenter 2015). Although both are US allies, and share similar security concerns over North Korea, they have struggled to institutionalize trust and confidence-building among their security and intelligence establishments, with efforts at establishing intelligence-sharing agreements undermined by occasional territorial spats and acrimonious exchanges over Japan's historical legacy in the Korean peninsula. Nonetheless, the majority of South Korea hydrocarbon imports pass through the South China Sea, so the country is alarmed by the increasingly militarized nature of the territorial disputes in the area.[11] South Korea–China territorial disputes in the Yellow Sea have not headlined global news as much as the South China Sea and the Senkaku/Diaoyu disputes. But they are real and often reach near-boiling point. In 2013 alone, the South Korean Coast Guard (SKCG) arrested more than 130 Chinese vessels, which strayed into waters claimed by Seoul. In the same year, a South Korean court sentenced a Chinese fisherman to thirty years' imprisonment for stabbing to death a SKCG officer. Then, in October 2014, a Chinese fisherman was killed during a scuffle with the SKCG (BBC 2014). Seoul's relations with China has also been affected by their Koguryo/Gaogeli history dispute – a national-identity-centred controversy over whether an ancient kingdom was exclusively part of Korea or China, or both – and a border dispute concerning Mt Paektu/ Changbai, a highly symbolic location to both countries' historical narratives (Erickson and Monti 2015). Despite facing pressure from China, South Korea, which is also intent on building a robust defence industry at home, is expected to export twelve FA-50 lead-in fighter jets (worth US$415.7 million) as well as donate a 'Pohang-class corvette' to the Philippines, which has desperately sought to develop a minimum deterrence posture against China (Agence France Presse 2014c). This way, South Korea has emerged as an important external player in shaping the evolving balance of power among competing claimant states in the South China Sea. To prevent isolation among its North-East Asian neighbours, Japan successfully pushed for a number of high-level diplomatic meetings with its South Korean and Chinese counterparts. In November 2014, Abe and Xi held a high-profile, albeit awkward and lukewarm, meeting, with both sides agreeing about the need to manage their territorial disputes and resume talks among their defence officials. In early 2015, the foreign ministers of Japan, South Korea and China met for the first time in three years, discussing the

[11] This section is partly based on exchanges with South Korean foreign ministry and Japanese defence ministry officials in 2014.

possibility of a trilateral meeting among their heads of state. By April, Japan and South Korea had held their first security talks in five years, involving their senior defence and foreign ministry officials (Agence France Presse 2015b). These high-profile meetings have raised hopes for normalization and restoration of bilateral ties between Tokyo and Seoul, two US allies, which have adopted divergent strategies on dealing with China.

Given the expansive nature of Chinese maritime claims and paramilitary patrols, Indonesia has also accelerated its efforts at streamlining its maritime policy. Under a proposed Sea Security Agency (Bakamla), Indonesia aims to place a dozen maritime agencies under the jurisdiction of an overall coordinating body. This will allow the South-East Asian power to develop a more coherent approach to the perceived threat posed by China. In a remarkable departure from its usually low-key pronouncements on the South China Sea disputes, high-ranking officials in Indonesia have begun to more openly discuss Indonesia's growing sense of vulnerability in the face of China's ever-expanding maritime patrols across the western Pacific. For instance, Vice-Admiral Desi Albert Mamahit, chief of the Sea Security Coordinating Agency and rector of Indonesia's Defence University, went so far as to portray China's manoeuvres close to Indonesian waters as 'clearly a real threat for Indonesia' (Jakarta Post 2014a). Since 2009, there have been several encounters between Indonesian and Chinese coastguard vessels, with the latter reportedly resorting to armed intimidation to prevent the former from apprehending Chinese fishermen entering Indonesia-claimed waters. For a long time, Indonesia chose not to publicize these incidents as part of its efforts to act as a credible mediator in the ongoing disputes in the South China Sea. Much to the delight of fellow ASEAN members such as the Philippines and Vietnam, Indonesia decided to openly question (March 2012) China's 'nine-dash-line' doctrine, arguing that it impinges on Indonesia's Riau province, which includes the hydrocarbon-rich Natuna islands. Since 2010, Jakarta has persistently sought Beijing's clarification as to whether there are any overlaps in their territorial claims (Kapoor and Thatcher 2014). Indonesia was concerned with the broader legal and practical implications of China's posturing on the sanctity of UNCLOS. As Anne Marie Murphy (2014) explains:

> For over two decades, Indonesia has positioned itself as an independent mediator in the South China Sea disputes between its partners in the Association of Southeast Asian Nations (ASEAN) and China … [But] at stake for Indonesia is not only the Natuna Islands and surrounding waters – critical through these are – but also the sanctity of UNCLOS. Indonesia is the world's largest archipelagic state and it lacks the naval capacity to defend its far-flung archipelago, which spans 3,000 miles (4,800 kilometers) from east to west. It has therefore always been a strong advocate of UNCLOS. Indonesia's conception of its national territory encompasses not only its 17,000 islands, but also the waters that connect them: the Indonesian word for country is tanah air, literally land and water. When UNCLOS came into force in 1994, it included the archipelagic principle that granted island nations sovereignty over their internal waters. Ensuring that larger powers adhere to UNCLOS, therefore, is a key Indonesian security interest.

Like the Philippines, Indonesia fell short of developing its maritime and naval capabilities owing to its disproportionate focus on domestic security concerns, from quelling the communist insurgency in the mid-twentieth century to silencing separatist movements across the country over the succeeding decades. But Indonesia's newly elected president, Joko Widodo ('Jokowi'), has called for the transformation of the country into a 'global maritime nexus', which prominently features in his forty-one-page 'Vision Mission' statement during his presidential campaign (Harding 2014). During his state visit to Tokyo in late March 2015, the Indonesian leader reiterated his country's willingness to act as a 'neutral mediator' in the South China Sea disputes, while openly criticizing China's sweeping territorial claims (Lumanauw 2014). A highly charismatic reformist, who rose through the ranks from his humble beginnings as the mayor of a small provincial town, Indonesia's new leader is expected to focus on, among other things, enhancing the country's maritime deterrence capabilities to secure the country's territorial integrity and reinforce Jakarta's bid to become a major regional power in the coming decades. Thanks to successive years of relatively robust growth, Indonesia is in a good position to expand its defence spending and close its conventional military gap with other regional powers. Since 2010, the country has accelerated its defence spending, which is now three times larger than the allocated budget in the 2005–09 period and five times larger than in the 2000–05 period. In 2014, Indonesia increased its defence spending by a staggering 14 per cent. But the total amount stood at US$8.1 billion, less than 1 per cent of the country's GDP (Grevatt and Caffrey 2014). As the country's threat perceptions expand, Jakarta will be increasingly compelled to ramp up its defensive military acquisitions. The country is looking at establishing an F16 squadron (in addition to the Hawk 100 and 200 weapons system jets in the area) in Pekanbaru, in the Riau islands, and an Apache helicopter squadron near the disputed waters of the South China Sea. Indonesia, as the country's defence minister Purnomo Yusgiantoro explained, was particularly concerned with protecting one of Asia's largest gas field explorations at the East Natuna field, formerly known as Natuna-D Alpha block, which is expected to become a huge source of energy security and revenues for the country's booming economy (Jakarta Post 2014b). Indonesia has also moved towards regularizing joint patrols and naval exercises with the USA near the Natuna islands, underlining Jakarta's quiet tilt towards Washington (Panda 2015). Responding to China's rapidly developing military capabilities, South-East Asian countries have augmented their defence spending, which amounted to US$35.9 billion in 2013 (a 5 per cent increase), and is expected to rise to US$40 billion by 2016 (Ngui 2014). From 2001 to 2011, the region actually saw a 42 per cent increase (in real terms) in defence spending. Indonesia aims to have about five submarines at its disposal, with three of them to be provided by South Korea (O'Callaghan 2012).

Many analysts hope that the entry of other Pacific powers (Australia, India and South Korea) into the equation, particularly the South China Sea disputes, could have a stabilizing impact, mitigating the lopsided power relations between China and rival claimant states such as the Philippines and Vietnam. But this is not a panacea, and there is risk of further escalation. There is a serious need for sustained and meaningful diplomatic engagement among disputing parties, while weaker parties should urgently enhance their minimum deterrence capabilities to dissuade further maritime adventurism on the part of more powerful countries. Ultimately, however, the ongoing maritime disputes in the western Pacific reflect a more fundamental challenge: the need for a reappraisal and reformulation of Sino-American relations, which have moved from decades of détente and increased economic interdependence towards greater geopolitical rivalry and military competition.

6 | AFTER HEGEMONY: TOWARDS A PACIFIC COMMUNITY

The pessimist complains about the wind; the optimist expects it to change; the realist adjusts the sails.

William Arthur

Arab chivalry, Persian poetry, Chinese ethics and Indian thought, all speak to a single Asiatic piece, in which there grew a common life, bearing in different regions different characteristic blossoms, but nowhere capable of a hard and fast dividing line.

Kakuzo Okakura[1]

The Mediterranean is the ocean of the past, the Atlantic the ocean of the present, and the Pacific the ocean of the future.

John Hay, US Secretary of State (1898–1905)

Almost a century earlier, Tokyo stood as the bastion of pan-Asianism, attracting leading intellectuals from across Asia – from fully colonized places such as the Philippines (under Spain) and India (under Britain), to semi-colonized civilizations such as China, teetering on the brink of disintegration – who sought to emulate in their respective nations Japan's astonishing success in defending its sovereignty against Western imperialism and modernizing without losing its traditional roots. Japan represented the future; and budding nationalist movements across the region converged in the country, relishing the richness of its intellectual debates and the comforts of its new-found wealth. After half a century of systematic imitation of Western technology and institutions, Japan became the first industrialized nation in Asia. And its stunning victory over Russia in the Battle of Tsushima (1905) debunked the myth of European racial superiority. It was more than just a military success.

[1]   Quoted in Mishra (2012: 230).

It marked the beginning of the end of Asian subservience to Western colonizers, reinforcing anti-colonial movements across the region and inspiring the dream of a rejuvenated, unified Asia. For the first time in hundreds of years, a major Western power was decisively defeated by a non-Western nation. American president Theodore Roosevelt aptly described the event as 'the greatest phenomenon the world has ever seen' (Mishra 2012: 1). Japan's highly symbolic humiliation of Russia captured the imagination of the Asian continent, driving people from Turkey and Iran to India and China into an ecstatic mood of celebration and pride. Through Japan's success, nationalist leaders across the region saw the potential of reviving the civilizational grandeur of their beloved homelands.

The dream of a unified Asia – a dynamic mega-civilization, eclectically combining traditional wisdom with modern technology – was quashed by the brutal transformation of Japan into an expansionist imperial power in the succeeding decades. The First World War not only failed to end colonialism, it also reinforced the greed and grip of western European powers, particularly Britain and France, over much of Asia. The dissolution of the Ottoman Empire and the advent of warlordism and civil war in post-Qing-dynasty China meant that there was hardly a single indigenous power in Asia (with the exception of Japan) capable of holding Western encroachments at bay. Failing to gain full acceptance into the elite club of Western imperial powers, with rampant European racism alienating Tokyo's political elite, Japan would eventually join revisionist states such as Nazi Germany in coercively reshaping the Eurasian geopolitical landscape. Surrounded by the ruins of ancient empires, Japan chose to mimic the vicious imperial doctrine of Western civilization. Pan-Asianism gave way to a Darwinian struggle between Japan and the West over the acquisition and subjugation of the riches of Asia. The sheer brutality of the Japanese occupation of neighbouring Asian countries, in the run-up to and during the Second World War, instilled a deep-seated animosity, if not hatred, towards a country that was once seen as the future of Asia. In places such as China and the Korean peninsula, where tens of thousands of civilians were massacred and systematically raped by the Japanese imperial forces, a new form of nationalism would emerge: beyond their hatred of the capitalist West, iconic Asian leaders such as Mao Zedong understood patriotism in light of their resistance against Japanese aggression (Pyle 2008; Shirk 2008; Mishra 2012).

Japan's determination to assert its national pride and protect its sovereignty against Western aggression ended up being primarily at the expense of fellow Asian nations. And in the end, Imperial Japan was crushed by the West. The demise of Imperial Japan paved the way for almost seven decades of relatively uninterrupted American hegemony in East Asia, despite successive efforts by the USSR and its communist allies to impose an alternative regional order. The end of the Cold War simply reinforced American ascendancy in Asia – but not for long. To reclaim its glory, China shed its communist past in favour of state capitalism. Yet its inexorable rise has not exactly rejuvenated pan-Asian solidarity. And the brewing Sino-American conflict has placed smaller Asian countries in a difficult position, forcing many to choose between Beijing and Washington. As for China, it is an indigenous powerhouse, which in the past enjoyed outright dominance in East Asia for more than a thousand years, and is committed to relegating its 'century of humiliation' (1839–1949) to the dustbin of history. Asia is once again confronting the spectre of collision between an indigenous powerhouse and the West.

Yet, whether one likes it or not, the USA, as a Pacific power, has been (and will continue to be) a key actor in East Asia, at least for the foreseeable future. In an age of tremendous connectivity and pan-regional trade, the USA stands not only as a North American nation, but also a Pacific one, with the islands of Hawaii and Guam, and major trading hubs like Seattle, serving as its bridge to the East. Keeping this geopolitical reality in mind, it is perhaps more appropriate to talk about a Pacific community rather than a pan-Asian community. In recent years, the USA has adamantly reasserted its leadership position in Asia, while China has stubbornly sought to regain its historical pride of place in the region. It is this historic struggle which is threatening decades of relative stability and undermining the autonomy of smaller nations across Asia. As impossible as it may seem, there is still time and enough strategic space to transform peril into opportunity.

More than ever, it is essential to establish the building blocks of a prosperous, peaceful Pacific community.

The dreams of early-twentieth-century idealists and pan-Asian thinkers – from Kakuzo Okakura (1862–1913) to Miyazaki Torazo (1871–1922) and Rabindranath Tagore (1861–1941), who envisioned an era of harmony and cooperation among Asian civilizations – are far from dead. Today, Manila and Beijing are locked in bitter territorial disputes; yet Chinese visionaries and nationalist thinkers such as Liang Qichao (1873–1929) were among the greatest admirers of the Filipino anti-colonial movement, which tragically struggled against both Spain and the USA. Liang admired Filipinos as the 'pioneers of independence for Asia', who could (if successful), along with Japan, form 'a united Asian force that could resist the thrust of Europe's drift eastward' (Mishra 2012: 158). China's dream of modern statehood and independence flourished against the backdrop of Filipino resilience and Japanese determination in the face of Western imperialism. And later, during the Cold War, the likes of Nehru (India), Nasser (Egypt) and Sukarno (Indonesia) sought to resuscitate early-twentieth-century pan-Asianism by establishing the Non-Aligned Movement (NAM), which continues to be among the major global platforms for revisiting, enhancing and propagating 'Third World' solidarity. The pursuit of the 'Pacific dream' – a stable, multipolar, harmonious order in the Asia-Pacific theatre, anchored by rule-based institutions and Sino-American cooperation founded upon mutual understanding – necessitates a reconfiguration of the existing security architecture in the region. Preventing a violent confrontation between China, on one hand, and the USA and/or its allies, on the other, demands a decisive move on at least three major fronts.

First, the establishment of various mechanisms that provide sufficient space for Beijing and Washington to institutionalize the negotiation of their 'great power relations' in the interests of stability – rather than hegemony – in the Asia-Pacific theatre. Secondly, forging a greater sense of urgency and collaboration on the part of middle powers – whether sovereign states such as Japan or regional organizations such as ASEAN – to foster a cooperative balance of power, and establish international regimes which facilitate effective conflict management and encourage the resolution of territorial disputes in accordance with international law. It is important for regional states to agree on a common set of rules in resolving their disputes. Lastly, it is high time for smaller countries such as the Philippines to develop their own defensive capabilities and chart a more independent path in terms of foreign and defence policy. But efforts at enhancing their minimum deterrence posture should go hand in hand with much-needed, urgent initiatives and confidence-building measures, which are crucial for a diplomatic management/resolution of ongoing territorial disputes in the western Pacific. Ultimately, the best solution to the disputes is through bilateral diplomatic engagement rather than a competitive arms race and hedging. It is about finding the perfect balance between engagement and deterrence.

A new security architecture

The USA's overwhelming military presence across Asia has been a great source of vexation for independent-minded states such as China. But to blame the USA for all the troubles in the region is more propaganda than an objective appraisal of the situation. Throughout East Asia and beyond, most independent analysts would point at China as the main culprit behind the rise in maritime tensions in the region – and the cascade of destabilizing behaviour unleashed by it. The USA's P2A policy may have contributed to growing tensions, but China carries much of the responsibility for the regrettable deterioration in regional stability. As Justin Goldman, Associate Research Fellow in Military Studies at the S. Rajaratnam School of International Studies (RSIS), argues, 'the uptick in tension in the South China Sea is a direct result of the increasingly assertive behaviour, seen by a variety of actors in the maritime space, from the People's Republic of China (PRC)'.[2]

From the mid-2000s onwards, China has sought to make the most out of what it saw as excessive American preoccupation with military interventions in the Middle East, evidenced by its noticeable absence at the first meeting of the East Asia Summit in 2005, which prompted then ASEAN secretary-general Ong Keng Yong to openly suggest

---

[2] Interview with the author, 23 September 2014.

a lack of commitment by the Bush administration to engage in the region.[3] America's perceived (diplomatic) neglect of the region went hand in hand with growing Chinese maritime belligerence, often at the expense of smaller claimant states such as Vietnam, which is a fellow communist country and has fought a series of heroic anti-colonial wars against Western powers. In January 2005, Chinese forces killed nine Vietnamese fishermen in Vietnamese waters. In 2007 and 2008, China threatened British Petroleum and Exxon Mobil, respectively, with economic sanctions if they didn't cease their joint hydrocarbon exploration ventures with Vietnam in the South China Sea. In 2009, Chinese maritime forces detained 210 Vietnamese fishermen and seized their seventeen boats. By April 2010, China had declared a unilateral fishing ban in the South China Sea. Interpreting its own EEZ as a no-go zone for foreign military powers, China also stepped up its confrontation with American forces in the South China Sea. In March 2009, five Chinese vessels – hailing from varying law enforcement agencies – staged a coordinate effort at harassing the USS *Impeccable* around seventy-five nautical miles from Hainan Island, China's southernmost province in the South China Sea, forcing the American vessel to make an emergency 'all stop' lest it collide with the Chinese paramilitary forces. A similar incident took place a few months later, with two Chinese fishing vessels similarly harassing the USS *Victorious* (Pedrozo 2010).

In recent years, China has also accelerated its construction activities at a frantic speed and with astonishing breadth. Figures 6.1–6.6 show China's construction activities across the Spratly chain of islands, particularly on Fiery Cross and Mischief reefs, demonstrating China's determination to step up its strategic footprint in areas that fall within in nine-dash-line claims. As Mira Rapp-Hooper,[4] the director of the Asia Maritime Transparency Initiative of the CSIS – an influential organization that was behind the release of numerous high-resolution images of China's construction activities in the Spratly chain of islands, which sparked a media frenzy and panic among South-East Asian claimant states – explains:

[3] Ibid.
[4] Interview with the author, 15 April 2015.

China's construction activities in the Spratly Islands have proceeded with stunning speed and scope, and this naturally raises concerns about its longer-term intentions amongst its neighbors. China has far superior dredging technology and naval and coast guard reach when compared to the other claimants, so the scale of this construction is probably unmatched. When it comes to the Spratlys, however, there is a transparency problem that is not unique to China – all of the other claimants have engaged in some construction on the land features they hold, and some have used land reclamation techniques. Other claimants should provide data on their own development work – when it took place, where, and what exactly was done – if they hope to build support for the narrative that China's activities are truly unprecedented. As to whether this recent building spree is a strategic game changer, that will be determined by what exactly China installs on its artificial islands, and how the international community reacts in the months ahead ...

Within ASEAN and beyond, many countries have been alarmed by China's decision to build 'facts on the waters'. Beginning in December 2013, China reclaimed 1170 hectares (2,900 acres) of land across the disputed waters over a span of 18 months. Disputed features such as Fiery Cross have been expanded by eleven times their original size, while other contested features such as Mischief, Johnson South and Gaven reefs are barely recognizable. It is nothing short of geo-engineering on steroids, as China artificially transforms contested rocks and reefs into island-like features, which can host airstrips, military personnel, radars and advanced weaponry such as missile defence systems. Fiery Cross, in particular, has become a military garrison, reportedly hosting up to two hundred PLA soldiers. It can also host fighter jets and surveillance aircraft, thanks to its 10,000-foot-long runway. As China builds a network of airstrips and military facilities across the Paracel and Spratly chain of islands, it will be in a position to impose an ADIZ across the South China Sea, which, in turn, will allow China to impose restriction on freedom of overflight in the area. Thanks to its military bases and facilities as well as expanding paramilitary patrols and military drills across the contested waters, China will be able to make it increasingly difficult for other countries – particularly Vietnam and the Philippines, which control the most features in the Spratlys – to resupply their personnel in features under their control (Asia Maritime Transparency Initiative 2015; Perlez 2015b). Astonishingly, China may even be considering the establishment of 2-kilometre-long floating sea bases in the South China Sea that would be mobile and suitable for conducting a range of military operations; they would be composed of multiple semi-submersible hull sections, which could be linked together through their component pieces (McLeary and Robinson 2015). As Professor Carl Thayer[5] of the University of New South Wales (Australia) puts it:

> [China is] ripping the maritime heart out of South-East Asia (defined in ASEAN's 1995 Southeast Asia Nuclear Weapons Free Zone Treaty as including the EEZs, continental shelves and seabed of ASEAN members). China is creating an interlinked network for intelligence, early warning, and forward deployment of commercial (fishing, oil exploration), paramilitary (coastguard) and military warships. China's artificial islands will serve as storage depots and maintenance and repair centres. Chinese forward-deployed paramilitary and military assets will be able to respond more quickly to adverse contingencies that arise. In other words, China will have shortened its logistics tail considerably.

Through its massive construction activities, China will not only be able to achieve de facto – rather than de jure, since artificial and permanent alteration of contested maritime features is not admissible before international law[6] – sovereignty over contested features it occupies, it will also be in a position to drive out other countries from features under their control. China's decision to accelerate its construction activities may have something to do with pre-empting two potentially significant

[5] Interview with the author, 19 March 2015.
[6] Since the UNCLOS (see Art. 121(1) on regime of islands) discusses 'naturally formed' features, artificial transformation of contested features, beyond the coastal state's EEZ, will have no legal bearing on claims to sovereignty and maritime delimitation. Not to mention that the principle of 'critical date', the period after which there is a legal recognition (by an arbitration body) of an existing dispute, precludes disputing parties from going beyond the normal resumption of prior activities by permanently altering the nature of features under dispute. For instance, see the presentation by Professor Yushifumi Tanaka (Copenhagen University) at the International Law of the Sea Conference (23/24 March 2015) at Hanoi Law of the University, Hanoi.

developments in 2016: first, the conclusion of the arbitration at The Hague, with the Philippines hoping that China's sweeping claims will be judged as inconsistent with international law; and secondly, the transition towards a leadership change in both Washington and Manila, as Obama and Aquino spend their final years in office. China wants to hand the arbitral tribunal, the Philippines and the USA a fait accompli before any major development in 2016 (Moss 2015).

China has also become more assertive in dominating and pushing the USA out of the Yellow Sea. In 2001, a Chinese frigate (Jianheu III class) ordered an unarmed American Pathfinder-class oceanographic survey ship (USNS *Bowditch*), which was conducting a routine survey in the area, to exit China's EEZ. In 2009, Chinese vessels undertook a similar operation against another US surveillance ship in the Yellow Sea. In July 2010, Beijing went so far as to openly oppose a planned joint military exercise – in response to North Korea's alleged sinking of a South Korean warship (*Cheonan*) in March 2010 – between

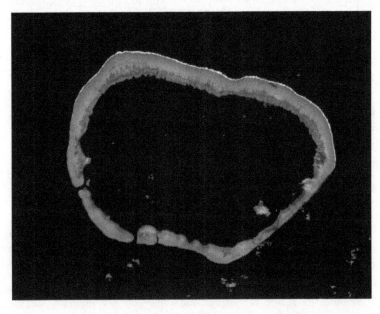

6.1 Mischief Reef before extensive Chinese construction activities (24 January 2012) (*source*: CSIS Asia Maritime Transparency Initiative/DigitalGlobe).

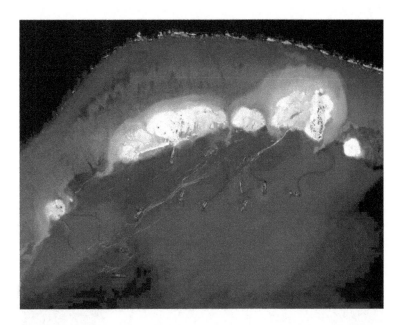

6.2 Mischief Reef after construction activities. Early 2015 saw extensive Chinese constructive activities on the reef, lying 129 nautical miles from Palawan (the Philippines' westernmost province), particularly on its western rim. The reef is claimed by Manila, which effectively lost it to China in 1994. The widening of the southern entrance to the reef and increased activities by PLAN forces around the reef signal China's possible long-term plans of establishing advanced military facilities on the contested feature. By 1998, China had already established a permanent multi-storey building, with troops and anti-aircraft guns stationed in the area (*source*: CSIS Asia Maritime Transparency Initiative/DigitalGlobe, amti.csis. org/mischief-reef).

Washington and Seoul in the Yellow Sea. China was specifically opposed to the deployment of the USS *George Washington*, which had conducted similar operations in the area earlier, describing it as a threat to China's national security. After the USA decided to withdraw the aircraft carrier from the military exercises, China conducted its own live-fire naval exercises in the Yellow Sea (ibid.). Chinese naval forces have also engaged in provocative actions in the East China Sea. Amid

6.3 The rapid transformation of Fiery Cross (August 2014–March 2015) Land reclamation activities began in August 2014, with Chinese dredges artificially creating a landmass covering the entire existing reef, approximately 200–300 metres wide and 3,000 metres long; the reef expanded from 0.8 square kilometres to 0.99 square kilometres (*source:* CSIS Asia Maritime Transparency Initiative/DigitalGlobe, amti.csis. org/fiery-cross/).

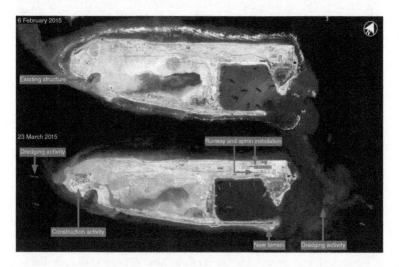

6.4 The accelerated transformation of Fiery Cross (February–March 2015) (*source:* CSIS Asia Maritime Transparency Initiative/DigitalGlobe).

the intensifying disputes over the Senkaku/Diaoyu islands, a Chinese naval vessel locked (January 2014) its fire-control radar on an SDF ship, which almost triggered a counter-manoeuvre by the Japanese

6.5 The airstrip on Fiery Cross. Images taken on 17 March 2015 show almost fifty metres of runway under construction at the northern corner of the (artificially constructed) island, with another 200 metres under construction in the southern portion. The runway is projected to be expanded to as big as 3,110 metres once construction is completed, possibly before the end of 2015 (*source*: CSIS Asia Maritime Transparency Initiative/DigitalGlobe, amti.csis. org/fiery-cross/).

side (Akita 2014b). Chinese jet fighters have also joined the fray, with ever-audacious, if not reckless, shadowing of American and Japanese aircraft in recent years. In May 2014, during Sino-Russian military exercises in the East China Sea, two Chinese SU-27 jets shadowed a Japanese SDF OP-3C surveillance plane flying close by, with one of the Chinese fighter jets getting as close as 50 metres to the Japanese aircraft. An hour later, two Chinese jets shadowed a SDF YS-11EB electronic intelligence aircraft, one of them flying as close as 30 metres to the Japanese aircraft. Reports suggest that a single pilot

6.6 Advanced facilities on Fiery Cross. China is estimated to have built more than sixty rectangular buildings, permanent or semi-permanent, on the northern side of the (artificially constructed) island on the Fiery Cross reef (*source*: CSIS Asia Maritime Transparency Initiative/DigitalGlobe, amti.csis. org/fiery-cross/).

was responsible for both dangerously close shadowing manoeuvres, raising the possibility of 'rogue' activities by individual Chinese fighter jet pilots (ibid.). In August 2014, the USA accused a Chinese J-11 jet fighter of performing an aerobatic manoeuvre to intercept a US Navy P-3 anti-submarine aircraft and a P-8 patrol aircraft flying 220 kilometres east of Hainan Island. The incident rekindled simmering concerns over the possible repeat of the 2001 incident in Hainan, when a Chinese jet collided with a US EP-3 surveillance plane. Back then, the Pentagon similarly accused the Chinese pilot of getting dangerously close to the American aircraft (Hutzler 2014). Some Japanese officials have ruled out the possibility of Chinese pilots engaging in such dangerous manoeuvres without clearance from above.[7] But there are reasons to doubt the extent of at least

[7] Based on a conversation with a high-ranking Japanese Maritime Self-Defence Force (MSDF) official, who visited Manila in October 2014.

some of the Chinese pilots' professionalism: in the past fifteen years, China has reportedly expanded its fleet of fighter jets by more than six times; the massive expansion within such a short period may have come at the expense of optimal training of new pilots, many of whom are the product of the 'patriotic education' of the early 1990s (Akita 2014b). China has upped the ante by also taking its military challenge (to the USA) into space. In 2007, China jolted Washington by conducting an anti-satellite (ASAT) test, shooting down a weather satellite with a ballistic missile. Given the US armed forces' heavy reliance on satellite technology for conducting and coordinating complex military operations across the globe, China's ASAT capability represented an important technological milestone – and a threat to American military supremacy (Bates and Kleiber 2007; Sanger 2010). Over the succeeding years, China conducted three more similar tests, raising genuine fears of an arms race in space (Lewis 2014). China has also been challenging the USA on the high seas, deep beneath the oceans' surface. In the 1980s, the founder of China's modern navy, Admiral Liu Huaqing, sketched out the role of nuclear attack submarines in China's evolving maritime strategy. He viewed the presence of the US forces in the 'First Island Chain' – an area that stretches from Japan in the north to the Philippines in the south, in the western Pacific – and the 'Second Island Chain' – an area that stretches from Japan to Guam and Indonesia – as a containing factor, preventing China from dominating what it saw as its natural backyard in the western Pacific (see Figure 6.7).

He called for China to achieve naval dominance in the first chain by 2010 and the second chain by 2020, with the country becoming a fully fledged global naval power by the middle of the twenty-first century (Page 2014). Since the 1970s, China has been slowly moving away from its diesel submarines in favour of nuclear submarines, which are less noisy and can remain hidden deep beneath the ocean's surface for an extended period. By 2014, China further pushed the envelope by launching 'boomer'-type submarines, with the capability to carry and launch nuclear missiles from the sea, placing East Asia, Hawaii, the continental USA and Alaska within its range. China is expected to keep

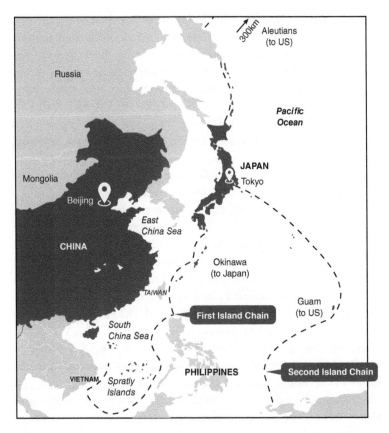

6.7 The First and Second Island Chains (*source: Economist* (2012)).

its boomers near its coastal waters, which may, some analysts argue, explain Beijing's increasingly assertive efforts at denying the USA easy access and routine surveillance operations across the South China Sea. With Chinese nuclear submarines reportedly roaming across the Indian Ocean and the western Pacific, surfacing in the Strait of Malacca, off Sri Lanka and the Persian Gulf, the North-East Asian powerhouse has joined an elite club of nuclear powers capable of straddling the high seas and projecting power well beyond their immediate coastal waters. Along with Russia and the USA, China is poised to become the third (and only Asian) country capable of launching nuclear missiles from air, sea and land (ibid.). Alarmingly, there are also some indications that China may be revisiting its 'no first use' nuclear policy, which, for decades, served as a reassuring reflection of Beijing's cautious and responsible approach to nuclear weapons. As Acton (2013) explains, China's 2013 defence White Paper 'omits a promise that China will never use nuclear weapons first. That explicit pledge had been the cornerstone of Beijing's stated nuclear policy for the last half-century. The white paper, however, introduces ambiguity. It endorses the use of nuclear weapons in response to a nuclear attack but does not rule out other uses.'

A grand bargain In many ways, however, China is simply replicating the USA's imperial approach in the nineteenth century, with naval strategists such as Alfred Mahan guiding the upstart North American power towards establishing naval hegemony, first in the western hemisphere, and later across the Pacific Rim, as part of a broader effort to drive European powers out of what Washington considered as its natural backyard and zone of influence (Bello 2010; Holmes 2011). At present, however, the USA still holds overwhelming advantage over China (see Table 6.1), but its quantitative (defence spending) advantage may not last for long (Figure 6.8). And this gives Washington enough strategic space to negotiate the parameters of a more stable great-power relationship in the Asia-Pacific region. The USA enjoys a wide array of military partnerships with more than sixty countries. Washington and its allies account for almost 75 per cent of global defence spending (Ikenberry 2014). In contrast, China can only rely on tenuous strategic partnerships (not treaty-based military alliances) with the likes of Russia and Iran, which harbour their own suspicions vis-à-vis China's rise and occasionally adopt contradictory positions vis-à-vis the West. For instance, under the Rouhani administration, which came to power in 2013, Iran has sought better, normalized ties with the USA, while Putin, who oversaw the annexation of Crimea in early 2014, has abandoned earlier efforts by the Medvedev administration to 'reset' Russia's relations with the West. While Moscow has resented China's growing reach across Central Asia, Iran, in turn, has been annoyed by China's opportunistic practices (e.g., barter trade deals, delay in oil payments, abandonment of major oil exploration contracts, etc.) when the West began imposing wide-ranging punitive sanctions against the Middle Eastern country over its nuclear programme (Heydarian 2012g, 2012h). Poor, dependent countries like Laos, Cambodia and North Korea – widely seen as China's satellite states – are hardly a major source of strategic support, if not an economic liability, for China's broader global ambitions. On its own, the USA continues to enjoy overwhelming advantage in naval power. In the Pacific alone, the USA has six nominal aircraft carrier strike groups. It has also deployed twelve guided missile cruisers in the region, while stationing twenty-nine guided destroyers. In contrast, China only has one aircraft carrier (a refurbished Soviet-era relic), no guided missile cruisers and only eight advanced destroyers (Kaplan 2014: 176–7). In light of China's rapid advances in the realm of asymmetrical warfare, particularly in terms of 'Area denial/Anti-access' A2/AD capabilities, the USA has developed the 'Air-Sea Battle' doctrine, which is designed to paralyse China's entire command-and-control structure in the event of a major crisis. In the short to medium term, the USA is the overwhelmingly superior military power in the Pacific. As Richard Haas (2014), former policy planning chief at the US State Department, puts it: '[the USA] is well positioned to thrive in the twenty-first century ... no other country is even close to having the necessary mix of capacity and commitment to be a challenger to the United States for global preeminence.' But this is expected to change in the coming decades, as China moves from mechanization (installation and deployment of new military platforms) to informatization (integrating them into an overarching network) as part of broader efforts to consolidate its Command, Control, Communications, Computers, and Intelligence (C4I) structure; upgrades its asymmetric warfare capabilities; and rapidly closes the conventional military gap with the USA (*Economist* 2012).

But as the leading liberal theorist John Ikenberry (2008) correctly points out: 'The rise of China does not have to trigger a wrenching hegemonic transition,' since 'China faces an international order that is fundamentally different from those that past rising states confronted.' As students of history, Chinese leaders have carefully studied previous power transitions (from one hegemonic power to the other), meticulously drawing valuable lessons from the experiences of Imperial Japan, Kaiser Germany, Nazi Germany and the Soviet Union, which unsuccessfully – and, ultimately, devastatingly – tried to challenge the hegemony of two Anglo-Saxon powers, Great Britain and later the USA. In 2006, China's CCTV launched a twelve-part Chinese documentary television series, entitled *The Rise of the Great Powers*, which assiduously analysed the conditions under which great powers, beginning in the sixteenth century, competed against each other for global dominance (Kahn 2006). Owing to the nature of and advances in military technology, it is in fact difficult to even conceive of an all-out war between the USA and China. They have both more or less reached a threshold whereby no side is capable of achieving a decisive military success without paying a considerable price. As Charles Glaser (2011) explains:

> Current international conditions should enable both the United States and China to protect their vital interests without posing large threats to each other. Nuclear weapons make it relatively easy for major powers to maintain highly effective deterrent forces. Even if Chinese power were to greatly exceed U.S. power somewhere down the road, the United States would still be able to maintain nuclear forces that could survive any Chinese attack and threaten massive damage in retaliation. Large-scale conventional attacks by China against the U.S. homeland, meanwhile, are virtually impossible because the United States and China are separated by the vast expanse of the Pacific Ocean, across which it would be difficult to attack. No foreseeable increase in China's power would be large enough to overcome these twin advantages of defense for the United States. The same defensive advantages, moreover, apply to China as well.

In fact, not all power transitions were as violent as those between Allied and Axis forces in the early twentieth century. The transition from Dutch to British hegemony, and later from Great Britain to the USA, was relatively peaceful. The rise of Japan in the second half of the twentieth century failed to trigger a major military confrontation between Tokyo and the dominant power of the time, Washington (Ikenberry 2008). To be sure, the structure of the international system hasn't changed, with anarchy (i.e. the absence of a world government) remaining its defining characteristic (Milner 1991). But power transitions are as much, if not more, shaped by the mindset and diplomatic capabilities of leading states as by the nature of the existing international order (Wendt 1992). In his celebrated work 'Anarchy is what states make of it', leading constructivist theorist Alexander Wendt analysed how the end of the Cold War had much to do with the endogenous transformation of the strategic calculus of the USSR under Gorbachev's leadership amid changes in the international order.

> If states find themselves in a self-help system, this is because their practices made it that way. Changing the practices changes the intersubjective knowledge that constitutes the system … Self-help systems, for example, tend to reward competition and punish altruism … The exceptional, conscious choosing to transform or transcend roles has at least two preconditions. First, there must be a reason to think of oneself in novel terms. This would most likely stem from the presence of new social situations that cannot be managed in terms of pre-existing self-conceptions. Second, the expected costs of intentional role change – the sanctions imposed by others with whom one interacted in previous roles – cannot be greater than its rewards. When these conditions are present, actors can engage in self-reflection and practice specifically designed to transform their identities and interests and this 'change the games' in which they are embedded. (Ibid.: 407–420)

For Wendt, a state's strategic calculus is not static and monolithic; political leaders' strategic introspection amid changes in the external security environment can produce new behavioural patterns among states. For Ikenberry (2008), 'even more decisive is the character of the international order itself – for it is the nature of the international order that shapes a rising state's choice between challenging that order and integrating into it'. For Ikenberry (ibid.), as Beijing chips away at Washington's advantages in almost every important arena of competition, there are three factors that underpin the endurance of the reigning liberal international order, which is expected to outlast American primacy per se: first, the relatively open and inclusive nature of the international economic system, which has allowed non-Western powers such as China, India, Russia, Brazil, Mexico and Turkey to rise through the ranks and develop robust economies; secondly, the coalition-based nature of American leadership, with Washington relying not only on its own hard power, but also the combined capabilities of the NATO alliance and a whole host of treaty allies across Asia and beyond which prefer the status quo; and lastly, the protection of state sovereignty and territorial integrity under the auspices of international law and intergovernmental organizations such as the UN. The problem, however, is that rising powers such as China tend to have a less sanguine view of the liberal international order. And they have sought to challenge the existing BWS by establishing alternative regional and global financial, security and development institutions and mechanisms (see Chapter 3). China, like Iran and Russia, views the US-led network of alliances, spread across the Eurasian landmass, as a deliberate effort at containing its ambitions – if not threatening its territorial integrity. In the post-Cold War era, Western unilateral interventions in the Balkans, Afghanistan, Iraq and across the developing world have also undermined the Westphalian principles of non-interference and state sovereignty. And huge powers such as China and Russia, which have historically dominated their respective regions, seem to resent the formal emphasis of the existing order on equality among nation-states (regardless of their size and influence) before international law. In short, Ikenberry (2008, 2011) tends to overestimate the attraction and influence of the liberal international order. As Nathan and Scobell (2012) describe, China views the USA as the 'most intrusive outside actor in China's internal affairs, the guarantor of the status quo in Taiwan, the largest naval presence in the East China and South China seas, the formal or informal military ally of many of China's neighbors, and the primary framer and defender of existing international legal regimes'. Nonetheless, Ikenberry is correct in pointing out that aspiring hegemons (China) risk massive (economic, diplomatic and military) backlash if they seek to coercively overturn the existing order, for this could trigger a counter-offensive by the dominant power as well as a whole host of like-minded allies which prefer the status quo. The way forward, as Zbigniew Brzezinski in (Rothkopf 2014) put it, is for the USA to treat 'China as a kind of co-equal stakeholder', with both sides recognizing each other's natural dominance in their respective regions.

TABLE 6.1 Comparison of US and Chinese military

	China	US
Defence budget 2010–11, $bn	89.8	739.3
Share of GDP, %	1.3[a]	4.9
Active personnel, m	2.3	1.6
Strategic and long range assets		
Intercontinental ballistic missile launchers	66	450
Bombers	132	155
Nuclear-powered submarines with ballistic missiles	3	14
Manoeuvre[b]		
Modern main battle tanks	2,800	6,302
Armoured infantry fighting vehicles	2,390	6,452
4th generation tactical aircraft	747	3,092
Attack helicopters	16	862
Heavy/medium transport helicopters	294	2,809
Power projection		
Cruisers/destroyers	13	83
Aircraft-carriers	0	11
Frigates	65	28
Nuclear-powered submarines	5	57
Principal amphibious ships	1	29
Heavy/medium transport aircraft	57	847
Tanker aircraft	13	550
ISTAR[c]		
AWACS[d]	14	104
Heavy unmanned aerial vehicles	na	370
Imagery satellites	15	10
Intelligence satellites	11	20
Navigational satellites	10	31

Source: IISS; *Economist* (2012).

a Official figure; excludes some military spending
b Combat units and formations capable of manoeuvring
c Intelligence, surveillance, target acquisition and reconnaissance
d Airborne warning and control system

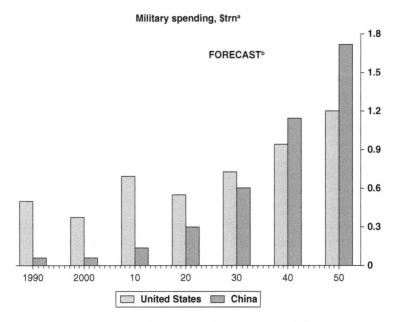

Military spending, $trn[a]

FORECAST[b]

United States | China

6.8 A comparison of actual and projected US and Chinese defence spending.
a 2009 prices.
b Based on US GDP growth of 2.7 per cent a year and military spending
   slowing to 3 per cent of GDP, and gradually slowing Chinese GDP with
   military spending of 2.1 per cent of GDP.

But this would require a genuine recognition of some fundamental
misunderstanding between the two powers, based on the difficult
realization that Washington and Beijing should explore a blueprint to
renegotiate the terms of their strategic relationship in Asia. As Henry
Kissinger (2011), the architect of the Sino-American détente in the
1970s, explains:

Some American strategic thinkers argue that Chinese policy
pursues two long-term objectives: displacing the United States
as the preeminent power in the western Pacific and consolidating
Asia into an exclusionary bloc deferring to Chinese economic and
foreign policy interests ... [For them] Beijing possesses the ability
to pose unacceptable risks in a conflict with Washington and is
developing increasingly sophisticated means to negate traditional

U.S. advantages. Its invulnerable second-strike nuclear capability will eventually be paired with an expanding range of antiship ballistic missiles and asymmetric capabilities in new domains such as cyberspace and space. China could secure a dominant naval position [in the region] ... [eventually] lead[ing] to the creation of a Sinocentric Asian bloc dominating the western Pacific ... On the Chinese side ... They see the United States as a wounded superpower determined to thwart the rise of any challenger, of which China is the most credible. No matter how intensely China pursues cooperation, some Chinese argue, Washington's fixed objective will be to hem in a growing China by military deployment and treaty commitments, thus preventing it from playing its historic role as the Middle Kingdom.

For starters, the two powers can ramp up as well as expand (existing and proposed) confidence-building measures (CBMs), which could help in preventing military conflict and managing strategic differences. As Steinberg and O'Hanlon (2014), authors of *Strategic Reassurance and Resolve: U.S.–China Relations in the Twenty-First Century*, explain, both sides will need a combination of restraint, transparency, resilience and reciprocity in order to establish and maintain a stable great-power relationship. Both countries could consider voluntary reductions in their defence spending in order to signal good intent. In terms of weapons acquisitions, China could exercise self-restraint in developing long-range anti-ship ballistic missiles and other related capabilities, which clearly signal the country's preparation for a naval showdown with and ejection of the US naval presence in the western Pacific. China could also signal goodwill by showing more transparency in its conventional and asymmetric defence spending. The USA, in turn, could better explain its 'Air-Sea Battle' (ASB) doctrine,[8] make it less lethal by modifying its 'offensive-minded' features, and give it a less provocative name such as 'Air-Sea Operations' (ibid.). It could also place a cap on its acquisition of strategic bombers, long-range, precision-guided ballistic missiles and other weapons. The two sides

---

[8] By 2015, there were reports that the USA had moved towards renaming the ASB 'Joint Concept for Access and Maneuver in the Global Commons' (JAM-GC), most likely to make it look less provocative and directly threatening to China.

could also extend their CBMs to nuclear, air, space and cyberspace realms. They could develop agreements on banning ASW (Anti-Surface Warfare), establish 'keep-out zones' around satellites, norms on acceptable behaviour in space competition and prevention of its full militarization. It would be best if China constantly reiterated its 'no first use' nuclear policy, with both sides negotiating a cap on their total stockpile of nuclear arsenals. The USA could show restraint by not deploying a significant number of ballistic missile interceptors to the Asia-Pacific theatre, which could effectively neutralize China's retaliatory capacity. They could also move towards ratifying the Comprehensive Nuclear Test Ban Treaty, accompanied by its strict and verifiable implementation. They could also enhance transparency by adopting an 'open skies' regime, allowing both parties to conduct overflights (at a certain agreed-upon number per year) over each other's territories. This could lessen China's frustration over and opposition to routine US reconnaissance flights close to Chinese territorial waters in the South and East China Seas. In cyberspace, both sides could look at mechanisms which would allow for greater mutual transparency, joint investigation of anonymous cyber-attacks, and a firm commitment not to target each other's civilian infrastructure (ibid.).

In terms of geopolitical hot spots, the two sides could look at varying actions and CBMs which would assuage China's strategic anxieties over Taiwan and potential reunification on the Korea peninsula. For instance, the USA could place certain limits on the volume and nature of its arms exports to Taipei. In exchange, Beijing could enhance cross-straits relations by communicating its willingness to rule out the forcible assimilation of Taiwan into Greater China, limiting military exercises that simulate a full-scale blockade and missile barrage of Taiwan, and establishing institutionalized dialogue with the top leaders in Taiwan. The USA could communicate its willingness to reduce its military presence in South Korea in the event of reunification on the Korean peninsula, while seeking China's help in containing the potential fallout of regime change in North Korea. Both sides should also focus on increasingly institutionalizing military-to-military dialogue at the highest levels, while fully operationalizing existing and proposed hotlines as well as incidents-at-sea agreements, which aim to manage/de-escalate tensions in times of crisis and accidental clashes (ibid.). While achieving the aforementioned CBMs is a tall order, both sides can significantly enhance their strategic relations by just committing themselves to negotiating such mechanisms. Thankfully, there has been some major breakthroughs in terms of negotiating CBMs in the western Pacific, with Obama and Xi, during their bilateral summit in late 2014, signing a number of agreements on how to avoid accidental clashes on the high seas and in the skies in highly contested areas such as the South China Sea. The agreements were inspired by existing international agreements such as the Code of Unplanned Encounters at Sea (CUES) and the 1972 Convention on the International Regulations for Preventing Collisions at Sea (COLREGS). The breakthrough came after sixteen years of hiatus following the establishment of the Military Maritime Consultative Agreement (MMCA) between the two powers in 1998. As Bonnie Glaser, a China expert at the Center for Strategic and International Studies (CSIS), explains:

> Two agreements on military confidence building measures were inked at the US–China summit in Beijing: notification of major military activities and a code of conduct for safe conduct of naval and air military encounters. Together, they hold out promise that despite persisting mistrust and ongoing preparations to deter and defeat the other side if conflict breaks out, the US and Chinese militaries can work together to reduce misperception, increase predictability, and lower the risk of accident that could result in inadvertent escalation in a crisis ... The two militaries will inform each other when they conduct major exercises in the Asia-Pacific region ... Agreement on these basic military CBMs is a good start. As maritime patrols and aerial activities have increased in disputed waters and near contentious territories, so too has the risk of an accident that could spiral out of control. These steps, if implemented and followed by additional measures, can reduce the potential for mishaps between the US and Chinese militaries, as well as provide a template that can be applied to other regional military rivalries, such as China and Japan. (Glaser 2014)

In the end, there would be a natural limit to the amount of transparency, reciprocity and restraint which the two powers can agree upon and fully commit themselves to. After all, it is still up to the two parties to determine, for instance, when to notify each other with respect to their military exercises in the western Pacific, while China continues to be non-committal vis-à-vis reciprocal notification of, for instance, ballistic missile launches (ibid.). This is why resilience is important: the USA will have to maintain sufficient residual capabilities in order to clarify red lines, place a marker in the sand, and demonstrate its capacity and willingness to defend its core, long-standing interests in the region, particularly regarding the security of its allies (e.g., Japan, South Korea and the Philippines) and freedom of navigation in international waters, especially the South China Sea. Beyond engagement, there should be a concerted effort by the USA, regional powers (e.g., India, Australia, South Korea, Japan and ASEAN) and other concerned parties (e.g., the EU) to constrain China's excesses (Segal 1996). Containment is not an option: China is a large, highly capable indigenous power, which is fully integrated into the regional and global economy, with legitimate interests in East Asia. It is no Soviet Union, and it is not engaged in an ideological competition with the West and its neighbours. China is a rational and broadly pragmatic power, which tends to respond to pressure as well as opportunistically take advantage of any power vacuum in the region. Almost two decades ago, Gerald Segal (ibid.) laid down the elements of a 'constrainment' strategy:

China's policy will remain softer only if pressure is maintained ... A policy intended to constrain China ... is intended to tell [her] that the outside world has interests that will be defended by means of incentives for good behavior, deterrence of bad behavior, and punishment when deterrence fails ... Constrainment of China can work, but its neighbors and powers further afield need to appreciate that they must act in a concerted fashion both to punish and to reward China; they must use elements from a strategy of engagement as well as the balance of power. Learning to constrain China is a necessity for all great powers, but most immediately for the East Asians ... Of course the United States cannot be expected to 'hold the ring' in East Asia unless the states of the region want and help it to do so. Northeast Asians have made some strides in this direction, but Southeast Asians, apart from Indonesia, have not. For the time being, it is the United States that provides the oxygen of security for the maritime states of East Asia.

For years, the USA has struggled to come up with an appropriate military strategy to counter China's 'salami-slicing' tactics in the South China Sea. A major problem with the ASB doctrine is that it is essentially useless when it comes to countering China's gradual, calculated and low-intensity territorial expansionism. Activating the ASB, or imposing a blockade (in tandem with treaty allies and India) on China's energy imports and trading commodities passing through the Indian and Pacific oceans, could not be justified unless Washington faces a major military conflict (think of a full-scale Chinese invasion of Taiwan) or an existential threat to its homeland (Keck 2014b). In recent months, however, the Pentagon has sought to develop and experiment with new tactics to constrain China's territorial assertiveness in the western Pacific. Careful not to fully provoke China, the USA has rejected options such as the deployment of US coastguard vessels to the disputed territories, or the establishment of US-led convoys to prevent the entry of and/or expel Chinese fishermen from the EEZ of the Philippines and other allied states. But Washington has considered the following options: the more extensive utilization of its surveillance aircraft to monitor developments on the ground; a PR offensive, whereby Washington would share images or videos indicating Chinese provocative actions (e.g., harassment of Vietnamese fishermen, construction activities on disputed features, massive paramilitary patrols within neighboring states' EEZs, etc.) on the ground; establishment of a regional information-sharing system; provision of advanced radar equipment to allies such as the Philippines and Japan; timely and calibrated deployment of US naval vessels and aircraft to the disputed territories as a show of force and an explicit sign of American opposition to China's actions (Dyer and McGregor 2014). These tactics should go hand in hand with intensified dialogue with Beijing under the auspices of existing (and expanding) diplomatic mechanisms. Any effort at renegotiating 'great power relations' with China, however, should be part of a broader strategy that involves other important players in the region. Otherwise, the USA could be accused of 'appeasement', which is perhaps one of the most abused words in Western history, thanks to the ill-fated attempt of the UK in the early twentieth century to acquiesce to Nazi

Germany's annexation (1938) of Czechoslovakia's Sudetenland in hopes of staving off a larger confrontation in Europe – to no avail. As eminent British historian Paul Kennedy (2010) argues: 'Nothing so alarms a president or prime minister in the Western world than to be accused of pursuing policies of appeasement. Better to be accused of stealing from a nunnery, or beating one's family.' This is precisely why it would be almost impossible, tantamount to political suicide, for any American administration to contemplate an exclusive Sino-American strategic settlement without involving allies and other important regional stakeholders. But this would also mean that other regional powers should step up to the task and contribute to the establishment of a viable regional security architecture which reflects the seismic shift in the regional balance of power and interests.

Middle powers and institutional innovation For decades, especially in the post-Cold War period, ASEAN has sought to occupy a central role in shaping the regional order. As a collection of smaller states – which are intent on preserving their national autonomy as well as expanding trade and investment opportunities across the region and beyond – ASEAN has pushed for a norms-driven order in East Asia; the main aim was (and continues to be) the transcendence of classical balance-of-power politics in favour of rule-based interstate behaviour and cooperative security. By 'socializing' major powers into appreciating and internalizing ASEAN-driven norms, the regional organization sought to prevent conflict among major powers, resolve disputes in accordance with established regional principles (e.g., the Treaty of Amity and Cooperation) and international law (e.g., UNCLOS), and prevent the domination of the region by a single state. For a certain period, especially from the mid-1990s to the mid-2000s, the 'ASEAN formula' worked: the USA became the main security guarantor, while China became the top economic partner of almost all its neighbours, with small South-East Asian countries as well as Japan and South Korea cautiously (and ever hopefully) welcoming China's seemingly peaceful rise. This 'golden age' of regional stability and prosperity was ultimately transient, owing partly to the failure of ASEAN to rise to the occasion (i.e. in the South China Sea disputes) and strengthen its institutional capabilities. Short-term complacency served as a major source of long-term failure: after signing the largely symbolic 2002 DOC on the South China Sea, ASEAN failed to even develop the guidelines for the operationalization of DOC; and there was hardly any genuine effort at negotiating a CoC in the following decade. Efforts at negotiating a CoC in 2011 were half-hearted, with Cambodia's chairmanship of ASEAN in 2012 shattering any hopes of a unified regional position on the South China Sea disputes. From 2013 to 2014, ASEAN simply restarted earlier, stalled talks on establishing a CoC, without any major breakthrough. In late 2013, China agreed, in an ASEAN–China meeting in Suzhou, to at least negotiate the guidelines of a CoC (Storey 2013). The following year, however, it once again dragged its feet on the issue, claiming that a discussion of the CoC was premature, since both sides had to first establish the guidelines for implementing the DOC (Dizon 2014). Later, China even turned down the Philippines' 'triple action plan', which called on rival claimant states to (i) observe the 2002 DOC by freezing construction activities and armed paramilitary patrols in contested waters; (ii) negotiate a CoC; and, finally, resolve disputes in accordance with the UNCLOS. During the ASEAN Defence Senior Officials' Meeting Plus, held in Kuala Lumpur in early 2015, China vetoed the call by ASEAN members to place the CoC issue on the agenda. When it comes to sensitive issues such as the territorial disputes, China has effectively become – mainly thanks to its huge economic sway over many South-East Asian countries – a veto-bearing honorary member of ASEAN (Mahdzir 2015). Far from a monolithic expansionist power, China is a calculating and perceptive power, which has leveraged both its economic power – by some measures it is now the biggest economy on earth – and traditional diplomacy to reassert its historical leadership in East Asia. Beijing has pushed its territorial claims across East Asia, while preserving sufficient stability and diplomatic goodwill to preserve intra-regional trade and investment networks, which have transformed China into a global manufacturing powerhouse. In short, the Chinese leadership wants to have its cake and eat it, too. China's strategic success rests on its unique ability to exploit power vacuums in East Asia, both during and after the Cold War, and recalibrate its actions once the balance of forces turns unfavourable. This is precisely what China has done after every major diplomatic crisis with its South-East Asian neighbours throughout the post-Cold War period, particularly after the 1995 Mischief Reef crisis and the 2009/10 territorial spats with the Philippines and Vietnam. In both instances, China first exploited the power vacuum created by the United States' withdrawal from the region (i.e. the closure of American bases in Clark and Subic in 1992) and/or perceived geopolitical decline, particularly after the 2007/08 Global Financial Crisis. But once China realized that it might have overplayed its hand and allowed its rivals to play on lingering anxieties among Asian states vis-à-vis China to mobilize a counter-coalition, there was a swift rethink in Chinese tactics – but not its long-term objective and strategy – with Beijing reverting to the language of diplomacy, trade and historical ties to calm down regional tensions (Fravel 2012). The Xi administration has deployed a similar strategy, using economic incentives and high-level diplomatic channels after every major escalation in the South China Sea, including the oil-rig crisis between China and Vietnam in mid-2014, which led to an almost total breakdown in bilateral ties, risked armed clashes on the high seas, provoked unprecedented anti-Chinese protests in Vietnam, and forced ASEAN to (indirectly) criticize China by expressing 'serious concern' over unilateral, provocative actions in the disputed areas (Heydarian 2014e).

A fundamental problem with ASEAN's consensus-based decision-making process is that it allows China to leverage its influence over a very few pliable countries such as Laos and Cambodia to block any decisive action on critical issues such as the South China Sea disputes. This means that China needs just one dissenting opinion to render ASEAN toothless, even though most ASEAN members, including Singapore, Malaysia and Indonesia, have expressed their alarm over China's actions and its rhetoric vis-à-vis the South China Sea disputes. For a long time, the Chinese Foreign Ministry (CFM) has been the key interlocutor between the leadership in Beijing and ASEAN. The early-2013 appointment of Wang Yi, a leading Asia expert, as China's foreign minister raised hopes of better relations between Beijing and its ASEAN counterparts. As the Asia hand at the CFM, Wang was directly involved in the high-stakes negotiations over the 2002 DOC in the South China Sea, and displayed tremendous diplomatic dexterity when he served as China's ambassador to Japan. The appointment signalled that Xi was perhaps serious about containing territorial disputes with neighbouring countries, as explicitly mentioned in his late-2013 speech on the centrality of 'peripheral diplomacy' to China's long-term interests, in which he called on China to 'strive to promote regional security cooperation' and 'insist on mutual trust and benefit, equality and cooperation, propose the overall, common and cooperative security idea to push ahead security cooperation with peripheral countries'.[9] To back up its rhetoric, during the ASEAN–China summit in October 2013 China proposed the '2+7 cooperation framework', which called for two-point political consensus on enhancing mutual trust and good neighbourliness and a seven-point cooperation scheme, primarily in the areas of trade, investment and infrastructure spending (Parameswaran 2013). But such uplifting pronouncements have been countered by lack of diplomatic subtlety on the part of the CFM. In recent years, not only has the CFM lost much of its influence in the crafting and conduct of Chinese foreign policy, thanks to the rise of other interest groups such as law enforcement agencies and the Hainan provincial government, China's top diplomats have also become increasingly bellicose and uncompromising in their rhetoric, further eroding trust and confidence in hopes of diplomatically resolving differences between Beijing and its South-East Asian neighbours. To the consternation of some ASEAN countries, Wang has sounded as hawkish as some of his hardline counterparts in the Chinese civilian and military bureaucracy. Unwilling to be outdone by (proudly nationalist) colleagues in other branches of the Chinese state, Chinese diplomats have tried to project toughness over the country's sweeping territorial claims in adjacent waters. Long gone are the days, especially under the Jiang Zemin administration, when the Chinese Foreign Ministry acted as the voice of reason and moderation in Chinese foreign policy (see Chapter 1).

---

[9]   See a summary of the speech at China Council for International Cooperation and Environment and Development, www.cciced.net/encciced/newscenter/latestnews/201310/t20131030_262608.html.

In a March 2015 press conference, Wang angered many ASEAN members by chastizing China's South-East Asian neighbours, particularly Vietnam, for supposedly engaging 'in illegal construction in another person's [China's] house'. He went so far as to brazenly claim that China 'does not accept criticism from others when we are merely building facilities in our own yard', since Beijing has 'every right to do things that are lawful and justified [within China's nine-dash-line]' (Xinhua 2015b). Far from ameliorating maritime tensions with neighbouring countries, Wang has increasingly sounded like his moderate-turned-hawkish predecessor, Yang Jiechi, who purportedly shocked his South-East Asian counterparts by crassly stating, while staring at his Singaporean counterpart, that 'China is a big country and other countries are small countries, and that's just a fact' during the 2010 ASEAN Regional Forum (ARF) meeting in Hanoi (see Chapter 3).

Meanwhile, reflecting their growing fears over China's designs in the South China Sea, Filipino officials made a decision to effectively evict eighteen Chinese nationals who had been working in the National Grid Corporation of the Philippines (NGCP). The Chinese technicians were working on behalf of the State Grid Corporation of China, which, quite astonishingly, happens to hold a 40 per cent stake in the Philippine national electricity grid. After months of constant warning about the possibility of China sabotaging strategic sectors like electricity in the event of outright conflict in the South China Sea, Manila implicitly mentioned national-security-related concerns as the basis for refusing to renew the visas of the Chinese nationals (Rappler 2015).

To reassert its relevance, ASEAN will have to swiftly forge ahead on at least three fronts. First, it has to forge a working agreement on the question of a CoC in the South China Sea. Moving from a consensus-based towards a more majoritarian decision-making approach – as the region does on questions of trade and economic integration – is one way to break the ongoing deadlock. If it can't bring China on board, then at least ASEAN countries can come up with a CoC among themselves, providing a living, operationalized regional principle to present to China and other strategic partners like India and the USA later. Secondly,

ASEAN should begin to consider the proposal for joint peacekeeping patrols in the South China Sea. There is already precedence for this in South-East Asia. In the Strait of Malacca, Thailand, Singapore, Indonesia and Malaysia have, since 2004, participated in joint patrols against non-traditional security threats, such as maritime piracy. The exact mandate and composition of any multilateral peacekeeping force in the South China Sea will certainly inspire a contentious debate. To be sure, China will exert tremendous pressure on its regional allies, particularly Cambodia and Laos, to block any such effort. But with key ASEAN countries, such as Indonesia, Singapore, Malaysia, Vietnam and the Philippines, consistently expressing their concerns about China's territorial assertiveness, there is enough reason to seriously consider such an option. External powers such as the USA and Japan could also play a critical supporting role. The US Navy's Vice-Admiral Robert Thomas, commander of the US Pacific Fleet, was among those who proposed the scheme and underscored that the US 7th Fleet 'would be ready to support' such operations. Washington has also asked the Japanese Maritime Self-Defence Force to contribute to such efforts. The Japanese Defence Ministry seems to be receptive to such a proposal, especially in light of the Abe administration's concerted effort at carving out a new security role for Japan in the region. The United States has also proposed the establishment of a South China Sea International Operations Centre in Jakarta, Indonesia – ASEAN's informal leader, which has been increasingly critical of China's territorial posturing. The International Operations Centre could provide critical logistical support for joint maritime patrols by the United States and its regional allies in the western Pacific and Indian oceans (Sharp and Shi 2015; Vu and Heydarian 2015). ASEAN could also develop an information-sharing system in the region, through which competing claimant states could share real-time, relevant data on developments in the contested areas and avoid unwanted clashes. In recent years, Japan and the USA have expressed their willingness to support such efforts, especially as they try to enhance the intelligence, surveillance and reconnaissance (ISRT) capabilities of partner nations such as the Philippines and Vietnam. Thirdly, ASEAN should also address the other major crisis in the South China Sea: the rapid deterioration of the ecological balance of one of the world's most biodiverse maritime zones. In one of its most recent and unusually detailed justifications of its sweeping construction activities in the South China Sea, the Chinese cited, among other things, 'environmental protection' and 'fishery production service' as among the core objectives of China's growing footprint in the contested waters (Tiezzi 2015). Other claimant countries, however, have retaliated, with the Philippines, in particular, claiming that China's construction activities may have damaged up to three hundred acres of coral reefs, leading to 'irreversible and widespread damage to the biodiversity and ecological balance' (Whaley 2014). Manila claims that China's activities have cost neighbouring countries up to US$100 million annually by virtue of damage to the coral reefs, which happen to be the breeding grounds for high-value fisheries. By some estimates, up to 70 per cent of coral reefs in the South China Sea have been undermined by a combination of unsound fishing practices, pollution, mechanical accidents and climate change (Hachigian 2015). With China expanding its reliance on fishermen-cum-militia forces to push its claims across the South China Sea, one can expect more congestion as well as illegal, underreported, unregulated (IUU) fishing in the area. Desperate to prevent IUU within its waters, which is costing the country billions of dollars every year, Indonesia has resorted to an aggressive 'sink the vessels' policy, while the Philippines has stepped up its apprehension of Chinese and Vietnamese fishermen poaching endangered species such as sea turtles. The Philippines' coral reefs have also been a victim of mechanical accidents, with major incidents involving American (USS *Guardian*) and Chinese vessels damaging the Tubbataha Reefs Natural Park (Heydarian 2015c). ASEAN should step up its efforts at establishing an environmental regime which protects endangered species and precious coral reefs against further deterioration, else the lives of tens of millions of coastal peoples, who depend on fisheries stocks, will be at stake. Rehabilitation of damaged reefs and a moratorium on fishing in certain areas should be seriously considered. As Professor David L Fluharty,[10] a leading environmental expert at the University of Washington, explains:

---

[10] Interview with the author, 9 February 2015.

What is important is to get lasting resolution of marine/environmental protection issues – independent of boundary issues. While the locus of sources for environmental impacts from land-based sources of pollution, for example, resides with the coastal state, fisheries management and conservation constitutes an important issue to be resolved under existing protocols ... I see it as a failure of coastal states and distant water states to mutually agree on management goals and allocation of benefits ... Best practices for environmental management [pollution control, permitting of activities, fisheries management] generally start from agreed national boundaries and transparent data for decisions. The South China Sea lacks this ... At a minimum, the claimant countries should develop a forum where discussion can occur about the documented and prioritized environmental issues. National action, independent of territorial claims, can occur ... The first issue is to identify where environmental protection is inadequate [for whatever reason]. The second issue is to agree on environmental goals for the South China Sea ... The main issue as far as I am concerned is that potentially sustainable fisheries and protection of marine biodiversity are not compromised by agreement on goals and commitment of national policy to achieve those goals.

As signatories to the UNCLOS and Convention on Biological Diversity, China and ASEAN claimant countries have an obligation to ensure their sovereignty claims and national economic priorities don't come at the expense of their obligations towards preserving the ecological balance in the South China Sea. There are already emerging environmental regimes in places such as the Yellow Sea, where China and South Korea have stepped up their efforts at protecting the ecological balance in their shared waters. Claimant states such as Taiwan have also pushed for a peace initiative in the South China Sea, focusing on environmental cooperation and joint exploration/exploitation of maritime resources.[11] But in order for ASEAN to be effective and relevant it also has to address its bureaucratic hollowness. Despite its ambitious plan to establish an Economic Community (a common regional market) by 2015, and maintain a central role

[11] Based on exchanges with Taiwan's Foreign Ministry and President Ma Ying-jeou on the sidelines of the 2015 Taiwan-US-Japan Security Dialogue.

in shaping the security architecture in East Asia, ASEAN has only 200 employees (compared to 30,000 in the EU) to oversee, facilitate and implement rules and regulations relevant to regional integration (*Economist Intelligence Unit* 2013). ASEAN completely lacks any effective compliance enforcement mechanism; its norm-driven advocacies have largely relied on the goodwill and receptiveness of great powers such as China. So far, there has been little indication that China has fully internalized ASEAN's fundamental principles on peaceful, rule-based resolution of territorial disputes. ASEAN is attached to an outdated form of super-nationalism: that is to say, the regional body has minimal political autonomy, and almost no independent power to shape the preferences and behaviour of its member states; it is largely a platform for the amalgamation/aggregation of the individual interests of South-East Asian states, with no core states (such as France, Germany, Italy and the UK in the case of the EU) effectively and coherently directing the agenda and evolution of the regional body. Unless ASEAN matures in institutional terms, and overcomes its inherent weaknesses, it will struggle to shape the broader regional environment. In the meantime, it is up to key ASEAN states such as Singapore (the most advanced nation in the region) and Indonesia (the largest state in the region) to compensate for ASEAN's institutional weaknesses in addressing critical issues such as the ongoing maritime disputes in the South China Sea. And there are indications that both states have been moving in the right direction. Aside from mediating in the disputes between China, on one hand, and rival claimant states such as Vietnam and the Philippines, on the other, Indonesia has more openly criticized China's excesses, while enhancing its own maritime capabilities to deter further Chinese adventurism (see Chapter 5). For its part, Singapore (the region's largest defence spender) has not only strengthened its military ties with the US Navy, which regularly conducts rotational visits to the city-state, it has also more explicitly criticized China's actions, calling for rule-based, peaceful management of the disputes in accordance with international law. In effect, Singapore has rejected China's nine-dash-line doctrine, which isn't consistent with the UNCLOS. As one Singapore-based maritime expert explained:

Singapore's position on the South China Sea is that while it does not have a claim in the South China Sea, it does have an interest in preserving peace and stability in the region, including ensuring freedom of navigation. This position has remained broadly consistent ... Singapore has strongly supported the US maintaining its military presence in Asia, with its officials consistently arguing that the US role as a provider of stability was critical to the remarkable Asian economic growth in the second half of the 20th century and beyond. In 2012 on the sidelines of the World Economic Forum, Prime Minister Lee stated in an interview that the US role in Asia in the Post-World War II period continues to be considered benign and that it is an example for the Chinese to emulate. While there are sensitivities to the appearances of the logistical support it provides the US through access to facilities, Singapore's role has been absolutely critical to ensuring a persistent presence of US forces in the region ... Singapore will continue to communicate to all claimants the importance of their exercising restraint and that disputes are to be resolved peacefully and in accordance with international law.

Other Pacific powers such as Australia, India, Japan and South Korea should also play a more constructive and engaged role in managing the South China Sea disputes – and constraining China's excesses. In 2012, in a controversial essay published before the parliamentary elections, Abe expressed his commitment to forging ahead with a more muscular and assertive foreign policy aimed at containing China and consolidating a regional democratic security diamond. 'I envisage a strategy whereby Australia, India, Japan, and the US state of Hawaii form a diamond to safeguard the maritime commons stretching from the Indian Ocean region to the Western Pacific,' he wrote. 'I am prepared to invest, to the greatest possible extent, Japan's capacities in this security diamond.' During the first round of foreign trips made by Japan's top leaders, Australia was the sole non-ASEAN destination. Canberra's significance lies in its status as the other spoke – together with Japan – in the US-based 'hub and spokes' alliance network in the Pacific. The three Pacific powers – Japan, the USA and Australia – have been in a constant state of interaction and cooperation under the Trilateral Security Dialogue (TSD), while the 2007 Joint Declaration on Security Cooperation has served as a linchpin in the evolving Japanese–Australian strategic partnership. Aside from a regular ministerial-level (2+2) dialogue, the two countries have also signed an intelligence-sharing agreement as well as an Acquisitions and Cross-Serving Agreement in recent years. In terms of enhancing interoperability, Japan and Australia have conducted joint naval exercises since 2009. Recognizing India's rising profile in the Pacific, especially given its direct energy investments in Vietnam-controlled disputed waters in the South China Sea, Tokyo also sought deeper strategic cooperation with New Delhi. In 2012, Japanese and Indian coastguards conducted a joint exercise known as 'Sahyog Kaijin XI' from India's port of Chennai. The Japanese Coast Guard ship *Settsu* (PLH-07), two interceptor boats and eight other coastguard ships participated in the exercise. Japan's navy is viewed as the main regional counterweight to China, which has rapidly developed its anti-access and blue-water naval capabilities in recent years. Japan has the world's sixth-largest military budget, while its navy boasts forty-eight major surface combatants; two large helicopter-carrying destroyers; an assortment of corvettes, frigates and stealthy diesel-powered submarines (considered the best of their kind); and a state-of-the-art Aegis combat system (Fackler 2012).

What the region needs is *minilateralism*: informal mechanisms aimed at enhancing partnership and cooperation among like-minded states on specific issues (i.e. the South China Sea disputes). China is the pre-eminent indigenous power in East Asia, with no peers in size and capability. But middle powers can collectively match China's outsized prowess: for instance, Japan, India, Australia and Indonesia have a combined population of 1.64 billion, a combined defence expenditure of US$127 billion, and a combined GDP of US$9 trillion (Mohan and Medcalf 2014). Together with ASEAN, these middle powers can create a formidable regional force, which could temper China's ambitions and territorial assertiveness. By coordinating their diplomatic efforts in various regional gatherings – from the ARF to APEC, ASEAN and East Asia summits – and enhancing strategic and defence cooperation among themselves, the middle powers can effectively signal the counterproductive nature of China's unilateral actions in the region. And there are some indications of the emergence of a quasi-constrainment strategy against China. For instance, India, despite China's vehement opposition, has not only stepped up its hydrocarbon investments in contested waters, with state-owned ONGC Videsh (OVL) acquiring new oil-exploration contracts (without bidding) in mid-2014, it has also been more assertive in defending its interests in the South China Sea and criticizing China's actions. And in the latest ASEAN and APEC summits, and other major regional gatherings, leaders from Australia, Japan, South Korea, Indonesia and India have more forcefully called for freedom of navigation in international waters and the resolution of maritime disputes in accordance with international law. Since the late 1990s, revisions in the USA–Japan defence guidelines have also progressively expanded Tokyo's zone of responsibility to the wider Asia-Pacific region, with the Japanese Maritime Self-Defence Force expected to play an increasingly important role in enhancing maritime security across SLOCs, aiding maritime civilian law enforcement capabilities and improving the intelligence, surveillance and reconnaissance (ISR) capabilities of the Philippines and Vietnam, as well as conducting joint naval exercises with like-minded Pacific powers such as Australia and India. China's assertiveness has provided the perfect impetus and justification for the re-emergence of its arch-rival, Japan, as a key security player in the region. China's ultimate nightmare is complete isolation within the region, with all relevant powers acting in concert with the USA. The Trilateral Security Dialogue (TSD) serves as the linchpin of the triangular Washington, Canberra and Tokyo hub-and-spokes alliance. Against the backdrop of growing Chinese power, India has moved closer to the USA, and there have been serious discussions on reviving the Quadrilateral Security Dialogue (QSD), building the foundations of an 'Asian Arc of Democracy' (Japan, India and Australia) in tandem with the USA (Khera 2015), which also hopes to strengthen the triangular Japan–USA–South Korea triangular alliance in North-East Asia. In his magisterial work *On China*, Henry Kissinger explains China's strategic culture by emphasizing the importance of concepts such as strategic momentum and the balance of forces in the foreign-policy calculus of Beijing. While China, like any astute realist actor, prizes hard power in its pursuit of national interest, psychological variables and perceptions of the shifting momentum in international configuration of power, in turn, also play a pivotal role in shaping the mindset of Chinese leaders. China may stand as the most powerful indigenous actor in Asia, but its leaders also know that hard power alone can't guarantee a successful bid for regional leadership. If China seeks to displace the United States as the pre-eminent power in Asia, Beijing can't afford to look like an aggressive power bent on pushing its interests at the expense of smaller states in the neighbourhood.

The ongoing disputes in the western Pacific, especially in the South China Sea, are dramatically undermining China's image among its neighbours – and in the wider world. For instance, a survey by the Pew Research Center in mid-2014 showed that majorities in eight Asian countries were alarmed by China's intensifying territorial spats with rival claimant states in the South and East China Seas. Panic is gripping some neighbours, which feel increasingly vulnerable to China's naval prowess and territorial assertiveness. In the Philippines, widely considered the weakest player among active claimants in the South China Sea, 93 per cent of respondents said that they were 'very concerned' about the ongoing disputes, followed by Japan (85 per cent) and Vietnam (84 per cent). Non-claimant states, such as South Korea, which heavily rely on the passage of imported hydrocarbon products through the contested waters, have also shown a deepening sense of alarm, with 83 per cent of respondents expressing similar sentiments. Even in China, the dominant player in the disputes, over 60 per cent of people expressed concerns over the prospects of an armed conflict over the disputed features. Worryingly, antipathy towards China has gone mainstream: the citizens of the Philippines, Vietnam and Japan consider China as the biggest threat to their national security, complicating the prospects for any meaningful diplomatic compromise in the near future. Meanwhile, regional concern over China's territorial assertiveness has facilitated a noticeable rebound in the United States' global image, especially in Asia, despite lingering concerns over the Obama administration's commitment and wherewithal to push back against rising powers such as China to protect its beleaguered allies (Harjani 2014). No wonder the United States has maintained extraordinarily high approval ratings among a number of Asian countries. It is, however, even more important for rival claimant states themselves to step up to the occasion by enhancing their own deterrence capabilities as well as exploring various diplomatic mechanisms to genuinely engage China (Santos 2014). In an April 2015 Pew Survey, Americans and Japanese expressed overwhelming trust towards each other, but only 30 per cent of Americans and 7 per cent of Japanese expressed similar sentiments towards China (Agence France Presse 2015c). Meanwhile, in a survey by the Perth USAsia Centre, a think tank focused on the Asia-Pacific region, 87 per cent of Chinese citizens expressed confidence over the PLA's ability to 'retake' the Senkaku islands, and an overwhelming majority thought China could face up to and beat the USA over the disputed features in the western Pacific, if Washington decided to intervene in support of its allies (FlorCruz 2015). In short, the polls reveal deep worries vis-à-vis China's behaviour in the western Pacific, but also an alarmingly high level of confidence among Chinese citizens that their country can achieve its aims, even if things deteriorate to a military showdown with Japan and the USA. Such a toxic combination of widespread hubris and panic is far from reassuring.

Self-reliance and engagement China's mid-2014 decision to dispatch an oil rig to Vietnam's EEZ sparked the greatest diplomatic crisis between the two communist states since the end of the Cold War. Throughout the months-long crisis over China's unilateral deployment of the US$1 billion Haiyang Shiyou 981 oil rig in Vietnamese-claimed waters, officials in Hanoi confronted an existential dilemma: on one hand, they were deeply alarmed by the explosion of nationalist fervour on the streets of Hanoi and across the country, which led to massive destruction of foreign-owned factories and the exodus of thousands of Chinese citizens, while facing the prospect of a devastating naval showdown with a better-equipped armada of Chinese paramilitary forces defending the oil rig, on the other. Still shocked by China's decision to torpedo previous bilateral negotiations aimed at de-escalating territorial tensions in the South China Sea, the Vietnamese government wasn't particularly reassured by China's announced plans to withdraw the oil rig by mid-August. As Vietnam's ambassador to Manila, Truong Trieu Duong, commented:[12] 'China's activities

---

[12] Interview with the author, 4 July 2014.

violated the high-level agreements of the two countries on non-aggravation and non-complication of the situation in the SCS ... we have consistently and vehemently protested against China's activities that violate Vietnam's sovereign rights and jurisdiction in its Exclusive Economic Zone and continental shelf.' One noticed a lingering sense of betrayal among many Vietnamese diplomats, who tirelessly sought to prevent armed confrontation and deepening territorial tensions with their powerful neighbour. There were genuine worries that China would consider a more permanent presence in the contested area, consolidating its claims by sending additional batches of oil rigs accompanied by a thicker protective flotilla of Chinese naval and coastguard vessels. After all, during the latter decades of the Cold War, China showed little hesitation in coercively expelling (South) Vietnamese forces from the Paracels island chain and, later, the (unified) Vietnam from strategic locations in the Spratly island chain. Hanoi anxiously wondered whether China could be deterred from more provocative actions. At the same time, the Vietnamese government was concerned with its domestic political legitimacy, especially amid an economic slowdown. There were also concerns about the prospect of a new wave of anti-China protests, which could irredeemably tarnish Vietnam's attraction to foreign investors, especially the Chinese (and Taiwanese) businessmen interested in the country's affordable labour costs and favourable location. After four months of intense maritime jostling between Chinese and Vietnamese naval forces, China decided to withdraw the oil rig, a month ahead of the announced schedule. To make sense of China's latest manoeuvre, analysts mentioned a number of motivating factors, ranging from the threat of maintaining a complex hydrocarbon exploration amid a stormy season in the area to speculations over a possible diplomatic bargain between Hanoi and Beijing (Abuza 2014). But a better explanation is that China may have (again) recalibrated its territorial posturing, falling back on its age-old strategy of employing temporary de-escalation measures to ameliorate international pressure and regional isolation. Vietnam's incessant efforts at finding a diplomatic compromise with China also played an extremely important role. To resolve the oil-rig crisis, Vietnam engaged in a proactive diplomatic offensive, culminating in the visit of

Vietnam's Politburo member Le Hong Anh to Beijing in late August. Since then, bilateral tensions have subsided, with both countries seeking to enhance existing crisis-management mechanisms to avoid a similar crisis in the future. Back in 2012, the foreign ministries of both countries established a hotline, which covers a comprehensive set of issues, including maritime disputes. In 2013, Vietnam's Ministry of Agriculture and Rural Development and China's Ministry of Agriculture also set up a hotline to prevent disputes concerning fishery resources. In late 2014, the two countries, according to Vietnamese officials, also agreed to establish a hotline between their defence ministries. As Ambassador Truong Trieu Duong explained:[13] 'Vietnam's strategy in dealing with the ongoing disputes could be termed a mixed or combined one. Above all, we use diplomatic measures and other peaceful means to solve the disputes ... It is Vietnam's position that issues, if involving only two countries, could be settled on a bilateral basis.' But there are signs, Vietnam experts argue, that Hanoi is increasingly tilting towards the USA. For Alexander Vuving, an associate professor at the Hawaii-based Asia Pacific Center for Strategic Studies (APCSS), a growing strategic alignment between Hanoi and the USA seems almost inevitable: 'Vietnam will continue to move closer to the USA as the China threat will continue to grow ... a de facto alliance between the USA and Vietnam is a likely future scenario.'[14] Beginning with Hillary Clinton's July 2012 visit to Hanoi, where she met Vietnamese Communist Party chief, Nguyen Phu Trong, bilateral ties have picked up momentum, paving the way for the establishment of the US–Vietnam Comprehensive Partnership in July 2013, when Obama met his Vietnamese counterpart (Truong Tan Sang) in Washington. In October 2014, John Kerry's visit to Hanoi coincided with the announcement that the USA was relaxing its age-old restriction on military exports to Vietnam to improve the latter's maritime capabilities (Vuving 2015). Bilateral ties between the two former enemies have not only normalized, they have moved closer to a full-blown strategic partnership. But this has not prevented the Vietnamese leadership from maintaining robust, party-to-party high-

---

[13] Ibid.
[14] Interview with the author, 13 April 2015.

level ties with China, evident in the timing and nature of the April 2015 visit of Vietnam's paramount leader, Nguyen Phu Trong, the Vietnamese Communist Party's general secretary, to Beijing ahead of his trip to Washington (Vu and Heydarian 2015). Meanwhile, Tokyo successfully pushed for a dialogue between Prime Minister Shinzo Abe and President Xi Jinping on the sidelines of the 2014 APEC in Beijing, which paved the way for the first meeting between their foreign ministers in three years and their first top-level security talks in four years in early 2015 (VOA News 2015). As a result, the two Asian powers are once again considering necessary CBMs to ensure their territorial spats don't evolve into a larger armed confrontation. Of particular importance are Abe's efforts to reach out to South Korea, ensuring their separate historical and territorial disputes won't allow China to drive a wedge between the two US allies. The Obama administration has repeatedly sought to facilitate a Japan–South Korea rapprochement to maintain a robust trilateral alliance in North-East Asia against common threats.

Meanwhile, Chinese president Xi Jinping has yet to hold a formal dialogue with his Filipino counterpart, Benigno Aquino, who is entering his final years in office. The Philippines stood as the only rival claimant state with no institutionalized, high-level dialogue with Beijing. (There is hope that this will change when the Philippines hosts the 2015 APEC summit, which will be attended by Xi.) In a dramatic display of strategic naivety, the Philippines decided (early October 2014) to suspend the repair and upgrade of its age-old airstrip on the Spratly island of Thitu (*Pagasa* to the Filipinos), among the biggest and most prized land features in the South China Sea, which can generate its own 200-nautical-mile exclusive economic zone (EEZ). Manila tried to justify the controversial move by emphasizing the (supposed) importance of maintaining 'the moral high ground' during the country's pending legal complaint, at a special arbitral tribunal in The Hague, against China's expansive maritime claims, as well as its increasingly aggressive posturing within the Philippines' exclusive economic zone.[15] In short, the Philippines prioritized an inherently

---

[15] Partly based on exchanges with Philippine Foreign Secretary Albert Del Rosario on July 29, 2015.

uncertain legal manoeuvre (see Chapters 4 and 5) at the expense of
investing in tangible mechanisms which could *actually* protect the
areas under its control.[16] The airstrip is critical to the Armed Forces
of Philippines' (AFP) ability to project power and defend its maritime
claims beyond its immediate territorial waters. Thanks to the strategic
foresight of the late Filipino dictator Ferdinand Marcos (1966–86),
who recognized the importance of establishing permanent, defensible
structures on contested features in the South China Sea, the Philippines
has managed to exercise effective and continuous sovereignty over the
island, which hosts a permanent civilian community and boasts its own
mayor. As veteran Filipino journalist Ellen Tordesillas explained, the
Philippines has failed to hold on to its initial advantage in the South
China Sea: 'It was during Ferdinand Marcos' time that the Philippines
made the official claim over the Kalayaan islands in the Spratlys by
making the discoverer, Tomas Cloma, execute a "Deed of Assignment
and Waiver of Rights" to the Marcos government – for a single peso
… In the post-Cold War era, President Fidel Ramos [1992–98] tried
to fortify Philippine claims by adding presence in the occupied islands.
They also planned to set up lighthouses. But this did not push through
due to interdepartmental wrangling.' In fact, throughout the entire
post-Cold War period, none of the Filipino administrations managed
to significantly build on the earlier efforts by the Marcos dictatorship
to secure the country's claims in the South China Sea. As Filipino
defence expert Alma Salvador[17] explains:

> Of course, history will bear us out that no serious upgrade was
> undertaken during the Arroyo administration [2001–10]. Even
> if Arroyo's National Internal Security Plan 2001 and the AFP's
> Strategy of Holistic Approach actually addressed the limits to the
> military approach to COIN [counter-insurgency], allocations for the
> military continued to focus on internal security operations. The AFP
> is thus very vulnerable to the politics of budgeting and prioritization

[16] Realizing the futility of its moralistic argument, the Philippines in succeeding
months (early 2015) reversed its initial decision to suspend upgrade of its
facilities on Thitu island, just to postpone it once again by mid-2015.
[17] Interview with the author, 24 July 2014.

of administration. The AFP's desire to shift to external defence is internally driven. Talk to most of them today and they will tell you that it is high time that they shift their role, although sometimes their actions demonstrate ambivalence ... Of course money is their greatest challenge; and policy continuity in the succeeding administration is far from assured. Whatever the case is, the current pace of AFP's modernization doesn't even come close to addressing the capability gap between it and the PLA.

Meanwhile, Manila and Washington also faced renewed legal and political obstacles to the implementation of the 2014 EDCA, which sought to upgrade the US–Philippine military alliance amid rising Chinese assertiveness. Constitutional restrictions over the establishment of permanent US military bases in the Philippines have prevented the immediate implementation of the EDCA. Bilateral relations were also tested by the public outrage over the alleged killing of a Filipino citizen by a US Marine in October 2014. The incident rekindled age-old concerns over criminal abuses by foreign troops. Nationalist figures and movements have stepped up their opposition to what they see as a violation of Philippine sovereignty by the presence of American troops on Philippine soil. Leading Senators such as Miriam Defensor-Santiago called for the VFA to be scrapped, while others called for a review of the bilateral agreement. Criminal jurisdiction continues to be a sensitive political issue in the Philippines, since the 1998 VFA stipulates that the host country does not have full jurisdiction over criminal cases involving American troops (see Chapter 4). In the meantime, practically all other claimant states have fortified their positions in the South China Sea. For instance, Taiwan, which controls the Pratas chain of islands in the northern portion of the South China Sea, is building a US$100 million port on Itu Abu (*Tai Ping* to Taiwanese), which already has a well-maintained military airstrip. The new port, expected to be finished by 2015, could accommodate coastguard cutters and heavy naval frigates. Taiwan is also upgrading the airstrip to accommodate its Hercules C-130 transport planes, while finishing an ambitious project of surveying the entire South China Sea through high-resolution satellite imagery. This would give Taiwan a more complete picture of the developments across disputed features, providing valuable intelligence for legal and military contingencies (Gold and Torode 2014).

With its recent acquisition of two Russian-made, state-of-the-art Kilo-class submarines (more advanced than those operated by China), Vietnam has also beefed up its minimum deterrence capabilities. Hanoi has also welcomed Washington's decision to relax existing restrictions on arms exports to Vietnam, which could aid Vietnam's efforts at developing its civilian law-enforcement capabilities. Unlike the Philippines, practically all active claimant states have adopted a combination of deterrence, engagement and long-term defence planning to protect their territorial interests in the South China Sea. The Philippines' weak hand in the ongoing disputes is largely a reflection of its excessive dependence on the USA and its lack of diplomatic dynamism and long-term strategic vision. After two decades of territorial jostling in the South China Sea, the Philippines has not even managed to establish a single hotline with any important agency or department in China. It has placed all its strategic eggs in the uncertain basket of legal arbitration, while constantly prodding Washington (to no avail) to more explicitly support its territorial claims in the South China Sea. To be fair, the Philippines has experienced its most significant defence build-up under the Aquino administration (see Figure 6.9). In his three years in office, Aquino allocated US$648.44 million to modernizing the AFP, with the year 2013 seeing a whopping 17 per cent increase in defence spending. He allocated US$1.73 billion for additional defence procurement for the 2013–17 period, while, in December 2012, overseeing the passage of the Revised AFP Modernization Act,[18] extending the AFP's modernization for another fifteen years. Under his watch, the Philippines will, for the first time in a decade, field modern fighter aircraft, thanks to the expected delivery of a few FA-50 lead-in fighter jets to be completed by 2017. Cognizant of the necessity to decouple the AFP from domestic counter-insurgency operations, which have absorbed the bulk of the country's military efforts, Aquino also engaged in high-stakes peace negotiations with the

[18] The Philippines' regular defence budget is mainly for compensation of personnel and maintenance, while the AFP Modernization Act is the primary source of funding for defence procurements.

leading and most enduring rebel groups, the Moro Islamic Liberation Front (MILF) and the communist insurgency (Heydarian 2015b). In terms of minimum deterrence, it is important for the Philippines to invest in its coastguard capabilities, given the immense capacity deficit of the Philippine Coast Guard (PCG). So far, the Philippines seems to be primarily relying on key strategic partners to augment the capability of the PCG. As Rudyard Somera, deputy commander at the PCG, highlights:[19]

> The PCG struggles with an insufficient number of air and marine assets to undertake maritime patrols over a wide area of operation … [But] in order to upgrade the fleet and personnel of the command, the PCG is regularly participating in combined exercises and conferences in order to enhance [its] interoperability and cooperation with allied countries and local authorities. These include the anti-piracy exercise with the Japanese Coast Guard, the CARAT exercise with the US and Philippine navies, and the fleet exercise with Australia. Such collaboration is not limited to sea exercises. The Japan International Cooperation Agency sustains support to PCG's capability-building and human resource development, by providing training to PCG personnel, providing equipment and extending grant aid to enhance the PCG's Communication System for Maritime Safety and Security. Likewise, Australia and the Philippines signed an MOU pertaining to the combating of international terrorism and transnational crime in 2003. The Philippines–Australia relationship is particularly important as both countries work together to improve international and national security and reduce the threat of terrorism. The cooperation on security issues is exemplified by the success of the Philippines–Australia Port Security Capacity Building Project, which has also benefited the PCG. The Philippine–US alliance has always promoted cooperation and force interoperability in the areas of maritime law enforcement and maritime security.

The PCG should ideally be at the forefront of defending the country's territorial integrity against China, which is mostly relying on well-equipped paramilitary patrols and fishermen-cum-militia

---

[19] Interview with the author, 29 July 2015.

forces. It is important to keep the ongoing territorial jostling among law enforcement agencies, and not involve conventional military forces. The ultimate strategic aim for the Philippines should be to at least develop a minimum deterrence capability, which will give China some pause before considering any further push against Philippine-claimed features in the South China Sea. Filipino defence experts such as Chester Cabalza, Associate Professor at the National Defence College of the Philippines, highlight the Philippines' appreciation of assistance from its strategic partners: 'The support we are gaining from our allies only reaffirms our common values. By renewing and cementing stronger alliances in the region, this can contain the expansionist ambition and military might of China.'[20] But given the sheer speed and scale of China's military modernization, the Aquino administration's efforts could end up as too little, too late. This is why the Philippines will continue to rely on multilateral diplomacy and bilateral security alliances to keep China at bay. Small powers such as the Philippines will have to intelligently combine engagement with deterrence, and make up for the lack of deterrence through proactive diplomacy. Often, the Philippines is accused of using ASEAN as a platform for China-bashing. Perhaps it is time for the Philippines to ensure that its advocacies within ASEAN are better coordinated with (or routed through) other like-minded member countries, particularly Vietnam and Indonesia, both of which have no explicit treaty alliances with any great power, and therefore can't be accused of acting as proxies for another external actor. The Philippines should also prepare itself for the post-arbitration phase, especially if, as some experts have speculated, the arbitral tribunal strikes down Manila's request for compulsory arbitration of the South China Sea disputes. In the first place, it remains to be seen whether the arbitration body will decide to exercise jurisdiction – a decision that is expected by late 2015. In the event that there is an exercise of jurisdiction, the question then is: how extensive would it be? That is to say, will the tribunal examine the merits of all the Philippines' arguments – from clarification of maritime delimitation-related concerns to questioning the validity of

[20] Interview with the author, 18 July 2014.

China's sweeping claims – or only some of them; the next question is whether the tribunal's final verdict will be a clear-cut victory for the Philippines, and whether China will be susceptible to any compromise down the road. Of course, there is the risk that any unfavourable verdict will embolden China to be more aggressive in consolidating its claims, defeating the very purpose of the arbitration process. The Philippines hopes that at least China will be forced to clarify the 'nine-dash-line' and that the tribunal will determine the exact nature of the disputed features in the South China Sea. But the Philippines should also be ready for a defeat if the tribunal refuses to, say, (i) exercise jurisdiction at all or (ii) falls short of coming up with an explicit verdict against China's sweeping claims and aggressive posturing in the South China Sea.[21] It is highly probable that the succeeding administration in the Philippines will try to adopt an alternative strategy, transcending the whole arbitration gambit in favour of economic engagement and diplomatic normalization with China. Current Filipino vice-president Jejomar Binay, who is widely seen among the top contenders in the next presidential elections, has for years been signalling his willingness to prioritize engagement rather than confrontation with China, often emphasizing how territorial disputes and the ongoing arbitration at The Hague should not undermine broader bilateral Philippine–China relations. In a recent interview (Esmaquel 2015), Binay bluntly said: 'China has money, [and] we need capital', highlighting his preference for reviving bilateral trade and investment relations with China, which has arguably become the economic pivot of Asia in recent years. Binay's pragmatism, however, should not be mistaken as capitulation; with the South China Sea disputes – and the image of China as a

---

[21] In fact, in the event of overlapping claims within a country's EEZ, the UNCLOS (Art. 59, Part V) states: 'the conflict should be resolved on the basis of equity and in the light of all the relevant circumstances, taking into account the respective importance of the interests involved to the parties as well as to the international community as a whole'. For this reason, some legal experts speculate that the arbitral tribunal could choose to defer either jurisdiction or a final clear-cut verdict (at China's expense) in favour of the formation of a conciliation commission (Art. 1, Annexe V). This would effectively mean the two parties getting back to the pre-arbitration scenario of bilateral negotiations.

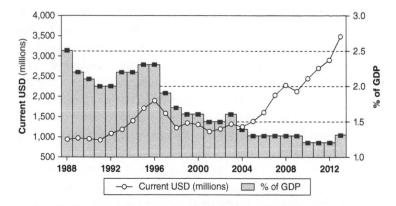

6.9 The Philippines' defence spending (1988–2012) (*sources*: Asia Maritime Transparency Initiative; Stockholm International Peace Research Institute).

'bully' – capturing the imagination of the Filipino population, any diplomatic manoeuvre even resembling capitulation is tantamount to political suicide – acting as a perfect rallying point for the opposition forces.

The ultimate decider The maritime disputes in Asia represent the intersection of the advent of popular nationalism, China's expanding regional interests, strategic complacency on the part of smaller powers such as the Philippines, and the inability of the existing regional security architecture to peacefully accommodate China's rising ambitions and constrain its destabilizing territorial assertiveness. Externally, China's neighbours should combine deterrence with engagement in order to temper Beijing's excesses. The ultimate source of change, however, is China. Sovereignty disputes are inherently intractable: they involve matters of national pride, identity and interest. No Asian leader, whether autocratic or democratically elected, can openly compromise on the territorial disputes without inviting political backlash at home. But as Xi emerges as China's new paramount leader – with an increasingly stable grip on the country's (civilian and military) bureaucracy – and consolidates his nationalist credentials (see Chapter 3), he will be in a strong position to resolve China's territorial disputes – and contemplate much-needed compromises. Recognizing the in-built risks of China's fragmented maritime bureaucracy, Xi has already pushed ahead with a series of initiatives to remedy the situation. On the one hand, he established the State Security Committee (SSC), which allows him to personally supervise and streamline the civilian and military aspects of China's foreign and domestic security policy. The SSC could also serve as a crisis-management body, especially as Beijing's territorial spats with neighbouring states and geopolitical tensions with the USA intensify. In addition, Xi has streamlined the maritime law enforcement agencies, potentially placing the 'Five Dragons' of the Maritime Border Police (formerly under the Ministry of Public Security), the Fishing Regulation Administration (FRA, formerly under the Ministry of Agriculture), China Marine Surveillance, General Administration of Customs (under the State Council) and the Maritime Safety Administration (under the Ministry of Transport) under the control and supervision of the State Ocean Administration (SOA). Figure 6.10 provides an illustration of reforms. Chinese scholar Nong Hong (2015) explains the relevance of the bureaucratic reshuffle:

> The reform aims at enhancing China's maritime law enforcement capacities in a more controlled and coordinated manner. Meanwhile, the reform could significantly improve response time, reduce redundancy, strengthen communication, and bolster overall command and control mechanisms. Two objectives may be achieved through the merger: First, a unified force will better be able to pursue national objectives; second, it will reduce the chance that uncoordinated actions by separate commanders trigger unintended escalation and conflict at sea ... There are at least three possible strategic and security implications derived from the ongoing structural reform of China's maritime law enforcement. First, a united agency, now officially called China's Coast Guard, reflects the decision of China's leadership to enhance its maritime law enforcement capability and to transform it into a maritime power ... The second major implication is that a stronger Chinese enforcement entity serves to promote China's rapidly growing 'soft power' both in the Asia-Pacific and around the globe. The third implication is the relationship between PLA[N] and the new China Coast Guard. The PLA[N] formerly had the capacity of only an elaborate coast guard and now

emphasizes technology-intensive warfare. It shows interest in issues that are traditionally coast guards' responsibility, including search and rescue, environmental protection, and piracy.

Overall, China moved towards creating a more versatile coastguard to manage its territorial affairs in adjacent waters. It remains to be seen, however, whether it is interested in any compromise at all; but at least China's neighbours can take comfort in the fact that China's maritime policy has become increasingly disciplined and centralized under Xi's watch. Deng's old formula of joint development and postponement of sovereignty-related concerns is still a viable option. Competing claimant states could agree upon a series of CBMs to de-escalate tensions. First, they could place a temporary freeze on all construction activities and paramilitary patrols across the contested waters. Instead of rival claimant states (think of the Philippines) or external powers (think of the USA) making such proposals, it is better if countries like Indonesia and Singapore – which have no direct territorial claims and are seen

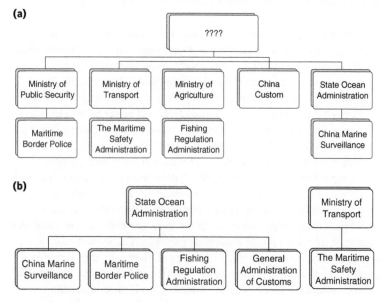

6.10 China's maritime law enforcement bureaucracy (a) before and (b) after reform (*source*: Hong 2015).

as honest brokers – are at the forefront of advocating such initiatives. Secondly, claimant states could begin dividing overlapping claims into two main areas: those that could be subject to joint development, on one hand, and those that are non-negotiable and have been firmly under the control of (and of primary strategic significance to) one party, on the other. Inevitably, there will be a lot of haggling in the process.

Rival parties could also consider mutual disengagement from highly contested areas, as a prelude to a broader joint-development scheme. With respect to joint development, rival claimant states could explore creative ways to enhance mutual trust and ensure no single party gains the upper hand. For instance, it is clear that China has the most advanced hydrocarbon exploration and offshore drilling capability among South China Sea claimant states. The parties can revisit the 2005 JMSU agreement, but with certain modifications: consultations with important domestic stakeholders could ensure greater transparency, which is especially important in democratic countries like the Philippines; it is also important to ensure that any agreement will be consistent with domestic legislation, constitutional provisions regarding the protection of national patrimony, and the international obligations of parties. Meanwhile, claimants can come up with an arrangement whereby national energy companies would be jointly involved in upstream activities, but downstream activities would be contracted out to an acceptable third party, i.e. a major multinational company or state-owned energy company (from a non-claimant state), which has amicable relations with all the parties. The strategic segmentation of the development of energy resources in the contested maritime zones would reduce the possibility of one dominant party outmanoeuvring its weaker counterparts. Thirdly, all parties should establish hotlines between their civilian leaderships as well as their armed forces. Fourthly, the parties could also focus on developing an 'environmental regime', placing a cap on the exploitation of marine resources, preserving endangered species, and developing guidelines on shared exploitation of the available resources. Many of the above CBMs could also be applied to the Sino-Japanese disputes over the Senkaku islands. Abe's purported decision to privately acknowledge the contested nature of the East China Sea features is a step in the right direction (Fifield and Wan 2014). Both sides can once again put aside the issue of sovereignty, and focus on negotiating mutually acceptable ways in which both countries could share the fisheries and hydrocarbon riches in the area. The effective negotiation of CBMs, however, will require diligence, imagination and a certain level of autonomy (and calibrated secrecy) on the part of negotiators and policy-makers. It is high time for competing claimant states to decouple the territorial disputes, which could be effectively managed through sustained dialogue and wide-ranging CBMs, from domestic politics and provocative nationalistic discourse. After all, China can't afford to continuously alienate its neighbours without risking a diplomatic backlash and strategic isolation; its smaller neighbours, meanwhile, can't contemplate submission to rising Chinese assertiveness without totally losing their sense of national autonomy and dignity. There are no easy solutions to these highly intractable disputes, but in times of great peril, when the stakes are high, there are also great opportunities for effecting much-needed change.

To overcome new challenges, the Asian security architecture must evolve and mature as never before. During his high-profile meeting with Obama in mid-2013, Xi declared, 'The vast Pacific Ocean has enough space for two large countries like the United States and China' (BBC 2013). To avoid hegemonic wars, however, the region needs to establish a truly multipolar, dynamic and cooperative Asia-Pacific community, rather than a Sino-American condominium, which sacrifices the interests of smaller powers like Japan, Vietnam and the Philippines. What is at stake is the future of the Asia-Pacific and decades of relative prosperity and stability in what has become the world's most dynamic and promising region.

REFERENCES

Abuza, Z. (2014) 'Vietnam buckles under Chinese pressure', *Asia Times Online*, 29 July, www.atimes.com/atimes/Southeast_Asia/SEA-01-290714.html.

Achariya, A. and A. Achariya (2007) 'The myth of the Second Front: localizing the "War on Terror" in Southeast Asia', *Washington Quarterly*, Autumn.

Ackerman, B. and T. Matsudaira (2014) 'Dishonest Abe: why we should be worried about the Japanese prime minister's move to amend the constitution', *Foreign Policy*, 24 June, foreignpolicy.com/2014/06/24/dishonest-abe/.

Acton, J. (2013) 'Is China changing its position on nuclear weapons?', *New York Times*, 18 April, www.nytimes.com/2013/04/19/opinion/is-china-changing-its-position-on-nuclear-weapons.html?_r=0.

Agence France Presse (2012) 'Philippines sends more troops to guard disputed islands', *Philippine Daily Inquirer*, 30 September, globalnation.inquirer.net/51834/philippines-sends-more-troops-to-guard-disputed-islands/.

— (2013) 'Southeast Asian nations tackle maritime security issues', *South China Morning Post*, 29 August, w.scmp.com/news/asia/article/1053186/southeast-asian-nations-tackle-maritime-security-issues.

— (2014a) 'Feuding China, PH can still do business – envoy', *Inquirer*, 2 July, business.inquirer.net/173975/feuding-china-ph-can-still-do-business-envoy.

— (2014b) 'Brunei disappointed by cancelled US President's visit', *Gulfnews*, 4 October, www.theborneopost.com/2013/10/05/brunei-disappointed-by-cancelled-us-presidents-visit/.

— (2014c) 'South Korea is giving the Philippine navy a free ship as tensions rise with China', *Business Insider*, 6 June, www.businessinsider.com/south-korea-donates-philippine-2014-6.

— (2015a) 'Bar ban for US troops in Philippines amid murder trial', *Yahoo News*, 18 April, news.yahoo.com/bar-ban-us-troops-philippines-amid-murder-trial-114739168.html.

— (2015b) 'South Korea, Japan hold first security talks for 5 years', *Yahoo*, 14 April, news.yahoo.com/south-korea-japan-hold-first-security-talks-5-072152405.html.

— (2015c) 'US, Japan trust each other but both wary of China: poll', *Yahoo News*, 8 April, news.yahoo.com/us-japan-trust-other-both-wary-china-poll-011821586.html.

Aitken, R. (2014) 'How long before China's renminbi becomes fully convertible?', *Forbes*, 7 July.

Akita, H. (2014a) 'US–Japan defense guidelines could see drastic changes', *Nikkei*, 20 February, asia.nikkei.com/

Politics-Economy/Policy-Politics/US-Japan-defense-guidelines-could-see-drastic-changes.

— (2014b) 'The truth about military aircraft encounters in East China Sea', *Nikkei Asian Review*, 10 June, asia.nikkei.com/print/article/35065.

Alagappa, M. (2015) 'Community building: ASEAN's millstone?', Pacific Forum, Center for Strategic and International Studies, 19 March.

Al Jazeera (2013) 'Wukan: after the uprising', Aljazeera English, 26 June.

— (2014a) 'China uses Deng's birth date to glorify Xi', Al Jazeera English, 22 August.

— (2014b) 'China attacks Japan for "barbarous" past', Aljazeera English, 4 July, www.aljazeera.com/news/asia-pacific/2014/07/china-attacks-japan-barbarous-war-past-20147462238353147.html.

— (2015) 'Transcript: Dr Zhang Weiwei', *Head to Head*, 9 March, www.aljazeera.com/programmes/headtohead/2015/01/transcript-dr-zhang-weiwei-150130115930963.html.

Allen-Ebrahimian, B. (2014) 'Chinese censors just had their busiest day of the year', *Foreign Policy*, 3 July.

Almario, M. (2014) 'US' unequal treaties', *Inquirer*, 26 April, opinion.inquirer.net/73941/us-unequal-treaties.

Anderson, B. (1987) 'Old corruption', *London Review of Books*, 9(3): 3–6.

— (1997) 'First Filipino', *London Review of Books*, 19(20): 22–3.

— (1998) 'From miracle to crash', *London Review of Books*, 1 March, www.lrb.co.uk/v20/no8/benedict-anderson/from-miracle-to-crash.

— (2001) 'Western nationalism and Eastern nationalism: is there a difference that matters?', *New Left Review*, 9, May/June, 31–42.

Andreas, J. (2008) 'Changing colours in China', *New Left Review*, 54: 123–42.

— (2010) 'A Shanghai model: on capitalism with Chinese characteristics?', *New Left Review*, 65: 63–85.

— (2012) 'Sino-seismology', *New Left Review*, 75: 128–35.

Aquino, B. (1968) 'What's wrong with the Philippines', *Foreign Affairs*, July, https://www.foreignaffairs.com/articles/asia/1968-07-01/whats-wrong-philippines.

Asahi Shimbun (2014) 'Abe playing catch-up to China as he travels to Latin America seeking allies', *Asahi Shimbun*, 25 July, ajw.asahi.com/article/behind_news/politics/AJ201407250067.

Asia Defence News (2012) 'Indian navy answer to Chinese rapid growing navy', *AsiaDefense.net*, www.asian-defence.net/2010/08/indian-navy-answer-to-chinese-rapid.html.

Asia Society (2015) 'US Treasury Secretary softens view on China-led infrastructure bank, but stresses "high standards" in Asia Society address', *Asia Blog*, 31 March, asiasociety.org/blog/asia/us-treasury-secretary-softens-view-china-led-infrastructure-bank-stresses-high-standards-a.

Asian Development Bank (2012) 'Public private partnerships key to meeting Asia's $8 trillion infrastructure needs – study', *adb.org*, 30 May, www.adb.org/news/public-private-partnerships-key-meeting-asias-8-trillion-infrastructure-needs-study.

Asia Maritime Transparency Initiative (2015) 'Island tracker', Center for Strategic and International Studies, amti.csis.org/island-tracker/.

Baldwin, R. (2013) 'The WTO and global

supply chains', East Asia Forum, Australian National University.

Baruah, D. (2014) 'Second Thomas Shoal: the new battleground', *The Diplomat*, 30 April, thediplomat.com/2014/04/second-thomas-shoal-the-new-battleground/.

Batongbacal, J. (2014) 'Bajo De Masinloc (Scarborough Shoal): maps and documents', Joint publication of UP Law Center's Institute for Maritime Affairs and Law of the Sea and the National Mapping and Resource Information Authority, Philippines.

— (2015) 'Arbitration 101: Philippines v. China', Asia Maritime Transparency Initiative, Center for Strategic and International Studies, 21 January.

BBC (2013) 'Chinese leader Xi Jinping joins Obama for summit', *BBC News*, 8 June, www.bbc.com/news/world-asia-china-22798572.

— (2014) 'Chinese fisherman killed during S Korean coastguard raid', *BBC News*, 10 October, www.bbc.com/news/world-asia-29564204.

Beckman, R. (2014) 'South China Sea conundrum: US and China differing views', *Straits Times*, 26 September.

Bello, W. (2005) *Dilemmas of Domination: The Unmaking of the American Empire*, New York: Metropolitan Books.

— (2010) 'From American lake to People's Pacific in the twenty-first century', in S. Shihematsu and K. Camacho (eds), *Militarized Currents: Toward a Decolonized Future in Asia and the Pacific*, Minneapolis: University of Minnesota Press.

— (2014) 'One-dimensional diplomacy: a cost–benefit analysis of Manila's security deal with Washington', *Inquirer*, 23 April, opinion.inquirer.net/73853/one-dimensional-diplomacy-a-cost-benefit-analysis-of-manilas-security-deal-with-washingt on#ixzz3XjsilFeS.

Bello, W. et al. (1982) 'Development debacle: the World Bank in the Philippines', Institute for Food and Development Policy, California.

Bensurto, H. (2011) 'Cooperative architecture in the South China Sea: ASEAN–China zone of peace, freedom, friendship, and cooperation', Center for Strategic and International Studies, 30 June.

Bitzinger, R. (2015) 'China's double-digit defense growth', *Foreign Affairs*, 19 March.

Bloomberg (2013) 'China eclipses U.S. as biggest trading nation', *BloombergBusiness*, 11 February.

Bonnet, F. (2004) 'The Spratlys: a past revisited', *World Bulletin*, Philippines: University of the Philippines Institute for International Legal Studies.

Bradsher, K. (2014) 'Philippine leader sounds alarm on China', *New York Times*, 4 February, www.nytimes.com/2014/02/05/world/asia/philippine-leader-urges-international-help-in-resisting-chinas-sea-claims.html?_r=0.

Bradsher, K. and N. Cumming-Bruce (2013) 'China cuts ties with North Korean bank', *New York Times*, 7 May, www.nytimes.com/2013/05/08/world/asia/china-cuts-ties-with-north-korean-bank.html.

Brattberg, E. and K. Tracz (2014) 'The hunt for Black October', *Foreign Policy*, 20 October.

Brookings (2012) 'Understanding the U.S. Pivot to Asia', Brookings Institution, 31 January, www.brookings.edu/~/media/events/2012/1/31-us-asia/20120131_us_asia_panel_one.pdf.

Brown, K. et al. (2010) 'Investment across the Taiwan Strait: how Taiwan's relationship with China affects its position in the global economy', Royal Institute of International Affairs, London.

Browne, A. (2014) 'China bypasses Philippines in its proposed "maritime Silk Road"', *Wall Street Journal*, 10 November.

Brzezinski, Z. (1998) *The Grand Chessboard: American Primacy and Its Geostrategic Imperatives*, New York: Basic Books.

Buckley, C. (2013) 'China leader affirms policy on islands', *New York Times*, 29 January.

Burns, K. (2000) 'China and Japan: economic partnership to political ends', Stimson, www.stimson. org/images/uploads/research-pdfs/ burnspdf.pdf.

Burns, N. (2014) 'Passage to India: what Washington can do to revive relations with New Delhi', *Foreign Affairs*, September/October.

Calica, A. (2012) 'Noy: Roxas, Xi talks good start for Phl–China ties', *Philippine Star*, 27 September.

Calonzo, A. (2014) 'DFA chief: US bound to defend PHL in case of attack in West Philippine Sea', *GMA News*, 30 April, www.gmanetwork.com/news/ story/358978/news/nation/dfa-chief- us-bound-to-defend-phl-in-case-of- attack-in-west-philippine-sea.

Campbell, K. and E. Ratner (2014) 'Far Eastern promises: why Washington should focus on Asia', *Foreign Affairs*, May/June.

Carpenter, T. G. (2015) 'The island dispute no one is talking about', *The National Interest*, 23 February, nationalinterest. org/feature/the-island-dispute-no- one-talking-about-12297.

Cayabyab, M. J. (2012) 'Philex rep denies Trillanes claim that Del Rosario favored MVP in West PHL Sea issue', *GMA News*, 20 September, www.gmanetwork.com/news/ story/274897/economy/companies/ philex-rep-denies-trillanes-claim- that-del-rosario-favored-mvp-in- west-phl-sea-issue.

CBS News (2014) 'China calls for new security pact with Russia, Iran', *CBS News*, 21 May, www.cbsnews.com/ news/china-calls-for-new-security- pact-with-russia-iran/.

Chang, G. (2013) 'The Chinese and Japanese economies are delinking: prelude to conflict?', *Forbes*, 16 February, www.forbes.com/sites/ gordonchang/2014/02/16/the- chinese-and-japanese-economies- are-delinking-prelude-to-conflict/.

— (2014a) 'Tiananmen: could it happen again?', *The National Interest*, 2 June.

— (2014b) 'China's "Gorbachev" is tearing the Communist Party apart', *The National Interest*, 14 August.

Chatterjee-Miller, M. (2014) 'Foreign policy à la Modi: India's next worldview', *Foreign Affairs*, 3 April.

Chaudhury, D. R. (2014) 'ONGC's presence in South China Sea: Beijing sets up oil rig to reinforce its territorial claims', *Economic Times*, 7 May, articles.economictimes. indiatimes.com/2014-05-07/ news/49689745_1_petrovietnam-oil- blocks-south-china-sea.

Chen, J. (2013) 'Xi–Obama summit ushers in new era of bilateral relations', *The Diplomat*, 18 June, thediplomat. com/2013/06/xi-obama-summit- ushers-in-new-era-of-bilateral- relations/.

Cheng, W. (2013) 'PNoy: no need to remove blocks in Scarborough',

ABS-CBN, 23 October, www.
abs-cbnnews.com/nation/10/23/13/
pnoy-no-need-remove-blocks-
scarborough.

Cliff, R. et al. (2011) *Shaking the Heavens
and Splitting the Earth: Chinese Air
Force Employment Concepts in the
21st Century*, Santa Monica, CA: Rand
Corporation.

Clinton, H. (2011) 'America's Pacific
century', *Foreign Policy*, 11 October,
foreignpolicy.com/2011/10/11/
americas-pacific-century/.

— (2012) 'The art of smart power',
New Statesman, 18 July, www.
newstatesman.com/politics/
politics/2012/07/hillary-clinton-art-
smart-power.

Colby, E. and B. Glosserman (2012) 'Asia's
real "America problem"', *Foreign
Policy*, 22 March.

Colby, E. and P. Lettow (2014) 'Have we
hit peak America', *Foreign Policy*, 4
July, foreignpolicy.com/2014/07/03/
have-we-hit-peak-america/.

Colmenares, N. (2008) 'Spratlys deal
unconstitutional: Joint Marine
Seismic Undertaking void', *GMA
News*, 17 March, www.gmanetwork.
com/news/story/85173/news/
specialreports/spratlys-deal-
unconstitutional-joint-marine-
seismic-undertaking-void.

Colvin, R. (2012) 'In China's shadow,
ASEAN leaders look to India
for maritime security', *Reuters*,
20 December, in.reuters.
com/article/2012/12/20/
india-southeastasia-
idINDEE8BJ07Z20121220.

Cook, M. (2014) 'The second wave:
Japanese FDI to Southeast Asia',
Perspective, Institute of Southeast
Asian Studies, Singapore, 29 May,
www.iseas.edu.sg/documents/
publication/ISEAS_Perspective_2014_
33_final.pdf.

Cooper-Ramo, J. (2005) 'The Beijing
Consensus', London: Foreign Policy
Centre.

Corr, A. and P. Tacujan (2013) 'Chinese
political and economic influence
in the Philippines: implications
for alliances and the South China
Sea dispute', *Journal of Political
Risk*, 1(3), www.jpolrisk.com/
chinese-political-and-economic-
influence-in-the-philippines-
implications-for-alliances-and-the-
south-china-sea-dispute/.

Davis, B. (2014) 'Beijing endorses market
role in economy', *Wall Street Journal*,
12 November.

Davis, J. H. and R. Archibold (2015)
'Obama meets Raul Castro, making
history', *New York Times*, 11 April,
www.nytimes.com/2015/04/12/
world/americas/obama-cuba-
summit-of-the-americas.html?_r=0.

De Koning, P. and P. Lipscy (2013) 'The
Land of the Sinking Sun', *Foreign
Policy*, 30 July, foreignpolicy.
com/2013/07/30/the-land-of-the-
sinking-sun/.

Dempsey, M. (2014) 'The bend of power',
Foreign Policy, 25 July.

Desker, B. (2012) 'Defusing tensions
in the South China Sea', RSIS
Commentaries, S. Rajaratnam School
of International Studies, 3 December.

— (2015) 'ASEAN integration remains an
illusion', Pacific Forum, Centre for
Strategic and International Studies,
16 March.

Diola, C. (2015) 'DFA chief: 50 meetings
with China reached dead end',
Philippine Star, 15 April, www.philstar.
com/headlines/2015/04/15/1444169/
dfa-chief-50-meetings-china-
reached-dead-end.

Dizon, D. (2014) 'China using dialogue to ward off ASEAN unity: analyst', *ABS-CBN*, 25 June, www.abs-cbnnews.com/nation/06/25/14/china-using-dialogue-ward-asean-unity-analyst.

Dreyer, J. T. (2015) 'The Asian Infrastructure Investment Bank: who will benefit?', Foreign Policy Research Institute, April, www.fpri.org/articles/2015/04/asian-infrastructure-investment-bank-who-will-benefit.

Du, R. (n.d.) 'The patriotic education campaign in China and the rise of Chinese Nationalism: a comparison between official doctrines and public opinion', Foreign Military Studies Office – Center for Global and International Studies (CGIS), fmso.leavenworth.army.mil/Collaboration/international/China/ChineseNationalism.pdf.

Dyer, G. and R. McGregor (2014) 'Pentagon plans new tactics to deter China in South China Sea', *Financial Times*, 9 July.

Economist (2012) 'China's military rise: the dragon's new teeth', *The Economist*, 4 April, www.economist.com/node/21552193.

— (2013a) 'China in Central Asia: rising China, sinking Russia', *The Economist*, 14 September.

— (2013b) 'India as a great power: know your own strength', *The Economist*, 30 March, www.economist.com/news/briefing/21574458-india-poised-become-one-four-largest-military-powers-world-end.

— (2014a) 'Japan's economy: consumptive', *The Economist*, 16 October, www.economist.com/news/asia/21625863-will-prime-minister-keep-his-nerve-over-consumption-tax-consumptive.

— (2014b) 'Japan's quantitative easing: a bigger bazooka', *The Economist*, 31 October, www.economist.com/blogs/banyan/2014/10/japans-quantitative-easing.

— (2014c) 'China and Russia: best frenemies', *The Economist*, 24 May.

— (2014d) 'China's far west: a Chechnya in the making', *The Economist*, 9 August, www.economist.com/news/leaders/21611067-iron-fist-xinjiang-fuelling-insurrection-chinas-leadership-must-switch-tactics.

— (2015) 'The Asian Infrastructure Investment Bank: American poodle to Chinese lapdog?', *The Economist*, 13 March, www.economist.com/news/business-and-finance/21646352-america-and-britain-odds-over-how-deal-china-american-poodle-pekinese-lapdog.

Economist Intelligence Unit (2013) 'Riding the ASEAN elephant: how business is responding to an unusual animal', Economist Corporate Network, www.inceif.org/download/ridingASEAN.pdf.

Economy, E. (2013) 'Secretary of State John Kerry on China', Council on Foreign Relations, 27 February, blogs.cfr.org/asia/2013/02/27/secretary-of-state-johnkerry-on-china/.

Egan, D. (2014) 'Rethinking War of Maneuver/War of Position: Gramsci and the military metaphor', *Critical Sociology* 40(4): 521–39.

Emmerson, D. (2012) 'ASEAN stumbles in Phnom Penh', Pacific Forum, Center for Strategic and International Studies, 19 July.

Energy Information Agency (n.d.) 'South China Sea', www.eia.gov/countries/regions-topics.cfm?fips=scs.

Erdbrink, T. and C. Buckley (2014) 'China and Iran to conduct joint naval exercises in the Persian Gulf', *New York Times*, 21 September, www. nytimes.com/2014/09/22/world/middleeast/china-and-iran-to-conduct-joint-naval-exercises-in-the-persian-gulf.html?_r=0.

Erickson, A. and E. de La Bruyere (2014) 'China's RIMPAC maritime-surveillance gambit', *The National Interest*, 29 July.

Erickson, A. and G. Collins (2013) 'New fleet on the block: China's coast guard comes together', *Wall Street Journal*, 11 March, blogs.wsj.com/chinarealtime/2013/03/11/new-fleet-on-the-block-chinas-coast-guard-comes-together/.

Erickson, A. and C. Kennedy (2015) 'China's island builders: the people's war at sea', *Foreign Affairs*, 9 April.

Erickson, A. and M. Monti (2015) 'Trouble ahead? Chinese–Korean disputes may intensify', *The National Interest*, 20 February, nationalinterest.org/feature/trouble-ahead-chinese-korean-disputes-may-intensify-12284?page=show.

Esmaquel, P. (2014) 'China offers PH "carrot" to quit case', *Rappler*, 26 February.

— (2015) 'Binay: "China has money, we need capital"', *Rappler*, 14 April, www.rappler.com/nation/89880-binay-china-philippines-south-china-sea.

Esposo, W. (2013) 'How our historic claim to Sabah supports China', *Philippine Star*, 17 March.

Esquerra, C. and T. J. Burgonio (2014) 'No firm commitment from US to defend PH', *Philippine Daily Inquirer*, 29 April.

Estévez-Abe, M. (2014) 'Feeling triumphalist in Tokyo: the real reasons nationalism is back in Japan', *Foreign Affairs*, May/June.

Fackler, M. (2012) 'Japan is flexing its military muscle to counter a rising China', *New York Times*, 26 November, www.nytimes.com/2012/11/27/world/asia/japan-expands-its-regional-military-role.html?pagewanted=all.

Fallows, J. (1987) 'A damaged culture: a new Philippines?', *The Atlantic*, www.theatlantic.com/technology/archive/1987/11/a-damaged-culture-a-new-philippines/7414/, accessed 7 October 2014.

Feigenbaum, E. and D. Ma (2013) 'The rise of China's reformers?', *Foreign Affairs*, 17 April.

Ferguson, N. and M. Schularick (2013) 'The U.S. and China both need economic rehab', *Wall Street Journal*, 5 November.

Fifield, A. and W. Wan (2014) 'China's Xi and Japan's Abe to hold long-awaited meeting at Apec', *Washington Post*, 7 November, www.washingtonpost.com/world/chinas-xi-and-japans-abe-to-hold-long-awaited-meeting-at-apec/2014/11/07/61e90e8b-75b7-489d-813b-a15b12dd2c5f_story.html.

Fish, I. (2014) 'Democracy is contagious', *Foreign Policy*, 1 September.

Fish, I. S. and H. Gao (2014) 'The dumpling effect?', *Foreign Policy*, 7 February.

FlorCruz, M. (2015) 'China's military can beat the US in South China Sea and Diaoyu/Senkaku Island conflicts: poll', *International Business Times*, 13 March, www.ibtimes.com/chinas-military-can-beat-us-south-china-sea-diaoyusenkaku-island-conflicts-poll-1846248.

Fravel, T. (2012) 'All Quiet in the South China Sea: Why China is Playing Nice (For Now)', *Foreign Affairs*. March 22.

— (2013) 'Xi Jinping's overlooked revelation on China's maritime disputes', *The Diplomat*, 15 August, thediplomat.com/2013/08/xi-jinpings-overlooked-revelation-on-chinas-maritime-disputes/.

— (2014) 'Hainan's new fishing rules: a preliminary analysis', *The Diplomat*, 10 January, thediplomat.com/2014/01/hainans-new-fishing-rules-a-preliminary-analysis/.

Fravel, T. and E. Medeiros (2003) 'China's new diplomacy', *Foreign Affairs*, November/December.

Fukuyama, F. (1992) *The End of History and the Last Man*, New York: Free Press.

Galeotti, M. (2014a) 'From chess player to barroom brawler', *Foreign Policy*, 14 March.

— (2014b) 'Putin's secret weapon', *Foreign Policy*, 7 July.

Gao, Z. and Bing Bing Jia (2013) 'The nine-dash line in the South China Sea: history, status, and implications', *American Journal of International Law*, 107(1): 98–124.

Garver, J. W. (1992) 'China's push through the South China Sea: the interaction of bureaucratic and national interests', *China Quarterly*, 132: 999–1028.

Gates, B. and M. Kleiber (2007) 'China's space odyssey: what the antisatellite test reveals about decision-making in Beijing', *Foreign Affairs*, May/June.

Glaser, B. (2014) 'A step forward in US–China military ties: two CBM agreements', Asia Maritime Transparency Initiative, Center for Strategic and International Studies, 11 November.

Glaser, C. (2011) 'Will China's rise lead to war?: why realism does not mean pessimism', *Foreign Affairs*, March/April.

Glenday, J. (2014) 'Tony Abbott and Barack Obama agree to new defence force posture, note different climate change approaches', *ABC*, 13 June, www.abc.net.au/news/2014-06-13/tony-abbott-and-barack-obama-agree-to-new-defence-posture/5520370.

Glennon, M. (2014) 'National security and double government', *Harvard National Security Journal*, 5, 1–113.

Glosserman, B. (2014) 'Japan and South Korea: headed towards extinction?', *The National Interest*, 1 September, nationalinterest.org/blog/the-buzz/japan-south-korea-headed-towards-extinction-11176?page=show.

Glosserman, B. and E. Colby (2013) 'Asia's real American problem', Center for Strategic and International Studies, csis.org/files/publication/Pac1216.pdf.

Glosserman, B. and D. Kang (2014) 'The myth of Japanese remilitarization', *The National Interest*, 15 October, nationalinterest.org/feature/the-myth-japanese-remilitarization-11470.

Glosserman, B. and D. Roy (2014) 'Asia's next China worry: Xi Jinping's growing power', *The National Interest*, 23 July.

GMA News (2010) 'PHL boycott of Nobel Peace Prize pleases China', *GMA News*, www.gmanetwork.com/news/story/207949/news/nation/phl-boycott-of-nobel-peace-prize-pleases-china, accessed 1 January 2013.

— (2015) 'PHL stops oil and gas drilling in Reed Bank, cites dispute with China', *GMA News*, 3 March, www.gmanetwork.com/news/story/445665/economy/companies/phl-stops-oil-and-gas-drilling-in-reed-bank-cites-dispute-with-china.

Go, F. (2013) 'Australia playing greater role in U.S. strategy to contain China', *Asahi Shimbun*, 7 October, ajw.asahi.com/article/behind_news/politics/AJ201310070001.

Gold, M. and G. Torode (2014) 'As Taiwan beefs up prized South China Sea outpost, barely a peep from China', *Reuters*, 25 May, www.reuters.com/article/2014/05/25/taiwan-southchinasea-idusl3n0070av20140525.

Gomez, J. (2013) 'Philex Petroleum-led forum, China's CNOOC eye deal in disputed sea', *GMA News*, www.gmanetwork.com/news/story/332202/economy/companies/philex-petroleum-led-forum-china-s-cnooc-eye-deal-in-disputed-sea.

Grevatt, J. and C. Caffrey (2014) 'Indonesia increases defence budget 14%', *HIS Jane's 360*, 17 August, www.janes.com/article/42069/indonesia-increases-defence-budget-14.

Groll, E. (2014) 'Russian military escalates provocation campaign in Europe', *Foreign Policy*, 20 October.

Gupta, S. (2014) 'Abe's quest for collective self-defence: will Asia's sea lanes bind or divide?', East Asia Forum, Australian National University, 25 May, www.eastasiaforum.org/2014/05/25/abes-quest-for-collective-self-defence-will-asias-sea-lanes-bind-or-divide/.

Gvosdev, N. (2014) 'The Bear awakens: Russia's military is back', *The National Interest*, 12 November.

Haas, R. (2014) 'The unraveling: how to respond to a disordered world', *Foreign Affairs*, November/December.

Hachigian, N. (2015) 'The other problem in the South China Sea', *The Diplomat*, 8 April, thediplomat.

com/2015/04/the-other-problem-in-the-south-china-sea/.

Hallinan, C. (2014) 'Will sanctions sideline the U.S. dollar?', *Foreign Policy in Focus*, Institute for Policy Studies, Washington, DC.

Harding, B. (2014) 'Jokowi's big maritime plans for Indonesia need international support', *World Politics Review*, 3 September, www.worldpoliticsreview.com/articles/14026/jokowi-s-big-maritime-plans-for-indonesia-need-international-support.

Harjani, A. (2014) 'China neighbors worry sea dispute will lead to war: survey', *CNBC*, 14 July, www.cnbc.com/id/101835607#.

Harris, P. (2012) 'Drone wars and state secrecy: how Barack Obama became a hardliner', *Guardian*, 2 June.

Hayoun, M. (2014) 'China returns to show trials of 1950s and '60s, legal experts say', Al Jazeera, 28 August.

Hayton, B. (2014a) 'China's false memory syndrome', *Prospect*, 10 July.

— (2014b) *The South China Sea: The Struggle for Power in Asia*, London: Yale University Press.

Hemmings, J. (2010) 'Understanding Hatoyama's East Asian Community idea', East Asia Forum, Australian National University, 22 January, www.eastasiaforum.org/2010/01/22/understanding-hatoyamas-east-asian-community-idea/.

Heydarian, R. J. (2010) 'The China–Philippines–U.S. triangle', *Foreign Policy in Focus*, Institute for Policy Studies, Washington, DC, 16 December.

— (2012a) 'Manila takes on the Goliath', *The Diplomat*, 7 June, thediplomat.com/2012/06/manila-takes-on-the-goliath/.

— (2012b) 'China splits Philippine politics', *Asia Times*, 10 October.

— (2012c) 'Philippines running out of options in the South China Sea', *World Politics Review*, 21 December.

— (2012d) 'Construction tensions in the South China Sea', *Asia Times*, 26 October.

— (2012e) 'Manila paddles harder in the South China Sea', *Asia Times*, 16 November.

— (2012f) 'Iran: running out of options', *The Diplomat*, 5 July, thediplomat.com/2012/07/iran-running-out-of-options/.

— (2012g) 'China and Iran breaking up?', *The Diplomat*, 8 March, thediplomat.com/2012/03/china-and-iran-breaking-up/.

— (2012h) 'Iran pays price for Chinese support', *Asia Times*, 10 November, atimes.com/atimes/Middle_East/NK10Ak02.html.

— (2012i) 'ASEAN's fast fade into irrelevance', *Asia Times*, 29 November.

— (2013a) 'New reef rift hits China–Philippines ties', *Asia Times*, 18 July.

— (2013b) 'More US boots on Philippine soil', *Asia Times*, 9 September.

— (2013c) 'New nadir for China–Philippine ties', *Asia Times*, 12 September.

— (2013d) 'Obama no-show isolates allies', *Asia Times*, 11 October.

— (2013e) 'Aquino rebalances his China position', *Asia Times*, 5 November.

— (2013f) 'Japan pivots south, with eye on China', *Asia Times*, 26 January.

— (2013g) 'Japan, US squeeze China's ADIZ', *Asia Times* 18 December, www.atimes.com/atimes/Southeast_Asia/SEA-03-181213.html.

— (2013h) 'US sincerity questioned in Southeast Asia', *Asia Times*, 23 July, atimes.com/atimes/Southeast_Asia/SEA-01-230713.html.

— (2014a) 'China casts red tape in South China Sea', *Asia Times*, 14 January.

— (2014b) 'The Philippines–China–US triangle: a precarious relationship', *The National Interest*, 1 May.

— (2014c) 'Obama's free trade strategy falters in Asia', *InterPress Service*, 19 June, www.ipsnews.net/2014/06/obamas-free-trade-strategy-falters-in-asia/.

— (2014d) 'The BRICS bank: multipolarity or Beijing consensus?', Al Jazeera, 21 July, www.aljazeera.com/indepth/opinion/2014/07/brics-bank-beijing-consensus-201472183428811634.html.

— (2014e) 'ASEAN unity and the threat of Chinese expansion', Al Jazeera, 26 May, www.aljazeera.com/indepth/opinion/2014/05/asean-unity-threat-chinese-exp-2014525165623437127.html.

— (2015a) 'The power of the new China-led investment bank', Al Jazeera, 31 March, www.aljazeera.com/indepth/opinion/2015/03/asia-infrastructure-investment-bank-china-150326071738756.html.

— (2015b) 'Catchup in Manila for minimum deterrence', Asia Maritime Transparency Initiative, Center for Strategic and International Studies, Washington, DC.

— (2015c) 'The other crisis in the South China Sea', Asia Maritime Transparency Initiative, Center for Strategic and International Studies, 21 April.

— (2015d) 'China's economy: Back to reality', *Aljazeera*, August 16, http://www.aljazeera.com/indepth/opinion/2015/08/china-economy-reality-150815165145072.html.

Hill, F. and B. Lo (2014) 'Putin's pivot:

why Russia is looking east', *Foreign Affairs*, 31 July.

Hilton, E. (2015) 'Speak bitterness', *London Review of Books*, 37(5): 22–3.

Holdstock, N. (2008) 'In Ürümqi', *London Review of Books*, 31(15): 29.

Holland, S. and D. Brunnstrom (2014) 'Obama, Modi work to deepen improving U.S.–India ties', *Reuters*, 1 October, in.reuters.com/article/2014/10/01/modi-obama-meeting-usa-india-idINKCN0HP1I320141001.

Holmes, J. (2011) 'What makes China "Mahanian"?', *The Diplomat*, 18 November.

— (2012) 'The Sino-Japanese naval war of 2012', *Foreign Policy*, 20 August, foreignpolicy.com/2012/08/20/the-sino-japanese-naval-war-of-2012/.

— (2014a) 'Asia's worst nightmare: a China–Japan war', *The National Interest*, 26 October, nationalinterest.org/commentary/asias-ultimate-nightmare-china-japan-war-9662.

— (2014b) 'Coming to the Indian Ocean, the Chinese navy: how should India respond?', *The National Interest*, 7 October, nationalinterest.org/feature/coming-the-indian-ocean-the-chinese-navy-how-should-india-11415.

— (2014c) 'Which Germany should modern China emulate', *The National Interest*, 5 July.

Holmes, J. and T. Yoshihara (2012) 'Is China planning string of pearls?', *The Diplomat*, thediplomat.com/2011/02/is-china-planning-string-of-pearls/.

Hong, N. (2015) 'China's maritime law enforcement reform and its implication on the regional maritime disputes', Asia Maritime Transparency Initiative, Center for Strategic and International Studies, 1 April.

Huang, Y. (2013) 'Democratize or die: why China's communists face reform or revolution', *Foreign Affairs*, January/February.

Hui, W. (2012) 'The rumour machine', *London Review of Books*, 34(9): 13–14.

Hutzler, C. (2014) 'Beijing denies fighter flew dangerously close to U.S. patrol plane', *Wall Street Journal*, 23 April.

Ikenberry, J. (2008) 'The rise of China and the future of the West: can the liberal system survive?', *Foreign Affairs*, January/February.

— (2011) 'The future of the liberal world order: internationalism after America', *Foreign Affairs*, May/June.

— (2014) 'The illusion of geopolitics: the enduring power of the liberal order', *Foreign Affairs*, May/June.

International Crisis Group (2012a), 'Stirring up the South China Sea (I): regional responses', www.crisisgroup.org/~/media/Files/asia/north-east-asia/223-stirring-up-the-south-china-sea-i.pdf, accessed 1 January 2014.

— (2012b), 'Stirring up the South China Sea (II): regional responses', www.crisisgroup.org/~/media/files/asia/north-east-asia/229-stirring-up-the-south-china-sea-ii-regional-responses.pdf, accessed 1 January 2014.

Jacques, M. (2012) *When China Rules the World: The End of the Western World and the Birth of a New Global Order*, New York: Penguin Books.

Jaishankar, D. (2012) 'India's ocean', *Foreign Policy*, 6 December, foreignpolicy.com/2012/12/06/indias-ocean/.

Jakarta Post (2014a) 'South China Sea conflict a real threat to Indonesia', *Jakarta Post*, 20 September, www.thejakartapost.com/

news/2014/09/20/south-china-sea-conflict-a-real-threat-indonesia.html.

— (2014b) 'RI to strengthen defense in South China Sea', *Jakarta Post*, 29 September, www.thejakartapost.com/news/2014/09/29/ri-strengthen-defense-south-china-sea.html.

Jiaobao, L. (2012) 'China–Philippines trade may be affected – experts', *China Daily*, 14 May, usa.chinadaily.com.cn/china/2012-05/14/content_15282715.htm.

Johnson, K. (2014a) 'Russia, China finally ink landmark energy deal', *Foreign Policy*, 21 May.

— (2014b) 'Cambodia sleeps with the fishes', *Foreign Policy*, 7 June.

— (2014c) 'Lord of the sea', *Foreign Policy*, 16 May.

Jones, J. (2014) 'Far fewer Americans now say Iran is No. 1 U.S. enemy: nuclear agreements may be fueling change', Gallup, www.gallup.com/poll/167501/far-fewer-americans-say-iran-no-enemy.aspx.

Kagan, R. (2014) 'Superpowers don't retire: what our tired country still owes the world', *New Republic*, 26 May, www.newrepublic.com/article/117859/allure-normalcy-what-america-still-owes-world.

Kahn, J. (2006) 'China, shy giant, shows signs of shedding its false modesty', *New York Times*, 9 December.

Kaplan, R. (2009) 'Center stage for the 21st century: power plays in the Indian Ocean', *Foreign Affairs*, March/April.

— (2010) 'The geography of Chinese power', *Foreign Affairs*, May/June.

— 2012. *The Revenge of Geography: What the Map Tells us about Coming Conflicts and the Battle against Fate*, Random House: New York.

— (2014) *Asia's Cauldron: The South China Sea and the End of a Stable Pacific*, New York: Random House.

Kapoor, K. and J. Thatcher (2014) 'Indonesia military worries over Asia arms race, territorial tensions', *Reuters*, 3 April, www.reuters.com/article/2014/04/03/us-indonesia-military-idUSBREA320GD20140403.

Katz, R. (2012) 'Mutual assured production: why trade will limit conflict between China and Japan', *Foreign Affairs*, July/August.

— (2013) 'Why Chinese–Japanese economic relations are improving', *Foreign Affairs*, 30 December.

— (2014a) 'China's treasury holdings climb to record in government data', Bloomberg, 15 January.

— (2014b) 'Voodoo Abenomics: Japan's failed comeback plan', *Foreign Affairs*, July/August.

Kazianis, H. (2014) 'The "House of Cards" lesson for the U.S. military', *Defense One*, 20 February, www.defenseone.com/threats/2014/02/house-cards-lesson-us-military/79091/.

Keck, Z. (2012) 'India's South China Sea gambit', *The Diplomat*, 5 December.

— (2014a) 'China's Communist Party and Japan: a forgotten history', *The National Interest*, nationalinterest.org/feature/chinas-communist-party-japan-forgotten-history-10533.

— (2014b) 'AirSea battle vs. Blockade: a false debate?', *The National Interest*, 6 January, nationalinterest.org/commentary/airsea-battle-vs-blockade-false-debate-9665.

Kennan, G. (1947) 'The sources of Soviet conduct', *Foreign Affairs*, July.

Kennedy, A. (2010) 'Rethinking energy security in China', East Asia Forum, Australian National University, 6 June.

Kennedy, R. (2010) 'The most abused

word in history', *The National Interest*, July/August.

Keohane, R. (1982) 'The demand for international regimes', *International Organization*, 36(2): 325–55.

Kesavapany, K. (2011) 'ASEAN and the Cambodia–Thailand conflict', East Asia Forum, Australian National University.

Khan, S. (2014) 'Suicide by drought', *Foreign Affairs*, 18 July.

Khera, P. (2015) 'Did Obama's India visit revive the "Asian arc of democracy" strategy against China?', *Huffington Post*, 28 January, www. huffingtonpost.com/pawan-khera/obama-india-quadrilateral-security-dialogue_b_6564544.html.

Kissinger, H. (2011) *On China*, New York: Penguin.

— (2014) 'Essay: Henry Kissinger on the assembly of a new world order', *Wall Street Journal*, 29 August.

Kondapalli, S. (2014) 'Dawn of a new era in India–Japan relations', *Reffif News*, 2 September.

Krishnan, A. (2011) 'India–China trade surpasses target', *The Hindu*, www. thehindu.com/news/international/indiachina-trade-surpasses-target/article1129785.ece.

Krugman, P. (2014) 'Apologizing to Japan', *New York Times*, 30 October.

Kundapali, S. (2014) 'Dawn of a new era in India–Japan relations', *RediffNews*, 2 September, www. rediff.com/news/column/dawn-of-a-new-era-in-india-japan-relations/20140901.htm.

Kurlantzick, J. (2007) *Charm-Offensive: How China's Soft Power is Transforming the World*, New York: Yale University Press.

— (2009) 'Taking the bosses hostage', *London Review of Books*, 31(6): 9–13.

Lam, W. (2015) 'Xi Jinping forever', *Foreign Policy*, 1 April, foreignpolicy. com/2015/04/01/xi-jinping-forever-china-president-term-limits/.

Law, V. (2014) 'Hong Kong's inconvenient truth', *Foreign Policy*, 21 August.

Lee, J. (2014) 'Nonmilitary approaches to countering Chinese coercion: a code of practice for the Asia-Pacific', Center for New American Security, September, www.cnas.org/sites/default/files/publications-pdf/CNAS_Maritime3_Lee_0.pdf.

Lewis, J. (2014) 'They shoot satellites, don't they?', *Foreign Policy*, 9 August, foreignpolicy.com/2014/08/09/they-shoot-satellites-dont-they/.

Li, N. (2010) 'Chinese civil–military relations in the post-Deng era: implications for crisis management and naval modernization', US Naval War College, January, www.usnwc.edu/Research--Gaming/China-Maritime-Studies-Institute/Publications/documents/China-Maritime-Study-No-4-January-2010.aspx.

Liff, A. (2014) 'Watch this space: "collective self-defense", constitutional reinterpretation, and Japan's security policy', Center for Strategic and International Studies, Washington, DC, 26 June.

Liming, W. (2013) 'Commentary: The Philippine's dual tactics doomed to fail', *Xinhua*, 29 August, news. xinhuanet.com/english/world/2013-08/29/c_125278022.htm.

Logan, J. (2013) 'China, America, and the Pivot to Asia', *Policy Analysis*, 717, Cato Institute, 8 January, www.cato. org/sites/cato.org/files/pubs/pdf/pa717.pdf.

Lourdes, N. M. (2006) 'Post-EDSA Philippine foreign relations, 1986–2001', in N. Morada and

T. Encarnacion Tadem (eds), *Philippine Politics and Governance: An Introduction*, Quezon City: University of the Philippines.

Lu, R. (2014a) 'A new definition of Chinese patriotism', *Foreign Policy*, 11 September, foreignpolicy.com/2014/09/11/a-new-definition-of-chinese-patriotism/.

— (2014b) 'Report: Hong Kong becoming "mere second-tier" Chinese city', *Foreign Policy*, 2 September.

Lumanauw, N. (2014) 'Jokowi clarifies: Indonesia still neutral in S. China Sea dispute', 24 March, thejakartaglobe. beritasatu.com/news/jokowi-clarifies-indonesia-still-neutral-s-china-sea-dispute/.

Luttwak, E. (2013) 'The enabler', *Foreign Policy*, 12 April, foreignpolicy.com/2013/04/12/the-enabler/.

Macaskill, A. and U. Krishnan (2014) 'Modi-led bloc wins biggest India mandate in three decades', *Bloomberg*, 17 May, www.bloomberg.com/news/articles/2014-05-15/india-to-count-551-million-votes-as-modi-projected-to-take-power.

Magkilat, B. (2013) 'CAEXPO invite signal of reconciliation', *Manila Bulletin*, 26 August.

Mahbubani, K. (2015) 'Why Britain joining China-led bank is a sign of American decline', *Huffington Post*, 16 March, www.huffingtonpost.com/kishore-mahbubani/britain-china-bank-america-decline_b_6877942.html.

Mahdzir, D. (2015) 'South China Sea issues blunt progress at ADSOM Plus', *Jane's*, 16 February, www.janes.com/article/49009/south-china-sea-issues-blunt-progress-at-adsom-plus.

Malig, J. (2012) 'Will the U.S. defend the Philippines if China attacks?', *ABS-CBN News*, 25 July, www.abs-cbnnews.com/-depth/07/25/12/will-us-defend-philippines-if-china-attacks.

Martin, P. and D. Cohen (2014) 'Mao and forever: Xi Jinping's authoritarian reforms', *Foreign Affairs*, 3 June.

Matlack, C. (2014) 'Are the BRICS nations too splintered to be a bloc?', *Bloomberg*, 15 July.

Mayeda, A. (2015) 'U.S. veto power at IMF said to face threat in rift on governance', *Bloomberg*, 30 January, www.bloomberg.com/news/articles/2015-01-29/u-s-veto-power-at-imf-said-to-face-threat-in-rift-on-governance.

Mazarr, M. (2014) 'The age of grievance: how to play resentment politics', *Foreign Affairs*, 3 July.

McCormack, G. (2013) 'Much ado over small islands: the Sino-Japanese confrontation over Senkaku/Diaoyu', *Asia-Pacific Journal*, 11(21), japanfocus.org/-Gavan-McCormack/3947.

McCurry, J. (2010) 'Japan's prime minister Yukio Hatoyama resigns', *Guardian*, 2 June.

McDevitt, M. (2013) 'Will China refashion the Asian maritime order?', *Journal of International Security Affairs*, December, www.cna.org/sites/default/files/McDevitt.pdf.

McLeary, P and A. Robinson (2015) 'Situation report: China looking at floating bases; Islamic State's weed; defense contractors eye two big prizes; and lots more', *Foreign Policy*, 29 April, foreignpolicy.com/2015/04/21/situation-report-china-looking-at-floating-bases-islamic-states-weed-defense-contractors-eye-two-big-prizes-and-lots-more/.

Mearsheimer, J. (2014a) 'Can China rise

peacefully?', *The National Interest*, 25 October, nationalinterest. org/commentary/can-china-rise-peacefully-10204.

— (2014b) 'Why the Ukraine crisis is the West's fault: the liberal delusions that provoked Putin', *Foreign Affairs*, September/October.

Medcalf, R. (2014) 'Asia's "Cold Peace": China and India's Delicate Diplomatic Dance' *The National Interest*. September 24, 2014, http:// nationalinterest.org/feature/asias-cold-peace-china-indias-delicate-diplomatic-dance-11338.

Meek, J. (2014) 'Putin's counter-revolution', *London Review of Books*, 36(6): 3–9.

Mendez, C. (2010) 'Senate duty-bound to review VFA', *Philippine Star*, 10 November.

Mendoza, A. and J. Heydarian (2012) 'China–Philippines', in F. Keith and K. Kemburi (eds), *ASEAN: China Free Trade Area Challenges, Opportunities and the Road Ahead*, Singapore: Nanyang Technological University.

Menon, R. (2014a) 'Modi's India: China's new friend or bitter foe?', *The National Interest*, 10 June, nationalinterest.org/feature/modis-india-chinas-new-friend-or-bitter-foe-10630?page=show.

— (2014b) 'The India myth', *The National Interest*, 23 October, nationalinterest. org/feature/the-india-myth-11517.

Miller, B. and T. Yokota (2013) 'Japan keeps its cool: why Tokyo's new government is more pragmatic than hawkish', *Foreign Affairs*, 21 January.

Miller, M. C. (2014) 'Foreign policy à la Modi', *Foreign Affairs*, 3 April.

Milner, H. (1991) 'The assumption of anarchy in international relations theory', *Review of International Studies*, 17: 67–85.

Mishra, P. (2012) 'The Gujarat massacre: New India's blood rite', *Guardian*, 14 March, www.theguardian.com/ commentisfree/2012/mar/14/new-india-gujarat-massacre.

— (2013) *From the Ruins of Empire: The Revolt against the West and the Remaking of Asia*, New York: Picador.

Mizokami, K. (2014) 'Australia's submarine play: run silent, run Japanese?', *The National Interest*, 14 September, nationalinterest.org/ feature/australias-submarine-play-run-silent-run-japanese-11273.

Mogato, M. (2013) 'Hagel assures Philippines no new permanent U.S. bases', *Reuters*, 30 August, www.reuters.com/ article/2013/08/30/us-philippines-usa-idUSBRE97T0AE20130830.

Mogato, M. and S. Wee (2014) 'Manila seeks clarification on Chinese fishing rules in South China Sea', *Reuters*, 9 January, www.reuters. com/article/2014/01/09/philippines-china-idUSL3N0KJ1OR20140109.

Mohan, C. R. (2012) 'The new triangular diplomacy: India, China and America at sea', *The Diplomat*, 5 November, thediplomat.com/2012/11/the-new-triangular-diplomacy-india-china-and-america-on-the-high-seas/ ?allpages=yes.

Mohan, C. R. and R. Medcalf (2014) 'The U.S.–China rivalry has Asia on edge: can "middle powers" create stability?', *The National Interest*, 15 August, nationalinterest.org/ feature/the-us-china-rivalry-has-asia-edge-can-middle-powers-create-11085?page=show.

Morada, N. (2006) 'Philippine foreign relations after September 11

(2001–2005)', in N. Morada and T. Encarnacion Tadem (eds), *Philippine Politics and Governance: An Introduction*, Quezon City: University of the Philippines.

Moravcsik, A. (1997) 'Taking preferences seriously: a liberal theory of international politics', *International Organization*, 51(4): 513–53.

Moss, T. (2015) 'U.S., Philippines add muscle to military drills', *Wall Street Journal*, 20 April, www.wsj.com/articles/u-s-philippines-add-muscle-to-military-drills-1429511920.

Murphy, A. M. (2014) 'The end of strategic ambiguity: Indonesia formally announces its dispute with China in the South China Sea', Pacific Forum, Center for Strategic and International Studies, csis.org/files/publication/Pac1426.pdf.

Nanning, B. Y. (2013) 'Philippines to welcome more Chinese funds', *China Daily*, 5 September, www.chinadaily.com.cn/bizchina/2013-09/05/content_16945953.htm.

Nathan, A. (2009) 'Zhao's version', *London Review of Books*, 31(24): 23–5.

Nathan, A. and A. Scobell (2012) 'How China sees America: the sum of Beijing's fears', *Foreign Affairs*, September/October.

Naughton, B. (2006) *The Chinese Economy: Transitions and Growth*, Cambridge, MA: MIT Press.

New York Times (1992) 'Excerpts from Pentagon's plan: "Prevent the re-emergence of a new rival"', *New York Times*, 8 March.

Ngui, Y. (2014) 'As China flexes maritime muscle, SE Asia builds home-grown defence industry', *Reuters*, 12 August, in.reuters.com/article/2014/08/11/southeast-asia-defence-idINKBN0GB23920140811.

Nikkei (2015) 'China needs to "purchase" friendships, scholar says', *Asia Review*, 2 March, asia.nikkei.com/Viewpoints/Perspectives/China-needs-to-purchase-friendships-scholar-says.

Nye, J. (2004) *Soft Power: The Means to Success in World Politics*, New York: Public Affairs.

— (2014) '1914 revisited?', *Project Syndicate*, 13 January, www.project-syndicate.org/commentary/joseph-s--nye-asks-whether-war-between-china-and-the-us-is-as-inevitable-as-many-believe-world-war-i-to-have-been.

O'Callaghan, J. (2012) 'Southeast Asia splashes out on defense, mostly maritime', *Reuters*, 7 October, www.reuters.com/article/2012/10/07/us-defence-southeastasia-idUSBRE8960JY20121007.

Office of the United States Trade Representative (2014) 'China's treasury holdings climb to record in government data', USTR.gov, 4 April, ustr.gov/countries-regions/china-mongolia-taiwan/peoples-republic-china.

Olson, W. (2014) 'Pentagon report finds sequestration cuts would reduce national security', *Stars and Stripes*, 16 April, www.stripes.com/news/us/pentagon-report-finds-sequestration-cuts-would-reduce-national-security-1.278153.

Orendain, S. (2014) 'Will new defense pact impact US support for Philippines in sea disputes?', *Voice of America*, 2 May, www.voanews.com/content/impact-of-us-philippines-defense-pact-on-s-china-sea-disputes-still-unclear/1906009.html.

Osborne, A. and P. Foster (2010) 'USSR planned nuclear attack on China in

1969', *Telegraph*, www.telegraph.
co.uk/news/worldnews/asia/
china/7720461/USSR-planned-
nuclear-attack-on-China-in-1969.
html.

Osnos, E. (2014) 'Born red', *New Yorker*,
6 April, www.newyorker.com/
magazine/2015/04/06/born-red.

Page, J. (2014) 'Deep threat: China's
submarines add nuclear-strike
capability, altering strategic balance',
Wall Street Journal, 24 October,
www.wsj.com/articles/chinas-
submarine-fleet-adds-nuclear-strike-
capability-altering-strategic-balance-
undersea-1414164738.

Palmer, J. (2014) 'Blood and fear in
Xinjiang', *Foreign Policy*, 2 March.

Panda, A. (2015) 'US, Indonesian navies
conduct air patrol exercise in South
China Sea', *The Diplomat*, 11 April.

Pant, H. (2014) 'Indian defense policy at
a turning point', *Foreign Policy*, 17
July, foreignpolicy.com/2014/07/17/
indian-defense-policy-at-a-turning-
point/.

Papa, A. (2009) 'Blackwater training
merceneries in Subic', *Inquirer*, 30
August.

Parameswaran, P. (2013) 'Beijing
unveils new strategy for ASEAN–
China relations', *The Jamestown
Foundation*, 13(21), 24 October,
www.jamestown.org/single/?tx_
ttnews[tt_news]=41526&no_cache=1#.
VK6ZM3uGPT8.

Pedrozo, P. (2010) 'Beijing's coastal
real estate: a history of Chinese
naval aggression', *Foreign Affairs*, 15
November.

Pei, M. (2014) 'How China and America
see each other', *Foreign Affairs*,
April/March.

Perlez, J. (2015a) 'Beijing, with an eye on
the South China Sea, adds patrol

ships', *New York Times*, 10 April.

— (2015b) 'China building aircraft runway
in disputed Spratly Islands', *New
York Times*, 16 April, www.nytimes.
com/2015/04/17/world/asia/china-
building-airstrip-in-disputed-spratly-
islands-satellite-images-show.html.

Philippine Daily Inquirer (2013) 'PH, US
tackling "gaps" in defense talks',
Inquirer, 4 October, globalnation.
inquirer.net/87051/ph-us-tackling-
gaps-in-defense-talks/.

Picardo, E. (2014) 'Why China's currency
tangos with the USD', *Investopia*,
14 March, www.investopedia.com/
articles/forex/09/chinas-peg-to-the-
dollar.asp.

Picq, M. (2014) 'The failures of Latin
America's left', Al Jazeera, 7
November.

Pillalamarri, A. (2014) 'Australian PM
visits India, signs nuclear deal', *The
Diplomat*, 6 September, thediplomat.
com/2014/09/australian-pm-visits-
india-signs-nuclear-deal/.

Pilling, D. and R. Landigin (2012)
'Philippines backs rearming of Japan',
Financial Times, 9 December.

Pinijparakarn, S. (2013) 'Some 1,000
mid-sized Japan firms eye Thai
bases', *The Nation*, 17 January, www.
nationmultimedia.com/business/
Some-1000-mid-sized-Japan-firms-
eye-Thai-bases-30198063.html.

Plumer, B. (2013) 'The U.S. gives Egypt
$1.5 billion a year in aid. Here's what
it does', *Washington Post*, 9 July,
www.washingtonpost.com/blogs/
wonkblog/wp/2013/07/09/the-u-s-
gives-egypt-1-5-billion-a-year-in-aid-
heres-what-it-does/.

Polling Report (2014) CNN/ORC Poll,
March, www.pollingreport.com/life.
htm.

Pomfret, J. (2010) 'US takes a tougher

tone with China', *Washington Post*, 30 July.

Porcalla, D. (2012) 'Asean leaders fail to agree on sea row', *Philippine Star*, 20 November, www.philstar.com/headlines/2012/11/20/868921/asean-leaders-fail-agree-sea-row.

Porter, P. (2013) 'Sharing power? Prospects for a U.S. concert-balance strategy', Strategic Studies Institute, www.strategicstudiesinstitute.army.mil/pdffiles/PUB1149.pdf, accessed 1 October 2014.

Putnam, R. (1988) 'Diplomacy and domestic politics: the logic of two-level games', *International Organization*, 42(3): 427–60.

Putz, C. (2015) 'Sold: Russian S-400 missile defense systems to China', *The Diplomat*, 14 April, thediplomat.com/2015/04/sold-russian-s-400-missile-defense-systems-to-china/.

Pyle, K. (2008) *Japan Rising: The Resurgence of Japanese Power and Purpose*, New York: Public Affairs.

— (2014) 'The sea change in Japanese foreign policy', National Bureau of Asian Research, www.nbr.org/publications/element.aspx?id=747.

Quilop, R. (2006) 'Nation-state formation in the Philippines', in N. Morada and T. Encarnacion Tadem (eds), *Philippine Politics and Governance: An Introduction*, Quezon City: University of the Philippines.

Rappler (2015) 'PH won't renew work visas of Chinese experts in NGCP', *Rappler*, 24 February, www.rappler.com/nation/84926-ph-chinese-experts-ngcp.

Rauhala, E. (2014) 'China now says almost 100 were killed in Xinjiang violence', *Time*, 4 August.

Rawski, T. and L. Brandt (eds) (2008) *China's Great Economic*

Transformation, Cambridge: Cambridge University Press.

Reuters (2012) 'China gives Cambodia aid and thanks for ASEAN help', *Reuters*, 4 September, www.reuters.com/article/2012/09/04/cambodia-china-idUSL4E8K41I320120904.

— (2014) 'Obama says disputed islands within scope of US–Japan security treaty', *Reuters*, 23 April, in.reuters.com/article/2014/04/23/japan-usa-obama-interview-idINKBN0D902F20140423.

Richardson, S. (2014) 'Hong Kong gets out the vote', *Foreign Policy*, 25 June.

Rodis, R. (2012) 'Trillanes may yet rule the Philippines', *Inquirer*, 26 September, globalnation.inquirer.net/51382/trillanes-may-yet-rule-the-philippines/.

Rodrik, D. (2011) 'The manufacturing imperative', Project Syndicate, 10 August, www.project-syndicate.org/commentary/the-manufacturing-imperative.

Romero, P. (2013) 'Phl, US eye new pact on "rotational presence" in time for Obama visit', *Philippine Star*, 19 September.

Ross, R. (2012) 'The problem with the Pivot', *Foreign Affairs*, November/December.

Rothkopf, D. (2014) 'A time of unprecedented instability?', *Foreign Policy*, 21 July.

Rothwell, D. (2013) 'South China Sea dispute dynamics', East Asia Forum, Australia National University, 16 June.

Rozman, G. (2014) 'Asia for the Asians: why Chinese–Russian friendship is here to stay', *Foreign Affairs*, 29 October.

Ruwitch, J. (2014) 'Satellites and seafood: China keeps fishing fleet connected in disputed waters', *Reuters*, 27 July.

Sanger, D. (1991) 'Philippines orders U.S. to leave strategic navy base at Subic Bay', *New York Times*, 28 December.

— (2010) *The Inheritance: The World Obama Confronts and the Challenges to American Power*, New York: Broadway Books.

Santos, M. (2014) '85% of Filipinos love US – survey', *Inquirer*, 22 April, globalnation.inquirer.net/102487/many-filipinos-love-us-survey/.

Sarotte, M. (2014) 'A broken promise? What the West really told Moscow about NATO expansion', *Foreign Affairs*, September/October.

Schell, O and J. Delury (2013) 'Chairman of the Board', *Foreign Policy*, 12 July, foreignpolicy.com/2013/07/12/chairman-of-the-board/.

Schmitt, E. (2002) 'A nation challenged: Pacific terror; U.S. and Philippines setting up joint operations to fight terror', *New York Times*, 16 January.

Segal, G. (1996) 'East Asia and the "constrainment" of China', *International Security*, 20(4), 107–35.

Severino, H. (2012) 'Sen. Trillanes accuses DFA's Del Rosario of treason over China', *GMA News*, 20 September, www.gmanetwork.com/news/video/134112/newstogo/sen-trillanes-accuses-dfa-s-del-rosario-of-treason-over-china-banner-story-ng-gma-news-online.

— (2013) 'How much can ASEAN do for a South China Sea code of conduct?', East Asia Forum, Australian National University, 30 October.

Sharma, R. (2012) *Breakout Nations: In Pursuit of the Next Economic Miracles*, New York: W. W. Norton.

Sharp, A. and Ting Shi (2015) 'Japan to mull expanding navy patrols to South China Sea', *Bloomberg*, 24 February, www.bloomberg.com/news/articles/2015-02-04/japan-to-consider-expanding-navy-patrols-to-south-china-sea.

Sheehan, N. (1989) *A Bright Shining Lie: John Paul Vann and America in Vietnam*, New York: Vintage.

Shih, T. (2014) 'China's surging investment in US heralds new multinational era', *South China Morning Post*, 4 August.

Shirk, S. (2008) *China: Fragile Superpower*, Oxford: Oxford University Press.

Slodkowski, A. (2013) 'Japan sees opportunity in Myanmar's emerging economy', *Reuters*, 4 January, www.reuters.com/article/2013/01/04/us-myanmar-japan-idUSBRE9030P220130104.

Smith, G. (2014) 'Taiwan's Sunflower Movement', *Foreign Policy in Focus*, Institute for Policy Studies, Washington, DC.

Smith, J. (2014) 'India and China: the end of cold peace?', *The National Interest*, 10 February, nationalinterest.org/commentary/india-china-the-end-cold-peace-9853.

Smith, S. (2015) *Intimate Rivals: Japanese Domestic Politics and a Rising China*, New York: Columbia University Press.

Song, Y. H. (2010) 'The application of Article 121 of the Law of the Sea Convention to the selected geographical features situated in the Pacific Ocean', *Chinese Journal of International Law*, 9(4): 663–98.

Steele, J. (2013) 'China in the Stans', *London Review of Books*, 35(20): 33–4.

Stewart, H. (2015) 'IMF spring summit: the same meetings, but different times', *Guardian*, 10 April, www.theguardian.com/business/2015/

apr/10/imf-summit-same-meeting-different-times.

Steinberg, J. and M. O'Hanlon (2014) 'Keep hope alive: how to prevent U.S.–Chinese relations from blowing up', *Foreign Affairs*, July/August.

Stiglitz, J. (2003) *Globalization and Its Discontents*, New York: Penguin.

Stone, I. and H. Gao (2014) 'The dumpling effect', *Foreign Policy*, 7 February.

Storey, I. (2013) 'China runs rings around Asean', *Wall Street Journal*, 2 October.

Sun, Y. (2015) 'China's AIIB challenges', Pacific Forum, Center for Strategic and International Studies, 11 March, csis.org/publication/pacnet-16-chinas-aiib-challenges.

Tagala, D. (2012) 'Del Rosario brings maritime dispute to UN', *ABS-CBN News*, 3 October.

Takahashi, M. and R. Katakey (2014) 'India warships off Japan show rising lure as China counterweight', *Bloomberg*, 30 July, www.bloomberg.com/news/articles/2014-07-29/india-warships-off-japan-show-rising-lure-as-china-counterweight.

Talley, I. (2014) 'IMF members weigh options to sidestep U.S. Congress on overhaul', *Wall Street Journal*, 14 April.

Talmon, S. and Bing Bing Jia (eds) (2014) *The South China Sea Arbitration: A Chinese Perspective*, London: Hart Publishing.

Tang, J. (2006) 'With the grain or against the grain? Energy security and Chinese foreign policy in the Hu Jintao era', Brookings Institute, Washington, DC, www.brookings.edu/fp/cnaps/papers/tang2006.pdf, accessed 1 January 2014.

Ten Kate, D. (2013) 'China to build structure on disputed shoal, Philippines says', *Bloomberg*, 3

September, www.bloomberg.com/news/articles/2013-09-02/philippines-rejects-chinese-demands-for-president-aquino-s-visit.

Thayer, C. (2014) 'Analyzing the US–Philippines Enhanced Defense Cooperation Agreement', *The Diplomat*, 2 May, thediplomat.com/2014/05/analyzing-the-us-philippines-enhanced-defense-cooperation-agreement/.

Thompson, T. (2012) 'Glowing pork, exploding watermelons', *Foreign Affairs*, 14 March.

— (2013) 'Choking on China', *Foreign Affairs*, 8 April.

Tiezzi, S. (2015) 'Revealed: China's reasons for island-building in the South China Sea', *The Diplomat*, 10 April.

Times of India (2014) 'Modi's world second-most followed politician on Twitter, Facebook', *Times of India*, 5 September, timesofindia.indiatimes.com/tech/social/Modis-world-second-most-followed-politician-on-Twitter-Facebook/articleshow/41735598.cms.

Tofani, R. (2013) 'Legality waves lap South China Sea', *Asia Times*, 8 February.

Tordesillas, E. (2014) 'Magdalo Rep scores neglect of PH-occupied territories in Spratlys', *Verafiles*, 29 August, verafiles.org/magdalo-rep-scores-neglect-of-ph-occupied-territories-in-spratlys/#sthash.IRJ7nu6W.dpuf.

Tsoi, G. (2014) '"Today's Hong Kong, tomorrow's Taiwan"', *Foreign Policy*, 9 August.

Twining, D. (2014) 'When Obama meets Modi: the superpower and the global swing state', *Foreign Policy*, 28 September, foreignpolicy.com/2014/09/28/when-obama-meets-modi-the-superpower-and-the-global-swing-state/.

Ubac, M. (2012a) 'Palace tells DFA chief, Trillanes to shut up on West Philippine Sea dispute', *Philippine Daily Inquirer*, 19 September.

— (2012b) 'It's official: Aquino signs order on West Philippine Sea', *Philippine Daily Inquirer*, 13 September.

Violet, L. (2014) 'Hong Kong's inconvenient truth', *Foreign Policy*, 21 August.

VOA News (2015) 'China, Japan hold first security talks in 4 years', *Voice of America*, 19 March, www.voanews. com/content/china-japan-hold-first-security-talks-in-4-years/2686505. html.

Vu, T. M. and R. J. Heydarian (2015) 'The tragedy of small power politics: Vietnam, the Philippines, and the great powers', *CogitAsia*, Center for Strategic and International Studies, 9 April.

Vuving, A. (2015) 'A breakthrough in US–Vietnam relations', *The Diplomat*, 10 April, thediplomat.com/2015/04/a-breakthrough-in-us-vietnam-relations/.

Walker, R. and D. Buck (2007) 'The Chinese road: cities in the transition to capitalism', *New Left Review*, 46, July/August.

Walt, S. (2014) 'Double diss', *Foreign Policy*, 13 August.

Walton, T. (2014) 'Are we underestimating China's military?', *The National Interest*, 19 May, nationalinterest. org/feature/are-we-underestimating-chinas-military-10479.

Wang, Z. (2013a) *Never Forget National Humiliation: Historical Memory in Chinese Politics and Foreign Relations*, New York: Columbia University Press.

— (2013b) 'Not rising, but rejuvenating: the "Chinese dream"', *The Diplomat*, 5 February.

Waxman, M. (2014) 'Intense maneuvers at the Hague', Asia Maritime Transparency Initiative, Center for Strategic and International Studies, 23 December.

Wei, L. and B. Davis (2014) 'China forgoes veto power at new bank to win key European nations' support', *Wall Street Journal*, 23 March.

Weisman, J. (2015) 'House rejects trade measure, rebuffing Obama's dramatic appeal', *New York Times*, 12 June.

Wendt, A. (1992) 'Anarchy is what states make of it: the social construction of power politics', *International Organization*, 46(2): 391–425.

Whaley, F. (2014) 'China's island-building is ruining coral reefs, Philippines says', *New York Times*, 13 April, www. nytimes.com/2015/04/14/world/asia/chinas-island-building-is-ruining-coral-reefs-philippines-says. html?_r=0.

White, H. (2014) 'Why Obama should abandon the pivot', East Asia Forum, Australian National University, 4 May, www.eastasiaforum. org/2014/05/04/why-obama-should-abandon-the-pivot/.

White House (2013) 'Remarks as prepared for delivery by National Security Advisor Susan E. Rice', www.whitehouse.gov/the-press-office/2013/11/21/remarks-prepared-delivery-national-security-advisor-susan-e-rice, 21 November.

— (2014) 'U.S.–India joint statement', Press release, 30 September, www.whitehouse.gov/the-press-office/2014/09/30/us-india-joint-statement.

Wolf, C., Xiao Wang and E. Warner (2013) 'China's foreign aid and government-sponsored investment activities:

scale, content, destinations, and implications', Rand Corporation, National Defense Research Institute, Washington, DC.

Wolf, J. (2013) 'Analysis: U.S. arms sales to Asia set to boom on Pacific "pivot"', *Reuters*, 1 January, www. reuters.com/article/2013/01/01/ us-usa-asia-arms-sales- idUSBRE90005D20130101.

Wong, E. (2014) 'China sentences Uighur scholar to life', *New York Times*, 23 September.

World Public Opinion (2014) 'Large majority of Americans favor making a deal with Iran on its nuclear program', World Public Opinion.org, 20 March.

Xinhua (2007) 'Hu Jintao calls for enhancing "soft power" of Chinese culture', 15 October, news.xinhuanet. com/english/2007-10/15/content_ 6883748.htm.

— (2012) 'Chinese military may establish presence in Sansha: defense spokesman', *Xinhua*, 28 June, news. xinhuanet.com/english/china/2012- 06/28/c_131682240.htm.

— (2014) 'Xi promises harsher anti- corruption drive', *Xinhua*, 14 January.

— (2015a) 'China completes fishery survey in South China Sea', *Xinhua*, 23 February, news.xinhuanet. com/english/china/2015-02/23/ c_134013151.htm.

— (2015b) 'China says island, reef construction in South China Sea lawful, justified', *Xinhua*, 8 March, news.xinhuanet.com/english/2015- 03/08/c_134048090.htm.

Yergin, D. (2008) *The Prize: The Epic Quest for Oil, Money and Power*, New York: Free Press.

Yu, A. (2015) 'Chinese rig finds huge gas reserve in South China Sea', *IHS Maritime 360*, 9 February, www. ihsmaritime360.com/article/16545/ chinese-rig-finds-huge-gas-reserve- in-south-china-sea.

Zhao, S. (1998) 'A state-led nationalism: the patriotic education campaign in post-Tiananmen China', *Communist and Post-Communist Studies*, 31(3): 287–302.

Žižek, S. (2013) *Less than Nothing: Hegel and The Shadow of Dialectical Materialism*, New York: Verso

INDEX

Page numbers in italic refer to figures and those in bold to tables; n following a page number denotes a footnote with the relevant number.

Indonesia: defence spending, 268; domestic security concerns, 267; hydrocarbon sector, **135**; military capability, *247*, 268; Natuna islands, 120, 268; South China sea disputes, *107*, 118–19, 266, 267
international order, 286–9; (*see also* Bretton Woods System)
Iran: and China, 285–6; nuclear programme, 61, 62; sanctions, 61–2, 96, 213, 286; and US, 61–2, 285
Iraq: extremist groups, 60, 61, 62; Filipino forces withdrawal, 153
Iraq War (2003–11), 54–5, 148, 231
Iroquois Bank, 172
ISIS (Islamic State), 60, 61, 62
Itu Abu (Tai Ping) island, 315

Japan: (*see also* Abe, Shinzo; Senkaku (Diaoyu) islands); ambitions as counterweight to China, 229–30; and Australia, 262–3; Battle of Tsushima (1905), 270–71; and China, 31, 106, 197–8, 220–21, 313; and China's air defence identification zone (ADIZ), 197–8; Constitutional reinterpretation, 230, 231, 233–4, 259; decline in trade and investment with China, 223–5; defence spending, **9**, 226, 231–2, 239; development aid, 38; economic decline, 13, 38, 221; economic indicators, *8*, *9*, **29**; engine of economic growth (flying geese phenomenon), 37–8, 232; External Trade Organization (ETO), 31; fiscal and monetary expansion, 235–6, *236*; Greater East Asia Co-Prosperity Sphere, 232; and Gulf Wars, 231; and India, 233, 234, 253–4, 259, 307; investment in South-East Asia, 227–8; naval strength, 307; Overseas Economic Cooperation Fund (OECF), 31; pacifist spirit, 230–31, 239–40; and Philippines, 202–3, 234, 317; Plaza Accord (1985), 30, 232; post-war US occupation, 217–18; regional cooperation, 306–8; security strategy, 226; self-defence, 229, 230; South China sea claims, **109**; South China sea security role, 302; and South Korea, 232–3, 264, 265–6, 313; and South-

East Asia, 226–9, 233; structural reform, 238–9; TPP negotiations, 216; trade and investment in China, 30–31; trade with Philippines, *154*, **154**; and US, 199–200, 201–2, 210, 217–19; US bases, 211; US Mutual Defence Treaty (MTD), 200; and World War Two, 30, 202, 236–8, 271–2
Jiang Zemin, 32–3, 47–8, 50–51, 70, 74–5
JMSU (Joint Marine Seismic Undertaking), 124, 155, 156–7, 185, 323
Johnson, Keith, 126
Johnson South Reef, 112, 276
Joko Widodo, 267
Joshi, Admiral D.K., 243–4, 251

Kagan, Robert, 7
Kang, D., 240
Kaplan, Robert, 21, 104, 208, 248
Kashmir, 42
Katz, Richard, 223, 238–9
Kazakhstan, border conflicts, 41
Kazianis, Harry, 23
Kennan, George, 11
Kennedy, Paul, 7, 13, 139–40, 297
Kerry, John, 214, 312
Kishida, Fumio, 227
Kissinger, Henry, 25, 45, 91–2, 291–2, 308
Koizumi, Junichiro, 213, 219
Kondapalli, Srikanth, 243
Korea *see* North Korea; South Korea
Korean War, 148
Kraft, Herman, 152
Kurlantzick, Joshua, 69–70
Kyrgyzstan, border conflicts, 41

Lam, Wily, 86
Laos, 115, 209
Latin America, 34–5, 96
Layang-Layang Reef, 173
Lee Hsien Loong, 191, 306
Lee, John, 128
Lee Kuan Yew, 10, 217
Lew, Jack, 3
Li Keqiang, 19, 193
Li, Nan, 73, 136
Li Xiaobo, Nobel Peace Prize, 175
Liang Qichao, 273

overlapping claims, *107*, 111; Sansha city, 167, 171, 172, 174; Vietnamese claims, 26, 171, 196; Yongxing Island, 171

Peng Liyuan, 75

People's Liberation Army (PLA): Cobra Gold regional exercises, 39–40; exercises off Taiwan, 48; modernization, 22, 75; role following pro-democracy protests, 72–4; Sansha garrison, 171; tensions in civil-military relations, 73

People's Liberation Army Navy (PLAN): lobbying, 142; patrol vessels, 14; in South China Sea, 139, 141; strategy, 137–8; upgraded equipment, 112–13

Philippine National Oil Company (PNOC), 124, 155

Philippines (*see also* Aquino III, Benigno; Philippines-China relations; Philippines-US relations): AFP (Armed Forces of the Philippines) modernization, 174, 314–15, 316; anti-colonial movement, 273; and Australia, 317; Coast Guard (PCG), 317; coral reef damage, 303; defence imports, 265; defence procurement, 316; defence spending, *320*; domestic security concerns, 173–4, 186, 187, 317; energy security, 184–5; independence, 148; and Japan, 202–3, 234, 317; reliance on bi- and multilateral alliances, 316–18; Spanish colonial rule, 145; withdrawal from Iraq, 153

Philippines-China relations (*see also* UNCLOS (UN Convention on the Law of the Sea)): accusations of Chinese harassment, *125*; Aquino visit invitation rescinded, 188–90; bilateral visits, 115–16, 151–5, **152**, 154–5; business interests, 166; Chinese tourists, 169; defence cooperation, 153; diplomatic forums, 175–8; economic sanctions, 169; eviction of Chinese nationals, 301; and Hainan's foreign vessel regulation, 196, 197; hydrocarbon sector, 124–5, **135**; investment, 180; lack of high-level dialogue, 313; Li Xiaobo's Nobel Peace Prize ceremony, 175; maritime law, 119; Mischief Reef tensions, 112, 150, 172, 276,

278, *279*, 279*n7*; NBN-ZTE scandal, 156; Reed Bank, 121, 125, *134*, 184–5, 194, 195; Scarborough Shoal crisis, 162–71, *162*; Second Thomas Shoal, 183–4, 190; South China sea claims, *107*, **109**, 117–18, 170, 171–5; Thitu Island, 163, 171, *173*, 313–14; trade, 153, *154*, **154**, 169

Philippines-US relations: Abu Sayyaf Group (ASG), 150–51; Blackwater's training facility, 151; Enhanced Defense Cooperation Agreement (EDCA, 2014), 199, 201, 202, 315; Filipino murder charges, 202, 315; historical military assistance, 186–7, *187*; military assistance, 209–210, 215; military bases, 110, 112, 147, 149–50; Mutual Defence Treaty (MDT, 1951), 149, 165, 188, 200; Obama's cancelled tour, 191–3; Philippines support for US wars, 148; proposal on rotational US military presence, 185–6, 188, 192, 194–5; trade, *154*, **154**; US colonial rule, 145–7; Visiting Forces Agreement (VFA, 1998), 150–51, 186, 202, 315; War (1899–1902), 145, 148; 'war on terror' allies, 150–51

Pivot to Asia (P2A) policy, 64–5, 142, 160–62, 204–216, 262

power transitions, 286–8

Proelss, Alexander, 130, 131, 182

public opinion, 5, 55–6, 309–310

Putin, Vladimir, and China, 65

Pyle, Kenneth, 218, 231

al-Qaeda, 54, 60

Qian Qichen, 36

Quadrilateral Security Dialogue, 308

Ramo, Joshua-Cooper, 92–3

Ramos, Fidel, 152, 314

Randt, Clark T., 157–8

Rapp-Hooper, Mira, 275–6

Ratner, Ely, 205

raw materials, 34–5, 132–3

Reed Bank, 121, 125, *134*, 184–5, 194, 195

Rice, Susan, 11

Rizal, Jose, 147

Romana, Chito Santa, 130